THE
NEXT
AMERICAN
CENTURY

Simon & Schuster

How the U.S.

Can Thrive as

Other Powers

Rise

Nina Hachigian
Mona Sutphen

NEW YORK · LONDON · TORONTO · SYDNEY

SIMON & SCHUSTER
Rockefeller Center
1230 Avenue of the Americas
New York, NY 10020

First Simon & Schuster hardcover edition January 2008

SIMON & SCHUSTER and colophon are registered trademarks
of Simon & Schuster, Inc.

For information about special discounts for bulk purchases,
please contact Simon & Schuster Special Sales at
1-800-456-6798 or business@simonandschuster.com.

Designed by Paul Dippolito

Manufactured in the United States of America

10   8   6   4   2   1   3   5   7   9

Library of Congress Cataloging-in-Publication Data

Hachigian, Nina.
The next American century : how the U.S. can thrive as other powers rise /
Nina Hachigian and Mona Sutphen.
p.   cm.
Includes bibliographical references and index.
1. United States—Foreign relations—21st century.   2. Great powers.
3. Security, International.   4. International cooperation.   5. International
economic relations.   I. Sutphen, Mona.   II. Title.

E895.H33   2008
327.73009'05—dc22   2007037541

ISBN-13: 978-0-7432-9099-9
ISBN-10:   0-7432-9099-2

For Sosi, Sydney, Avo, and Davis,
who inspire us

Contents

THE
NEXT
AMERICAN
CENTURY

The United States and the Pivotal Powers

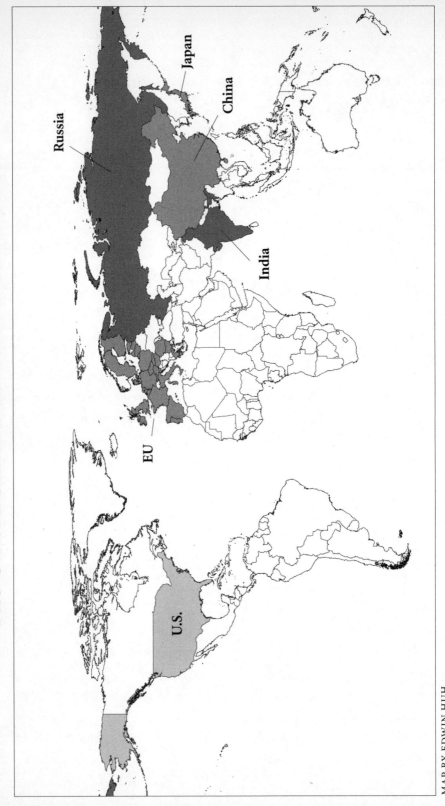

Russia

Japan

China

India

EU

U.S.

Preface

Our political coming-of-age was marked by the fall of the Berlin Wall, not by the Vietnam War. In 1989, just months after graduating from college, we witnessed the Cold War coming to an end. We launched our professional careers as America emerged as the lone superpower and began to chart the untested waters of unipolar global leadership. It was a moment of opportunity, for the country and for us personally. We took different paths in law, policy, and diplomacy before we met in a converted broom closet in the West Wing of the White House. In that tiny, shared office, we labored at the National Security Council, sometimes fifteen hours a day, in the frenetic guts of America's foreign policy machine.

At the turn of the millennium, we left the NSC optimistic about the future and America's role in defining it. Yes, the world was fraught with peril. Yes, terrorists were targeting us. But the economy was humming, we had a budget surplus for the first time in decades, and the U.S. had hit its stride in leading the world toward solving shared problems—bringing countries together to end conflicts and breaking down barriers to trade and travel. U.S. relations with the major powers reflected the optimism of that time. President Clinton had taken historic trips to China and India. Russia was struggling, but the U.S. wanted it to succeed again. Relations with our closest allies—Japan and Europe—continued to flourish. As his second term came

to a close, Clinton was greeted by mobs of cheering crowds everywhere he went.

We moved on with our lives. Nina focused on democracy, technology, and national security policy, directing the Center for Asia Pacific
Policy at the RAND Corporation, and later joining the Center for
American Progress. Mona went into the private sector, eventually becoming Managing Director at Stonebridge International, a consulting firm advising multinationals on business opportunities and
challenges around the world. We had children.

Meanwhile, the new Bush administration opted for an ABC—
"Anything But Clinton"—approach to foreign policy. The downing
of a U.S. surveillance plane in Chinese airspace just after Bush's inau-
guration allowed hawks in the administration to portray China as the
next monolithic state threat. Then the attacks of September 11, 2001,
reshuffled the deck. Yet initial sympathy for the U.S. soon dissipated
in the face of the Iraq war.

While U.S. foreign policy makers had less and less time for issues
outside the Middle East and terrorism, Americans became keenly
aware of the rise of China and the economic ascension of India, with
headlines devoted to steel shortages, our trade deficit, global job
flight, and immigration. What did their rise—or that of a resurgent
Russia, a rearming Japan, and an expanding Europe—really mean for
America's way of life? Washington was not saying. If anything, in the
case of China it looked like we were headed down the same well-worn
path of major power divisiveness.

We knew that couldn't be right. So much had changed since the
Cold War, the challenges so much less categorical and so much more
diverse. We thought, how could anyone conclude the China of today
would be a Soviet Union–style enemy of the U.S. when it is a major
trading partner and a key actor in halting North Korea's nuclear program? In the face of threats like terrorism, weren't our interests with
China as well as Russia and India more aligned than at odds?

Our instincts aside, however, we didn't have a clear idea of what

America's strategy toward the great powers ought to be. Which issues were really worth worrying about? Was India really taking all our jobs? Could China really outflank us in Asia? We wrote this book initially to answer these questions for ourselves.

When we told friends we had decided to write about big powers like China and India, their response was often fatalistic:

—"We should try to keep them down, right?" one joked. "But how?"
—"How is the environment going to weather the impact of two billion new cars and refrigerators?"
—"Travelling to China and India, you can just feel the momentum. . . . Despite every advantage, I worry that my kids won't be able to get a decent job."
—"Well, the Chinese are going to be our masters in fifty years, so we better learn how to get along with them."

Fortunately, our conclusions do not bear out pessimistic and confrontational reflexes like these that have marked major power relations in the past. America has great prospects ahead—if it does its homework. We had no idea we would end up writing so much about what America has to do at home. But that's our new world. The domestic is international, the international is domestic.

We have tried to develop a framework in which to ask and answer questions about America and the big powers. We also hope this book reenergizes a debate about America's relationship with existing and emerging power centers. In the end, we are still very optimistic about America's future. We see it daily in our children's eyes.

Acknowledgments

We could not have written this book without the insights, guidance, support, and feedback provided by so many of our friends, colleagues, and family.

We were fortunate to work with stellar young research assistants, Michael Beckley, David Shullman, and Jessica Sung, who were invaluable in collecting and compiling materials for this book. It would be a shadow of itself without their help.

We are also deeply grateful to the Center for American Progress, the Center for International Security and Cooperation at the Freeman Spogli Institute for International Studies at Stanford University (CISAC), Columbia University Libraries, the RAND Corporation, and the Stanley Foundation for their institutional support.

Along the way, many took their valuable time to guide us and share their expertise. We are grateful to have learned so much from these extraordinary individuals: Elshan Alekberov, Montek Aluwalia, Steve Andreasen, Bill Antholis, Phil Anton, Caroline Atkinson, Byron Auguste, Jeremy Azrael, Jeff Bader, Charlene Barshefsky, Jim Bartis, Nora Bensahel, Christophe Bertram, Chip Blacker, Tony Blinken, Lael Brainard, Steve Brock, Tom Carothers, Peter Chalk, Chris Chyba, Roger Cliff, Charlie Cook, Gerald Curtis, Robert Day, Larry Diamond, Susan Eisenhower, Diana Farrell, Irmgard Maria Fellner, Dick Foster, Frank Fukuyama, Scott Gerwehr, Jim Goldgeier, Mary

Goodman, Matt Goodman, Phil Gordon, Charles Grant, Michael Green, Richard Haass, Kirk Hachigian, Salman Haidar, David Halperin, Mikkal Herberg, Eric Higinbotham, Bruce Hoffman, Michael Hynes, Evelyn Iritani, Brian Jenkins, Jia Qingguo, Jin Carong, Omatunde Johnson, Edgard Kagan, Larry Korb, Lisa Kountoupes, Steven Kull, Charlie Kupchan, Tony Lake, Rollie Lal, Maxence Langlois-Berthelot, Jean-Pierre Lehman, Alex Lennon, Hank Levine, Ken Lieberthal, Ed Lincoln, Charles Ludolph, Michael Maclay, Kishore Mahbubani, Andrew Marshall, Michael McFaul, Diane McMahon, Tom McNaugher, Evan Medeiros, Mark Medish, Mike Mochizuki, Raja Mohan, Satoshi Morimoto, Dick Morningstar, S. Narayan, Gen. Bill Nash, George Nolfi, Joe Nye, Michael O'Hanlon, Jed Peters, Daniel Pink, Ken Pollack, Bill Potter, Jack Pritchard, Rob Ricigliano, Paul Romer, Joe Romm, Jeremy Rosner, Mara Rudman, Roald Sagdeev, Michael Schiffer, Howard Schultz, Brent Scowcroft, Kiyoyuki Seguchi, David Shlapak, Susan Shirk, Jake Siewert, Stefan Spinler, Steve Steadman, Rachel Swanger, Eric Talley, Donald Tang, Ratan Tata, Ashley Tellis, Maurice Templesman, Dmitri Trenin, Justin Vaisse, Joel Velasco, Ray Vickery, Stephen Walt, Andrew Weiss, Christian Weller, Ted Widmer, Frank Wisner, Charles Wolf, and John Yochelson. We especially want to thank the participants in the November 2006 workshop hosted by the Stanley Foundation and CISAC, whose input helped us work through some especially thorny issues.

We owe a special debt of gratitude to those who read the manuscript, and provided helpful, thorough comments: Sandy Berger, Grey Bryan, Susan Everingham, Olati Johnson, Warner Johnson, Abraham Lowenthal, Jack Sava, Michael Schiffer, and Sussan Sutphen. In particular, we want to thank Jim Steinberg, who somehow always had the time to advise us and never failed to challenge us in a constructive way.

It has been a privilege to work with our brilliant editor, Alice Mayhew, whose wise hand guided us every step of the way. Her unwavering focus on the core message of the book was the lodestar that kept us on course. Roger Labrie's consistently thoughtful advice and Serena Jones's skilled assistance were invaluable to us. Without our fantastic agent, Andrew Wylie, this book would have remained a nice idea, and we appreciate the confidence he had in us and in the project from the very beginning.

Nina would also like to thank: John Podesta and the rest of the team at CAP for being patient. My mother, father, and brother, who were always ready to help—reading passages, clipping articles, and offering ideas. Your cheerful support has always been the wind at my back. Finally, from deep in my heart I want to thank Joe for his optimism, faith, and good humor. Without you, I probably would not have thought of writing a book in the first place. I could not have done it without your intellectual, logistic, and loving support.

Mona would also like to thank: Everyone at Stonebridge International for their support and flexibility throughout this project. My father, sisters, and brother, who provided the much-needed encouragement to make the book a reality. And last but not least, my husband Clyde, who is always my biggest supporter and fan, and who showed the utmost patience in the face of numerous late nights and weekends spent away from the family. You are my rock, and I could not have done it without you.

Introduction

The fragrant lavender fields of Provence make an unlikely backdrop for the most ambitious science experiment of our time. Yet within a decade, the most distinctive structure in Cadarache, France, will not be the fifteenth-century stone castle, but a twenty-thousand-ton tokamak, a Soviet-designed, doughnut-shaped nuclear reactor. In it, deuterium nuclei, extracted from ordinary Mediterranean seawater, will collide with such force that they will fuse. The energy from this reaction—clean, massive, leaving no radioactive waste—may well be the answer to global warming and the destructive politics of oil. Already, over four thousand scientists from around the world are planning their multiyear collaboration in the International Thermonuclear Experimental Reactor (ITER) under the leadership of Japan's Dr. Kaname Ikeda. China is sending thirty scientists to help with construction.

What is even more remarkable than ITER's nuclear fusion is the political fusion it generated. In November 2006, officials from each of the world's biggest powers—China, the European Union, India, Japan, Russia, and the United States—shared a stage and together agreed to become partners in ITER. Each is contributing cash and technology. None could have built ITER on its own.

ITER ought to be the model of the future. We live at an extraordinary moment in history when the great powers of the world can align on the issues most critical to American safety, freedom, and prosperity. These powers want what America wants: a stable, peaceful, prosperous world organized around nation-states. No fundamental, intractable dispute divides us. None are ideological adversaries. This book argues that rather than worrying about these powers' relative gains, the United States should focus on renewing itself, and take advantage of this moment to work with them to solve humanity's pressing problems. This is a departure from America's current approach, but a different era calls for a different strategy. The pure zero-sum days of great power relations are behind us.

The Pivotal Powers

We call America's five big partners in the fusion experiment—China, Europe, India, Japan, and Russia—the "pivotal powers." These powers have the resources to support or thwart U.S. aims, to build the world order or disrupt it. Each has a significant capacity to get others to do what they want them to and to resist coercion. Through a combination of key traits—a large, educated population, vibrant economy, abundant natural resources, technological capability, capacity to innovate, military might, supporting infrastructure, cultural cachet, efficient governing institutions, ability to convert resources into effective power, current engagement with the world's rules and institutions, and ambition to play a major role—these powers, above others, are critical to the future order of the world.

Europe's $13 trillion economy is larger than America's, and the European Union is playing a part in every significant international institution and initiative. We treat the EU as one power because on global issues—be it climate change or peace in the Middle East—its member countries are increasingly speaking and acting with one voice. The European Union has its own central government, with a president, parliament, cabinet, central bank, and even an armed force (its sixty-thousand-strong rapid-reaction force). Further, a sense of

European identity is slowly emerging, especially among the younger generation, who have no direct memory of the conflicts that racked the continent in the twentieth century.

Japan has the world's second largest national economy, is actively engaged in Asia's regional architectures, and at approximately $330 million annually is the second-largest contributor to the United Nations. China and India have the world's largest populations by far, growing scientific capital, and skyrocketing economic growth. China's diplomacy is now decidedly global. Russia's vast natural resources and massive nuclear arsenal make it a force to be reckoned with. Each pivotal power has global interests and is now, or has the ambition and qualities to become, a world power.

Some may argue that other countries, representing other geographies, belong on this list, such as Brazil, South Africa, and Iran. While important regional players, these countries do not have the combination of assets or inclinations to make them influential global actors to the same degree as the other five. Brazil might be considered a pivotal power by the time our toddlers can read this book, with its large population, growing economy, resources, and cultural sway, but, at present, is not an essential player globally except on a few issues, like trade negotiations, and does not yet appear to have the clear determination to become a great power. South Africa, while a critical influence on issues across sub-Saharan Africa, has a modest economy and military. Iran is a strong regional player with an educated population and a history of being a great power, but its economy is one-dimensional and relatively small.

For now, it is China, Europe, India, Japan, and Russia, though all very different from each other, whether democratic or authoritarian, developed or developing, allies or rivals (or both), which have the most pivotal role to play in making the world a better place or not, supporting the United States or frustrating its plans.

America worries that the pivotal powers will reduce its geopolitical freedom, lure away its R&D, compete for the oil America needs, give solace to its enemies, and reduce the sway of liberal democracy. There is truth in some of these claims, but viewed through a pragmatic lens, the growing strength of the pivotal powers offers opportunities along with challenges and the need for adjustments. Taking as our starting point Thomas Jefferson's "life, liberty and the pursuit of happiness," in Chapters 1–5 we analyze how the pivotal powers affect these fundamental American interests.

It turns out that great powers do not inevitably threaten them. On the contrary, these powers often further American security, ideology, and prosperity. American CIA and FBI agents rely on their European, Russian, and Indian counterparts to foil terror plots. Keeping weapons of mass destruction away from terrorists is a joint endeavor. The road to a rollback of North Korea's nuclear program goes through Beijing. Each is critical to preventing a flu pandemic. Liberal pivotal powers like Europe, India, and Japan will become important partners in spreading our shared ideology as the backlash against America's misguided methods to bring democracy to Iraq continues to unfold. On the economic front, trade with pivotal powers, though it causes painful disruptions, grows the U.S. economy, and vice versa. To the extent that their growth does harm U.S. interests, America, often only America, can take the steps to put it right.

Even so, five hundred years of history tell us that when a dominant power is faced with the rapid rise of another nation, things will not go smoothly. America itself has never reacted calmly to the rise of another major power. Nazi Germany, Imperial Japan, and the Soviet Union rightly became enemies. Even the economic ascent of Japan in the 1980s—an official military ally, a democracy, and a country that had renounced the use of force—generated fear and fury in America before its economy faltered.

Today, the great power landscape is complicated. Europe and Japan remain old friends of the United States, but the prospect of a united European Union rattles some Americans, and Japan may yet chart a more independent course. The reemerging powers—China,

India, and Russia—all seek more recognition and influence. They are not adversaries, but neither have they been long-standing U.S. allies.

A New Era

In the days when royalty still lived in the Cadarache castle, the great powers were almost always at war. It could be different this time. New technologies and globalization have shaped the world and, with it, great power incentives. There is less room for great powers to turn on each other. We live, first, in the nuclear era. Alone these weapons pose an overwhelming deterrent to direct military confrontation. Also, unlike in the past, an increase in territory does not necessarily improve a country's prospects, eliminating one common reason for past wars between great powers. Commodities markets make conquering for land economically pointless, and it would be nearly impossible to occupy a country and make its knowledge workers productive at the same time.

Further, newly virulent threats profoundly affect pivotal power relations. The pivotal powers provide essential help in the battle against the true forces of devastation America now faces—like terrorists and pathogens. Terrorists have already killed thousands of Americans; viruses—millions. The more America and the pivotal powers cooperate on life-or-death matters of security, the higher and more evident become the costs of aiming at each other. A future great power that seeks to become safer by fighting America would also necessarily become less safe by forfeiting security cooperation. This security interdependence is genuinely new.

Economic interdependence has grown deeper too. Britain and Germany also traded heavily before plunging into World War I, but the degree and nature of economic interdependence in the world today is unprecedented. A bad day on the Shanghai stock exchange in February 2007 sent the Dow Jones down 400 points. Not only is the level of worldwide trade (measured as a ratio of exports to gross domestic product) nearly twice as high as before World War I, but foreign direct investment among pivotal powers is pervasive; we literally own pieces of each other's economies. Those relationships are much harder to replace than the portfolio investing of the pre-1914 era.

No pivotal power demands allegiance to a worldview at odds with our own. The fact that all pivotal powers are dependent on open trade and global stability for their economic growth, and the fact that our enemies are shared, increases the costs of conflict, and thus the chances for accommodation. Interdependence is no guarantee that peace will prevail, but mutual, deep dependence linked to prosperity raises the stakes of any contest.

Fear Itself

Pivotal powers will not pose a grave threat to the United States anytime soon. On the other hand, they do challenge American dominance and impinge on the freedom of action the U.S. has come to enjoy and expect. Their interests and ours will not always easily align and disputes will be intense and frequent. With China and Russia, these conflicts may be magnified by American distrust of opaque, illiberal regimes. Their economic rise, while ultimately growing our own economy, will cause painful change. Enemies they are not, but rivals they will sometimes be.

We also cannot rule out the possibility that a pivotal power will become a capable, aggressive challenger to vital U.S. interests. Nationalism remains a potent force that could push a pivotal power toward hostility. America must be prepared for this long-term possibility and continue to invest in a cutting-edge, sophisticated military. Here is where Washington will have to be careful, though, not to overdo it. In preparing for a possible clash, there is a danger America can inadvertently create the exact future for which it prepares. Each side's military precautions can be interpreted by the other side as confirmation of its worst fears. Preparation for conflict can become its cause.

The Certainty of Uncertainty

Another danger in overanxiety about pivotal powers is choosing the wrong target. Great powers have done this before, to their detriment. In the late 1800s, the Russian preoccupation with Japan led to an ill-advised intervention in Manchuria and Korea, and ultimately Russia's defeat in the Russo-Japanese War. Just a few decades later, fears of Bolshevik Russia left Great Britain ill-prepared to counter Nazi Germany at the onset of World War II.

Writing today, it seems unassailable that of the pivotal powers, China is America's biggest challenge. China's momentum seems unstoppable. In nine short years, it has doubled per capita income, a feat that took the U.S. and Britain fifty years to accomplish when they were industrializing. It attracted over $70 billion in foreign direct investment in 2006, and has been building a California's worth of expressway each year. Because America can tend to focus—like a cat—only on what is moving very quickly in the present moment, Washington has become a "cauldron of anxiety" about China, in the words of former Deputy Secretary of State Robert Zoellick. "Let's all wake up," warns Richard Fisher, vice president of the International Assessment and Strategy Center. "The post-Cold War peace is over. We are now in an arms race with a new superpower whose goal is to contain and overtake the United States." (Because of Washington's current focus on China, we often use China examples in this book.)

In reality, no one knows which, whether, or how fast any of the pivotal powers will rise. (We avoid the common term "rising powers" for this reason.) A brief review of "threatening countries of the recent past" is revealing. In 1988, just twenty years ago, the Soviet Union and Japan were the unquestionable focal points of American fears. By 1993 Germany and Japan were identified as potential threats, but the Soviet Union had vanished. By 1996, Japan had dropped out, but Germany remained. The year 2000 saw dire warnings about China and a newly integrating European Union, but not Germany. In 2005, the

EU also dropped out. Now conventional wisdom says China, and increasingly India and Russia, but not Europe or Japan, will rise to challenge America.

Even if China were hell-bent on fighting America one day, that day might never come. China faces a set of hurdles difficult even to enumerate, let alone solve. China's income gap is yawning; over 800 million of its citizens live on less than $2 a day. Social unrest is on the rise, the health care system is in shambles, fresh water is in very short supply, and the People's Republic is home to twenty of the thirty worst cities for air pollution in the world. India too is a tale of two nations. With its schools and demographic composition, India could have the world's largest pool of educated workers by 2020. But Bollywood and Bangalore aside, India is still a country in which two-thirds of households do not have an indoor toilet, and nearly half the children are malnourished, a higher percentage than in Sudan.

America cannot know the pivotal powers' future growth patterns, and furthermore, as Council on Foreign Relations president Richard Haass has observed, "the United States is not in a position to prevent the rise of other powers." The factors that determine growth—demographics, educational systems, economic policy, political stability, culture, individual opportunity, legal frameworks—are largely beyond the control of outsiders.

Moreover, straight-line forecasts are limited in value when history is an irregular sequence of major events. (Military strategists use the term "VUCA" to describe the international environment—volatile, uncertain, complex, and ambiguous.) In the end, as Robert Jervis, an influential scholar of international relations, observes, "History usually makes a mockery of our hopes and expectations." For example, in what is known as the "butterfly effect," simple changes can lead over time to far-reaching results. Quite literally: if George W. Bush had not been elected in the year 2000, America almost surely would not have invaded Iraq in 2003. Who could have guessed the profound impact of Florida's butterfly ballot on the future of the Middle East?

All of which is to say that America has to prepare prudently for the potential threats of tomorrow, and it has plenty of time to do that given the enormous lead it has in military strength. America should not, however, allow anxiety to lead it to waste precious resources on overpreparing in the short term for one particular scenario or another. As we see in Table A, China is a much more ambiguous potential foe than are terrorists, the true threat of today.

Table A: Jihadists and China: A Comparison of Threats

	RADICAL ISLAMIC TERRORISTS	CHINA
Number of Americans it killed on U.S. soil in U.S. history	3,000	0
Enabled by U.S. friends	Yes (e.g., Saudi Arabia)	Yes (China is Japan's, the EU's, South Korea's largest trading partner)
Functioning aircraft carriers	None	None
Proliferation of WMD	Want to increase	Wants to decrease
Copyright infringement	Little—denounce U.S. culture and ideas	Massive—great demand for U.S. culture and ideas
Contributes directly to U.S. GDP growth	No. 9/11 triggered a recession	Yes. China is the U.S.'s largest trading partner
Believe in free trade and capitalism	No	Pretty much
Announced policy toward liberal world order	Destroy	Join
Resentful of U.S.	Yes	Yes
Causing U.S. to undermine its own values in America	Yes (Patriot Act, NSA wiretaps)	Rarely these days
View of U.S. power	Evil	Harmful and helpful
Ideologically expansionist	Yes	No, has no coherent ideology to export

The Home Front

One thing is for certain—these pivotal powers are not going anywhere. A remarkably consistent cast of great powers has been milling around for a dozen or so centuries. America should assume very long-term relationships with all of them. Thus the real question is not "What are we going to do about China and India?" but "How can America continue to thrive in an age of multiple strong powers?"

Above all else, America must get its own house in order. The greatest risks to America's prosperity and way of life start and end at home. America has to invest anew in the strengths that propelled it this far. America's fiscal mess, underperforming education system, oil dependency, broken health care system, inadequate worker protection, and crumbling infrastructure are all things America needs to fix to ensure that the rise of other strong powers will be a benefit. Our innovation system demands special attention, as we discuss in Chapter 5. It is often these underlying problems that cause much of the pain and disruption Americans attribute to actions by pivotal powers. If the United States invests in its long-term economic vitality, and makes strategic investments in a sophisticated military, it will be able to take advantage of the growth of other powers.

A More Perfect World Order

As we describe in Chapter 7, the pragmatic approach to the pivotal powers is one of "strategic collaboration." America should draw in the reemerging powers—China, India, and Russia—and make room for them at the table with the EU and Japan, while being sure they all pay for the privilege. With their new status would come a new responsibility to rebuild the liberal world order.

Why should the goal be fixing the world order? Because institutions such as the World Trade Organization, World Health Organization, NATO, the United Nations, and many others—in addition to a variety of other international architectures like the one regulating airplane safety—have a strong track record of furthering U.S. interests. America needs them more than ever to help organize the collective effort to ensure that our children are safe. These institutions reflect and reinforce the "liberal" qualities of rule of law, transparency, accountability, and respect for individual rights that Americans cherish.

For now, the pivotal powers want in. China, India, and even Russia to a lesser degree, are knocking on the door of a system that the U.S. painstakingly built and maintained, with assistance from Europe and Japan, for over fifty years. This is welcome news, because only with help from the great powers can America hope to salvage the liberal world order. Every institution needs reform. Some regimes, like the Biological Weapons Convention, were flawed from the start. Others are no longer effectively addressing humanity's most pressing problems.

With help from the pivotal powers, they could. America needs to persuade the pivotal powers to tackle with new vigor the thorny problems that plague the world, be it disease, Iran's nuclear program, genocide, unsecured nuclear material, failing states, biological weapons, or global warming. Together with America, the pivotal powers represent over half the earth's population and over three-quarters of its GDP. The small group of pivotal powers are the fulcrum to move the world. With a great power alignment, we can make real progress toward a world in which Americans can continue to thrive whether or not America remains the sole superpower by a gigantic margin.

Even with effective rules and pivotal power buy-in, we can move forward only if America leads. Instead of leading, America has been busy alienating big powers and dismantling the world order, operating in an outdated paradigm that presumes power alone can deliver security. Even though America is more dominant, along more dimensions, than any other leading state in modern international history, it needs partners and it needs rules. It is not enough that our economy is the largest in the world, our military light-years ahead of the rest, our technology the envy of the globe, and our culture pervasive, if we cannot work with others to fight the true forces of disorder.

How can it be true that ultimate power does not bring ultimate security? Just ask yourself, what has primacy done for us lately? It tempted our leaders into a war in Iraq whose repercussions will haunt our grandchildren. U.S. primacy has not made Afghanistan a stable, liberal success story. With all its strength, America cannot effectively address Iran's and North Korea's nuclear programs without Chinese and Russian help. Americans are completely reliant on Scotland Yard to arrest terrorist suspects in the London suburbs. Alone, even if it wanted to, America could not reduce carbon emissions enough to avoid climatic disaster. Our bullets and borders cannot stop viruses.

Pivotal powers certainly want more influence, and that can complicate, even derail, U.S. plans. At the same time, as we discuss in Chapter 6, no pivotal power is out to dethrone America, and, to further their own interests, all want a positive relationship with the United States. They may not do what America wants them to, but neither are they trying to kill us. Together we can defeat those who are. Rather than fending off their attempts to take over the world, the greater challenge for the U.S. will be coaxing these big powers to pay for and play a constructive role in making it better. Pivotal powers ought to be America's sparring partners. We can knock each other around, but we are not each other's true battle.

New Thinking

During the Cold War, America's statesmen were highly focused on great power relations. Not only was the relationship with the Soviet Union itself critical, but the alignment of other power centers was also a major concern. During the 1990s, other than a period of worrying about the stability of Russia, and the economic rivalry with Japan, policy toward the biggest world powers was not on the front burner. India and China were weak, and transnational threats seemed in check. Post 9/11, America should return its focus to the big powers. Not as threats, and not as pawns in a balance-of-power system, but as partners against forces of destruction.

America needs to move away from its current amalgam of ad hoc, reactive, and inconsistent policies, and toward pragmatic cooperation with the pivotal powers, working with them and not against them. If we don't, we could awaken from our Iraq nightmare to a world not organized in our best interests. As Chapter 8 suggests, this shift will not be easy because America's political culture encourages our politicians to find foreign scapegoats for our problems. It can promote rejection of international cooperation, even though decade after decade, polling reveals that Americans are inclined to multilateralism. Much of the media, loving a fight because their viewers and readers do, does not tend to contribute to a reasoned discourse about the rise of other nations. If we are not careful, these factors, especially combined with a recession, could easily push Americans into unwarranted, extreme hostility directed at China or the next power du jour. Some Americans are already there.

More than anything, America must step back into the shoes of the world's reasoned leader and relinquish its role as the world's revolutionary power. America can then leverage the resources, skills, and experience of the pivotal powers to advance the many goals it shares with them, building a future in which Americans will thrive. In today's world, great powers pose no obstacle to American success. They will even help us, if we are brave enough to let them.

1. *Safety in Numbers*

On December 13, 2001, two months and two days after the attacks on September 11, five men stormed India's capitol building during a session of Parliament. Carrying AK-47s and hand grenades, the assailants killed seven and wounded eighteen in a bloody standoff with police before they succumbed. The attack sent tremors throughout India and was aimed, the prime minister later suggested, at decapitating the Indian government, eliminating all its top political leadership. Lashkar-e-Taiba (LeT), a hard-line radical Sunni Muslim group based in Lahore, Pakistan, claimed responsibility for the attack.

Fast-forward some eighteen months, to a U.S. District Court in Alexandria, Virginia. There, in June 2003, eleven American Muslims, called the "paintball terrorists," after a favorite pastime of theirs, were charged with training with and fighting for LeT. Six of the men eventually pleaded guilty, three were convicted at trial, and two were acquitted, making it the domestic terrorism case that has produced more guilty verdicts than any since September 11.

From halfway around the globe, the LeT threat came to haunt America's suburbs. Back when the LeT, "Army of the Pure," focused on "liberating Muslims" in the remote mountains of the disputed Kashmir region between India and Pakistan, it was of little direct concern to Americans. Now, like many other small terror groups, LeT has joined the global jihadist bandwagon, linked with al Qaeda, and views

23

as its chief priority "to select and train persons to wage war against nonbelievers, and especially the United States." Osama bin Laden has reportedly asked LeT to recruit Pakistanis for suicide missions. As it encounters new threats, America has to find new partners. America's ally in thwarting LeT is an aspiring great power, India, which has tracked this group for years.

In this chapter and the next we discuss American security. One of our less celebrated founding fathers, John Jay, wrote in 1787 in a newspaper column that became one of *The Federalist Papers*: "Among the many objects to which a wise and free people find it necessary to direct their attention, that of providing for their *safety* seems to be the first."

After over two hundred years of relative freedom from external threats, most Americans have grown accustomed to a sense of personal security unimaginable in many corners of the world. We need only look to Iraq, or to crime-ridden neighborhoods, to see that without freedom from physical violence, a society cannot prosper or progress. As anyone who has experienced it knows, there is little that is more preoccupying, and more draining to happiness and productivity, than deep fear for the safety of oneself and family members.

How do pivotal powers affect American security? Do they help or exacerbate the threats confronting Americans? Do they pose a direct threat? To answer these questions, we must first discuss what the principal threats to American security are. Traditionally, when most national security experts discuss threats, they have in mind actions by other states. We instead focus on a broader set of threats to Americans, in America, because if some external force (not a car accident or earthquake, but actors from outside, like terrorists) threatens to harm your family, you would want the government to try to stop it, even if it was not a state. In this chapter we examine how pivotal powers have an impact on threats that could kill a lot of Americans and wreak havoc with their lives. In the next, we look at how pivotal powers affect a variety of indirect threats to American security. In Chapter 3 we discuss the effect of pivotal powers on American ideology, and in Chapters 4 and 5, their economic effect.

Which Threats?

The most dire potential threats to American security are a large-scale terrorist incident with a weapon of mass destruction, particularly a nuclear weapon, and a major pandemic of contagious disease. These threats could directly kill hundreds of thousands of Americans or more on U.S. soil, and could occur soon. We add to this category of dire threats an invasion or large-scale attack by another country. Though this threat is unlikely to materialize in the near term, it is the only other outside force that could destroy American lives on a large scale. Each of these dire threats has the potential to cause disruptions so massive as to alter life in the United States as we know it.

Next on the list are serious, direct threats that would likely kill fewer people, are less mature, more deterrable, or involve a degree of culpability on the part of individual Americans who are victims. A hostile state, such as North Korea, does not yet have the capacity to attack the U.S. directly with a missile, nor launch disabling cyber attacks, and can be deterred to some degree. Nevertheless, it seeks destructive capacity, and could acquire it. Global warming could well prove a grave threat, though its most extreme effects are decades away, and Americans have some ability, if not yet the will, to mitigate the impact. Narcotrafficking ultimately results in many American deaths a year, but demand is a domestic phenomenon.

Finally, as we discuss in the next chapter, there are important American security interests that are several steps removed from a direct and immediate menace to citizens in America. They include potential threats to the wide network of key U.S. allies around the world, to regional stability, to America's ability to act exactly as it might wish in any given situation, and to American pride. In this last realm, pivotal power influence is undeniable, anxiety-producing, and hard to evaluate.

Table 1.1: External Threats to the United States

	Threat	Timeframe in which incident is likely to occur	Potential deaths in the U.S.	Degree to which individual American victims contribute to harm	Deterrable
D I R E	Terrorists, especially using WMD	Now	Extremely high	None	Unlikely
	Influenza or other epidemic	Now	Extremely high	Variable	No
	Massive attack or invasion by state	Distant	Extremely high	None	Yes
S E R I O U S	Limited attack by hostile state (including cyber)	Medium term	High	None	Yes
	Global Warming (extreme effects)	Medium term	High	In aggregate, high	No
	Narcotrafficking	Now	High	High	In some cases
I N D I R E C T	Threat to U.S. friend or ally from state	Medium term	None	n/a	In some cases
	Threat to stability, U.S. freedom of maneuver, U.S. pride	Now	Unclear	n/a	In some cases

Technology and globalization have made nonstate or small state threats far more potent than in the last century. Terrorists and traffickers are greatly empowered by the Internet. Hostile regimes have access to technical information once only available to the most sophisticated militaries. Diseases spread more rapidly because of cross-border travel of people and animals. Global warming is a direct product of human technological advances. The potential for "catastrophic damage" from weak nonstate actors is an unprecedented security challenge. Today, pivotal powers actually improve America's security from the clearest present dangers.

Jihadists, Nukes, and Germs

We first consider two enemies that have killed and will likely continue to kill large numbers of Americans: terrorists (especially if armed with a nuclear, chemical, or biological weapon) and contagious pathogens. These are the rotten fruit of globalization—transnational threats that fear no punishment civilization can dole out. How do other strong powers affect U.S. security from these agents?

THE TRUE THREAT OF TERROR Terrorists pose the most dire threat to American security today. The "gold standard in terror," according to expert Daniel Benjamin, remains "mass casualty attacks against Americans." A series of terror attacks on America's soft institutions—hospitals, schools, shopping malls—could change life as they know it for countless Americans.

In the last ten years, and particularly after 9/11, two trends have changed the nature of the terrorist threat America faces. On the one hand, the principles of terror have whipped their way around the world. Al Qaeda now exists "more as an ideology" than a unitary organization, but it has bonded hundreds of groups that once had parochial, local objectives. Now a diffuse jihadist network, living online and off, dedicates itself to "avenging the shedding of innocent Muslim blood." The new terror is a global problem in need of a global solution.

At the same time, the nuts-and-bolts execution of attacks is increasingly local. The 9/11 hijackers used mobile phones and crossed international borders many times. Now terrorists have gone to ground. Jihadists operate quietly in small cells, communicating with outsiders only when absolutely necessary. Many are "self-starters," operating without any guidance from al Qaeda or other international terror organizations.

To fight the evolving terrorist threat, the United States is tremendously and increasingly reliant on cooperation with other governments, including those of the pivotal powers. As powerful as the U.S. is, its intelligence services cannot know everything that thousands of terrorists are discussing and planning in some sixty countries. Much of the time, it does not even know who these individuals are. America's vast array of powerful satellites, flying drones, spy airplanes, and other impressive machinery that provide imagery and signals intelligence, or SIGINT, cannot track whispered conversations in markets or mosques. What's more, "the U.S. simply could not replicate an intelligence capability for all of the countries where we would have an interest," according to Brian Jenkins of RAND, one of the world's foremost terrorism experts. U.S. human intelligence (HUMINT)—old-fashioned spying—is notoriously inadequate, with major shortages of Arabic, Farsi, and Pashto speakers. Moreover, terror cells are incredibly difficult to penetrate even for those outsiders who do speak the language.

That leaves the U.S. "highly dependent," says Jenkins, on foreign intelligence services. A former official on the CIA's al Qaeda desk agrees, writing to us in an e-mail that counterterrorism cooperation with other countries is "VERY VERY VERY important." The 2006 National Intelligence Estimate on global terrorism trends concluded that "Countering the spread of the jihadist movement will require coordinated multilateral efforts that go well beyond operations to capture or kill terrorist leaders."

Each pivotal power faces what each considers a terrorist threat: Chechnyans in Russia, Uighurs in China, Islamic extremists in India and Europe (with the first two, at least, counterterrorism has also been a cover to target legitimate political activity). Japan is the only country to have suffered a deadly chemical terrorist attack. In 1995, the Buddhist cult Aum Shinrikyo released the nerve agent sarin gas into the

Tokyo subway, killing twelve. A subsequent raid on the cult's compound turned up samples of Ebola and anthrax along with enough sarin gas to kill four million people. Pivotal powers are motivated partners that see the terrorist threat as a very high security priority.

India has long defended itself against violent extremists of all stripes from Nepalese Maoists to Kashmiri separatists to Pakistani nationalists. With the third largest Muslim population in the world, and Pakistan still a key terror hub next door, India has diligently monitored and countered radical Islamic groups for decades. Suddenly, the U.S. badly needs this expertise.

The terrorist group LeT has been actively pursuing its new international and anti-American agenda. In addition to the paintball connection, the FBI has suggested that Mohammed Ajmal Khan, who held a leadership position in LeT (this according to the British judge that sentenced him to nine years in March 2006), discussed bombing East Coast synagogues with extremists in the U.S. Beyond the LeT, Jaish-e-Mohommed (JeM), another militant Islamic group battling Indian rule in Kashmir, also has ties to al Qaeda.

Fortunately for the U.S., Indian security forces have been carefully tracking LeT and JeM, relying on superior counterterror capabilities. After 9/11, India offered its full support for the U.S.-led fight against terrorism—including intelligence on al Qaeda and the use of port facilities for U.S. naval vessels. In June 2005, India and the U.S. signed a ten-year defense pact that promises continued counterterror operations, and a few weeks later, before a joint session of Congress, Indian prime minister Manmohan Singh pledged to make "common cause" against terrorism. India's pledge of "unlimited support" for the U.S. action in Afghanistan was also a welcome signal of a shared outlook.

European countries have been high-profile partners in fighting jihadist plots. Europe is itself a prolific source of new recruits, one of two great "fields of jihad." Europe was home to the terrorists responsible for the 2004 Madrid and 2005 London bombings. Three of the 9/11 hijackers lived in Hamburg. Only local police and intelligence agencies rooted in communities have any chance of gaining knowledge of terrorist plans. As a legacy of colonial relationships, European officials also have ongoing intelligence channels in Northern Africa that the U.S. lacks. Only through information sharing can America hope to monitor individual extremists from Algeria, Morocco, or Somalia as they travel to terrorist training camps in the Middle East or South Asia.

Happily, counterterror cooperation with Europe is robust and reciprocal. According to a U.S. military officer based in Europe, American and European intelligence services are cooperating closely in tracking suspected radical Islamic extremists. Without tip-offs from European law enforcement, the U.S. may not know of certain citizens, for example, raising money for known terrorist groups. At the same time, without the help of the U.S. the Europeans could not track these suspects as they travel to various countries in the Middle East and back again. Examples of this kind of cooperation are "infinite," he states, though details remain classified.

To take a public example, without British (and Pakistani) vigilance, the United States might well have witnessed another 9/11-scale attack on its landmark financial buildings. British counterparts told the Department of Homeland Security in July 2004 of a plot by a British cell to blow up the New York Stock Exchange and five other sites. A few days later, in "Operation Rhyme," British authorities arrested the key suspects. Without the British, U.S. law enforcement would not have known about this plot and, even if it had, would not have had authority to arrest suspects in London. America was completely reliant on careful British police work, just as with the August 2006 foiled plot to blow up ten airplanes bound for the United States with liquid bombs. Some Americans alive today owe their good fortune to MI5 and Scotland Yard.

Some facets of counterterrorism will benefit as Europe integrates and "seals up the cracks" between countries, says Nora Bensahel, a terrorism analyst. Terrorists will no longer be able to "shop" for countries with more favorable laws.

China is not on the front lines in the struggle against the militant Islamic threat, as the Uighur Muslim population in Xinjiang Province is small and its extremists comparatively feeble. Nevertheless, Beijing stepped up, arresting numerous suspects with ties to al Qaeda in the wake of 9/11. At a critical time, China also pressured its close ally, Pakistan, to cooperate with the U.S. in counterterror operations and to accommodate the war in Afghanistan. Beijing agreed to freeze the accounts of terrorist suspects in Chinese banks. China has acceded to eleven of twelve international counterterrorism conventions. The FBI now has an office in Beijing.

Most important, China has signed up to a major American anti-terrorism program, the Container Security Initiative (CSI), designed to prevent terrorists from smuggling a nuclear weapon into the United States in a shipping container. "The container is the potential Trojan horse of the twenty-first century," says the head of U.S. Customs, Robert Bonner. Because American ports are vulnerable, CSI is aimed at finding WMDs before they are loaded onto ships. Each year over 3.2 million containers leave China's ports bound for the U.S., more than from any other country. U.S. customs officials are now welcomed in the ports of Hong Kong, Shanghai, and Shenzhen.

Russia has also acted as a partner in counterterror. During the early stages of the campaign against the Taliban in Afghanistan, Russia proved as crucial as many NATO allies, if not more so. At their May 2002 summit, Vladimir Putin and President Bush founded the U.S.-Russia Working Group on Combating Terrorism and a number of bilateral treaties that, according to then–U.S. Ambassador Alexander Vershbow, have facilitated "unprecedented forms of intelligence sharing that have helped prevent attacks and shut down terrorist groups." To find a foreign jihadist training in Chechen camps, the U.S. must rely on Russia.

The last issue regarding terrorists is how they come to be in the first place. The factors that turn people into terrorists are complex and debated. Bruce Hoffman of Georgetown University has testified that until America recognizes the importance of understanding its enemy, it will remain forever on the defensive, unable to neutralize terrorist propaganda, nor successfully penetrate terrorist ranks to sow dissension from within, nor prevent operations. Because of their long experience with terrorists, pivotal powers like India and Europe can assist in this critical endeavor. A professor at the National Defense University concludes that China now understands, better than the U.S. does, that a terrorist movement must be fought politically more than militarily. As we discuss in Chapter 3, pivotal powers may also be able to help America to counter radical ideology, the "center of gravity" of the global jihadist phenomenon.

It is clear that failing, poor states without functioning governments provide sanctuary for training, planning, and recruiting. As much as with the other facets of counterterror operations, the U.S. needs pivotal powers to reform dysfunctional countries. The regional expertise and resources of pivotal powers, as well as the United Nations, would increase the odds of a successful outcome in any effort to build or rebuild a nation, be it in Afghanistan, Somalia, or elsewhere. Fortifying weak states is a central task for the big powers.

Pivotal powers and the U.S. both benefit from energetic cooperation on combating terrorism. However, to optimize these relationships, the U.S. should make some adjustments. It ought to refrain from "treating foreign intelligence services as if they are in the employ of the U.S. government," says Brian Jenkins, demanding all their intelligence relevant to the U.S., but not sharing much in return. Inadequate sensitivity to local political conditions is also a frequent complaint of governments who are cooperating with the U.S. Governments sometimes take big political hits at home when they help the U.S., as the administration of Chancellor Angela Merkel did for Germany's aid in renditions and in sharing Iraqi plans before the U.S. invasion in 2003. Finally, the U.S. would be more successful at rallying support for its struggle against terrorism if it were not presented as a purely American endeavor. After all, says Jenkins, "we are all in this together." In the realm of counterterrorism, the U.S. should want prosperous and stable rising powers.

WMDS ON THE LOOSE Even with cheap, crude technology, terrorists have succeeded in killing large numbers of innocent civilians. With weapons of mass destruction—chemical, biological, or nuclear—the death toll could rise by many orders of magnitude. Stopping the spread of WMDs to terrorists is thus an urgent goal, perhaps the most urgent goal, of U.S. foreign policy. This section focuses on nuclear weapons, as an atomic blast in a dense urban area would cause uniquely catastrophic results, even when compared to chemical or biological weapons—hundreds of thousands of people would die. Even a simple "dirty bomb," which combines a conventional explosive with radioactive materials, could cause widespread radiological contamination. Osama bin Laden has declared it a "religious duty" for Muslims to acquire nuclear weapons, and the intelligence community is "extremely concerned" with accumulating evidence that terrorists intend to use WMDs in attacks against the United States.

Says Michael Hynes, a nonproliferation expert, "the need for international cooperation in stemming the nuclear threat is paramount." Every layer of the nonproliferation web (controlling existing weapons, nuclear materials, and programs in development) requires the assistance of other countries, especially the pivotal powers.

Until recently, the international regime controlling nuclear materials had been effective in limiting nuclear programs and thus potential access by terrorists. The centerpiece is the Nuclear Non-Proliferation Treaty (NPT), but also included are the Comprehensive Test Ban Treaty (CTBT), the Nuclear Suppliers Group (NSG), and others. The International Atomic Energy Agency (IAEA) monitors civilian nuclear programs and conducts spot checks. Says nonproliferation expert Joe Cirincione of the Center for American Progress, "Despite serious setbacks . . . the nonproliferation regime remains the most successful international security arrangement in history.

Rather than the twenty or thirty nuclear states that many feared would emerge in the 1960s, we have only nine, including North Korea. There is every reason to believe we can decrease that number." That said, nonproliferation rules need reform, as we discuss more in Chapter 7.

A first-order nonproliferation priority, where pivotal power help is crucial, is preventing a terrorist group or hostile state from acquiring a "loose" nuclear warhead. Though the U.S. has already spent millions of dollars (through the Nunn-Lugar program) securing these bombs, Russia remains by far the largest potential source with thousands of warheads stored in hundreds of buildings littered throughout the vast country. Senior Russian officials confirmed four incidents in 2001 and 2002 of terrorists carrying out reconnaissance on nuclear weapons facilities and, through 2005, nearly one hundred incidents of trespassing at Russia's nuclear facilities. (Of minor comfort is the fact that many of these Russian warheads are old and might not detonate.)

The next concern is radioactive material. The fissile material of choice for terrorists would be highly enriched uranium (HEU) because making it detonate is easy for anyone with experience with large-scale weaponry. According to a report from the National Defense University, some two-thirds of Russia's six hundred metric tons of bomb-ready material, enough for "tens of thousands of nuclear weapons," remains inadequately secured. Some 128 civilian nuclear research reactors around the world each hold enough HEU for a bomb.

The IAEA reports ten incidents of disrupted illegal transactions involving HEU over a twelve-year period ending in 2005. Not including likely incidents that remain classified, that makes at least eleven separate occasions in which German, Russian, French, and other police forces arrested enterprising individuals illegally trying to sell radioactive material. In July 2001, for example, Paris police arrested four suspects for hawking uranium likely stolen from Ukraine. In October 2006, Beijing confirmed the arrest of two suspects reportedly trafficking uranium. Keeping nuclear materials out of terrorists' hands depends on skilled law enforcement in cities like St. Petersburg, Prague, Beijing, and Landshut, Germany.

Even if efforts to safeguard warheads and prevent the purchase of nuclear materials were funded in the U.S. and elsewhere at the level that they ought to be (much greater than at present) they will never be completely effective. Nuclear programs under development also have to be a target. If a terrorist group were to acquire a quantity of HEU from the black market successfully, according to expert Michael Hynes, they "wouldn't need a Manhattan Project" to turn it into a weapon. "They'd be set if they took over the bottom level of a parking lot in Karachi." Fortunately, the combination of tools and materials needed for fashioning a bomb, and the chemical residues, are unique, and can, in theory, be tracked. As with counterterror operations, the United States is reliant on foreign governments to track these groups, monitor their activities, share intelligence, and interdict them. As it sits thousands of miles away from the origins of the threat, Washington needs partners.

For the most part, and driven by their own interests, pivotal powers have been helpful in halting the proliferation of nuclear materials. As we discuss later, China has become a member in good standing of the nonproliferation community. Since the mid-1990s, China has greatly improved its domestic control over the flow of sensitive technologies, signed bilateral agreements with the U.S., and joined international conventions such as the NPT, the Chemical Weapons Convention, the Comprehensive Test Ban Treaty, the Nuclear Suppliers Group, and others, all of which require adherence to specific guidelines on the transfer of nuclear materials. The People's Republic was instrumental in felling the most notorious nuclear swap meet of our time, run by Pakistani scientist A. Q. Khan, whose customers included Iran, Iraq, North Korea, and Libya. That said, the U.S. government still regularly censures Chinese companies for illegally selling weapons' components to states hostile to the U.S. like Iran and Syria.

While trends are encouraging, China's export controls are still very leaky.

Japan is an active member of America's Proliferation Security Initiative (PSI), which calls on countries to interdict shipments of illegal goods, including WMDs. Administration officials have frequently praised Japan's "leadership role" in PSI. Japan also enforces its export controls carefully. In August 2006, Tokyo police arrested five in connection with the sale of a precision tool to Iran, which could be used to measure centrifuges for uranium enrichment.

To a large degree, Moscow also cooperates with the U.S. to secure its nuclear materials and weapons. While much work remains to be done, since 1991, five thousand nuclear warheads in Russia have been deactivated and fifteen thousand former weapons scientists have been involved in collaborations with Western researchers, reducing their incentives to sell their knowledge to terrorists. For the first time in a decade, Moscow issued a paper on its nonproliferation policy in 2006. Russia is also the cofounder and cochair with the U.S. of the "Global Initiative to Combat Nuclear Terrorism." A group of now fifty countries, some of which would have been reluctant to join if not for Russia's participation, the initiative seeks to develop a framework in which they can cooperate to prevent, detect, protect against, and respond to potential radiological attacks. Russia is doing this for its own reasons, which, other than counterterrorism, include wanting to address concerns that might limit profits in its civilian nuclear power sector. That said, like their Chinese (and European) counterparts, Russian defense companies circumvent export control laws to sell illicit items abroad. The Europeans are also engaged, with the European Commission, the U.K., Germany, Italy, and France pledging billions in a new initiative through the G8, the forum of the world's major industrialized economies, to secure weapons and materials of mass destruction.

India too has been increasingly willing to strengthen its domestic export control laws. While it undermines the NPT, the recent civil nuclear agreement between the U.S. and India commits India to greater controls over its nuclear energy infrastructure.

For the worldwide nonproliferation regime to continue to remain effective with the pivotal powers and the rest of the world, the U.S. has to show leadership in reforming it. Washington also has to get back in line, as an obstacle to an effective nonproliferation regime, Cirincione says, is now "U.S. policy itself." In recent years, America has failed to ratify the Comprehensive Test Ban Treaty, undermined the fundamental premise of the NPT by slow-walking reform efforts, and, far from emphasizing disarmament, is researching new nuclear weapons, including "bunker buster" bombs. Without a commitment by America to lead the nuclear pivotal powers toward disarmament, nonnuclear powers have less incentive to cooperate. Their agreement in the NPT to repudiate nuclear weapons was predicated on the nuclear powers reducing their own arsenals.

America's apparent disdain for international nonproliferation conventions extends beyond the nuclear. In a particularly egregious example from 2001, the U.S. delegation obliterated six and a half years of negotiations on the Biological Weapons Convention in a single, unexpected statement. Not only was the draft text of the agreement unacceptable, the leader of the U.S. delegation announced, but it could not be fixed. The net effect was to slow the momentum against biological weapons proliferation and thereby weaken U.S. security.

PATHOGENS Even a terrorist attack with a dirty bomb could not match the destruction of a highly pathogenic virus. With this threat too, the pivotal powers prove to be on the same page with the United States. While most discussions of national security focus on the threat posed by other people or countries, infectious diseases are the number one killer of human beings. In the last fifty years, an alarming number of new diseases have emerged, some quite gruesome— Ebola, mad cow, Legionnaires', hantavirus, and West Nile, to name a few. AIDS has already killed more than 25 million people.

A 2000 U.S. National Intelligence Estimate on the threat of global infectious disease identifies a global pandemic as an important threat to the global economy, and notes that "Emerging and reemerging in-

Figure 1.1: Emerging and Reemerging Diseases, 1996–2001

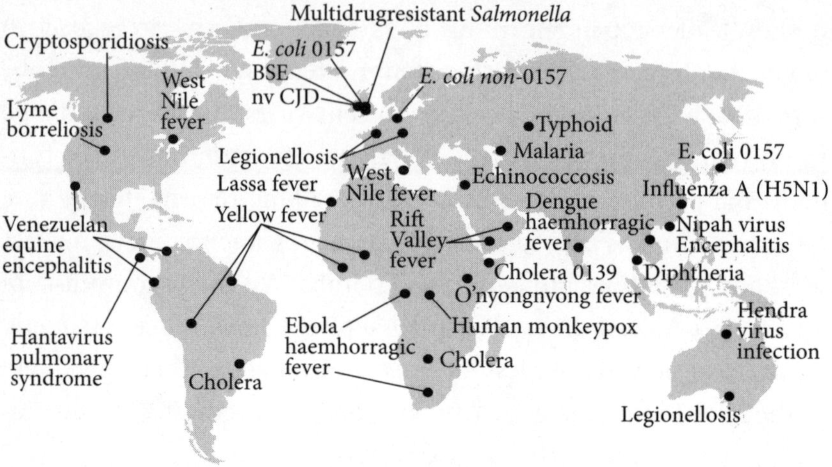

SOURCE: Klaucke D. 2002. *Globalization and Health: A Framework for Analysis and Action.* Presentation at the Institute of Medicine Workshop on the "Impact of Globalization on Infectious Disease Emergence and Control: Exploring the Consequences and Opportunities," Washington, D.C. Institute of Medicine Forum on Emerging Infections. Reprinted in Stacey Knobler, Adel Mahmoud, Stanley Lemon, Leslie Pray, eds., *The Impact of Globalization on Infectious Disease Emergence and Control: Exploring the Consequences and Opportunities, Workshop Summary—Forum on Microbial Threats* (Washington, D.C.: National Academies Press, 2006)5, available at http://www.nap.edu/catalog/11588.html (accessed May 22, 2007).

fectious diseases, many of which are likely to continue to originate overseas, will continue to kill at least 170,000 Americans annually." We focus here on naturally occurring diseases though many of the same issues are relevant to a bio-attack.

During the last major "Spanish flu" influenza pandemic in 1918, nearly one out of every two deaths in the U.S. were flu-related. The U.S. life expectancy dropped from fifty-five in 1917 to thirty-seven the next year. In eighteen months, on the order of 600,000 Americans (the percentage equivalent of some two million today) died horrible deaths, turning blue and coughing up blood. The global death toll may have been as high as 100 million. Recently linked to birds, the Spanish flu virus, shockingly, killed only 1 percent of those it infected—a mortality rate much lower than what is estimated for the avian flu circulating around wide swaths of Asia and Europe today.

Table 1.2: U.S. Cases of Infectious Diseases from Abroad

DISEASE AND YEAR	THOUGHT ORIGIN	ESTIMATED WORLDWIDE MORTALITY	ESTIMATED U.S. CASES	ESTIMATED U.S. MORTALITY
HIV/AIDS 1981–2005	Sub-Saharan Africa	25 million+	1.2 million	550,395
Tuberculosis 2005	Undetermined	1.6 million	10,236	1,347
Hepatitis C 2005	Undetermined	366,000	4.1 million	8,000–10,000 annually
Influenza Pandemics				
1918–19 "Spanish flu"	U.S. and Europe suspected	20–100 million	750,000	500,000–675,000
1957–58 Asian flu	China	2 million	Undetermined	70,000
1968–69 Hong Kong flu	Hong Kong	1 million	Undetermined	34,000
SARS (As of 2005)	China	774	8	None
West Nile 1999–2007	Uganda	Undetermined	23,969	566
Monkeypox 2003	Central and West Africa	Undetermined	37 (confirmed) 72 (being investigated)	None

SOURCES: UNAIDS; CDC; WHO; HHS; FDA; Mississippi Department of Health; Laurie Garrett, "The Next Pandemic?", *Foreign Affairs* 84, no. 4 (July/August 2005): 3–23; Joseph F. Perzl et al., "The Contributions of Hepatitis B Virus and Hepatitis C Virus Infections to Cirrhosis and Primary Liver Cancer Worldwide," *Journal of Hepatology* 45, no. 4 (October 2006): 529–38.

Even with medical advances, the world is more vulnerable to contagious disease than it was at the turn of the last century. In 2007, for the first time in history, over half the world's population lived close together in cities, often without adequate sanitation. Further, people are far more mobile than they were a hundred years ago. Now some 800 million people cross national boundaries every year. Disease-carrying mosquitoes can hitch rides in the wheel wells of airplanes and diseased animals are ferried across borders too. Along with the overuse and misuse of antibiotics in people and farm animals, and climate change, which is increasing the geographic range of pathogens, these factors make the world, and Americans, especially susceptible to a pandemic.

The outbreak of SARS (severe acute respiratory syndrome) in 2003 is a taste of what may come. The six-month SARS epidemic virtually shut down Hong Kong's vibrant economy and cost the region some $40 billion. SARS spread because one infected doctor from China's Guangdong Province stayed a single night in a Hong Kong hotel, infecting twelve other people. These travelers, in turn, seeded outbreaks in Singapore, Vietnam, and Toronto. Once SARS emerged in rural China, it spread to six countries in a matter of *hours*—and to thirty countries within a few months. SARS was not a particularly contagious or lethal virus: fewer than 8,500 people were infected and only 774 died.

A prominent example of American vulnerability to contagious disease from abroad is influenza. Another flu pandemic "cannot be avoided," in the words of one expert, and avian virus A(H5N1) could be the strain the global health community has long feared. Dr. Nancy Cox, the chief influenza scientist at the U.S.'s Centers for Disease Control, warns that further mutation of the avian flu—allowing it to spread from human to human—could precipitate the worst pandemic in human history. Mutations have made the virus "supervirulent" and extremely lethal—killing, as Table 1.3 shows, on the order of half the humans it has infected (though milder cases may not have been reported). "This is the worst flu virus I have ever seen," Robert Webster, a leading expert on the virus, says. If it becomes transmissible from human to human, Webster concludes, "God help us."

A worst-case scenario predicts sixteen million flu deaths in the U.S. alone. Given the extent to which the global economy relies on the movement of people, goods, and services, the economic impact could be staggering. The World Bank estimates an $800 billion price tag for a flu pandemic. The combination of travel restrictions and impact on the labor force would mean that all countries would experience major shortages of the most essential commodities and major industries

Table 1.3: Cumulative Number of Confirmed Human Cases of Avian Influenza A(H5N1)

	2003	2004	2005	2006
Cases	3	46	95	116
Deaths	3	32	41	80

SOURCE: Epidemic and Pandemic Alert and Response, "Cumulative Number of Confirmed Human Cases of Avian Influenza A(H5N1) Reported to WHO," World Health Organization, January 12, 2007, available at http://www.who.int/csr/disease/avian_influenza/country/cases_table_2007_01_12/en/index.html (accessed January 30, 2007).

would grind to a halt. As one expert puts it, "In short order, the global economy would shut down." The world is due for an influenza outbreak, and only governments working together can mitigate its devastation. Developed countries are only as secure as the world's weakest public health system.

How do the pivotal powers affect U.S. security from viral and bacterial agents? Combating infectious disease, whether influenza, TB, SARS, or a new pathogen, is a three-step process. First is preparedness, next surveillance and detection in human, livestock, and wildlife populations, and finally response and containment. Pivotal power cooperation is essential to each one.

When it comes to influenza, China is both the problem and the solution. Asia, especially southern China, is ground zero for flu outbreaks. Healthy wild ducks, geese, and herons play host to the influenza virus. Commercial development along their traditional migration routes means these wild birds encounter domestic birds in the farms and parks where they land looking for food and water. Once in domestic poultry, the virus will typically mutate to infect pigs. In the case of A(H5N1), it appears to be able to infect humans directly. In either case, the genetic leap is made much easier when birds, pigs, and humans live close together, as they do in "backyard flocks." With the largest rural population in the world as well as the largest poultry industry, China has all the ingredients of an avian flu incubator. Its efforts, therefore, in preparation, detection, and containment are critical.

China tried to cover up the first cases of SARS, but the international opprobrium, and devastating financial impact of SARS, seem to have taught at least some officials in Beijing a lesson. American and Chinese officials had repeated meetings in the fall of 2005 to "establish an effective cooperation mechanism" for the avian flu. China co-hosted a major avian flu conference in January 2006. It is also building in Wuhan a P4-level laboratory, one of only a few in the world, designed to research highly lethal and rare pathogens such as Ebola and SARS. The facility would become Asia's most sophisticated for the handling of deadly pathogens.

Only effective government can prevent a pandemic once a disease has emerged. SARS died down and did not return in force because Chinese government officials cracked down on the wildlife markets in Guangdong Province where the disease first spread to humans. In 2005, China slaughtered millions of chickens that may have been in contact with flu-infected birds. Over the long run, the U.S. will want to work with China to develop safer ways to raise and kill ducks, chickens, and pigs and to keep migratory birds, and bats, away from livestock. In the meantime, Americans can hope China's aggressive response continues.

Japan has also been active in combating the spread of avian flu, and the EU is also a key player in stemming an influenza epidemic, among other reasons, because the most common anti-influenza drug is produced only in Europe. Russia and India are also home to a variety of infectious diseases, from HIV to tuberculosis to typhoid. The U.S. has an interest in seeing their public health systems improve so they can battle diseases at home, before they spread.

None of these powers can act effectively alone. The World Health Organization's Global Outbreak Alert and Response Network is the central hub for all information on reports of new cases. Once the potential epidemic is spotted, a global network of virologists gets to work to identify and understand the associated pathogens. Coordination and cooperation are essential. One of the teams that traced bats as the original source of the SARS virus drew members from the U.S., China, and Australia. A well-developed science community in big countries is a direct boon to Americans in this case.

All the necessary ingredients for preventing outbreaks of contagious disease—better hygiene, fewer people living with animals, improved sanitation, sophisticated public health surveillance, more labs, and new drugs, not to mention demands from a growing middle class for an effective response to an outbreak—will improve as emerging economies grow wealthier. In its struggle against pathogens, the U.S. should encourage strong, wealthy, and able pivotal powers.

The Rest of the Worst

Beyond terrorism, proliferation, and contagious disease, other forces, like smaller, hostile states and global warming, can challenge U.S. security. How do pivotal powers affect these threats to U.S. safety? We find that here too international cooperation is key. Given space constraints, we do not discuss drug trafficking in detail, but pivotal power drug enforcement agents are cooperating with America's in combating it.

HOSTILES Today, the potential threat from hostile states is less acute than that posed by terrorists or disease. The United States can deter them, and they do not yet have the capability to launch significant attacks on the U.S. directly. In this chapter we will discuss North Korea because it has a long-range missile program that could, years from now, allow it to deliver a weapon, even a nuclear one, to the U.S. Iran, on the other hand, is more of an indirect threat to Americans, so we discuss it in the next chapter because it is likely never to be able to launch a direct attack on the U.S., though it could do so through a terrorist intermediary. In general, the more states that go nuclear, the

more likely a weapon will be sold to terrorists, stolen, set off acciden-
tally, or used in battle.

North Korea has greatly increased its stockpile of fissile material since October 2002, when negotiations with it broke down, and
in October 2006, Pyongyang tested a nuclear weapon. The regime,
though it ultimately wants diplomatic relations with the U.S., is
openly hostile, lambasting "the wicked nature and brazen-faced
double-dealing tactics of the U.S." How do pivotal powers affect this
threat?

Every pivotal power shares the goal of a nonnuclear North Korea
that plays by the rules of the international community. Though its
priorities and tactics differ, China has been an active player in trying
to bring around its longtime ally. At the outset of the North Korean
nuclear crisis in October 2002, diplomacy stalled for many months
as the U.S. refused to talk to Pyongyang directly and differences
within the U.S. government paralyzed North Korea policy. At Washington's invitation, Beijing stepped in and kept the negotiations moving forward. While American officials were frustrated that China
would not take a harder line earlier, Beijing hosted all the rounds of
the Six Party Talks, which also included Japan, Russia, and South
Korea. After Pyongyang tested, China did vote for tough U.N. sanctions, to the delight of U.S. officials. Japan is also a key ally of the
United States in addressing the North Korea nuclear program and
imposed particularly stringent sanctions on Pyongyang following its
nuclear test. While none of this involvement could substitute for U.S.
leadership, pivotal powers were playing a constructive role. When
smaller states choose to go down the nuclear road, pivotal powers are
critical to both detect such programs and to conduct the diplomacy
to convince the state to give it up. Only collective pressure can offer a
lasting solution.

HOT, HOT, HOT Harvard professor and co-chair of the National
Commission on Energy Policy John Holdren warns that without an

immediate reversal of polluting trends, the earth will be hotter than at any time in the last 160,000 years and that climate change will "adversely impact every dimension of human well-being that is tied to the environment."

A 2006 report prepared for the British government on the economic impact of climate change warned that inaction "could create risks of major disruption to economic and social activity, on a scale similar to those associated with the great wars and the economic depression of the first half of the 20th century."

American lives are directly at risk from a likely increase in extreme weather events—more frequent heat waves, droughts, wildfires, floods, and hurricanes. As global warming may allow disease-causing bacteria, viruses, and fungi to move into new areas, the United States could find itself fighting malaria and dengue fever in the future. The melting of Greenland's ice sheet, which many scientists think is likely to happen in another hundred years, would submerge many densely populated areas like Florida, along with places like Bangladesh and Shanghai. That melting is happening much more quickly than scientists estimated even five years ago. American security could also be threatened indirectly by crises around the world exacerbated by climate change, from strife over water resources, to weaker states, to the mass migration of "climate refugees."

All the pivotal powers contribute to global warming with their greenhouse gas emissions. China is the fastest-growing polluter, emitting approximately 15 percent of the world's yearly total emissions, and India is at over 5 percent. The U.S. is the largest culprit, accounting for 25 percent though China is likely to inherit that mantle soon. Unlike the rest of the world's rich countries (including Japan and Europe) the U.S. has not signed onto the Kyoto Protocol, which requires developed countries to cap their carbon emissions, nor offered a genuine alternative. As long as the U.S. resists, no long-term solution to climate change is possible because there is a widespread feeling in the emerging economies that the developed world, "which

Figure 1.2: Global Temperature: Land-Ocean Index

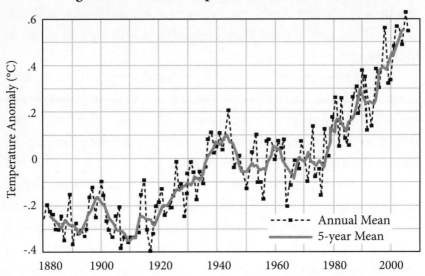

Line plot of global mean land-ocean temperature index, 1880 to present. The dotted black line is the annual mean and the solid gray line the five-year mean. SOURCE: NASA GISS Surface Temperature Analysis, May 2006, available at http://data.giss.nasa.gov/gistemp/graphs/ (accessed August 28, 2006).

grew rich while freely spewing carbon," should shoulder much of the responsibility for climate change. U.S. inaction gives China and India a free pass.

Global warming and its likely devastations can only be mitigated with multilateral cooperation. All big emitters must slow down emissions and deforestation and increase the use of alternative energy to reduce future levels of CO_2 and other agents that are causing the environment to change. And they have to do so quickly. NASA scientist James Hansen, a leading climate researcher, warns that if the world does not alter its behavior within the next decade, catastrophic effects would be unavoidable.

Pivotal powers are developing the technologies and societal adjustments that will help to solve this problem. Japan is a model of energy efficiency, and some European countries, like Germany, have successfully embraced alternative energy sources and reforestation.

As Europe and Japan work to meet their targets under Kyoto, they will garner "an immense amount of experience in what works and what doesn't. Hopefully we will have a lot to learn from them," says Joe Romm, a climate change expert.

King of the Hill

What about the pivotal powers themselves? Are they not a direct military threat to the United States? After all, before the days of suicide bombers and loose nukes, it was the fear of being conquered that haunted leaders of dominant states. The "king of the hill" dynamic has been a recurring theme in international relations for thousands of years.

Fortunately, despite hand-wringing in Washington, there is no need to fear an invasion or major attack by the Chinese, Indian, Japanese, Russian, European, or any other military anytime soon. Even leaving aside the reduced incentives for major power war that we discussed in the Introduction, it is not militarily plausible. First and foremost, America has a great strategic location. Jules Jusserand, France's ambassador to the United States from 1902 to 1925, observed that America is "blessed among the nations. On the north, she had a weak neighbor; on the south, another weak neighbor; on the east, fish, and the west, fish."

As Figure 1.3 suggests, pivotal powers have extremely limited capability to project their power across thousands of miles of water. No country today could successfully take over Los Angeles, let alone the nation. China has no operational aircraft carriers, no long-range heavy bombers, and, as of this writing, no programs to develop these capabilities. India has a single used aircraft carrier, built in 1953, and Russia has one. All the wealthy European countries combined have but a handful. Under no plausible scenario could a pivotal power, or even a coalition, acquire the capacity to take over and subdue the continental U.S. by force. And, as we have seen in Iraq, overtaking and managing even a medium-sized country far from home and against its will is highly challenging even for the world's best armed forces.

As discussed in the Introduction, a second reason the U.S. does not have to fear being conquered by a pivotal power is the extent to which nuclear weapons have changed the strategic landscape. Even if pivotal powers coalesced against the U.S., America could deter them with the threat of unacceptable damage to each.

The final reason the U.S. is not vulnerable to a traditional invasion or large-scale attack is precisely its uniquely capable military, which can take the fight to its enemy, wherever it is. The U.S. armed forces are so mighty that they defy comparison and even description. Never before in modern history has a great power's military been so vastly superior to that of its contemporaries. The U.S. spends more on its military each year than the rest of the pivotal powers combined, and roughly half of what the entire world spends. Washington's nonwar military budget, around $500 billion, is twice the size of the Russian federal government's entire 2008 budget and roughly five times the size of China's 2007 defense budget. This gulf is mirrored in every consequential measurement of military power, be it R&D, hardware, training, logistics, information warfare, sustaining troops in theater, or command and control capabilities.

The 2006 Quadrennial Defense Review, the every-four-year report on U.S. military priorities, suggests that of the pivotal powers "China has the greatest potential to compete militarily with the United States." More than half of Americans surveyed in 2005 were concerned about China growing militarily stronger in the next decade.

A head-to-head comparison of China's military with that of the U.S. is like comparing a rusty old pickup to an eighteen-wheeler. While it is easy for observers to take one statistic or another out of context to make Chinese capabilities seem foreboding, a complete comparison reveals the chasm that separates them. In terms of its nuclear arsenal, China has 110 or so missiles armed with nuclear warheads, including approximately twenty CSS-4 intercontinental

Figure 1.3: All the World's Aircraft Carriers
depicted at common scale

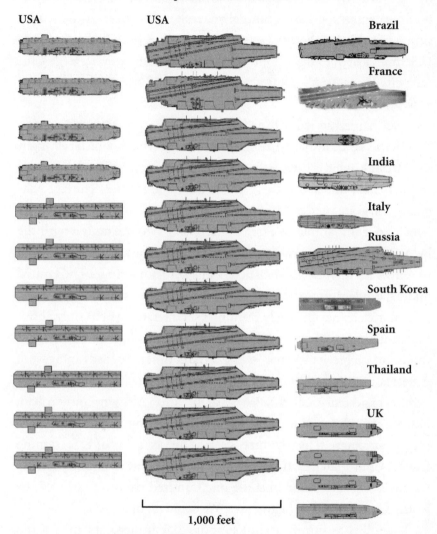

1,000 feet

SOURCE: http://www.globalsecurity.org/military/world/carriers.htm. ©GlobalSecurity.org (as of August 2007)

ballistic missiles (ICBMs) that can reach any target in the U.S. That number is sufficient to constitute a minimal deterrent (as the once popular bumper sticker said, "even one nuclear bomb can ruin your whole day"). In comparison, though, the U.S. has about a thousand warheads on top of five hundred Minuteman ICBMs, ballistic submarines with over two thousand warheads, and more than one hundred heavy bombers that can deliver nukes anywhere in the world. China is unlikely to use ICBMs against the U.S. because, in total, the U.S. military could deliver enough nukes to destroy every large Chinese city, every small Chinese city, and a good percentage of towns as well.

Also, as mentioned, China has no ability to project power across the Pacific. Its mothballed aircraft carrier, the *Minsk*, which it bought used from Russia, is the rusty star attraction of a military theme park in Shenzhen, and two others are equally inoperable. The U.S. has eleven carriers that hold seventy planes each and another eleven which are comparable to carriers in most services. Though with the help of Russia, China is building a few capable nuclear subs, its current fleet is either noisy (i.e., detectable) or short-range. The United States has fifty-five nuclear attack submarines in its fleet.

America also completely dominates the air. China has only about four hundred modern fighter aircraft; America has well over three thousand. Experience and training are other key advantages of America's military. Almost all highly ranked American officers have combat experience. China's People's Liberation Army, in comparison, has no experience with modern warfare, having not engaged in a major campaign in nearly thirty years. The vast array of U.S. training facilities is unmatched, by any standards, by any other military. America has troops stationed in some one hundred countries around the world. China has no foreign bases. We could go on.

The full facts simply do not support the notion that China could pose a direct, major military threat to the U.S. As a China military analyst at RAND put it, "The idea that China is our military peer is a joke." Twenty years from now, the picture may be somewhat different. China appears to be spending increasing percentages of its national budget on modernizing its armed forces, although, with massive domestic concerns, there are limits on what China can devote to its military if it wants to avoid the fate of the Soviet Union (and it does). Using sensible assumptions about economic growth and budgets, China will likely be spending on the order of $200–300 billion on defense by 2025 (still a fraction of U.S. spending). At that point, for conflicts on China's immediate periphery, China's capabilities could match those of the United States. In a conflict over Taiwan or elsewhere in Asia where it had the advantage of proximity, China would have a formidable capability. China's military growth will raise the costs to the U.S. of a conflict in ways that could certainly affect U.S. choices. But you have to project out some forty-five years, to 2050, before China could become a true military rival to America. Even then, it could not "take over" the U.S. Further, the ability to predict with certainty anything about the world's geopolitical state that far ahead approaches nil.

Simply put, and fairly obvious, short of the Chinese learning to control gravity, as envisioned in Kurt Vonnegut's 1976 novel *Slapstick*, China is not, and will not become in the imaginable future, a direct security threat to the U.S. Nor will any other pivotal power. Russian newspapers have reported malnutrition and even starvation among its soldiers. The combined military might of the EU is significant on paper, but, in addition to being longtime security partners of the U.S., military integration is not on the horizon. India's and Japan's capabilities remain regional. In the unlikely event of a head-to-head battle, the U.S. would vanquish any of these powers now, and for decades to come. Nevertheless, all these powers, with the possible exception of Europe, intend to invest in their militaries. This is not a sign that they plan to battle the U.S., but that a capable military protects them, and ensures they will be heard and will have leverage in the security debates of our time. Few big powers in history have ever turned down the chance to grow their military power.

To say that big countries cannot take over the United States or launch massive attacks does not rule out attacks using "asymmetric" means—not meeting the world's most powerful military head on, but fighting in ways that neutralize its advantages. Nevertheless, knowing the consequences of starting a war with the United States, a pivotal power is unlikely to lob a nuclear warhead onto an American city, hack into an urban electric grid, or destroy U.S. military satellites. That big powers are deterrable separates them from many terrorists, viruses, and climate change.

Could a great power emerge to become a hostile hegemon? We cannot rule out that possibility in the long term. Important, though, U.S. foreign policy will have a major impact on whether that future is realized, as we discuss later.

When it comes to the dire and immediate security threats that can kill Americans where we live—terrorists and viruses—the message is clear. Large, responsible powers are indispensable to the United States. British police and Chinese lab workers have American lives in their hands.

Alliance against these enemies, as well as global warming, flows from the broad harmony of self-interest among the world's largest powers. They have a stake in the stability of the world system just as the U.S. does, perhaps an even larger one, as they are still growing. Even though pivotal powers have different notions of tactics when it comes to dealing with hostile countries like North Korea, they want the same result. For the United States, there is safety in numbers.

Next we turn to the effect pivotal powers have on less direct threats to American security. Here the picture is far more ambiguous.

2. Indirect Threats: The Queasy Feeling

Beyond those threats that we discussed in the last chapter, which can directly take the lives of Americans, like a terrorist plot, outbreak of lethal disease, or the ravages brought on by global warming, lies a vast realm of situations in which American lives are not directly at stake. In these cases, America has a security interest nonetheless because an ally's security may be at risk or regional stability threatened or America's freedom of action compromised. These concerns are far afield from Americans dying in their own cities, but they remain relevant. First, threats to allies and stability can escalate into broader struggles, and second, Washington has grown accustomed to calling the shots on every important, and not so important, matter just about everywhere.

With pivotal powers on the scene, many American officials are left with a queasy sense that it will be harder to protect American interests. It is not so much their military power, but their economic, political, diplomatic, and cultural cachet that will increasingly allow the pivotal powers to reduce America's ability to determine outcomes of consequential struggles. Pivotal powers do and will prevent the United States from getting its way. They will do so in situations where their interests diverge from the U.S.'s, typically when a historical relationship (as in the case of Taiwan), resources (as in the case of oil and gas in Iran), or strategic location (e.g., Kashmir) are at stake.

The ways pivotal powers could frustrate U.S. aims are numerous. At one extreme, they could be willing to use force in opposition to U.S. goals. Short of that, they could themselves deny basing, over-flight rights, or troops for a military action (as in Iraq) and persuade others to do the same. They could attempt to delegitimize the U.S., give smaller states cover from U.S. influence, or simply outmaneuver the U.S. diplomatically. China, Russia, Britain, and France are mem-bers of the P5, the five permanent members of the U.N. Security Council, and can veto measures the U.S. seeks.

Asian Influence

This dynamic holds true, to some degree, with all the pivotal powers. The clearest example of the new dynamic is in Asia with China's growth. For over fifty years, and through ten presidents, the U.S. has named itself a "Pacific power." It has long been the most power-ful actor in Asia, politically, economically, and militarily. The U.S. has formal alliances and strong security ties with close to a dozen Asian nations. Its role as a security guarantor after World War II kept regional animosities at bay, allowing many Asian nations to boom. Now a growing China seeks a greater leadership role in its own neigh-borhood.

China's clout with every government in the region is increasing. China expert David Shambaugh writes that "the sheer volume of diplomacy and discourse" China is conducting in Asia is "staggering." Beijing is preaching development and cooperation at every turn, to draw a contrast with what Asia sees as American unilateralism. China is "expanding multilateral organizations like they are going out of style," China expert Evan Medeiros observes. It is settling border dis-putes with its neighbors and pursuing popular measures to advance free trade, while America's agenda has been "all terrorism, all the time." J. Stapleton Roy, a former U.S. ambassador to China, says "China is running circles around us" in Southeast Asia.

One Australian newspaper opined in the wake of back-to-back visits of President Bush and President Hu: "China, once a revolutionary threat to the global system, is now stakeholder. The US, once an architect of this global order, now seeks its radical redefinition." Asian neighbors see China's economic growth (but not military strength) as a positive development. All of America's Asian allies, including South Korea, Thailand, the Philippines, Singapore, and Australia, even, in some ways, Japan, have increasingly close relationships with China, grounded in booming trade.

What do China's friendly advances to its neighbors mean for the U.S.? First, China's growing influence in Asia could limit America's ability to "contain" China, to the extent it tries. Asian governments do not want to be forced to choose between Beijing and Washington, and America could have a difficult time gaining acceptance or assistance for overtly anti-China measures. In some cases, as Andrew Hoehn, a former Pentagon official and now a vice president of RAND, fears, as China becomes more proficient in balancing "hard" and "soft" power, it might "gobble up our allies," making it more difficult to line up partners on key political issues. China's influence may constrain America's heretofore almost boundless geostrategic freedom in Asia.

Over time, China's military modernization and pervasive friend making in the region could also limit America's ability to intervene successfully in the case of a military confrontation over Taiwan. While a Chinese attack on Taiwan would not directly harm American security, Taiwan is a U.S. interest because Washington has declared it is. America has long committed to help Taiwan defend itself, and America would be loath to see a vibrant democracy harmed. Taiwan has become America's litmus test for China. Former U.S. Secretary of State Colin Powell observed that "whether China chooses peace or coercion to resolve its differences with Taiwan will tell us a great deal about the kind of relationship China seeks not only with its neighbors, but with us."

For the most part, however, explains expert Robert Sutter, "China's rise in Asia does not come at the expense of US interests." Asian governments have misgivings about China, and they continue to value the role of the U.S. as an economic engine and security guarantor. China's diplomacy and trade overtures focus on low-hanging fruit to improve relations, but it is the United States that has the track record of coming through with tangible benefits. The response to the December 2005 tsunami that killed 170,000 in Southeast Asia was telling. America contributed $950 million ($346 million was in immediate relief), and sent 16,000 troops and twenty-one ships, including an aircraft carrier. China's pledged contribution of $63 million was comparatively meager. Asian countries know that America can deliver in a way that China may never be able to match. American influence in Asia is not being trumped. America, Sutter concludes, retains "the top security position" as Asia's "least distrusted power."

China Going Global

China's "charm offensive" has also spread to Africa, the Middle East, and Latin America, as China searches for commodity deals. In doing so, China supports some very repressive regimes, and while not unique among the pivotal powers (or the U.S.), such assistance offends America's ideals of justice and human rights, as we discuss in the next chapter. Do these efforts also affect, indirectly, U.S. security?

Over time, if you squint your eyes, you can begin to imagine that China's or other pivotal powers' actions might cause anti-Americanism or regional instability. The only places where Chinese and Indian companies can compete for oil and other resources are where U.S. interests have not locked everything up—often in countries under sanctions or otherwise hostile to the U.S. Venezuela's president Hugo Chávez is a thorn in the U.S.'s side, preaching disgust for America in its backyard. He is delighted to have China as a customer. "We have been producing and exporting oil for more than 100 years," he has said. "But these have been 100 years of dominion by the United States. Now we are free, and place this oil at the disposal of the great Chinese fatherland." An August 2006 deal has China helping to build twenty thousand homes for the poor and supporting Venezuela's bid for one of the fifteen seats of the U.N. Security Council. China is giving political solace to a regime inimical to the U.S. (But if China did not buy Chávez's oil, someone else would. In fact, India and Japan do. And so does America.)

China's Africa diplomacy is also in high gear as it strikes deals for energy and mineral supplies. In November 2006, Beijing hosted a summit of leaders from almost every African country, including some forty heads of state, something Washington has never attempted. Chinese investment in Africa reached over $1 billion in 2006 and two-way trade increased to nearly $55 billion that year. Beijing predicts that Chinese foreign direct investment in Africa will reach $100 billion by 2010, and this estimate does not appear to be exaggerated. China's practice of funding African governments without any conditions has undermined years of painstaking negotiations in the West to establish a harmonized set of rules for aid and lending used to counter corruption. The West has been attempting to enhance the transparency in the oil and mineral sectors, for example, through the Extractive Industries Transparency Initiative led by Great Britain with strong U.S. support. According to Africa experts this effort is "vital to the stability as well as the long term health" of African nations that are plagued by corruption. Now some countries, such as Angola, one of Africa's largest oil suppliers, have been able to resist this pressure, in part because of China's unrestricted and generous lending. Similarly, the World Bank warned China's banks against ignoring the Equator Principles, a voluntary code pledging that projects financed meet social and environmental standards. Its president cautioned Beijing against making the same mistakes as France and the U.S. did in supporting President Mobutu Sese Seko, who bankrupted Zaire (now the Democratic Republic of Congo), leaving it to swing in and out of conflict since Mobutu's rule came to an end in 1997.

In sum, China complicates existing U.S. relationships with many countries. As former Reagan-era Assistant Secretary for Africa Chester Crocker puts it, as Africa has become "a more competitive playing field, it gives greater influence to African leaders as well as to potential competitors or 'balancers' of U.S. diplomatic leverage." However, he goes on, "It is not just China: it is Brazil, the Europeans, Malaysia, Korea, Russia, India." Other pivotal powers can have similar effects in other regions, too. Having Russian backing makes some countries in Central Asia less susceptible to U.S. pressure. Europe's greater involvement in Middle East affairs could also come to complicate U.S. efforts there. It is not hard to imagine the Europeans and the United States on different sides of a deal to broker peace between Israel and the Palestinians, for example.

Iran

Iran is another example of dubious pivotal power influence. Iran's president Mahmoud Ahmadinejad has made no attempt to hide his hostility toward America, accusing it of "spending billions of dollars to humiliate other nations, destroy their love and compassion for each other, and remove divine aspirations from their minds." He has also dramatically threatened Israel. Iran funds Hezbollah, a terrorist group that has killed Americans. If Tehran some years from now builds a nuclear weapon, as it seems to desire, it could spark a regional arms race in the Middle East and become an even more destabilizing, dangerous force.

Pivotal powers, to a one, have close relationships with Tehran. Because American companies are prohibited from doing business there,

China, Japan, Europe, and India (in that order) are among Iran's biggest energy customers and investors—China is Iran's largest customer. In March 2006, India and Iran, who consider each other "strategic partners," held a joint naval exercise and are contemplating a major natural gas pipeline project to travel through Pakistan. Russia has been selling billions of dollars of weapons to Tehran for decades. In 2005, European governments provided $18 billion in government loan guarantees to Tehran. In 2006, Washington sanctioned six Chinese, two Indian, and an Austrian company for providing Iran with weapons technology. Japanese companies stand accused of doing the same.

Despite these troubling ties, though, pivotal powers are contributing to diplomacy that could halt Tehran's nuclear program. None wants Iran to go nuclear, though the issue is not as urgent to them as to America. Japan is using its leverage with Iran behind the scenes and has divested itself of an investment in a major oil field there. The EU3 (Germany, France, and the U.K.) have also taken stabs at bringing Iran to the table, and Russia has offered ideas for possible deals as well. Russia and China have weighed in to block some U.N. measures against Tehran, but have supported others. As we discuss in more detail when we lay out our pivotal power strategy in Chapter 7, the only way to address Iran's nuclear ambitions is through pivotal power buy-in. If America and pivotal powers do not close ranks, Iran will have plenty of political leeway to continue to brush off international pressure.

Ganging Up

The danger to U.S. security interests can be amplified when pivotal powers come together to frustrate U.S. security aims. For example, though during the Afghan war, China and Russia supported U.S. actions, later, the Shanghai Cooperation Organisation, of which they are the leading members, called for a timetable for the withdrawal of U.S. troops from Kyrgyzstan and Uzbekistan. China and Russia may want to foster a strategic partnership aimed at reducing America's ability to extend its global dominance in Central Asia. Despite its growing relationship with the United States, India would not "rule out" forming an anti-U.S. alliance with Russia and China on some issues. Finally, it took a surprising amount of U.S. diplomacy to convince Europe not to revoke its arms embargo against China. As scholars Francis Fukuyama and G. John Ikenberry note, "Europe might also see China as a potential ally in the restraint of the United States." All pivotal powers share concerns about U.S. unilateralism, and they are busy forming partnerships, as we will discuss in Chapter 6.

Flash Points

Another indirect danger to American security is the possibility of an accident or a small-scale dispute escalating and drawing in America. Flash points like Taiwan or Kashmir, or elsewhere where U.S. and pivotal power interests may clash, are candidates. The answer to this problem, of course, is better and more structures for communicating with pivotal powers, especially at times of crisis. Hotlines worked well for the U.S. and Soviet Union during the Cold War, but America doesn't yet have one with Beijing.

Pivotal powers themselves going to war would be a disaster for U.S. security and world stability. However, the chances of such clashes may not rise along with pivotal power stature. India and China, for example, are closer to solving their long-standing border dispute than they have been for years. Japan and China have the most contentious relationship of the lot. Both claim the right to natural gas and oil resources in the East China Sea and have also been vying for pipelines from Russia and Kazakhstan. (Of course, no matter whether a pipeline ends where China wants it to or Japan does, both countries would benefit by the increase of oil on the market, as we will see in

Chapter 4.) Historically, China and Japan have never been power-ful at the same time. Even as they vie for influence, they remain very busy trading partners, and Japan's prime minister Shinzo Abe as well as China's leaders are eager to keep their relationship on an even keel.

Indirect Upside

Though pivotal powers, or groups of them, may thwart U.S. aims or comfort U.S. enemies, growing and engaged powers can also help to solve regional security problems. We discussed how this is true in the case of North Korea and Iran. China has also deployed one thousand peacekeepers under U.N. auspices to help stabilize Lebanon, its first such action in the Middle East, and seeks a larger role in the Israeli-Palestinian conflict to help bring stability to a re-gion with energy supplies it needs. Europe is ever more active in diplomatic efforts in the Middle East and Africa. NATO's role in pro-viding security in Afghanistan is one of the most challenging the largely European alliance has ever undertaken. Japan, meanwhile, has taken a lead role in reconstruction there. From East Timor to Haiti, Russia is a regular contributor of police and military personnel to U.N. peacekeeping missions. India played a vital role in resolving the crisis in Nepal after the king dismissed the government there in Feb-ruary 2005.

Even the Taiwan question is fundamentally a political one and could be aided by China's growth. Taiwan may become, in effect, a high-risk detour on China's otherwise fairly direct path to status as a powerful, respected member of the international community. Simi-larly, now that India's economy has taken off, there are signs of politi-cal momentum to find a final solution to the Kashmir dispute. Great powers want stability, as we do, and are willing, under the right cir-cumstances, to be America's partners in achieving it.

Stepping Up

To make sure its strategic options do not erode unacceptably, American reengagement in Asia, Latin America, and Africa is necessary. Viewed from Asia, for example, writes analyst Eric Heginbotham, "U.S. treatment of allies often appears arrogant and unpredictable." Accusations of neglect are common in African and Latin American diplomatic circles. The U.S. should reinsert itself in the economic growth of key smaller countries, positioning itself as the leader who wants to promote their growth and "helped them when they were down." Former U.S. Trade Representative Charlene Barshefsky recommends that the U.S. consciously use economic agreements to their full strategic potential.

In the future, the United States will have to manage its expectations in light of greater pivotal power influence. In particular, America will need to distinguish situations where pivotal power actions taken without its blessing are truly harmful to its interests from those that only generate that uncomfortable feeling of not being in control. We must remember, too, that while threats we discuss in this chapter, as toward Taiwan, are very important, they do not compromise American security interests to the same degree as the threats we discussed in the last chapter that can kill Americans at home.

De-Fence

Threats, both direct and indirect, are only one side of the security equation. The other is preparedness. America must be able to defend itself from attacks, resist compromising a vital interest, avoid being compelled to do something it does not want to do, and continue to convince adversaries that attacking the U.S. would trigger unacceptably damaging retaliation.

First, the United States needs always to retain a highly sophisticated and extraordinarily capable military. Overspending on the armed forces, however, has been the economic doom of great powers in the past as it drains resources away from important domestic priorities. America therefore needs a military well tailored to threats it actually faces. We have just suggested that terrorists, proliferators, and disease, not big countries, are the biggest threats Americans face for the foreseeable future. The Defense Department's 2006 Quadrennial Review agreed, prescribing a shift in funding to areas such as counterterrorism, counterinsurgency, stabilization, and reconstruction operations, in order to win the "Long War" on terror. But the Department of Defense's 2007 budget does not heed its own advice. Much of the increase in spending is for new, huge weapons systems only useful for fighting other states and of "dubious" utility even for that, lesser-

Figure 2.1: National Defense Budget Authority, FY 1998–2008

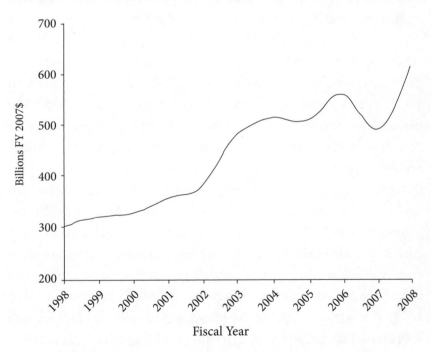

SOURCE: Center for Strategic and Budgetary Assessments, Analysis of the FY2007 Defense Budget Request. Includes $70b FY06 supplemental appropriations request, $50b downpayment request toward FY07 war costs, and FY08 base and war budget request.

priority, mission. The department's base proposed budget increased 48 percent from 2001 to 2007, yet Special Operations Forces to fight terrorists account for only around 1 percent of the total.

If the country were not so far in debt, perhaps America could afford all this. In reality, there are real trade-offs between conventional forces, anti-terror capabilities, and investing in technologies of the future. An important way to prepare militarily for a distant state threat, which we cannot rule out, is by discovering "breakthrough" or "leap-ahead" technologies. The Pentagon has not made anywhere near good on its promise to devote 20 percent of its procurement budget to these technologies, according to defense analyst Kori Schake, among others. Instead, tens of billions of dollars are devoted to massive weapons programs like the F-22A Raptor fighter plane, which were designed for the Cold War, offer incremental conventional advantages, at best, and do nothing for the priority battle against terrorists.

Waste is a perennial problem, but it has gotten much worse with escalating defense budgets. Says Larry Korb, an assistant secretary of defense under Ronald Reagan, now with the Center for American Progress, "It's always been bad, but I've never seen it this bad." The Government Accountability Office determined in 2006 that cost *over-runs* in weapons systems it studied amounted to $23 billion. Contractors involved in the F-22 have been paid $849 million in bonuses even though the current phase of the program is $10 billion over budget. Cost overruns ultimately mean fewer weapons are produced. Also appalling are the delays in delivery of up to four years. In fact, the procurement cycle of the Pentagon is so long that new systems are often already obsolete when they are delivered. It is more urgent than ever to remedy these misallocations, or America will be left with a host of wildly expensive, politically expedient, but not very useful weapons systems that do nothing to stem terrorism and leave it too broke to invest in the defenses we may need in the future.

Maintaining a strong military involves hard choices, but they are ones Americans have experience making. Other necessary national security reforms—developing a cogent plan for fighting terrorism over the long run, integrating U.S. homeland security bureaucracies, improving public health systems, training and equipping first responders, securing nuclear and chemical facilities, reducing carbon emissions, and supporting international regimes that address these threats—are equally urgent but not nearly as straightforward. Nor, as we discuss in Chapter 8, will it be politically easy to make the necessary shift of even a small percentage of funds from military to nonmilitary national security spending. Without that adjustment, though, America will not be able to engage diplomatically as it should with smaller countries, let alone the pivotal powers. Pivotal powers can assist with some threats, but they cannot help the United States make these important investments in its own capacity.

In sum, pivotal powers have a shared stake in foiling agents that would disrupt world order, and they do not pose a direct military threat to the U.S. At the same time, they will lessen the nearly unlimited freedom of action the United States has enjoyed within that order. They do and will challenge U.S. leadership. As they grow, they will become more involved in the politics of other regions. Sometimes that will play to the U.S.'s advantage; sometimes not. The challenge for the United States is not to turn this manageable security threat into an existential one.

Later in the book, we will suggest a strategy for how America can maximize pivotal power help with dire threats and minimize the obstacles these powers pose. Next, though, we look at how pivotal powers affect America's ideological priorities.

3. The Battle of Ideas?

In the last two chapters, we focused on the ways in which pivotal powers affect American security. Here we focus on the principles of individual rights, rule of law, capitalism, and democracy that together form America's unique "creed." How do the pivotal powers affect America's way of life at home and its ability to spread its ideals abroad?

Values at Home

The answer to the first half of the question is simple. Pivotal powers do not affect Americans' ability to live by their ideals at home. They cannot conquer America, and do not threaten to do so. None aspires to dismantle America's ideology, as we will see below, and they do not have much of an impact on how America's values are realized in America. That could change if, for example, elected officials became overly anxious about possible technology transfers to China and began a wide-ranging campaign to prosecute Chinese-American scientists over their research. For now, though, there is no measurable impact.

Contrast the impact of big powers with terrorists. The actions of terrorists, past and potentially future, have greatly affected the degree to which America lives by its ideals. In the wake of 9/11, the federal government has taken a slew of steps that many argue play fast and loose with Americans' constitutional rights—from provisions of the Patriot Act that allow expanded surveillance of Americans without judicial review, to cases involving the legal rights of detainees held as "enemy combatants," among others.

Beyond Borders

We turn now to the harder question. Will other pivotal powers undermine America's ability to extend its ideas abroad? In all likelihood, yes—but at the margins.

America is not unique in its passion to see its system reflected around the world. Throughout history, the world's greatest powers have all wanted to spread their ideology. Says political scientist Robert Art, none has been "content merely to stand as a shining example" of a certain form of government; they have been vigorous missionaries, to a one. Some ideas, like Roman concepts of the republic or Great Britain's adherence to laissez-faire economics, were adopted and propelled further by subsequent dominant powers like the U.S.

In the case of capitalism, U.S. promotion efforts have achieved stunning success. Every pivotal power has embraced this economic model. All want and need relatively free trade and open markets. Except for Russia, which is on its way, they are all members of the WTO. And even the Russians, according to prominent scholar Dmitri Trenin, see their "bigger is better" approach to capitalism as akin to America's. Of course, each pivotal power implements capitalism in its own way. The state still has its hands in many industries in China, and the Russian government is busily reinserting its fingers in the oil and media sectors. Most European governments spend a significantly higher percentage of GDP on social programs (23.3 percent of GDP versus 16.2 percent in the U.S. as of 2003) and there often is a stronger regulatory impulse there than in the U.S. Yet none of the pivotal powers would dispute the fundamental importance of competition and private industry.

Liberty for All

The export of liberal democracy, on the other hand, while a permanent fixture in American foreign policy, has a mixed track record. (Here we use "liberal democracy" as shorthand for the complex set of principles and values the U.S. promotes abroad, including the rule of law, individual rights, and an independent media, to name a few.) How will the pivotal powers affect this American practice?

The question for U.S. policymakers has long been how best to encourage liberal democracy abroad, not whether to do so. U.S. policies to this end have fallen somewhere on the spectrum from "exemplarism" to "evangelist and missionary." In America's earliest days, the concerns about "entangling alliances" constrained a more activist stance abroad, although the expansionist impulse was arguably in full view at home. By the eve of World War I, however, President Woodrow Wilson's declaration that the U.S. should make the world "safe for democracy" marked a turning point. Since the end of World War II, every presidential inaugural speech has included a reference to America's need or wish to promote liberty and democracy around the world. Over the years, the United States has moved along the spectrum toward more active proselytizing, as America's national identity, power, and sense of purpose have evolved. "If Americans know one thing for certain," writes senior *Newsweek* editor Michael Hirsh, "it is that their values are not just right for them, but for the world."

During the Cold War, America sought to shore up European democracies as a bulwark against Soviet expansionism (while at the same time Washington supported numerous anti-communist dictators). New institutions like the Organization for Economic Cooperation and Development (OECD)—the club for industrialized democracies—and initiatives like the Fulbright Educational Exchange Program were founded to spread liberal democratic princi-ples. Later, Jimmy Carter focused on promoting the universality of human rights, and Ronald Reagan founded the National Endow-ment for Democracy, the first institution that overtly funded pro-democracy nongovernmental organizations in foreign countries. At the end of the Cold War, Bill Clinton brought American attention to bear on dozens of electoral transitions around the world and used the threat of military force to uphold democracy in Haiti. Seen through this lens, President Bush's disastrous decision to invade Iraq was not unusual in its goal, just in its method.

Why is America so devoted to seeing its system replicated? A cot-tage industry explains the reasons for America's drive. Some analysts concentrate on the purported security benefits. As President Bush put it in his second Inaugural Address, "the survival of liberty in our land increasingly depends on the success of liberty in other lands." Advocates of the "democratic peace" theory suggest that mature democracies will not go to war with each other and that conflict be-tween them is necessarily bounded. Others believe that liberalism is an antidote to extremism (a 2006 National Intelligence Estimate pre-dicts that greater pluralism in Middle East governance will reduce the growth of jihadists); or that expanding the number of democra-cies will make American leadership more palatable by aligning their ideals with ours.

Yet others focus on more philosophical motivations, arguing that the American penchant for proselytizing can be traced back to America's religious founders. Alternatively, Georgetown University scholar Charles Kupchan argues that "unlike most other nations that define themselves via cultural symbols, America's identity is in-exorably linked to its political system," and thus its democracy pro-motion efforts validate that national identity.

Average Americans are of two minds. On the one hand, bringing democracy to other countries ranked dead last in a fourteen-item list of U.S. foreign policy goals in a 2006 survey. On the other, Americans clearly seek to do good, and a large majority see democracy promotion as at least a "somewhat important" goal. For the most part, Americans, including us, believe that liberal democracy, with all its flaws, is better than any other form of government around in delivering "ordered liberty" to its people.

The debate about why America does it is the subject of many volumes and need not be settled here. What is clear is that like dominant nations in the past, the U.S. will attempt to spread its ideology while it has the power and resources to do so. Democracy promotion efforts have been a staple of American foreign policy for a long time and will doubtless continue, even after the predictable backlash against them that Iraq will generate. We can only hope that the debate about whether democracy can be induced through military force is now firmly settled.

A Helping Hand

As the pivotal powers gain power and influence, how will their goals, interests, and ideals intersect with America's values promotion? Some pivotal powers will help. Of the five, three—Japan, Europe, and India—are thriving liberal democracies. Already, the expansion of the European Union has roped much of Eastern Europe into a system in which liberal democracy and open markets are literally required by law and expected by culture. The EU is a staunch promoter of shared values, declaring, for example, that "the EU will ensure that the issue of human rights, democracy and the rule of law will be included in all future meetings and discussions with third countries and at all levels."

While Japan and India are not as active as they could be in promoting democracy beyond their borders, both are crucial demonstrations of how democracy can thrive in a non-Western context. India is especially important in this regard. As the largest democracy on the planet, India represents, observes leading analyst C. Raja Mohan, "the most enduring example of the pursuit of the enlightenment project outside Europe and North America." Delhi may take a lower-key approach than Washington to promoting liberal ideals, but it does do it, and India is warming to the idea of playing a more active role in democracy promotion. Recently, Delhi and Washington worked together to bring about a peaceful democratic transition in Nepal, for example. Another positive trend is the work of Japanese NGOs in places like Afghanistan, where they assist in sectors like education and health.

America's ideals do not map exactly with these pivotal powers. All three may permit commercial dealings with oppressive regimes that Washington would rather they did not. Nevertheless, as we suggest in Chapter 7, it is only logical that America work harder with these likeminded democracies to further liberal norms.

A Mixed Bag

As China and Russia gain ground, their impact on America's ideology promotion efforts is less certain. Thus far, the energies of Russia and China have largely been focused inward. "The Chinese communist party today does not even seem to possess an ideology to export, even if it were inclined to do so," says China scholar David Shambaugh, and the Russians too are adrift ideologically. Unlike the Cold War era, notes China expert Bates Gill, "Beijing does not seek to spread Communist ideals, establish global networks of ideological client states, or foment revolution in the developing world." The same is true for Russia, which has turned toward "economic nationalism" as a guiding principle. For both, pragmatism, not ideology, is the touchstone, and each remains on the defensive about its approach toward civil liberties and governance.

In practice, both Russia and China have been tinkering with the mix of individual freedom and state control in an "economy first" approach to governance. In Russia, this dynamic is best demonstrated in the controversial moves to renationalize strategic oil assets, crackdowns on the press and civil society organizations, and efforts to centralize political power. As troubling as these developments are to Russia's fragile democracy at home, Putin is not advocating them assertively elsewhere.

Ideology Impact?

In contrast, even though China is not an active proselytizer of communism, some observers raise several ways in which China could pose an ideological challenge to America down the road. (With much of Russia's foreign policy focused predominantly on neighboring states, it has yet to figure prominently in such discussions.) First is the idea that as China's alternative economic development model gains headway around the globe, it will undermine the central tenet that economic growth and political freedom go hand in hand. The second concern is that China's firm principle of "nonintervention" in the internal affairs of other countries will constrain U.S. actions to promote democracy, human rights, and other liberal principles. Third, China's foreign assistance policy of "no questions asked" will reduce America's ability to demand concessions on human and political rights. Finally, some argue that the rise of a nondemocratic China will undermine liberal norms of international governance.

Let us examine each of these concerns more carefully. Some argue that under the banner "peaceful rising" China is promoting itself in Africa and Latin America as the model for ending poverty. This argument suggests that China is offering an appealing alternative to governments from Azerbaijan to Zimbabwe that would prefer not to relinquish political control in the quest for economic growth.

The appeal is there, no doubt, but mainstream China analysts do not see the evidence of a concerted effort by Beijing to push an alternative growth model for developing economies. Chinese relationships and investments are driven by pragmatism. Unlike during the 1960s, Beijing is not establishing "thought centers" or posting liaisons in foreign countries to market its system. Its Confucius Institutes teach Mandarin, not Mao. No political parties in developing countries are actively modeling themselves on China's. China simply does not care about the quality or type of domestic government it engages with. This absence of ideology poses a problem for the U.S. but it is infinitely less troubling than the challenge of an active ideological opponent.

Also, while it is not fully consistent with the U.S. approach, China's "market-lite" model is not diametrically opposed either. China does not advocate political repression (though some foreign leaders may nonetheless take that lesson away from Beijing's actions at home). Further, if the Chinese "model" ultimately proves successful, it will have helped some of the world's most impoverished people improve their daily lives—again reinforcing the benefits of capitalism and perhaps even leading to political pluralism. Democracy theorists have long argued that the more wealthy a nation is, the greater its chances of sustaining democracy.

A second area of concern is China's policy of "nonintervention" in the domestic affairs of other nations. Chinese views on sovereignty are born of a long history of losing territory to foreign aggressors and wanting to safeguard its claim on Taiwan. However, it is not alone in its devotion to the standard of nonintervention in the internal affairs of a sovereign state. The United Nations was founded on this notion, and most U.N. member states staunchly defend it. At the same time, the norm of sovereignty is evolving, and China is not bucking the trend. In 2005, the U.N. General Assembly, China included, agreed for the first time that the international community has "the responsibility to protect" individual citizens from genocide, war crimes, and ethnic cleansing. (Interestingly, it was India that held out the longest among pivotal powers before endorsing this concept.)

The record shows China's conception of sovereignty is neither static nor absolute. China did not vote against American intervention in Afghanistan or Iraq as it had earlier with Kosovo, and it also voted in favor of tough sanctions against North Korea after its nuclear test. Further, with its 1,861 troops, China is second only to France as the largest contributor to U.N. peacekeeping and police forces among the P5 U.N. Security Council members.

The places where China's pragmatism bumps up against U.S. ideology will continue to trigger friction. Business is business, says China's government, no matter how unspeakable the acts perpetrated by the party on the other end of the transaction. Darfur is a case in point. China, keen to protect its 40 percent stake in Sudan's oil industry, serves as Khartoum's protector in the U.N. China blocked U.N. Security Council efforts to sanction Sudanese officials and others implicated in Darfur abuses; abstained (along with Russia and Qatar) on the August 2006 U.N. Security Council resolution authorizing a force of up to 17,500 peacekeepers; and has been unwilling to use the full extent of its leverage to force the regime to accept U.N. peacekeepers (although in early 2007, President Hu Jintao took the unprecedented step of meeting with the Sudanese leadership to encourage their cooperation, and even the U.S. envoy for Sudan defended China's diplomatic efforts, saying they complemented, rather than undercut, the U.S. approach).

China is not alone in its appetite for Sudan's oil. Democracies also support Sudan's government. In February 2005, India's Oil and Natural Gas Corporation was awarded a contract to build a $1.2 billion oil refinery there. In January 2005, French oil concern Total (with its Houston-based partner, Marathon Oil) renewed exploration rights for southern Sudan, and Canadian oil company Arakis Energy has been actively involved in the development of two oilfields going back to 1996. Further, most observers agree that if the United States and Europe had the political will to take more decisive measures, including military ones, Beijing would not stand in the way. Instead, the People's Republic has probably concluded America values its cooperation on Iran and North Korea more than Sudan, and the West remains content to blame China for continued inaction.

Burma is a similar case. The military junta there has kept the country in a stranglehold since the 1990s, holding pro-democracy leader and Nobel Peace Prize winner Aung San Suu Kyi under house arrest, continuing the widespread use of child soldiers, and becoming one of the world's largest suppliers of heroin. China has embraced this neighbor to the southeast, driven by the desire to reduce cross-border drug shipments, gain naval access, and prevent regional instability from spilling over. (China's concern about northern Burma goes back many decades because nationalist pro-Taiwan troops sought refuge inside Burma and periodically attacked China's Yunnan Province.) Cross-border trade and investment has flourished, reaching nearly $600 million in 2002; the Chinese currency is now the principal trading currency across the northern third of the country.

Again, China is not alone in supporting the junta government. In 2006, during the first visit of an Indian president to Rangoon, India and Burma agreed to a long-term plan to provide gas to India via a pipeline; French energy giant Total has likewise been a longtime investor in Burma's natural gas sector. In January 2007, the Russians and Chinese vetoed a U.N. Security Council resolution on the situation in Burma, but were also supported by Japan in opposition to U.N. action. Japan remains Burma's largest foreign aid donor, and has refused to join the United States in imposing sanctions. These are all troubling ties, and the U.S. should continue to shine a light on these dealings. At the same time, it is important to recognize that they also can provide leverage, as we discuss in Chapter 7. The ideal approach is to try to forge a consensus and use the collective political weight of the pivotal powers to push for change.

On the question of aid and investment, as we discussed in the last chapter, China's approach—"no questions asked"—has increased its influence in the developing world and helped prop up distasteful regimes. If not altered, over time, China's approach will gradually undermine Western efforts to encourage better governance and more respect for individual rights. China has shown little interest in programs that help improve civil society, the touchstone for recent Western aid efforts.

In Africa, over eight hundred Chinese-funded aid projects are under way to build schools, hospitals, stadiums, and the like. To be fair, much of this aid goes to countries the U.S. also actively supports, like Liberia's newly elected government and Sierra Leone, both struggling to rebuild after decades of violence. But China's aid floats despotic leaders too. China is the principal supporter of Zimbabwe's regime of Robert Mugabe, one of Africa's most oppressive governments. In its quest for access to Zimbabwe's gold and platinum reserves, China supplies Mugabe with everything from jets to roof tiles for his new mansion.

China's aid gives despotic leaders more political wiggle room. Mugabe heralds China as the creator of a "new global paradigm." He can take China's unconditional aid or comply with multiple Western demands for fair elections, greater transparency, media freedoms, and human rights. Not a difficult choice. Despots aren't the only ones who welcome China's approach. As Garth Shelton of Wits University in South Africa put it, "if we deal with the United States or West European governments they would bring a list of 33 items requiring restructuring of your democracy, your human rights issues. China would arrive and say we accept you as you are. And that's a refreshing change."

It is unclear how long China's honeymoon in Africa will last and whether its short-term thinking will backfire in the end. Some argue China should prepare itself for a backlash because its actions are reminiscent of "old fashioned colonial powers, using cheap labor—sometimes imported from China—to extract natural resources . . . and selling manufactured goods which undermine local producers." Already, such complaints are surfacing. During President Hu's February 2007 trip to Africa, he canceled a visit to Zambia's copper-producing area for fear of public protests over poor working conditions and low pay; in South Africa, President Thabo Mbeki cautioned against allowing China to replicate Europe's "neocolonialist adventure." Further, though Chinese investments in Africa are up substantially in recent years, reaching just over $1 billion in 2006, these figures still pale in comparison to British and American investment, which topped $30 billion and $19 billion respectively that year.

Finally, there is the question of China's relationship to liberal international norms. As China's influence in the international arena grows, some worry that its very presence will erode liberal norms such as transparency, accountability, and anti-corruption entrenched and reflected in international institutions. As we discuss later in the book, the evidence for this thesis is slim. Moreover, liberal norms have such a large incumbency advantage that they will not easily be supplanted. At any rate, the best antidote is to bring China into the debate and shape its conceptions of how the international order ought to operate, gradually winning over its officials and thus slowly building up a core of right-thinking leaders in Beijing.

Powers on Their Own Turf

We've discussed how pivotal powers affect American values at home and abroad. What about how they treat their own citizens? Russia and China both repress freedom of speech and assembly, deny religious rights, refuse or rig local elections, imprison democracy advocates, prohibit or limit unions, permit deplorable working conditions, limit the independence of judges, torture prisoners, and censor the media, among many other illiberal and abusive practices.

Chinese and Russian abuse of their own citizens rightly angers and offends Americans, but the question is what can we do about it? Can America somehow force China and Russia to treat its citizens better or become liberal democracies as we would like? As Jeffrey Bader, long-time diplomat and now director of the John L. Thorton China Center at the Brookings Institution, explains, "I have spent my whole career pursuing human rights in China, and all we have done is gotten a few prisoners out of jail. The only things that work are being a role model and supporting local NGOs. The other stuff just makes us feel good." Says Susan Shirk, former deputy assistant secretary of state, "Our hopes for political reform in China . . . will never be realized through outside pressure." Public upbraidings on human rights can give solace to pro-democracy activists, and some on-the-ground programs like those helping individuals bring lawsuits against the government are worthwhile, but the main tool America has is to show these illiberal pivotal powers, through the example of a vibrant democracy with strong rule of law, the advantages of our system. After all, says Beijing University's Wang Jisi, "in China's modern history, the United States has always served as its reference for modernity, nation building and great power status." More on this below.

America has little direct leverage to promote individual rights and political liberalization in Russia or China, however much we wish otherwise. This is especially true considering that large majorities of the citizens of these countries appear willing to accept the implied trade-off between economic stability and greater political and civil rights. In a 2006 poll, 85 percent of Russians approved of Putin's move to renationalize the oil industry, and a plurality (44 percent) also endorsed a "more centrally controlled government." As the World Opinion pollster put it, "A liberal democracy, often bringing in tow messiness and inequalities, is not the majority goal."

Similarly, polling shows that 78 percent of Chinese think the way the Chinese government "manages its economy and its political system" is more of an advantage than a disadvantage for China. In part this approval reflects the fact that China has lifted hundreds of millions of citizens out of poverty in the last decade. In this way, growing pivotal powers, even illiberal ones, can contribute to better living conditions for many. A Chinese journalist suggested her American colleagues would have a different point of view: "They have not had to struggle just to survive, so they do not understand that human rights for many people . . . is simply having something to eat."

The Actual Obstacles

In assessing threats to America's ability to spread its ideals abroad, there are much more serious contenders than the pivotal powers. First is the growing popularity of radical Islam. Violent jihadists are advocating a form of theocracy antithetical to liberal democracy. Further, as counterterrorism expert Daniel Byman put it, "Al-Qaeda seeks America's unconditional surrender. It wants all forms of U.S. influence—including cultural—withdrawn from the Muslim world." Jihadist attacks are a way to further the struggle against the U.S. by "humiliat[ing] and slaughter[ing] those who defied the hegemony of God."

Their ultimate objective of reasserting the golden age of Islam remains unlikely, but, as the National Intelligence Council report on global trends has concluded, "a Caliphate would not have to be entirely successful for it to present a serious challenge to the international order." It is not outside the realm of possibility that a fundamentalist wave could take over successive Middle East governments from Egypt to Saudi Arabia to Pakistan, with serious strategic implications beyond individual rights and conceptions of the nation-state, involving control of the majority of the world's energy resources, state-sponsored terrorism, and access to nuclear weapons.

To the extent that the campaign against terrorists must counter their fundamentalist ideology in order to be successful, the pivotal powers could be important partners. Each of the pivotal powers is a current or potential jihadist target, and each has a keen interest in maintaining the international order upon which their economic prosperity has been built. Counter-radical messages coming from America have next to zero credibility in the Muslim world. Other pivotal powers may be better vectors and, at the very least, public diplomacy coordinated with them is more likely to succeed.

Actions Speak Loudest

Perhaps the largest obstacle to America's ability to promote its ideals abroad is its own actions. Always complicating America's democracy promotion efforts has been a fundamental tension, captured by Henry Kissinger: "As a people, we have oscillated between insistence on our uniqueness and the quest for broad acceptance of our values." How can America replicate its own system when it is intrinsically unique? For that reason and many more, promoting liberal democracy abroad has never been simple.

Two success stories occurred after World War II when the world watched as the U.S. nearly single-handedly funded the rebuilding of Germany and Japan, turning them into stable, democratic, and economically powerful nations. They became the best possible advertisements for the American system, but, for a variety of reasons, their cases were unique. For one thing, the amount America spent per capita in those countries was far in excess of any effort it has undertaken since; planning for post-war reconstruction was rigorous.

More recent, the U.S. track record has been less than stellar. Today, fewer than 20 percent of the one hundred nations once described as "transitional" are clearly on the path toward stable, functional democracies. Most are stuck in a semi-authoritarian twilight zone. Millions of taxpayer dollars of development assistance, civil society programs, retraining of judges, and reforming legal systems have made some progress, but corruption and institutional dysfunction remain stubbornly intact in many aid-recipient countries. The fact that America and its partners have not been able to bring about the transformations they say they will, writes noted political theorist Francis Fukuyama, "undercuts the higher ends they seek."

Friendly Fire

Not only do American efforts sometimes not deliver as promised, but they can actively do harm in the name of democracy. As Stanford

University democracy expert Michael McFaul has said, "In the world we have, current U.S. tactics for spreading its ideology are much more destructive to it than any competing ideology of a big state." The Iraq War is the extreme case. While President Bush declares the "grand ambition" to spread democracy worldwide, "[d]emocracy promotion has come to be seen overseas," says Carnegie Endowment democracy expert Thomas Carothers, "not as the expression of a principled American aspiration, but as a 'code word' for 'regime change.' "

The backlash is not just over Iraq. Across the developing world, there are fresh memories of U.S. complicity with corrupt, murderous leaders despite strong rhetorical support for democracy. In Africa, after decades of propping up corrupt dictators during the Cold War, the U.S. largely disappeared, leaving dysfunctional societies to fend for themselves. In too many cases, U.S. disengagement helped unleash conflict, which continues to plague the continent today. This same backlash dynamic is part of what propelled the rise of Venezuela's Hugo Chávez. In many ways, the United States is now paying the price for a history of questionable tactics.

Do as I Say

American efforts to promote liberal democracy continue to be undermined by its own hypocrisy and inconsistency. All across the world, from university conferences to dinner tables, for example, American torture of prisoners in Abu Ghraib was a daily topic of discussion in 2004 and 2005.

President Bush could not say a word about torture in Beijing when he visited President Hu in November 2005 at the same time as the U.N. rapporteur on torture was also in China conducting an investigation on prisons. It would have been a perfect moment to praise China for allowing the U.N. access (after ten years of stalling), and emphasizing the importance of treating prisoners humanely, but because of U.S. actions at Guantánamo Bay and Iraq had to be forfeited. As Human Rights Watch's executive director Ken Roth put it, "this catastrophic path has left the United States effectively incapable of defending some of the most basic rights . . . knowing how easily an interlocutor could turn the tables and cite US misconduct as an excuse for his government's own abuses." Further, as Jeffrey Bader explained, American misdeeds send the message that "any government under stress routinely resorts to extreme measures, and that U.S. preaching on human rights and democracy is designed to weaken and divide China, not to live up to some ideal that we ignore under stress." Hypocrisy, real or even apparent, casts doubt on U.S. credibility and moral stature, which in turn strengthens the hands of U.S. detractors and undermines our legitimacy. In addition, concludes analyst Wang Jisi, "So long as the United States' image remains tainted, China will have greater leverage in multilateral settings."

America's inconsistency is also a liability. Venezuela's record on political rights and civil liberties is no worse than America's friend Pakistan's. The U.S., forever a champion of the Geneva Conventions, decided abruptly they do not apply to the prisoners at Guantánamo Bay. Growing connectivity means such contradictions are exposed at the click of a mouse. For example, in 2001, when Secretary of State Colin Powell pressed Qatar's foreign minister to rein in Arab news channel Al Jazeera's negative coverage of the U.S. it triggered a flurry of on-air and Internet opinion pieces, highlighting the contradiction with U.S. proclamations about the need for independent media.

From these inconsistencies and scores of others, outside observers take away a clear message that the U.S. cares about its principles only when its other interests are so aligned. According to Qazi Hussain Ahmad, the head of Pakistan's Islamist party, "the most enduring factor of the U.S.-Islamic world relations is the sheer inconsistency between the high moral ideals that the United States advocates and the practice of successive U.S. governments in their relations with the Islamic world." As democracy expert Thomas Carothers advises, "pursuing democracy as a matter of principle does not mean focusing only on lofty ideals and ignoring hard interests. But it does mean acting with at least a modicum of consistency."

Getting Back on Track

Despite America's recent shaky record, democracy has retained its near-universal appeal around the world. To find further success, America needs to once again become an example of the liberal democratic values it preaches. During that transition and beyond, democracy promotion could use a new, and less American, "face." Seventy percent of Americans in a 2005 poll said the U.S. should promote democracy through the U.N. "because such efforts will be seen as more legitimate." Working together with Europe, India, Japan, and other liberal democracies is the other solution. Together, they can chart a course toward reinforcing shared liberal ideals. America also has to realize that its version of democracy is unique and be willing to support other ways to provide citizens abroad "liberty under law." Finally, America must take a long, hard look at the methods it uses to promote its ideals, to make sure they are as sound as the ideals themselves. Only slow, small, and steadfast steps over a long time horizon will succeed in building stable liberal governments in the end.

The conclusions we reach here are consistent with our security analysis. Pivotal powers pose no threat to America's ability to live by its values at home and the three liberal powers help the U.S. with its mission abroad. While China and Russia do not accord their own people the rights Americans think they deserve, and undermine America's democracy promotion efforts to some degree, their actions are not the biggest obstacle in American efforts to promote U.S. ideals.

This is not to say that a values-driven clash is impossible. Recent wrangling with Russia over U.S. policies toward newly democratized Ukraine and Georgia and ongoing tensions with China over Taiwan prove issues that evoke ideology could evolve into serious conflicts.

That there is a "trust gap" between America and these pivotal powers because they have opaque, illiberal regimes, adds to the possibility of a clash. Yet no pivotal power is an active ideological adversary of the United States. Moreover, in confronting the real ideological challenge facing us—jihadism—the pivotal powers are willing and necessary cohorts. In its quest to promote its ideology abroad, America must start at home. First and foremost by leading by example, but also ensuring its rhetoric and practice are in step.

4. U.S. Prosperity and the Pivotal Powers

In 2004, when American Airlines was weeks away from bankruptcy, its employees faced a stark choice: work differently or not at all. The six thousand mechanics at the American aircraft maintenance facility in Tulsa, Oklahoma, conceded to significant cuts in salary, benefits, and vacation in return for equal input in running operations. American promised its Tulsa workers that if they could reduce the time it took to do a major overhaul by half, executives would not outsource their jobs overseas like other airlines had.

Drawing on their years of expertise, AA mechanics completely reconfigured the overhaul process and designed their "dream" machine to make it easier to move airplane engines around. AA executives, keeping up their end of the bargain, took a risk and green-lighted the new design, to the mechanics' utter amazement. As a result, an aircraft overhaul at the AA facility now takes 450 mechanics thirteen days instead of 800 mechanics twenty-five days. Costs have been slashed by 55 percent, union workers kept their jobs, and they are working closely with management. "When I have my union meetings now, and I've got two hundred guys in there," says Dennis Burchette, president of the Transportation Workers Union Local 514, "instead of complaining about management, they sound like business people."

American is profiting from a new revenue opportunity as it makes the operation a service provider to other airlines. AA says it now has fifty customers who bring their jets to Tulsa for overhaul from as far away as South America. American turned a profit in 2006 for the first time in six years, in no small part because of the Tulsa operations. The mechanics' contract comes up again for negotiation in 2008, and they are now in a good position to demand a share of the profits they helped to generate.

There is a tension between the two things Americans want—high standards of living and predictability. A pink slip is awful, even if another job is around the corner. To thrive, though, an economy must adjust just as the airline mechanics did. "There is no choice but to embrace change," states Ron Blackwell, director of corporate affairs at the AFL-CIO. "The world doesn't stand still. It's going to move forward, one way or the other, with us or without us." By accepting change, American workers and consumers can be better off in a world with growing international competition.

America's economy is still the largest in the world, twice as large as number two, Japan, but reemerging pivotal powers China and India (and, in a different way, Russia) are on a fast track to growth. They are succeeding, somewhat ironically, by doing exactly what America has been preaching for decades—opening their economies and letting the private sector loose. China and India are investing in education and infrastructure, looking to the U.S. and Europe for examples of laws, policies, and actions to drive their progress. They are harnessing the very capitalist principles that America champions, in search of better lives, replete with plumbing, heat, and cars. The emergence of these nations as economic powers represents the triumph of American economic gospel.

What will their success mean for Americans? The important question is not whether America's relative dominance is diminishing in the face of these new economies. It is. The unsustainable degree of U.S. control, autonomy, and privilege in the economic arena, as in geopolitics, is eroding. The right question is: Does it matter? Is there a limit to the mutual prosperity of the United States and pivotal power economies? If America makes sound domestic economic and political choices, the rise of other major economies will support American prosperity, not undermine it.

The Benefits of Big Powers

To economists, the notion of nations "competing" economically is ridiculous. Companies can be pure rivals, but nations are not. Their firms may sells goods that compete, but unlike McDonald's and Burger King, nations are also each other's main markets and suppliers of useful imports. Economic theory predicts a multitude of rewards for countries that trade with one another. Going back to the turn of the nineteenth century, economist David Ricardo predicted that countries that freely trade will prosper, even when they import more than they export. The world economic system is a giant bathtub. Though they may cause waves, the more people who get in, the higher the water rises for America.

History has accommodated the economists thus far. There is a tight fit between theory about free trade and American experience. As Figure 4.1 illustrates, from the 1950s until today, U.S. economic growth occurred in parallel with the expansion of other economies. As the shattered economies of Germany and Japan took off after World War II, so did America's. As South Korea's GDP per capita grew from $194 in 1960 to $16,346 in 2005, American GDP grew along with it, only faster.

Likewise, as we see in Figure 4.2, as U.S. trade with these countries mushroomed in the last thirty years, China, India, and Russia grew in parallel with, not at the expense of, the American economy, U.S.-China trade exploded from $5 billion in 1980 to over $340 billion in 2006, and both countries' economies have expanded. One study predicts that U.S. GDP will be larger by a modest amount (0.7 percent) in

Figure 4.1: Real GDP per Capita in Post-WWII Economies, 1953–2005

(2005 U.S. Dollars)

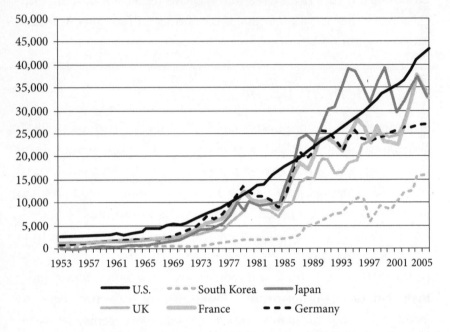

SOURCE: GFD Database Search Engine, Global Finance Data, available from http://www.global financialdata.com (accessed February 14, 2006). Data for Germany uses West German numbers from 1953–1996 and unified Germany data from 1997–2005.

2010 as a result of increased trade and investment with China alone. Another suggests that the American economy has gained $1 trillion per year due to international trade in recent decades.

A world where great power economies stagnate or decline would be a much less prosperous one for Americans, and vice versa. Moreover, as *The Economist* notes, "The emerging economies are helping to lift world GDP growth at the very time when the rich world's ageing populations would otherwise cause growth to slow." In fact, far from fearing pivotal power growth, the U.S. needs to be concerned about the risk of their economic stagnation.

How specifically does America benefit from economic interactions with large and growing economies? First, these countries are big

Figure 4.2: GDP of Reemerging Powers and U.S., 1975–2004

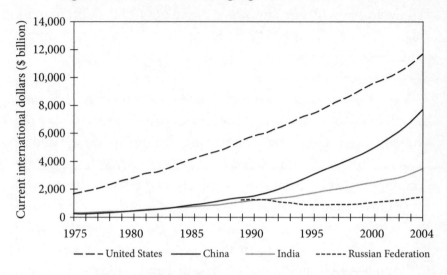

SOURCE: World Bank estimates.

export markets. Europe has served this role for some time, and to a lesser degree, Japan, but now India and China offer promising opportunities. During 2000–2005, U.S. exports to China increased by 158 percent compared to 12.6 percent for the rest of the world. In 2005, India was the fastest-growing U.S. export market. Many American companies, including Yahoo!, Wal-Mart, and KFC, expect that China will soon become one of their largest markets. Yum! Brands CEO David Novak told *Fortune* magazine in 2004 that KFC "makes almost as much money in China today as it makes in the U.S." Starbucks CEO Howard Schultz thinks that soon only North America will be a bigger market for its company than China, and he plans to open stores in India. If General Motors avoids bankruptcy, one reason will be the profits it has made from soaring sales of its cars in China. While its U.S. sales dropped 8.7 percent in 2006, they grew by nearly 32 percent in China. American agriculture is also a clear beneficiary—U.S. agricultural exports to China tripled from 2000 to 2004 to $5.5 billion. Both India and China have bought billions of dollars' worth of American airplanes. Toward the end of 2006, Westinghouse Electric, the U.S. nuclear power company owned by Japan's Toshiba Corporation, announced that China had awarded it a multibillion-dollar contract to build nuclear reactors in China, in a deal expected to create some 5,500 American jobs.

More exports mean more wealth and more American jobs, even though other jobs are lost, and workers displaced, as we discuss later. The gains from these new markets will continue to grow if and as these economies continue to expand; as Chinese and Indians leave grinding poverty by the millions to join the middle class, they too will eat fast food and fly in planes. Over the next decade almost a billion new consumers will enter the marketplace. Further, China's appetite for raw materials has boosted many other economies, whose citizens in turn buy American exports. Chinese demand is a key stimulant to the global economic growth on which American prosperity hinges.

Cheap manufacturing abroad has lowered the price of consumer goods for average Americans, thus allowing paychecks to go further and, in effect, increasing standards of living. Remember when the price of household goods used to go up each year? This reversal is significant, especially for low-income Americans whose wages have stagnated. Michael Cox of the Dallas Federal Reserve Bank writes that the material possessions of Americans at the poverty line in 2000 more or less equaled those of middle-class Americans in 1971. (Despite that, income inequality remains a real and troubling trend, as we discuss later.) In total, a Morgan Stanley study estimates that imports from China alone have saved U.S. consumers $600 billion over ten years. That amounts to $521 in disposable income for every American household each year for ten years. Manufacturing abroad has also lowered the cost of production for American companies, in some cases keeping companies open and growing net U.S. jobs.

Pivotal powers are also a critical source of investment in U.S. industry. European firms held $1.4 trillion in U.S. assets in 2005. Chinese and Indian firms are also beginning to invest. This capital can mean job growth in the United States. Pivotal economies also help to finance the U.S. debt. The net result has been lower interest rates, more affordable mortgages, and a general stimulus to the U.S. economy.

Though it is the very thing that Americans fear, competition from strong economic players may well be what is most beneficial about them. Explains Harvard's Michael Porter, "international competition helps upgrade productivity," as new multinationals from China, India, Russia, and Brazil give U.S. companies a run for their money, so to speak, forcing them to innovate faster and improve their products. One study suggests that U.S. manufacturing productivity will get a significant boost by 2010 in part because of competition with China. "Competition with China keeps us on our toes and sharpens our wits, forcing us to move up the value-added ladder to new and better jobs with higher pay," says the CEO of the Federal Reserve Bank of Dallas. "Sure Chinese companies are tough competitors," explains the head of consulting giant Deloitte. "But competition makes us better." In rivalry, vitality.

Though certainly a major stimulus to American growth, the pivotal powers have no control over who in America benefits from that growth. As we discuss later, the fruits of this economic symbiosis are these days enjoyed disproportionately by the well-off.

The pivotal power economies benefit the U.S. in a final, important way—they are as invested in economic stability as America is. This distinguishes them from past rivals and proto-rivals: the Soviet Union, communist China pre-1978, and Japan in the 1980s were not nearly as integrated into the global economy as China, and Europe, and, to a lesser extent, India and Russia are now. China may be the most open large economy the world has ever seen. These countries want to play a role in the world's financial institutions like the World Trade Organization (WTO), Organization for Economic Cooperation and Development (OECD), International Monetary Fund (IMF), G8, and World Bank, even though they are largely America's brainchildren and continue to reflect its preferences. China was so determined to join the WTO that it accepted terms that Chinese economy expert Nick Lardy describes as "so onerous they violate fundamental WTO principles."

All the big powers are in the same economic boat, and no one wants to rock it too hard. American leaders rarely acknowledge this potential benefit, but it means that these economies are a force for stability. There is another benefit of pivotal economies rarely discussed. Large, organized market economies also help the U.S. in regulating multinational corporations. Without the assistance of foreign regulators, wayward companies could evade taxes, fix prices, export tainted food, and transport hazardous waste with abandon. Efforts in multiple countries are also necessary to track down hackers and virus creators whose cyber attacks can cause huge economic damage. Every day, American officials cooperate with their counterparts, particularly in Europe, and increasingly in other pivotal powers, to investigate and prosecute these kinds of offenses.

Moreover, over the longer term, some theory suggests that economic development and international economic integration, especially of the kind we are now witnessing, could contribute to stability within countries and regions. In the case of China, a growing Chinese middle class could push that country toward a more pluralistic political system, which, while possibly chaotic in the short term, could benefit the U.S. and world stability in the long term.

We started this chapter by saying that the right question was not about America's relative decline compared to the reemerging pivotal powers but whether America could continue to thrive. This is correct, but for one nuance. It turns out that when it comes to happiness, a person's perception of his or her standard of living as compared to others actually matters more than the absolute level. (This is why relatively poor countries can rank highest on happiness indexes, and also, in part, why America's growing income stratification is problematic.) Even considering this dynamic, though, the day when average Americans could compare their lives with those of an average Indian,

Chinese, or Russian and come up wanting is not foreseeable. If or when China's economy grows to be as large as America's, the average American will still be three or four times richer than an average Chinese person.

Despite the measurable benefits, historical evidence, and mainstream economic theory, many Americans remain worried that they will ultimately lose out. We hear that they (China and India, usually) are taking our jobs, buying our companies, luring away our capital, gobbling up our oil, trading unfairly, and trying to rewrite the rules of the game. Let's take a look at each of these concerns. In the next chapter we look at one more worry: that pivotal powers are out-innovating us. We will find throughout that many of these presumed ills are either real, but America's to cure, or psychosomatic.

Outsourced and Offshored

A continuing fear about the growth of the Chinese and Indian economies is that they will take U.S. jobs. The phenomenon began in manufacturing, but jobs in services are moving quickly too—Indians now interpret American CAT scans. This trend is undeniably painful to workers in those jobs, and the burdens of free trade and capitalism fall on those least able to shoulder the weight. The losers are those like Melissa Knight, a twenty-eight-year-old single mother who was laid off from a Hoover plant facing competition from cheap vacuum cleaners made in China. But Melissa understands the trade-offs better than many pundits. "It's all our fault," she told *BusinessWeek.* "The American economy wants cheaper things . . . I'm guilty of this too." Americans as employees and Americans as consumers are at odds.

Worker displacement is not new. The entire history of the American economy is one of disruption. Technological innovation necessarily puts people out of jobs as it creates new ones. When combines were invented, ranch hands lost work. The U.S. has gone from some 95 percent of the labor force working on farms in the 1700s to some

40 percent in the early 1900s to less than 2 percent today. Meanwhile, farming output increased many-fold.

In the end, the number of jobs in America, explain Lael Brainard and Robert Litan of the Brookings Institution, "has closely followed the growth of the labor force," despite great increases in foreign trade and the "advent of a host of new job-displacing technologies, such as voicemail, word processors and optical scanners." The U.S. economy added some thirty million workers to its payroll since 1985. In the last ten years, firms have created tens of thousands of jobs for nurses, financial advisors, and architects. "Someone will always work cheaper," former governor of Virginia Mark Warner once said. "We have to work smarter."

Offshoring, whereby firms move parts of their internal business to other countries to take advantage of lower costs, and outsourcing, where firms give functions to other companies, foreign or not, is the latest way American companies are attempting to get a competitive edge. Job churn is an inevitable by-product of the very same forces that make the U.S. such an economic powerhouse in the world—the ingenuity and flexibility of American firms. What is new is that foreigners are getting the jobs, they are sometimes decent jobs, and the transition is happening at lightning speed. Due to digitization, "the normal adjustment process simply can't take place in a socially acceptable or politically meaningful time," explains Yale's Jeffrey Garten. The economic shifts are outpacing our public debate.

Though it is of little comfort to displaced workers, offshoring creates value for the U.S. economy and even jobs. Catherine Mann of the Institute for International Economics has estimated that between 1995 and 2003, the U.S. economy would have grown 0.3 percent slower without offshoring in information technology. McKinsey's Diana Farrell estimates that every dollar of U.S. services offshored generates $1.14 for the U.S. in the form of cost savings to companies, profits from additional exports, increased productivity, and wages for workers that find new jobs. Some businesses use offshoring and outsourcing to sustain profitability and thus preserve other U.S. jobs. For example, a high-tech computer parts company in Minnesota was able to stay in business because of low-cost manufacturing in China. The low prices fed demand for computers and MP3 players, and the company therefore *added* nearly two thousand jobs in Minnesota in 2003 because of outsourcing.

In addition, offshoring may speed up the formation of innovative products and services, by using low-cost workers in China and India to build prototypes and do initial exploratory work. U.S. firms that employ highly skilled Americans may thus be able to bring products or services to market at a lower cost and more quickly than before.

The number of jobs already lost overseas is relatively tiny in the context of the U.S. economy as a whole. Estimates vary because the government does not keep these statistics. The hawkish U.S.-China Economic and Security Review Commission estimates that the U.S. lost 1.5 million jobs—manufacturing and service—to China over the fourteen-year period from 1989 to 2003, or roughly 100,000 per year. Forrester Research predicts that some 340,000 a year will move offshore by 2015. In the one month of January 2007 alone, however, nearly five million Americans joined the payrolls. Some 25,000 jobs are destroyed and slightly more created every *hour* America is open for business. Losses to offshoring from all countries represent only some 2 percent of the fifteen million Americans who are laid off every year.

Moreover, there is a limit to the number of jobs that could be shipped overseas. Many jobs just have to be done face-to-face, or very nearby—think of pediatricians, pilots, plumbers, performers. Regulatory barriers and skilled labor shortages in India and China (the United States has ten times the number of skilled workers that China has) will also limit the flow.

We should also keep in mind that offshoring is a two-way street, and American workers are also at the receiving end of the offshoring phenomenon. In industries where low cost is not the only criterion, the U.S. often wins out. Foreign corporations employ 6.4 million Americans working in America, and they pay 14 percent higher wages than American firms, on average. The Chinese appliance maker Haier has opened a plant in South Carolina and a design center in Los Angeles. Japan's Toyota accounts for 27,000 manufacturing jobs in the United States.

Helping Workers Adjust

When their jobs go overseas, most workers find new jobs within six months, but not all do. For those who do, their wages may be lower. Part of the reason for this is the flood of low-wage workers entering the world market that puts pressure on wages. (Boeing employs Russian aeronautical engineers for a third of the cost of American ones.) This is part of an alarming trend of income stratification also caused by technology, de-unionization and tax policies. Princeton University Economist Paul Krugman points out that "Globalization can explain part of the relative decline in blue-collar wages, but it can't explain the 2,500 percent rise in C.E.O. incomes." A 2007 Center for American Progress report explains that "Inequality has reached record highs. The richest one percent of Americans in 2005 had the largest share of the nation's income (19 percent) since 1929. At the same time, the poorest 20 percent of Americans had only 3.4 percent . . ." The vast majority of Americans' total earnings have been falling since 2000 even though productivity has risen.

Discussing the causes of and solutions to income stratification goes beyond the parameters of this book. But on the narrower question of offshoring, the right answers are, first, helping workers cope with disruptive change and, second, ensuring that America is the best environment on earth for innovative business. Protectionist measures send resources to old, unproductive industries that cannot compete, and drain them from those that can. America should protect workers, not firms, and tariffs are not an effective way to do that. Even with heavy tariffs and quotas, the textile industry hemorrhaged jobs from 1994 to 2000. Also, studies have shown that the poorest Americans are disproportionately harmed by textile tariffs because they have to pay the higher prices for goods. Protectionist policies are politically popular, however, for reasons we will examine in Chapter 8, and if workers are not helped with better programs, pressure for protectionism will mount.

Fortunately, there are powerful policy tools America can and should use to help its dislocated workers as the economy adjusts. Currently, the U.S. spends far less than other developed nations on programs for displaced workers. While American incomes are benefited to the tune of $1 trillion per year from trade, the lifetime wage losses of trade-displaced workers in a given year are around $54 billion. Federal spending devoted to these workers is just $2 billion.

One idea, wage insurance, could offer compensation to laid-off service workers for the lower salaries they are forced to accept—but (to keep incentives in line) only after they've found a new job. The current unemployment insurance system, which is very out of date, needs real reform. Another idea gaining currency is a universal 401(k) plan to give workers a private retirement account on top of Social Security, providing a measure of future financial security and enabling them to move from job to job without jeopardizing their retirement. Economist Alan Binder of Princeton University suggests reorienting the U.S. education system to train future workers for the face-to-face jobs that will remain in the United States. A recent report suggests that Congress identify certain communities facing significant pressure from international competition for targeted tax breaks and other benefits designed to attract new investment.

Companies that benefit from offshoring also have an obligation to help their former workers. Firms could make up for 70 percent of lost wages and provide health care subsidies for two years, at a cost of only 4 to 5 percent of their cost savings from offshoring. Economist Catherine Mann suggests tax credits for companies that train and retrain workers.

There are some steps the United States could take to encourage firms to keep jobs in the U.S. America would do well to ensure that the tax code does not reward offshoring. Developing a more educated pool of Americans and encouraging more R&D are also important steps, as we discuss in the next chapter. Portable national health care would address an increasingly prohibitive cost for businesses in the U.S. and would simultaneously help displaced workers. Intel opened a large new chip facility in China in part because it doesn't have to pay for health care there. Thomas Friedman writes that "Virtually every entrepreneur I talked to for [*The World Is Flat*] cited soaring and un-controlled healthcare costs in America as a reason to move factories abroad."

America's infrastructure also needs attention, as brownouts and failed levies have a way of discouraging investment. America has slipped from being third in the world for broadband access in 2000 to twelfth in 2006. A 2005 survey by the American Society of Civil Engineers estimated it would cost the U.S. $1.6 trillion to shore up America's aging infrastructure—bridges, roads, the power grid—just to bring it up to the bare minimum standards. That is two-thirds of the entire federal budget today, and has prompted several propos-als, including the creation of a national investment corporation and special-purpose, long-duration bonds for financing major invest-ments.

Owning U.S.: Foreign Ownership of U.S. Companies

In the 1980s, Americans feared "The Buying of America" by Japan. In reality, Japanese investors never owned more than a small fraction of American capital and eventually sold iconic businesses and buildings like Rockefeller Center at a steep loss. In 2005, when the Chinese com-pany Lenovo bought the struggling PC division of IBM, these same concerns resurfaced.

Does it matter whether foreign firms own American ones? No. In fact, it is a sign of health that foreigners want to invest here. While commentators seize on Asian deals, the long-standing trend of European companies directly investing billions in the U.S. has not abated. Europe's direct investments in America dwarf all others; in 2004, Europe and Canada together accounted for 90 percent of all new foreign investment in the U.S.—Asia, as a whole, accounted for only 6 percent. Some of the biggest names in American commerce are owned by European concerns—Burger King, Jeep, 7-UP, Holiday Inn, Arco, Shell. The fact that this trend never makes headlines points to the reality that unless the assets in question are truly relevant to national security, and the federal government already has a sensible process in place to deal with those cases, the nationality of the company that owns them does not matter.

Multinationals, whether headquartered in the United States, Europe, or China, employ Americans, pay taxes, and provide goods and services to American consumers. American mayors understand this and they are bending over backward to convince Chinese investors of the advantages of investing in their cities.

Notwithstanding the political outcry, Chinese computer company Lenovo's purchase was a windfall for IBM—allowing it to unload a division that was losing hundreds of millions of dollars each year and to use the proceeds, $1.75 billion, to invest in growth areas. Further, as part of its drive to become a respected, globally competitive player, Lenovo decided that it had to preload legal operating software onto its computers. When it became clear that this would put it at a competitive disadvantage compared to other Chinese computer manufacturers, Lenovo was instrumental in successfully petitioning the Chinese government to require all computers manufactured or imported into China to have preloaded software, thus striking a major blow against piracy. IBM also ended up owning nearly 19 percent of Lenovo after the deal (U.S. private equity firms bought another 10.8 percent stake). Americans are sure to hear more in the coming years about Chinese and Indian companies buying American ones. If their jobs remain, American workers need not worry about the nationality of their boss's boss.

Capital Flight

Another concern about the growth of pivotal power economies is their competitive capital markets. Well-functioning capital markets have played a vital role in the U.S. economy. For decades, established American companies, the main users of these markets, have been able to raise capital on better terms—rates up to one percent lower than their foreign counterparts. They also play a vital role in innovation, as we discuss in the next chapter, and create jobs. For sixty years after World War II, firms seeking capital naturally came to the U.S. Now, because of technology and the growth of other markets, they have more choices. The concern is that America's capital markets, though big, will have a harder time competing with those in London and Hong Kong. Indeed, only 5 percent of the value of global initial public offerings was raised in the U.S. last year, compared to 50 percent in 2000. America is still ahead of Europe in hedge fund and mutual fund assets, but the gap is narrowing. London is now seen as the logical home for firms pursuing transactions in emerging markets like Russia.

Again, these are American problems to fix in order to prosper in a more competitive world. Experts point to a host of issues that contribute to the downward trend—the cost of complying with the Sarbanes-Oxley regulations enacted in the wake of the Enron scandal, the difficulty of getting visas to the U.S. for routine business travel, the risk of complex litigation, and weak shareholder rights when it comes to electing board members, among other important areas. Each of these is well within the power of America's government to adjust.

Fossil Fight

As big economies grow, they will use more resources. How will that affect security for Americans and the availability of important natural resources like clean water, rare elements, and energy? We focus in this section on the most anxiety-producing of resources, oil.

Oil is critical to America's economy because the price of oil affects the cost of just about everything and oil price spikes have triggered global recessions three times. Many observers predict a future of aggressive competition over energy resources. One Stanford University geophysicist warns that the war in Iraq could "pale in comparison" with the "looming potential conflict" over oil with China. China is now the second largest consumer of oil in the world, using about a third of what America does. Japan comes in third, Germany fifth, and India sixth (Russia is fourth but is a net exporter). Because of demand growth, many assume a return to an earlier era in which the great powers competed, sometimes militarily, for access to resources.

This prediction might prove true, but not because there is economic logic to such competition. Misperceptions and "mythology," in the words of energy expert Mikkal Herberg, rule the day when it comes to "energy security." The conceptions of many policymakers as well as average citizens are often rooted in the oil crises of the 1970s. But this is not your daddy's oil market. Oil is now a global commodity. With allowances for quality and transport costs, the wholesale price is more or less the same everywhere. OPEC can raise the world price by reducing supply, but it cannot embargo one country any longer. Back in the 1970s, when oil flowed according to rigid contracts, countries without supply contracts, or with unfavorable pricing in their contracts, suffered. No longer. If one producer refuses to sell, many others will. Consumers can purchase oil on the spot market if all else fails. For those of us who have flashbacks to the long gas lines the easiest way to understand today's reality is to imagine that all the oil in the world resides in one huge barrel. The price is calibrated every nanosecond in real time according to global supply and demand. While it may seem logical that owning oil wells will somehow ensure price and supply, it does not. In terms of access to supplies, it simply does not matter who owns what.

Nevertheless, at the direction of their national leaders (whose fear about adequate energy supplies they have often stoked), Chinese, Indian, and Japanese oil companies are traversing the world putting flags into every oilfield they can find and often paying above-market prices for the privilege. These countries are paying a premium but not getting any more security of supply than if they relied on global markets. The idea that owning a field will improve energy security is an illusion from the point of view of anyone in the oil business. The global market and the balance of supply and demand set the price of oil. In a crisis, countries with oil simply do not have to honor existing contracts. Owning assets does not really assure access either. That mostly depends on secure shipping lanes and pipelines, which, in turn, depend largely on the good graces of the U.S. military. Ironically, Americans benefit from these deals economically. Though China's oil investments through 2005 represent only 0.5 percent of global oil production, these deals ultimately bring more oil to the market than would be there otherwise, lowering the price for Americans.

Capitol Hill, however, is concerned. "Congress does not understand the modern oil market," Mikkal Herberg explains. Because of that, America is responding to Chinese policy, which is based on an illusion, with signals that reinforce that illusion. That Congress unleashed its fury when a Chinese oil company, CNOOC, tried to buy California-based Unocal, simply confirmed to the Chinese that they cannot trust the markets. Despite Congress's assertion that the sale would "threaten to impair the national security of the United States," Unocal sells oil to the highest bidder like any other oil company. If Unocal's oil went to China, that would free up other supplies for the U.S. and neither the price of oil nor the access to it would change for Americans.

Are there areas where Asian oil demand could have a negative impact on the U.S.? Yes. One is price. Even though coal provides some 70 percent of its energy needs, China has gone, since 1993, from being a net exporter of oil to the second largest importer, and is likely to double its usage within twenty years, as Figure 4.3 shows. (The growth in U.S. demand from 1995 to 2004 was significantly higher than China's, however.)

Figure 4.3: Projected Oil Consumption, 1990–2030

(million barrels oil equivalent per day)

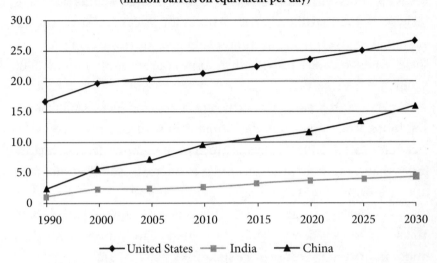

SOURCES: Energy Information Administration, Office of Energy Markets and End Use, "World Petroleum Consumption, Most Recent Annual Estimates, 1980–2006," April 20, 2007, available at: http://www.eia.doe.gov/emeu/international/RecentPetroleumConsumptionBarrelsperDay.xls (accessed July 11, 2007) and International Energy Outlook 2007, Table A5, "World Liquids Consumption by Region, Reference Case, 1990–2030," May 2007, available at: http://www.eia .doe.gov/oiaf/ieo/excel/ieoreftab_5.xls (accessed July 11, 2007).

India too could be importing over two-thirds of its oil and nearly half its gas by 2030. In addition to industrial growth, the number of cars in China is set to rise from 23 million in 2005 to some 130 million in 2030, and even then, nine in ten Chinese will not own one. If China followed a similar pattern of development as the U.S., it would eventually have 1.1 billion cars (there are 800 million in the world today). The world's resources cannot support this path.

Meanwhile, because there is a finite amount of oil in the world, the long-term supply of cheap oil is diminishing. The consensus among geologists, famously first articulated by M. King Hubbert in 1949, is that sometime between tomorrow and twenty years from now we will pass the "peak" point after which there will be less and less conventional oil available each year. With demand rising and supply declining, in the long run, prices will rise. Yet oil expert Daniel Yergin believes oil prices will decline in the near term. Moreover, there is lots of oil left—around a trillion barrels. Also, as the price of oil rises, unconventional sources of oil become profitable. In the U.S. alone, "oil shale" could, one day, provide three times the amount of oil in all of Saudi Arabia's reserves.

Current high prices only partly reflect demand increases in China and India. More important, the ultimate cause of high oil prices is the fact that a cartel, OPEC, controls much of the supply. Because historically they have had little incentive to increase supply (and thus decrease price), OPEC countries have chronically underinvested in their oil industries, and capacity has been stagnant since 1980. Today's increased demand has eliminated spare capacity and thus minor interruptions cause price spikes.

It is true that Americans will pay higher prices at the pump because average Chinese and Indians will drive their first cars and use machines instead of their hands to harvest crops. However, it is hard to make an argument that India and China do not have a "right" to more energy. From 2001 to 2005, per capita oil consumption in the U.S. was about twenty-five barrels per person per year. In China it was less than two barrels.

There are other areas where big power oil policies can negatively impact Americans. Climate change is one, as we discussed in Chapter 1. As the largest carbon emitter, the U.S. has to take a leadership role on this issue or it will allow China and India to continue to duck international pressure. We also discussed how pivotal powers are supporting hostile states and horrible dictators as they search for resources. Finally, while it may not be economically logical, the possibility of geopolitical conflict over oil remains. Maritime gas and oil deposits are claimed by a slew of countries in East Asia, including Japan and China.

China's approach toward sea-lane protection is a related concern. The world has come to accept and appreciate the U.S. Navy's role in protecting shipping routes for oil and gas. Eighty percent of China's oil passes through the Strait of Malacca. Given the loud voices in Washington calling China a threat, Beijing is concerned that the U.S. could try to blockade its oil supply. Xuecheng Liu of the Chinese Institute for International Studies in Beijing writes: "China's energy strategy is rooted in the vulnerability of its access to external energy resources and defensiveness against the United States curtailing its energy supplies." He argues that the so-called Chain of Pearls, China's port agreements with seaside states from the Middle East to East Asia, are a "preventive strategic consideration." A Chinese naval capacity sufficient to protect its oil would greatly alarm the U.S. and neighboring countries.

The U.S. could do quite a bit to reduce the risk of conflict over energy supplies. In general, the United States should encourage multilateral energy solutions and counter the "energy nationalism" that drives flawed policy. Such steps begin with Washington recognizing China's and India's legitimate need for oil and bringing them into the global institutions that debate and form energy policy. China and India must become partners, if not members, of the International Energy Agency, the organization that advises governments on energy policy and coordinates action during energy emergencies. That would help the IEA maximize its effectiveness during a supply crisis and expose Beijing and Delhi to a range of sophisticated energy policies.

Pivotal powers could work together to increase their negotiating power. Together, as energy expert Amy Myers Jaffe points out, China, India, the U.S., and Europe would have substantial market clout to pressure OPEC. After all, it is the cartel that is profiting from high prices, not the pivotal powers (save Russia).

The U.S. should welcome the cooperation that is already occurring in Asia. In January 2006, India and China, despite their history of fierce competition for oil deals, signed an agreement to cooperate on securing oil assets. They have already bid jointly on ownership stakes in Middle Eastern oil companies. What is needed and missing is a regional energy forum to diffuse tension and discuss ideas. The Asia Pacific Partnership on Clean Development and Climate, which met for the first time in January 2006 and includes China, India, and Japan, among others, is a welcome start. The Department of Energy's opening an office in Beijing in 2005 was also a step in the right direction.

If the U.S. wants to discourage Chinese, Indian, and Japanese policies that may distort the free market, it also has to be a consistent champion of it. As politically natural as they are, the U.S. ought to refrain from actions, like blocking the Unocal deal, that justify energy insecurity. Not only should the U.S. allow, it should encourage American oil companies to enter into joint ventures with the Chinese, giving them a sense of energy partnership with the U.S. and demonstrating the U.S. approach. (U.S. companies are already investors in Chinese state oil companies.)

To lessen China's incentives to build a strong navy, the U.S. should reassure China that it intends to keep open sea-lanes from the Persian Gulf to China. If the U.S. were to attempt a blockade (which might not even be feasible), oil prices, at least in the short term, would spike dramatically, and naturally limit the use of this lever. A cooperative understanding of sea-lane policing among Japan, China, India, and the U.S. should be explored. Given the potential for terrorist actions in maritime Asia, where piracy is commonplace already, it would seem there is common ground for such an arrangement. In the end, all these big economies want the same thing—stability in general and stability of oil supplies in particular.

Perhaps most important, for economic and security reasons, the U.S. should encourage energy efficiency and joint research into clean energy. China and India are highly inefficient users of energy, consuming some four times as much energy for each dollar of GDP as does America. Japan, the most energy-efficient country in the world, is the model to emulate. There, for example, government-subsidized hydrogen fuel cells in homes heat the bathwater. Afterward, a tube sucks the remaining water to the washing machine. Conservation, clean energy, and climate change are all common goals that joint research can address. In 2006, China and India both joined the U.S.-initiated FutureGen project to develop a zero-emissions coal-fired power plant by 2012. We need more multilateral alternative energy projects, like FutureGen and nuclear fusion, that put Asian scientists to work on problems Americans want to solve also. Such initiatives and similar ones would address the pollution from China's energy policies that also affects American quality of life. The Environmental Protection Agency estimates that, on some days, 25 percent of the particulates in the air in Los Angeles is from dust and coal burning in China.

Of course, the U.S. badly needs to address its own demand for oil as well. Dozens of creative ideas are on the table, among them tax incentives for purchasing ultra-efficient cars, stronger mandatory standards for fuel efficiency, establishing an agency in the Department of Energy to sponsor cutting-edge research, and a "counter-cyclical" tax on cars, trucks, and airplanes that is triggered only when the price of oil is low. These and other ideas need not come at the expense of growth. Since 1975, U.S. GDP has grown by 150 percent while energy consumption has grown by only 25 percent. As oil expert Daniel Yergin puts it, "conservation has worked."

In the Red

Trade deficits are another sticky issue between the U.S. and the pivotal powers. America's trade deficit with China was $232.5 billion in 2006, the largest with any country, ever. Many policymakers claim that the reason for this deficit is that China is trading unfairly—that it is keeping the value of its currency, the renminbi, or yuan, artificially low, and thus harming American exporters.

Reasonable people can differ on whether this is true—many economists do not think so. In any case, the trade deficit with China is only 30 percent of America's total, and small relative to the trade deficit with the oil exporting economies who enjoy growing surpluses, as we see in Figure 4.4. (And while China is showing a bit of flexibility about taking steps that increase the value of the yuan against the dollar, many of these oil exporters are keeping their currencies firmly fixed.) Moreover, almost 60 percent of Chinese exports to the United States are produced by non-Chinese companies, many of them American, operating in China. Also, component parts are often imported from the rest of Asia and just assembled in China. The share of America's trade deficit with Asia as a whole has actually decreased over the last ten years. So the large imbalance between the United States and China does not accurately reflect the underlying economic realities.

It's true that if China let its currency float today, and it appreciated, the trade deficit with China would be reduced. In the category of "be careful what you wish for," a risk of China devaluing its currency

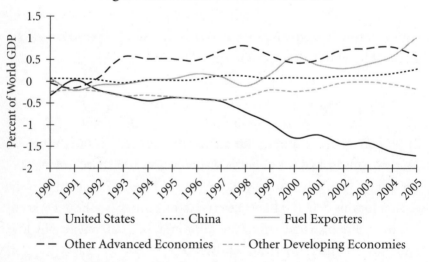

Figure 4.4: Current Account Balances

SOURCE: IMF; Department of Commerce; JP Morgan.

is that it would have fewer reserves to buy Treasuries, and that would put pressure on U.S. interest rates to rise. Moreover the overall U.S. trade deficit would not budge, however, unless the pattern of savings and consumption in the U.S. also changed. Why is that? The nation's current account deficit represents the fact that America (meaning its people, companies, and the government) consumes more and saves less than other countries do—leading to a trade deficit. (This is the case because in order to maintain our lifestyle, we have to borrow money from abroad—the money has to come from somewhere. That means that foreign capital is coming into the U.S. That inflow, in turn, increases demand for the dollar, which raises the value of the dollar relative to foreign currencies, which makes imports cheaper to Americans, encouraging them to buy more from abroad, and thus generates a trade deficit.) America's dependence on foreign oil imports is a major contributing factor.

In order for the trade deficit to be smaller, America would have to save a lot more, consume a lot less, or both. Americans' savings patterns can only change over the very long term and are historically low now. In 2005, American households saved less than 0 percent for the first time since 1933, declining from 10 percent in the 1970s.

An area where America can potentially begin to reverse its appetites quickly is through the federal budget, which represents a huge chunk of American consumption. America has careened from a $236 billion federal budget surplus in 2000 to a nearly $250 billion deficit in 2006, one of the largest swings in U.S. history. Interest payments alone on the nearly $9 trillion national debt, the result of accumulated deficits, were over $400 billion in fiscal year 2006. This was over 15 percent of the federal budget—taxpayer dollars that did not educate children, build roads, or improve homeland security—a growing "debt tax" of some $3,600 for every American household. As economist Paul Krugman puts it, America is a "superpower living on credit."

To finance its budget deficit, America borrows from abroad—to the tune of about $2 billion per day. The result is that foreign countries now finance America's government programs, owning over $1 trillion in U.S. Treasury Bonds. China and Japan account for nearly 80 percent of that. Might China sell its Treasuries in an aggressive move during a confrontation with the U.S.? Highly unlikely. If the dollar slid against the renminbi, the value of its foreign reserves would plummet.

Low-income China is loaning money to the world's richest nation. Why? Like a massive company store, China loans money to the U.S. to ensure that Americans can afford to keep buying its exports. As Jacob Weisberg, editor of Slate.com, has observed: "Borrowing to consume, which is what the U.S. is doing, as opposed to borrowing to invest, is a lousy long-range strategy unless you plan to die young."

While the ratio of America's deficit to its GDP has stabilized recently, lowering the federal budget deficit remains a matter of some urgency. Federal Reserve chairman Ben Bernanke warned in early 2007 that the budgetary impact of safety net programs could cause a "fiscal crisis" in the U.S. one day. The tax cuts of 2001 are the primary culprit in building unsustainable budget deficits. The concern is that investors will judge that the risk of an overleveraged U.S. is too great. When that happens, foreign investors will stop buying Treasury Bonds, or will sell their bonds, the dollar will fall, interest rates will shoot up, and sectors like the U.S. housing market or consumer durables could take a sudden fall, among other painful scenarios. The Fed might not be able to forestall "a meltdown," and America could witness an Asian- or Mexican-style financial crisis. David Walker, the comptroller general of the U.S. in the current Bush administration, admits: "I think the greatest threat to our future is our fiscal irresponsibility."

The Almighty Dollar

There is another reason to address the budget deficit. An extended period in which the dollar shows volatility could weaken its place as the world's reserve currency, prematurely ceding ground to some pivotal power currencies. The privileged status of our currency is a huge boon to the U.S. Because it is accepted everywhere, people are willing to take the images of our forefathers in exchange for their goods. China sends us DVD players and we send them paper they can put in a vault. While other countries have to earn dollars to buy oil or wheat on the international market, we can just print them. It is only because the United States can borrow in its own currency that it is able to sustain its enormous trade deficits. Argentina or Belgium could never sustain trade deficits like those of the U.S.

The dollar became the currency of choice because America had the strongest, most vibrant, most stable economy after World War II and in the decades since. No other currency, not for fifty years at least, will supplant the dollar as the reserve currency, according to many experts. But the strength of the dollar could erode as pivotal economies grow and their currencies become alternatives. Central banks are moving to a mix of currencies, now holding yen and euros. Someday they will also hold renminbi. The U.S. has everything to do with the pace of that shift. If the U.S. stops eroding the dollar with huge deficits, it will be a very long time before the dollar loses its special status.

U.S. deficits have another, more subtle effect as well. They diminish the authority of U.S. officials in urging policies on others. Even when U.S. officials advocate sensible ideas, they are seen as attempts to relieve pressure on the U.S. economy, not as a prescription for shared growth. U.S. credibility is low when it is seen as unwilling to do what it needs to help itself.

Adjustments All Around

We can hope that concern about China forces the U.S. to take on the work of lowering the budget and trade deficits as a similar fear did once before. Says John Yochelson, former president of the Council on Competitiveness, "Competition from Japan in the 1980s prompted us to face our own problems. They were telling us in our trade talks that our budget situation was a mess."

Even so, the American consumer cannot remain such a disproportionate engine of growth for the global economy. While America is fixing its own savings/investment balance, other countries need to make room for American exports. Japan and Europe also enjoy trade surpluses with the United States and they could, today, take steps to stimulate consumer spending and close the trade gap. Chinese and Indian consumers will eventually buy more high-quality U.S. goods as they become wealthier, but those countries too could do more today to stimulate domestic consumption. China knows it eventually needs to shift away from its export-led growth of the last decade, but the steps must begin sooner rather than later.

Certainly, American officials must continually pressure China to improve access for American firms in Chinese markets, especially for strong U.S. industries that employ many Americans, like financial services. It should bring WTO cases where justified. Washington should likewise allocate more generous funding to promote American goods abroad, as many European countries do, especially in foreign cities where there is no American embassy or consulate.

Who Writes the Rules?

The final worry about new economic actors is their effect on global financial rules and standards. As the world's most powerful country, the United States is accustomed to scripting the economic play. Even though Washington is increasingly constrained by the wishes of foreign countries and firms, and by international rules it has helped to implement, America still enjoys an unusual ability to shape economic parameters. Will growing economies usurp that authority, rewriting the rules so that their industries benefit instead of America's?

They have, and will continue to try and do so. Why wouldn't they? But let's be clear that trying to gain advantage is different from trying to change the norms of economic institutions, the procedural rules, or their guiding principles.

Europe and Japan often challenge the U.S. and its firms. European environmental and consumer protection standards are a clear example. American companies that want to compete in the nearly 500-million-person EU market have to comply with much stricter regulations than they face at home. A recent law banning lead and mercury has spawned a multibillion-dollar effort by the U.S. electronics industry to wean itself off toxic chemicals. Other examples include regulations requiring that genetically modified foods be labeled, implementing Kyoto Rules on auto emissions, imposing tougher radiation-dose standards for X-ray equipment, and guaranteeing online privacy.

In many international financial organizations, the U.S. has only one vote against coordinated votes of EU member states. Getting the IMF, the powerful organization that can extend large-scale loans to countries in need, to help Mexico in 1995 thus required intense U.S. lobbying, as, without a shared border, this was not a priority for Europeans. Japan, India, and the EU have challenged the U.S. using the WTO dispute settlement process and won.

As China and India gain strength, they too will want to have a say in setting the rules of the game. This will mean more difficult encounters over trade. In the Doha Round, India and Brazil, along with China, banded together to try to gain concessions in agriculture, for example. On the other hand, China as a fellow free trade champion also helps the U.S. China has brought actions in the WTO against Japan and South Korea, markets the U.S. has tried to crack.

As it grows, China will also push for a greater say in standards. For example, China has proposed a homegrown set of technical specifications for wireless communications. Chinese business leaders want to reduce the stream of license payments to the U.S. patent holders, especially because China's cell phone market at 460 million and counting dwarfs that of the U.S. What is encouraging is that, so far,

China is appealing for its alternate standard through established channels of the International Organization for Standardization, not unilaterally mandating them.

The U.S. government and companies will need to continue to fight these skirmishes over standards, though they largely impact the profits of particular firms, and sometimes only particular American billionaires, not the overall U.S. economy. U.S. companies also need to ensure that domestic disputes will not cripple their international competitiveness. In the case of cell phones, failure to agree on domestic standards for mobile phones is seen as a principal reason why foreign firms were able to capture both technological and market leads over their U.S. competitors. In general, if U.S. firms continue to innovate, as we discuss more in the next chapter, the standards will follow.

In some cases, emerging economies are not enforcing agreed-upon rules, to the detriment of U.S. firms. Abuse of intellectual property rights is one example. Losses from illegal copyright and patent infringement in 2006 were estimated to be some $2 billion in China, $2 billion in Russia, and $500 million in India.

Authorities in these countries claim to enforce the rules, but the damage continues on a huge scale. The natural evolution of China and India will begin to resolve this issue because the pressure for respecting intellectual property is beginning to come from their own domestic firms. After the U.S., China is the country with the largest losses due to piracy of computer software. Bill Gates predicts that within ten years, intellectual property rights will no longer be a problem in places like China and India. Until then, the U.S. has few options but to continue to press aggressively for better enforcement at the local as well as national level.

America cannot have an economic policy based on the hope that poor countries remain poor. The benefits to the United States from emerging great economies are large, broad, and lasting. Cheaper goods, more profits, lower inflation, more innovation, and greater overall economic growth. Paradoxically, the growing economic inter-dependence that erodes U.S. economic power is a stimulus to growth in America. The potential harms from this expansion are finite or specific, like jobs lost in certain sectors and forgone royalties.

Further, many of the perceived threats from the emerging economies of China and India are fundamentally problems America must and can solve itself. Despite the increase in trade, American living standards are "overwhelmingly determined" by domestic factors. Trade with China only accounts for about 4 percent of total economic activity in the U.S. The globalized economy magnifies the outcomes of our own choices, for good and for ill. Thus, the U.S. has to protect its workers from the disruptions of outsourcing; continue to attract foreign businesses; bring other countries into the energy club and promote serious conservation; reduce the federal budget deficit; and pursue opportunities for its companies abroad.

Will Americans continue to face economic disruptions? No question. The steps to address those disruptions are America's to take, however. If America can tackle its significant domestic economic challenges, and encourage its companies to face the competition head-on, other strong economies will not pose obstacles to American economic prosperity. Indeed, the opposite. It's America's fear of China's and India's growth, not the growth itself, that could endanger its economy.

5. Repairing the Innovation Engine

As we saw in the last chapter, many of the most common concerns about the role of pivotal powers in shaping America's economic future are not well founded. America's actions, not those of others, will largely determine our future prosperity. Here we examine one last issue that also generates great angst about the pivotal powers generally and the rise of China and India in particular—the prospect of America losing its innovation edge. We find that the danger to America's innovation culture does not emanate from any race with foreign competitors, but from the potential crumbling of its foundations at home.

The Case for Unthought Thoughts

There are myriad factors influencing the U.S. economy, but innovation ultimately drives the U.S. standard of living. Here is why: economists agree that economic growth is the key ingredient to improving standards of living. Even slight improvements in economic growth, when compounded over time, can make enormous differences in per capita income. The linchpin to U.S. economic growth is productivity growth. Productivity growth allows companies to make more with less—less money, fewer workers, fewer machines. The money left over can be passed to consumers, workers, or leveraged and reinvested. Each of these uses ultimately translates into better jobs and greater wealth for Americans. (Of course, there is no guarantee that wealth will be distributed evenly.) What spurs productivity growth? As the McKinsey Global Institute's Diana Farrell says, "[T]he key to productivity growth is innovation," and many have argued it will be the most important factor driving American economic success this century. Technological improvements have accounted for up to 50 percent of U.S. GDP growth, and some 65 percent of productivity growth since World War II.

Innovation can take many forms—new products (Post-it notes or diabetes drugs), production methods (just-in-time manufacturing), ways of doing business (big-box retailing), or even new industries (genomics). Innovation can also come from mundane improvements in the way a company does business. Small changes can beget great efficiencies, higher productivity growth, and, ultimately, economic growth. As Stanford economist Paul Romer explains, the introduction of the one-size lid for all sizes of coffee cups made the whole business slightly more efficient.

There are several reasons for the U.S. to ensure the continued health of its innovation system. First, America is counting on innovation in a very high-stakes game. Given its national debt, America's productivity growth stands between it and financial ruin. If American innovation slips and economic growth slows, America's fiscal situation would deteriorate further, rendering some otherwise pressing budget problems like Medicare and Social Security financially catastrophic.

Second, unlike in commodities markets, location matters with innovation. Innovation tends to occur in geographic "clusters," where talented people from rival companies can feed off each other's ideas and energy and where specialized knowledge, often unrecorded, accumulates. When an innovation occurs in Pittsburgh, U.S. firms can pick it up quickly. If more and more innovation happens in Bangalore, however, the benefits to American consumers may be delayed and inspiration for new innovation may not benefit U.S. firms as easily.

A third important reason for innovation to remain in the United States is because certain inventions and new technologies have important military applications that America will want to be the first to discover. Fourth, American companies can profit from being the locus of innovation, though earnings to firms are a minor benefit compared to the rewards to consumers. For example, first movers in an industry can maintain their position for decades, particularly when an innovation can lead to natural monopolies, as in the case of Microsoft's Windows. Similarly, the first mover in a given technology can have a strong role in setting the technical standards and can then earn lucrative licensing fees. Moreover, even as more innovation happens abroad, America will need scientists and engineers to spot and adapt those improvements for American industry. Finally, and perhaps most important, innovation in America can create good jobs here.

Better Living Through Chemistry

The example of Germany shows that an innovative sector can pay benefits for generations. In the late nineteenth century, Germany developed organic chemistry technology that laid the foundation for the massive pharmaceutical and chemical industries that remain fixtures of the German economy today.

The U.S. and Great Britain, though keen to capitalize on Germany's technological advances, found it difficult to catch up because they lacked the scientists and networks to commercialize those innovations. For starters, the superiority of German science education not only produced greater numbers of German chemists, but also meant that American and British students needed to study in Germany.

The language of chemistry was German, and German manufacturers were able to draw on a large reservoir of capable German-speaking chemists. The academic environment in Germany also helped facilitate communication among universities, research institutes, and industry so scientists were able to publish and share their latest developments. These links in turn helped drive venture capital into investments in new technologies.

Germany's technology lead fostered further, unforeseen innovations. German research yielded indanthrene, which became the base dye for jeans in the mid-twentieth century. Other spin-offs had direct military applications, such as the development of synthesized ammonia, which subsequently played a major role in explosives production during World War I. In the end, the wealth creation and self-sustaining cycle of innovation were mutually reinforcing, making it that much more difficult for others to break into a field dominated by the Germans, even through the upheaval of two world wars.

America, the Innovative

Happily, America remains the world's foremost innovative society—by a long shot. With less than 5 percent of the world's population, the United States accounted for 40 percent of all R&D spending in 2005. China's $93 billion in R&D spending in 2004 roughly equaled U.S. levels back in 1983.

The World Economic Forum's 2006 Global Competitiveness Report ranked the U.S. number two after Finland, based on the unparalleled strength of its innovation system. (China placed 49th, India 50th.) In 2005, India and China together generated less than three times the number of U.S. patents as the University of California, and most of the world's best research institutions are in the United States. There is more foreign-funded R&D in the U.S. than American-funded R&D overseas, and scientific articles by Americans are still cited more than any other. The U.S. also leads the major global technology markets such as aerospace, computers, and scientific instruments.

Beyond the numbers, the strengths of America's innovation society range from the society's tolerance of failure, its political stability, to its embrace of foreigners (once they get in). America's dynamic capital markets deserve special mention, suggests Richard Foster, a former director at McKinsey & Co., and author of *Creative Destruction*, as they are the ultimate drivers for private investment in new technologies. Venture capitalists will lend $1 million to a risky venture only because the markets will offer up $10 million if the technology pans out. Two hundred years of legal and regulatory evolution have yielded sophisticated, trustworthy capital markets. Not too underregulated, not too overregulated—usually just right. No other country has them.

Innovation as Destiny

Given America's strong culture of innovation and entrepreneurialism, it is hard to envision how a downward spiral might take hold. But as one Alcoa executive put it, "There is no God-given right to have tech centers in the United States."

Already, more and more innovation is taking place overseas. U.S. multinationals are fast establishing research labs in China, India, and Russia, capitalizing on rapidly growing infrastructure, talent, generous tax breaks and other financial incentives. In 2006, Google established an R&D facility in Moscow and announced plans for another in St. Petersburg, joining other major U.S. multinationals like Boeing, who are taking advantage of Russia's engineering talent. Boeing's Moscow Design Center employs 1,400 Russian engineers. India also houses hundreds of foreign research labs. As a senior vice president at Cisco said: "We came to India for the costs, we stayed for the quality, and we're now investing for the innovation."

China is the real comeback story, however. While it has a long road to travel, its top leaders are set on reclaiming China's legacy as a "nation of innovation." National spending in China on all R&D activities rose 500 percent from 1991 to 2002 and is set to increase dramatically through 2020. Its R&D spending is now second only to the U.S.

In 1997, China had fewer than fifty research centers managed by multinationals; by 2004, there were over six hundred. Bill Gates asserts that the Microsoft research center in Beijing is the company's most productive research lab based on the "quality of ideas" it generates. Procter & Gamble runs five R&D facilities in China with some three hundred researchers who work on innovations for Crest toothpaste and Oil of Olay cream. The research centers run by multinationals are undoubtedly the brightest jewels in China's innovation crown. Nevertheless, as a whole, one brokerage report concluded flatly, "China is not an innovative economy and has no innovative companies." Plagiarism plagues research, and China ranks 124th in the average number of times its research papers are cited.

As their massive domestic markets grow, however, the need to design products for Indians and Chinese customers will send even more R&D there. Only a design team based in India will know that washers sold there need a "sari cycle." Many products now optimized for the U.S. market will instead be optimized for Asians and adjusted for the U.S.

Positive Sum

In the end, does it matter whether China, India, and Russia are home to more innovation? The short answer is no—assuming America continues to nurture its own innovation system. That is because, unlike cheap oil, the amount of future innovation is not fixed. More innovation abroad does not mean less in the United States. In fact, more innovation abroad could trigger more here. There is no limit to innovative ideas because the problems and desires of the human race are infinite.

Because innovation necessarily grows from thoughts no one has had yet, it is hard to be confident that more innovation is always possible. Paranoia about the decline of innovation is therefore commonplace. Steven Popper, an innovation expert, tells us that policymakers and scientists he has met from China, Korea, Canada, Mexico, Sweden, Israel, the Netherlands, and the U.K. all convey a common fear that they are losing the race for innovation's future.

Yet think about all the many important inventions that do not yet exist—a cure for breast cancer, a cost-effective way to desalinate water, or a safe way to dispose of nuclear waste. Paul Romer likes to point out that possible combinations of four elements (not to mention five or six) from the periodic table, any of which could yield breakthrough new compounds, number 330 billion. If labs evaluated one thousand of these a day, it would take almost a million years to review them all.

How could someone living even twenty-five years ago predict a world where an average person could talk on a cell phone while walking down the street, duck into a gourmet coffee shop, log on to something called the Internet, and use it to get a good look at the roof of her house, or almost anyone's house, on Google Earth? Without fail, each generation brings inventions the previous one could not have imagined.

Furthermore, Americans benefit directly by discoveries made elsewhere. In general, the more innovation there is, wherever it occurs, the better off Americans ultimately will be because consumers of innovations reap the greatest rewards, not the firms that commercialize them. If an Indian pharmaceutical company were to invent an Alzheimer's cure, Americans would rejoice. American companies have been conducting research in Europe for decades, with no ill effect; in 2004, approximately two-thirds of U.S. corporate R&D outside the U.S. was conducted in Europe.

Moreover, in many areas of science, no one nation can make the investments needed to stay ahead: the economies of scale demand cooperation. In subatomic physics, discoveries made at the brand-new CERN collider in Geneva will be dependent on earlier measurements from the Beijing collider. American and EU scientists have been working together for decades on critical projects like next-generation nuclear power plants. The research party is just getting bigger with nuclear fusion, as we discussed in the Introduction.

Finally, innovation is not zero-sum. Competition is one of the most important stimulants to innovation. Increased innovation by scientists and engineers in China and India could end up creating more innovation everywhere. Although America's overall percentage of innovation is likely to be smaller in the future, Americans will still be better off.

America has little to fear from more innovation happening abroad, but at the same time there is no guarantee that its own robust innovation society will last. Through active mismanagement or benign neglect, the United States could let its innovation system deteriorate, potentially endangering its future prosperity.

History Lessons

This is exactly what has happened to many big powers in the past. All great powers have been keen innovators, but some allowed innovation to stagnate. As the cases of Imperial China and Great Britain show, innovation is not necessarily self-perpetuating.

MING CHINA: ENLIGHTENMENT DIMS Over seven hundred years before any European even lit a kerosene lamp, Imperial Chinese engineers, scientists, and craftsmen had racked up a startling list of achievements. Beyond tea and gunpowder, early Chinese innovators can take credit for the decimal system, the compass, the wheelbarrow, paper, paper money, movable-type printing, and even dominoes. In many areas, China was literally thousands of years ahead of other civilizations. Iron production was fully under way in China by the ninth century, nearly one thousand years before the same technology took hold in Europe.

In the tenth and eleventh centuries, China already had developed sophisticated sea ships, with watertight compartments, multiple decks, four to six masts, and the ability to transport nearly one thousand sailors. The largest vessels, known as "treasure ships" had nine masts and were over four hundred feet long, with 2,500 tons of cargo capacity. (By comparison, Christopher Columbus's ships, launched over two hundred years later, were only 125 feet long with 280 tons of capacity.)

China was poised to become a dominant maritime force, but ultimately reversed course. After a series of successful expeditions in the fifteenth century, Ming Dynasty leaders chose to shutter much of China's maritime industry, closing the door on a four-hundred-year technology lead. It was an ill-fated decision, leaving China vulnerable in the face of the threat posed by Japan and the new European invaders arriving just a century later.

This decision reflected a broader pattern of slowing innovation in Imperial China, the causes of which scholars debate. In the specific case of shipbuilding, many have argued it was a preoccupation with the land-based Mongol threat to the north that drove funding priorities away from naval investment. Others focus on cultural factors and shifts in official attitudes toward the sciences that resulted in a more insular and traditional outlook, undermining the overall environment for intellectuals. Regardless, as China's innovation society continued to slip away during the last decades of the Ming Dynasty and its Qing Dynasty successor, so too did its economy and position as a global power. Greater innovation alone would not have arrested this decline, but China would arguably have been better prepared to face future challenges had it maintained its technology edge.

BRITISH EMPIRE: SHORT-TERM THINKING The British similarly lost their innovation lead, but for different reasons. In the early 1760s, British clockmaker John Kay and inventor Thomas Highs partnered to solve the challenge of improving cloth weaving speeds. Their invention, the water frame, helped revolutionize the textile industry, and in turn sparked the larger Industrial Revolution in Great

Britain. Just one hundred years later, Great Britain realized the vast fruits of inventions like Highs and Kay's. Britain had gone from being the laggard in European manufacturing to the dominant global manufacturing base. At the height of its power in the mid-nineteenth century, Great Britain controlled a quarter of the world's land and its oceans, and ruled over nearly 350 million subjects.

However, after reaping the benefits of early industrial advances for almost a century, the British began to lag. Across the economy, as new technologies were developed elsewhere, British industry did not keep pace. It was easier and cheaper to repair and replace machines than to scrap and innovate. The focus on short-term profits meant industry after industry (textiles, dairy processing, milling, agricultural machinery, metals, mining, glassmaking to name a few) lost their edge in the face of the widespread complacency among British business—and government—leaders.

As in the U.S. today, the dominant orthodoxy of nineteenth-century Britain espoused the merits of limited government, low taxes, and balanced budgets. The government consciously pursued a minimalist bureaucracy, spending a relatively small percentage of gross national product on government expenses. The low level of public spending was not driven by fiscal constraint, but by choice, reflecting popular attitudes about the negative impact of excessive government influence in society.

By the turn of the twentieth century, savvy observers had the nagging sense that Great Britain, seemingly at the zenith of its power, was living on its past accomplishments. However, both major political parties clung to optimistic projections about the future of the British economy. So limited was the belief in the role of government in the economy that no one even bothered to compile detailed economic statistics. As historian Aaron Friedberg explains:

> After 1903, Englishmen tended to divide into those who . . .
> refused to acknowledge any difficulties and those who blamed
> all their country's woes on foreigners. A smaller and more

discrete group recognized the onset of relative decline, but believed that nothing could be done to arrest its progress. The possibility that limited government action could have improved the nation's overall economic performance by promoting research and development, encouraging domestic investment and seeking better access to overseas markets was not given serious consideration.

As calls for more social and public spending increased, British politicians retreated behind the familiar orthodoxy of low taxes and limited government. Many argued the nation could not afford to raise taxes to fund such public investments.

Nowhere was the lack of investment more decisive than in the field of public education. Until the end of the nineteenth century, education was not even seen as a responsibility of the state. Compulsory primary education was not instituted fully until 1880 and state-supported secondary education followed only in 1902. The first public grant to fund science education was awarded in 1890, and by 1901 the government's total investment in its universities was only £25,000.

Great Britain was caught flat-footed, having failed to make the kind of investments necessary to excel in the twentieth-century age of innovation. And even as some observers understood the necessity of major structural change, British society was unable to overcome strongly held ideological and cultural constraints—ultimately failing to confront head-on the challenges it faced.

Asleep at the Switch

Despite America's great entrepreneurial history, the trend lines of U.S. innovation today are not encouraging. As a share of GDP, U.S. federal funding for research in the physical sciences and engineering has been on a steady decline, dropping by half since 1970. Moreover, federal agencies that grant research funds have become "increasingly risk-adverse and focused on short-term results." Likewise, private funding for R&D, two-thirds of the U.S. total, while on the rise, is overwhelmingly devoted to near-term, narrowly commercial activities. Only 5 percent of funding is devoted to basic research. Europe's and Asia's shares of science and engineering publishing is growing while America's shrinks.

A smaller share of American undergraduates study engineering (6 percent) than in any other industrialized nation save one (Sweden). Tuition is up, but scholarship funds are shrinking, making college especially difficult for low-income students. Yet the number of jobs requiring science and engineering skills is growing nearly 5 percent a year.

So far, America has addressed this imbalance by importing much of its innovation talent; 55 percent of America's doctoral students in engineering are foreign-born. Immigrants like Russian Sergey Brin, who co-founded Google, and France's Pierre Omidyar, who started eBay, have created some of America's most successful companies. "If you took all 'foreigners' out of Silicon Valley," says McKinsey director Byron Auguste, "the place would completely collapse."

Importing creative talent has worked, but it may not last. Post-9/11 immigration laws and research constraints have gotten much tougher, just at the moment when other nations are becoming more attractive alternatives. As a result, overseas Chinese are "flocking back from top U.S. institutions" like Harvard University and Lawrence Livermore National Laboratory. In 2006, two prominent cancer researchers cited politics and cuts in research funding as their reasons to move to Singapore. A recent book, *Flight Capital*, makes the case that, for the first time, America is on the wrong end of a fast-flowing brain drain.

The next generation of American students is woefully unprepared to step into the breach. A troubling OECD study of forty industrialized countries found American fifteen-year-olds placing 28th in math and 29th in problem solving, "significantly below" the OECD average and well below South Korea, Iceland, Latvia, and Poland. A recent blue-ribbon commission organized by the National Academies, graced by such luminaries as the chairman of Intel and president of Yale University, argue in their report, *Rising Above the Gathering Storm*, that the U.S. is experiencing a "creeping crisis" and that "the scientific and technical building blocks critical to our economic leadership are eroding." The Hart-Rudman Commission on National Security for the 21st Century—the one that called, before 9/11, for much stronger defenses against terrorism—wrote in 2001 that "the inadequacies of our system of research and education pose a greater threat to U.S. national security over the next quarter century than any potential conventional war that we might imagine."

Homework

In Thomas Friedman's *The World Is Flat*, the founder of an Indian video gaming company advises Americans to think about "how you can raise your bar." He goes on to observe, "Americans have consistently led in innovation over the last century. Americans whining— we have never seen that before." Amen. Though the innovation trends in America today are not rosy, America can change that.

The best thinkers in the country have recommended myriad steps the United States should take to tackle the deficiencies in America's innovation investments. Increasing and expanding federal grants and tax credits for basic R&D is one important step. America also should start tracking its progress, assessing weak spots, and prioritizing responses. A periodic report card on the U.S. innovation system, just like the regular assessment of national defense strategy undertaken by the military, could help America focus its energies and inspire the nation's researchers with national missions.

Most critical, though, are investments in human capital. Tax incentives to promote "insourcing" in rural America and making it easier for foreign scientists and engineers to come and stay in this country are two areas for improvement. Intel chairman Craig Barrett likes to say that a Green Card should come stapled to every foreign student's science diploma.

Portable health care, mentioned earlier, would also help fuel entrepreneurism. Many people have faced the quandary typical would-be entrepreneur Rob Ricigliano did in the year 2000. He wanted to start his own consulting business, based on thirteen years of experience in conflict resolution. When he investigated health plans, the insurers told him they would not cover him (he had had a benign brain tumor removed and doctors told him there was no chance of a recurrence), his wife's allergies, or his eight-month-old because she had a harmless birthmark. What they would cover would have cost $800 a month. He gave up and accepted a university job instead.

Then there is educating our own. America has known for a long time that it needs to improve pre-K–12 education, especially in math and science. It has been twenty-five years since the Reagan administration released *A Nation at Risk* in 1983, and since then the number of panels, studies, high-level commissions, and books that have similarly pointed to shortcomings of American elementary education and suggested solutions could fill a barn. There is no shortage of ideas about what to do. The Teaching Commission, chaired by former IBM CEO Lou Gerstner and made up of several ex-governors and other high-caliber experts, recently issued a study recommending steps to upgrade America's K–12 teachers. Another blue-ribbon panel sponsored by the Center for American Progress suggests, among other ideas, increasing the number of hours children spend in school to levels in other industrialized countries. Other experts suggest new charter schools that specialize in math and science, or government scholarships in technical fields.

Many of these ideas have merit, and America has been debating them for a long time. It is now time to take the plunge and try some of them. While it is fine for America to track the activities of other nations, its central objective must be improving itself, to remain a strong player in a more competitive game. As historian Arnold Toynbee is credited with saying, "Civilizations die from suicide, not by murder." Or, as Jon Stewart has put it, "The only thing that can destroy us is us." Innovation is America's to lose.

6. The Powers' Perspectives

Before we turn to our ideas about how the United States should approach pivotal powers, let's first hear their side of the story. How do pivotal powers view America? How do they see the future of their relationship with the United States? Are they seeking to usurp America's dominant role?

Obviously, in one chapter we cannot accurately sum up the complex views of five great powers, over three billion people, on such weighty questions. These powers are not monolithic, either. Myriad interests compete within each government and society. Drawing definitive conclusions is even more difficult given the flux in each: Japan is debating becoming a "normal" nation with fewer strictures on its military. India, China, and Russia, in very different ways, are in the midst of a series of fundamental economic changes, and Europe is debating its collective identity and long-term potential as an integrated power. We will have to settle for some overarching impressions. We offer ten, about how the pivotal powers see their own priorities, the U.S., each other, and the world order.

Self-Reflection

1. The pivotal powers think of themselves as vulnerable and relatively weak, yet most believe in their destiny as great powers.

Pivotal powers have dueling inferiority and superiority complexes. China, India, and Russia all believe in their historical destiny as great powers, yet are simultaneously preoccupied with a raft of daunting internal challenges. In China's case, such bifurcated attitudes come from a millennial history of cultural and technological superiority, followed by a "century of humiliation" and economic backwardness. Chinese government officials and analysts consistently emphasize the monumental domestic problems China faces, whether a shortage of resources, staggering environmental degradation, a failing social safety net, or others. Chinese analysts will remind foreigners that despite its fantastic growth, China, per capita, remains a low-income country, ranking 123rd in the world in 2006. At the same time, the sense that China is destined to be a great nation again is strong. The Chinese public is confident that, within ten years, China will match the United States' level of influence.

In India, the mood is buoyant. While Indians readily admit India's many overwhelming hurdles—India consistently ranks in the bottom third of nearly all global human development statistics—they are confident of being on the right path. As analyst C. Raja Mohan puts it, "India's greatness is so self-evident, Indians don't even debate it." Indians believe they are a great civilization and are entitled, destined, to become a great power. This sense of entitlement is rooted not just in having a large population, an ancient civilization, and a booming economy, but also being the "world's most important democracy." In recent polling, Indians declared themselves as a very powerful country, second in influence only to the United States, and slightly ahead of China.

Russia too is at once triumphant and weak. On the margins of their July 2006 summit, Russian president Vladimir Putin turned to President Bush, pointed to his Labrador, Koni, and said, "Bigger, tougher, stronger, faster, meaner—than Barney [the president's terrier]." The Bush team was inclined to dismiss the remark as Putin's weak attempt at humor, but Russian observers saw a more telling message: don't question our status.

Putin's comment reflected a broadly held consensus across the political spectrum that Russia is a force to be reckoned with. Russians see themselves as the third most influential power in the world, after the U.S. and the European Union. The debate inside Russia, therefore, has not been about whether Russia's destiny is as a great power, but rather the precise meaning of "great power" and how to reclaim Russia's place in the world. For Putin, strengthening the power of the state is necessary to achieving that greatness.

However, for all of Putin's recent swagger and confidence, there is a sense that his "irresistible urge" to remind everyone that Russia has recovered its power suggests underlying insecurity. This lack of confidence lingers just beneath the surface of Russian elites' worldview, as they are keenly aware of the host of short-term and long-term social and economic problems facing their country. At a deeper level, like China, Russia also is trying to come to terms with its legacy of retreat, humiliation, and economic weakness, but it is a more recent, painful history. The devastation of going from the world's second superpower to a collapsed empire helps explain the motivation behind Russia's desire to climb back onto the world stage as well as Putin's efforts to project strength.

If China, India, and Russia are weak states with great state mentalities, where does that leave Japan and Europe? Everyone would agree both are major global powers, and they work in tandem with the U.S. to solve world problems. However, both also are less enamored with the trappings of traditional demonstrations of power, which sets them apart from the other three pivotal powers.

Europeans seek to be a different kind of power. European attitudes have been shaped significantly by memories of two world wars that devastated the continent. As a result, Carnegie Endowment fellow Robert Kagan writes that "Europeans today are not ambitious for power, and certainly not military power . . . [and] have developed a genuinely different perspective on the role of power in international relations." Of course, Europe can "afford" the rejection of traditional military power, since its security is implicitly guaranteed by the U.S. via NATO. Europeans have more appetite for being a leading "force" in global affairs than a traditional great power.

Japan's self-conception is one of a small, vulnerable, resource-poor nation. Whereas the U.S., India, Russia, and Europe seek to shape the world in various ways, the Japanese preoccupation for most of the last 150 years has been survival. Yet this humble goal is mixed with memories and some hopes of future greatness. Leading Japan scholar Gerald Curtis captures this contradiction when he describes Japan as a "huge economy with a small country mentality that wants to be respected as a great power." A recent poll also shows this ambivalence—nearly 40 percent of people surveyed from around the world named Japan a "world power," third after the U.S. and China, but only 16 percent of Japanese polled did so. For Japan, a permanent seat on the U.N. Security Council, which it seeks, is an end in itself. The seat would be a fitting recognition of Japan's generosity to the U.N. and an important symbol of status, but not necessarily a platform for a more aggressive push to shape global events.

In sum, pivotal powers operate from a complex place of vulnerability and pride—much like the U.S. Unlike the U.S., though, their recent histories evidence violence at the hands of foreigners on a scale that the U.S. has never experienced. In World War II alone, millions of citizens of Japan, Germany, China, and Russia were killed on their own soil. Dr. Jia Qingguo, associate dean of the School of International Studies at Peking University, explains the difference in mindset: "The U.S. has been secure for many years, so any change is viewed as increasing insecurity. But China has been insecure for many years, so any change is likely to be viewed as an improvement."

Because of these radically different histories, both pivotal powers and America have difficulty understanding each other's strong sense of vulnerability. Pivotal powers tend to see the U.S. as "unassailably powerful, proud and strong." In each, there are nationalist elements (sometimes stirred up intentionally for domestic political purposes) that have the potential to spiral out of control in dangerous ways—especially in reaction to perceived humiliation inflicted by another power (recall violent anti-American protests across China after the U.S. bombing of its embassy in Belgrade in 1999). For its part, America has its own nationalist voices to contain, and is biased toward focusing on the strengths of pivotal powers, paying less attention to their weaknesses and traumatic histories.

2. The pivotal powers seek prestige, influence, and freedom to maneuver, particularly in their own regions. While they want a voice in the issues of the day, their priorities are generally in line with America's.

We start with Japan, which is not as preoccupied with increasing its influence as China, India, Russia, or even Europe. Though being treated as a pivotal power is important to Tokyo (as it is with the others), as the world's second largest economy, Japan believes it has already arrived and wants others to recognize that status.

India's aspirations are more ambitious. It wants to be second to none in Asia (that means you, China). As former Indian foreign secretary Salman Haidar explained it, Delhi wants a say as "part of the future of the world" and to be recognized as a "significant and powerful country." But while India seeks a prominent role in the future balance of power arrangements in the Indian Ocean and Asia-Pacific regions, it does not want primacy in the region and certainly not the world. India wants to move from being a reactive power to one that influences events abroad, but does not seek to be the dominant power player on the world stage.

Russians do not aspire to the same type of global superpower role they had during the Soviet era. Russian foreign affairs scholar Dmitri Trenin concludes that "Russia today is not and is not likely to become a second Soviet Union . . . [an] imperialist aggressor bent on reabsorbing its former provinces." At the same time, Moscow does seek sufficient power to exert influence in the region—the ability to thwart what it sees as "inappropriate" U.S. influence in countries like former Soviet republics Ukraine and Georgia and across Central Asia. As longtime Russia expert Susan Eisenhower has pointed out, while the U.S. takes issue with their position, Russians believe their traditional ties (ethnic, cultural, economic, historical) to bordering states justifies the desire to assert dominance there.

In the past, Russia may have been too weak to confront the U.S. over perceived transgressions like NATO expansion or the war in Kosovo. From these two experiences, Russians concluded that a close relationship with the West meant a subservient one. Now, with economic strength at hand, Putin has opted for a more independent course as a way to gain operational flexibility—whether complicating America's military presence in Central Asia, wresting control of lucrative assets in Eastern Europe, or supporting alternative regional bodies like the Shanghai Cooperation Organisation designed to serve as a counterweight to U.S. power.

As U.S. strategic interests in the Caucasus and Central Asia increase (because of local energy supplies and counterterrorism efforts), the U.S. should expect more of this confrontational behavior, with Russia competing to regain its footing in the region and trying to force the U.S. to engage with Moscow on more equal terms. Though the Cold War is over, as Carnegie Endowment Russia expert Mark Medish put it, "Russia is still trapped in a twentieth- and even nineteenth-century mind-set," with zero-sum thinking about the merits and uses of power. Columbia University Professor Stephen

Sestanovich sums up Russians' approach as follows: "Its main goal is to regain power for leverage and think of its specific purpose later."

The two remaining pivotal powers—Europe and China—are more serious contenders for global influence. In some areas, like steps to address global climate change, Europe already rivals U.S. influence and expects its voice will remain strong. Europe relies primarily on its "soft power"—diplomacy, foreign aid, and culture— to build currency (although by July 2006, their revamped European Security and Defense Policy framework had supported sixteen civilian, police, and military operations around the world). In much of the world, European foreign assistance has more clout than America's because there is more of it—$36.5 billion versus $13.3 billion spent by the U.S. (not including in Iraq) in 2003—and because the Europeans distribute their aid more widely; former colonies are the main recipients of European aid, which means that expenditures span the globe.

China's activities and its influence are increasingly global. Two of China's pressing foreign policy goals, both of which are essential to the Communist Party's legitimacy, are to: 1) foster economic growth, and 2) prevent the permanent separation of Taiwan. Most Chinese foreign policy decisions are driven, in one way or the other, by those two priorities. Beijing's active diplomacy and development programs in Africa further largely the first; its military modernization is geared toward the second. Its desire to have a stable and positive relationship with the U.S. is motivated by both.

For the same reasons, China seeks greater influence and strategic freedom, especially in Asia; a stable neighborhood is key to continued prosperity. A stronger hand in Asia also will help increase its options toward Taiwan, and more generally facilitate Beijing's ability to resist any American attempts at containment. As much as China wants more international standing and respect, its leaders continue to see its global engagement as serving China's domestic goals of economic development and social stability. With as many as three hundred separate mass protests in China each day, their focus on global affairs is necessarily partial.

Beyond having a voice in issues affecting them, the foreign policy priorities of all the pivotal powers are generally in line with America's. The challenges of economic growth, disease, terrorism, and the environment top each of their lists. Surveys of Indians, for example, reveal that the top three foreign policy goals are combating terrorism, preventing the spread of nuclear weapons, and protecting Indians' jobs—exactly the same as those of Americans, though in a different order. Building superior military power in Asia ranks near the bottom (though, interestingly, it is more of a priority for Indians surveyed than for Chinese). When ranking threats to China's vital interests, its citizens see global warming, along with disease, terrorism, and energy disruptions, as even more critical than the U.S. military.

Views of America

3. The pivotal powers are troubled by recent U.S. actions, yet acknowledge they benefit from a strong America.

In every pivotal power, *qinmei* (pro-American), *fanmei* (anti-American), and *kangmei* (America-phobic) feelings, to use Chinese terms, coexist. Feelings toward the American people (versus its policies) remain quite positive in every pivotal power. In Britain, for instance, 69 percent still view Americans favorably (down from 83 percent in 2000). In India, Japan, and Russia, majorities hold favorable opinions, and in China, it's nearly half. According to another poll, overwhelming majorities in China had favorable impressions of Americans as "warm and open." By comparison, far fewer citizens of the Muslim world think highly of Americans; in Pakistan and Turkey (U.S. allies), favorable ratings of Americans are held by a dismal 27 percent and 17 percent of those polled, respectively.

While the American people may be holding their own, support for the nation and its foreign policy is down dramatically among some pivotal power publics and has remained low in others. Dropping from 78 percent in 2000, in 2006, 37 percent of Germans expressed positive views of the U.S. The trends in Japan and Britain are similarly on the decline. Russians and Chinese have remained skeptical, with more variability among Indians. In every pivotal power but Japan, publics polled in 2006 thought the U.S. role in Iraq was more dangerous to world peace than North Korea.

America pays a price for all this distrust. Foreign governments find it more difficult to support the U.S. when their own populations think the U.S. acts without legitimacy. Moreover, if anti-Americanism persists, younger leaders who come to power may prove harder to win over than their predecessors. Some in Europe are beginning to see a more fundamental questioning of the merits of the U.S. system around the world. German scholar Christoph Bertram commented, "The doubt in the American system of government is much deeper around the world than you think. [There is] a growing feeling that America is no longer the ideal model, and that has an impact on the credibility and legitimacy of what the U.S. does and says." The great powers acknowledge benefits of U.S. power but also express strong ambivalence, at best, about whether the exercise of that power contributes positively to global peace and security. Perhaps most troubled are officials of America's European allies.

Europeans think the United States "continues to shoot itself in the foot," leading many to conclude the U.S. is increasingly threatening to global stability. Europeans were more inclined to look the other way in the face of U.S. aggressive action during the Cold War, but in the post–Cold War era, they are quite concerned about U.S. unilateralism. Within Europe, solid majorities express such concerns—France (82 percent), Great Britain (66 percent), Germany (59 percent), according to recent polls. Michael Maclay, a former senior advisor to British foreign minister Douglas Hurd, notes that the American unilateralist trend was already well under way during the Clinton administration, but differences over Iraq brought the disconnect to the surface.

However, policy elites (if not general publics) also will readily admit that U.S. power is essential. While Iraq may have taught America a painful lesson about unilateral military action, it raises a different concern for Europeans. As Maclay suggests, "the bigger worry is the possibility of U.S. isolationism in reaction to Iraq. Retrenchment is even more dangerous to the system."

Unlike America's European allies, Russian elites are not particularly surprised by the U.S. "go it alone" attitude, as it is what they naturally expect from America. Even still, over 70 percent of the Russian public expresses concern with U.S. unilateralism. Russia is ambivalent about any direct benefits it may gain from U.S. power. Elites concede that Russia benefits from the "strategic balancer" role the U.S. plays in specific instances like northeast Asia, but this is offset by deep unease with America's policies elsewhere. As former Russian parliamentarian Roald Sagdeev put it, "Moscow is extremely bitter about the demonstration of U.S. power in places like Iraq, but also will admit that the U.S.-led war on terror has been advantageous to Russia."

In the case of China, the policy elite are likewise pointed in their criticism of U.S. foreign policy, with many finding it increasingly capricious, unrestrained, and aggressive. According to Wang Jisi, dean of the School of International Studies at Peking University, the Chinese view of America as an "insatiable, domineering country" intent on establishing an unassailable hegemony is common. The Iraq War is proof of this intent, but of greater concern is U.S. policy toward China because Chinese strategists are "acutely aware" that U.S. power could be turned on them. Says Wang, "Many Chinese still view the U.S. as a major threat to their nation's security and domestic stability."

Even though many Chinese analysts are convinced of American hostility, they also see the benefits of U.S. power in the security and stability it has provided to Asia, the protection of oil transit routes, and delivery of other public goods. A 2006 poll found that a strong majority in China think that the U.S. is playing an either somewhat or very positive role in Asia. Further, they admit that seeing another nation supplant the U.S. would be far worse. Surprisingly, a majority of Chinese surveyed thought it would be "mainly negative" if the U.S. became "significantly" less powerful either militarily or economically. The consensus in China, albeit a "sullen" one, is that at least for twenty years, China should encourage the U.S. to remain the world's leader. And while Beijing is worried about a U.S. policy of containment, the idea of America hedging against China is viewed as a natural element of geopolitical strategy.

Indians and Japanese are relatively more sanguine about U.S. power. America's might has benefited Delhi in specific ways, like helping to manage tense relations with Pakistan. Japan is even more welcoming of U.S. power—and most ready to endorse U.S. actions. Unlike in Europe and China, there were no major demonstrations in Japan against the Iraq War because the Japanese, as scholar Gerald Curtis says, "cannot even afford to think about being critical of the U.S." A nuclear North Korea that has launched missiles into Japanese territory, and a rising China still smarting over Japan's brutal occupation, means the U.S. alliance is crucial to Japan's security.

In short, the publics and elites in most pivotal powers do not like American foreign policy, but governments do see benefits of American power to varying degrees. In each, majorities believe America wants to serve only itself and is not concerned with the views of others. Not surprising, the intensity of such sentiments is tied closely to whether America's policies toward their own country are perceived as friendly or hostile.

4. The pivotal powers express bitter frustration with American disregard for the established rules of the system.

Officials and analysts from every pivotal power expressed disappointment, if not outrage, over America's flouting of international rules. According to a hierarchical, Confucian worldview common in China, the leader ought to be a benevolent, restrained force, acting as a moral example. Instead, the United States shows "contempt" toward the power of the international community, the Chinese think, and plays by the rules only when it suits U.S. interests. The expression Chinese policy analysts will use to describe American hypocrisy translates as "Officials are allowed to burn houses but ordinary people can't even light lamps." Chinese often ask: "Why does a domestically democratic nation act in such an undemocratic way in world affairs?"

Their sentiment is echoed in Europe and Russia. Europeans' plea is for the U.S. to stop pretending America has different rules than everyone else. From the Russian point of view, a major problem with the U.S. is America's inclination to "equate its national interests with global interests." As Stanford University Russian foreign policy expert Coit D. Blacker explains, "Russians see the United States as the single most duplicitous power in the international system. America says things it expects others to accept as 'the truth,' but the U.S. then feels completely free to operate as it sees fit." But perhaps most annoying for the Russians is the fact that the U.S. has managed to get away with "global interest" rhetoric as a thinly veiled cover for self-interested action for many years—at least until Iraq.

5. All the pivotal powers want good relationships with the United States, but also want independence.

With the sometime exception of Russia, pivotal power governments desire a productive, stable relationship with the United States. All realize their interests are tied up in U.S. decisions and actions. At the same time, while there is a high degree of acquiescence to America's wishes, no pivotal power (with the partial exception of Japan), wants to play second fiddle to the U.S. They do not want to be dictated to.

Despite its misgivings about American foreign policy, China places "enormous value" on maintaining a positive relationship with the United States. American markets, investment dollars, and technology are key to China's economic growth. A stable relationship with America also is central to "a peaceful international environment" that China needs so it can devote its full attention to its legion of domestic challenges. China, though, will quietly go its own way when America's path does not serve Beijing's interests, signaling disagreement with Washington's policies but avoiding confrontation. China's low-key diplomacy at the U.N. in opposing the Iraq War is a case in point of such behavior. Only on issues that Beijing judges as core national interests, such as Taiwan, is it willing to challenge the United States publicly.

For India, the possibility of a positive bilateral relationship marks a radical departure from earlier times. During the Cold War, India led the Non-Aligned Movement (NAM), had a close security relationship with the Soviet Union, and policymakers reflexively railed against Western imperialism and exploitation. Indians were "congenitally anti-American," as expert Ashley Tellis puts it. (The feelings were mutual. Following a 1971 meeting between President Nixon and Prime Minister Indira Gandhi, the president referred to her as an "old witch" and Secretary of State Henry Kissinger called the Indians the "goddamn most aggressive people around.")

A variety of factors have since shifted Indian attitudes, among them: the collapse of the Soviet Union, an economic opening (which made India more dependent on the global trading system), as well as a turn in U.S. strategic thinking. A warmer relationship is now seen by many to have benefits for India. Standing with America can signal to China that India "has options," and better U.S. ties can help India gain access to sensitive technologies. A close relationship is also an "entrée card" onto the world stage, signaling to other great powers that India has come into its own. That the U.S. is more accepting of India as a great power feeds their sense of self-esteem. Being "de-hyphenated" from Pakistan is an important component of that.

Because "no page in history turns neatly," elements led by the political left continue to warn against a hegemonic U.S. that will try to put India "in its vest pocket." So while there is a tentative consensus in the policy community that now India can and should have a close strategic relationship with the U.S., India is highly protective of its independence. "There is no support here for the role of 'junior partner' " explains analyst C. Raja Mohan.

In particular, India is wary of appearing to be part of any Washington plan to "contain" China. Neoconservatives in Washington may daydream about India and the U.S. together beating up on the People's Republic, but it's not going to happen Indian analysts warn. India will never allow a situation where, as Brookings scholar Stephen Cohen put it, "the United States will fight China to the last Indian."

Though segments of the policy community remain distrustful of U.S. intentions, most in the policy mainstream are not concerned that the U.S. would seek to quash its growth. Shared interests in modernizing the Muslim world and managing China's rise will ensure that, they believe.

In the case of Russia, since the fall of communism, Russian attitudes toward the U.S. (and vice versa) have experienced pendulum swings between hope and despair. In the early 1990s, when Russia was most vulnerable, many accused the U.S. of poking around in the open wound. As Dmitri Trenin has observed, some are resentful that the U.S. treated Russia "as a 'defeated state,' " at the end of the Cold War, unlike post-communist nations like Poland, the Czech Republic, and others, which were welcomed. Pointing to evidence such as NATO enlargement, the pursuit of national missile defense, the war in Kosovo, and economic reforms pushed by the U.S. and the IMF that empowered corrupt oligarchs, there is a sense that the "U.S. took advantage of Russia when it was weakest." In reality, neither side was willing to commit to truly integrating Russia into the West.

Now, Russia is ultimately pragmatic, "neither anti nor pro-Western." But any attempt at salvaging ties will need to be on equal terms, Russians warn. Russia is determined to relinquish its "junior status," and reassert its independence and freedom to maneuver. Russia analyst Lilia Shevtsova suggests that attempts at a hollow partnership will only lead to dissatisfaction and trigger yet another swing of the pendulum.

The extent and degree of European comfort with the status quo of a close U.S. relationship has been hotly debated for decades. The Suez Crisis of 1956, in which the United States forced the U.K., France, and Israel to back down in their confrontation with Egypt, led the British to conclude they should be on the side of the U.S. on any global strategic issue. The French concluded the opposite, and the split more or less endures today. Generally, though, there is an assumption of a continuing, thick transatlantic partnership; policy elites assert that there are real advantages to staying close to the US.

Unlike the others, Japan is hanging on to the U.S. alliance for dear life. The Japanese are no longer worried, as they were in the 1980s, that the U.S. will try to keep them down (though they still resent it). There is a broad consensus in Japan that no strategic option is more attractive or viable than sticking to the U.S. like glue. With a growing China and a nuclear North Korea on their doorstep, Japan needs to keep America close. Though Tokyo is more and more convinced that the U.S. relationship is critical, it also increasingly feels the need to hedge against uncertainties in the relationship. Without the shared threat of the Soviet Union, the United States could abandon Japan one day, so the U.S. alliance may not always guarantee Japanese security. In developing independent capabilities, though, Japanese officials are wary of striking out too far on their own.

In sum, each of the pivotal powers believes a good relationship with the United States is desirable, though all seek more independence and to avoid playing Robin to the U.S. Batman.

6. Their future relationship with the United States is a topic of heated debate among the pivotal powers. All believe that the United States is in the driver's seat in setting the tone and direction of the bilateral relationship.

Within each pivotal power, the future relationship with the U.S. is contested. On one extreme are those advocating close ties to the U.S. well into the future. On the other are those who argue that with adequate future strength, their nation or group of nations could afford to distance itself and should.

In India, to use Stephen Cohen's taxonomy, the elite is split four ways. The "enthusiasts" are confident they can manage America and think a closer relationship, on the model of Israel, is the best course. The "free riders" think cooperation is fine, but do not envision an enduring alliance in the long run because America is "too fickle and powerful to be trusted." The "doubters" think Washington remains a potential threat to India, as it was during the Cold War, whereas the "hostiles" think America, intrinsically opposed to India, will exploit and corrupt it. Those on the fence want the United States to demonstrate that it is serious about having a long-term relationship with India.

Many in India would agree there is far more congruence than competitiveness among U.S. and Indian objectives, and thus room for continued cooperation. The dominant view recognizes that India's capacity to act on its own remains limited, but that India's rise creates opportunities for joint endeavors because India increasingly has assets to bring to the table.

Similarly in China, while the direction for the next generation is basically set, the debate in China about the future relationship with America is "pluralistic" as one scholar put it. Several schools of thought compete for currency. The first argues that more power for China is better because it provides more security. Those who think China is already powerful believe China should build a bigger military now. Those who see China as less powerful are concerned about provoking the U.S. and believe China should accumulate more capability over time. The second school argues there is no fundamental conflict with the U.S. and, as such, the two countries can work together. These first two schools compete in policy circles. In the last camp are the emotional hard-liners, usually found in online chat rooms, who would argue that China should build its economy so the U.S. cannot bully China in the future. If China becomes strong, it can later take revenge for U.S. mistreatment. China needs to be able to stand firm, these proponents would say, because America respects power and toughness. If China gives an inch, the Americans will take a mile. As these varying opinions suggest, and former Defense Secretary William Perry has pointed out, Americans must appreciate that China's future intentions "are not a *secret* they are keeping from us, they are a *mystery* to both sides."

Across the spectrum, Chinese policy elites believe that America does not want China to become a great power and seeks to contain, constrain, slow, or pin down China. Creating and confirming this view is a series of unilateral actions by the U.S. that the Chinese believe have directly harmed Beijing's interests, including the strengthening of the U.S.-Japan defense relationship as well as other alliances in Asia; America's determination to build a missile defense system, perceived as a means to neutralize China's nuclear deterrent; and even America's opposition to China's 2000 Olympics bid, seen as a deliberate jab. To this day, worldly, America-friendly Chinese believe that the accidental U.S. bombing of the Chinese embassy in Belgrade was Washington's intentional, humiliating punishment for China's opposition to the war in Kosovo. America's clear, constant, and public disapproval of China's political system also reads to many as a desire to foment political instability in China.

However, it is U.S. policy toward Taiwan that grates the most. The loss of Taiwan in 1895 as war booty to a previously weaker Japan is one of the greatest humiliations in Chinese history. A very popular view in China is that America's commitment to Taiwan's defense is a strategy designed to keep China fragmented, unable to unify and become a great nation. Otherwise, Chinese ask, why does the U.S. seek "peaceful resolution" of the Taiwan Strait situation, instead of "peaceful reunification"? When America and Japan issued for the first time, in 2005, a *joint* statement about Taiwan policy, it "woke up a thousand ghosts from Chinese history." It is deeply uncomfortable to the Chinese that the U.S. holds a trump card on an issue as existential to them as Hawaii might be to Americans. To the Chinese, America has China's big toe in a vise grip. So Chinese leaders do what they can, slowly and carefully, to loosen America's hold.

Europe's debate is less stark, with all European powers recognizing the centrality of America to Europe's security and interests into the future. Even those who claim that more independence from the United States would be better, theoretically, cannot hope for real separation. As leading French political scientist Justin Vaisse put it, "whether we share the same policy objectives or not, we Europeans find ourselves stakeholders of the same international order as the Americans . . . and others see us as part of 'the West,' so we cannot pretend we're on our own. All this makes true independence wishful thinking." However, Iraq taught Europe that it could not afford to sit back while America was engaged on major global issues that had serious consequences for the EU.

In Russia, the debate about a future warm relationship with the U.S. is all but over. According to former parliamentarian Roald Sagdeev, "across the political landscape, there is an increasingly solid anti-U.S. consensus." Russians who have argued for a more positive relationship with the U.S. or U.S.-style democracy in Russia have been pushed to the sidelines.

Some see U.S. power as nefarious, and more conspiratorially minded Russians believe the U.S. has a "master plan" for subverting Russia. There is a perception the U.S. wants to "keep Russia in a box," and for the Russians, evidence of this strategy abounds. The U.S. support of the "Orange" and "Rose" revolutions in Ukraine and Georgia or the prospect of further NATO enlargement are interpreted as parts of a concerted effort to impinge on Russia's traditional sphere of influence. U.S. policies, like the outdated Jackson-Vanik Amendment tying Most Favored Nation trading status to Soviet emigration policies or U.S. laws restricting Russian companies from competing for space cooperation–related contracts, are examples, for those who seek them, of the U.S. conspiracy against Russia.

Post-9/11, both sides thought counterterror cooperation might jump-start the whole relationship, but instead the last seven years have ushered in an anti-Western flavor to Putin's efforts to rebuild Russia as a great power. Putin's increasingly assertive and autocratic style, in turn, has prompted unease in the U.S. Though it is no longer fashionable to be pro-U.S., some Russians do quietly fear the implications of a chilly relationship with the West, and potential Russian isolation. (The moneyed elite have a self-interest in maintaining their savings and investments linked to Western banks and the routine of vacationing in the U.S.)

In Japan, how close to remain to the U.S., as well as how much to pay to maintain the alliance, are questions not yet answered, with a spectrum of views represented in policy circles. That discussion interacts with another about the degree to which Japan ought to be willing to use force to shape its environment. Four camps result. The "middle power internationalists" think Japan ought to use prosperity to achieve prestige and aspire for Japan to become a country close to the U.S. with a role akin to Australia's. The "neo-autonomists" would keep their distance from the U.S. and build an independent, full-spectrum military including their own nuclear deterrent. Pacifists would eschew force as well as the U.S. while the "normal nationalists" think Japan can stand on the international stage shoulder to shoulder with America.

Whether they are comfortable with it or not, all the pivotal powers recognize that the U.S. largely sets the tone of the bilateral relationship. "Everything Americans say and do regarding China reverberates through Chinese domestic politics," says Susan Shirk, former deputy assistant secretary of state. In an instant, U.S. actions can put those arguing for a cooperative U.S. relationship on the defensive. Russians similarly see the agenda in the U.S.-Russian relationship as driven by American concerns, given the asymmetry in American and Russian power. As a result, as scholar Michael McFaul has suggested, "the main impetus for the drift in U.S.-Russian relations is not the growing authoritarianism within Russia, but shifting American foreign policy priorities." Indian analysts also believe that the U.S. is "in the driver's seat" in the bilateral relationship. When asked about the future Indo-U.S. relationship, Ratan Tata, a prominent Indian CEO replied, "The answer to that will lie in the United States, not in India."

What the U.S. does and says has a profound impact on the domestic debates within each pivotal power about its future relationship with America.

Conscious Courtship

7. The pivotal powers are systematically improving relations with one another, but distrust lingers in many relationships. With the exception of China, each is more concerned about the potential threat from another pivotal power than from the United States.

As we see in Table 6.1, recent years have seen a flurry of activity among pivotal powers, from state visits to technology-sharing agreements to military exercises. No pivotal power, no matter how close to the U.S., is putting all its eggs in America's basket. For China, Russia, and India in particular, other pivotal power relationships are a way to garner strategic space in the face of a strong America. Academics call this "soft" balancing because it does not involve direct military competition.

Pivotal powers are courting one another with vigor. Chinese president Hu visited India in 2006 with great fanfare. Europe is China's largest trading partner and Brussels contemplated dropping its arms embargo on China in 2004 before the U.S. quashed the idea. In 2005, Russia and China held their largest-ever military exercises. India and Japan recently unveiled an "Eight-fold" initiative. China and Japan have the only frosty relationship among the lot, yet China is Japan's largest trading partner.

This chumminess has some natural limits. Underneath almost all relationships flows a current of distrust. For example, while India and Russia have again drawn closer, announcing a "strategic partnership,"

Table 6.1: Pivotal Power Interactions

	INDIA	JAPAN	EU	CHINA
R U S S I A	"Strategic partners." Vow to reach $10 billion in trade by 2010. Moscow is Delhi's largest defense partner. Space agreement made Russian law, November 2006.	Bilateral trade in 2006 reached highest level. Japan is largest investor in Russian oil and gas.	Free trade agreement proposed in 2006.	Major military exercise held and "strategic alliance" reaffirmed in 2005.
I N D I A		Major state visit in 2008. "Strategic partner-ship" announced in 2005. "Eight-fold" initiative issued. India is the largest recipient of Japanese development assistance.	In 2006 the U.K. pro-posed India and EU enter into free trade agreement. Memo-randum of under-standing on training and employment signed in November 2006.	"Strategic partner-ship" announced in 2005. Major summit in November 2006 with pledge to double trade by 2010. Border deal signed in 2005. Agreed in June 2007 to hold first ever joint army exercise.
J A P A N			Japan is Europe's 2nd overall trading part-ner. EU ranks 2nd in Japan's imports and 3rd in exports.	2006 summit in Beijing ends 5-year hiatus. In 2006 began considering bilateral free trade agreement.
E U				China is EU's 2nd largest trading partner, and EU is China's largest.

neither wants their relationship to be seen as directed against China, Pakistan, or the U.S. Similarly, Russia and China flirt, and conduct major joint military exercises, but unease lingers. After all, Russia must manage its long, energy-rich, undefended and underpopulated eastern border, with an energy-hungry and overflowing Chinese population on the other side. Already, Russians jokingly refer to the rush of Chinese across its "Mexican border," and express quiet concern about de facto Chinese dominance in Russia's Far East. Such concern about China is shared among the nearby pivotal powers; a recent poll found that 93 percent of Japanese respondents, along with 76 percent in Russia and 63 percent in India, held a "negative view" of China's growing military might. Further, for all their recent friendliness, India has a history of tensions with China, including a war fought along India's northeast border in 1962, and an "undeclared rivalry." Europe worries about the long-term implications of energy reliance on an autocratic and aggressive Russia.

The Pivotal Powers and the World Order

8. No pivotal power is aiming to unseat the United States as a superpower, nor do the pivotal powers seek a weak United States. At the same time, the pivotal powers want a more multipolar world.

Leaders in every pivotal power have at some point called for a more multipolar world—but they have differing views on which powers could or should serve as the other poles. The Chinese, for example, think they should have a lot more power, Europe and India a little more, but Japan and the U.S. less. The Indians think they should have a lot more power, Europe and China a little more, Japan the same and the U.S. less.

According to recent Pew polling, majorities surveyed "favor another country challenging America's global military supremacy." In Western Europe, nearly 70 percent would welcome such a development, as would 74 percent of Russians and Chinese, and 80 percent of

Indians. (Japan was not part of the survey.) In a different poll, a majority or plurality of citizens in twenty out of twenty-three countries surveyed, including European countries, China, and Russia thought it would be mainly positive for Europe to become more powerful than the U.S.

While all pivotal powers believe the world would be better off if the U.S. were more constrained, none is volunteering to try to weaken America's role directly. Tokyo is most supportive of American power, and if anything, worries because it already sees U.S. diplomacy, moral authority, and economic appeal waning.

Many Chinese believe the decline of U.S. primacy and a transition to a more multipolar world is "inevitable" over the long term, but that America's power is unlikely to diminish in the short term. This realization has been one of China's greatest disappointments in the post–Cold War era. Because of America's staying power, and the great importance to China of the U.S. relationship, China has gone out of its way to reassure Washington that it has no intention of trying to dethrone the U.S. Beijing is framing its path to reemergence as a "peaceful rise," with emphasis on "win-win" solutions and China's adherence to the principles of peace, equality, openness, and cooperation. Chinese thinkers claim that China is blazing a "new strategic path" that "transcend[s] the traditional way for great powers to emerge."

Indians also believe that having a single superpower is "not so good for the unipolar power or for the world," explains Montek Ahluwalia, deputy minister of planning, and one of India's highest-regarded intellects. At the same time, India would deeply regret the dramatic dilution of U.S. power, as it often serves India's purposes.

In the case of Russia, as Dmitri Trenin put it, "Russia is realistic. It would like to see the U.S. have slightly reduced power, but wants it to be above all the others." Russians are not instinctively opposed to U.S. power, but see every issue through an interests lens. Therefore, a U.S. military base in Central Asia would automatically generate

Russian opposition because it implicitly increases U.S. leverage, even if the purpose of the U.S. presence is ultimately consistent with Russian interests.

The European desire for constraint on U.S. power is driven much more by dissatisfaction with the way the U.S. has played its dominant role than by its own ambitions. As Justin Vaisse commented, "the hegemon is supposed to be conservative in using its power to reinforce the world order, but American power is not being exercised in that way today." In a region that emphasizes multilateralism, unilateral action is anathema. Europeans presume that Europe will inevitably become one of the pillars in a multipolar world, though some analysts have noted that Europe's preference for "soft power" may leave it ill-prepared for the "rough and tumble world of a true multipolar order."

In sum, for various reasons, the pivotal powers (except, to a large degree, Japan) see benefit in a more multipolar world, either as a reflection of their own rise or to ensure a more stable global environment. However, none are preparing to wrestle America for the superpower title.

9. The pivotal powers have all bought into the current liberal world order to a greater or lesser extent, but many want a stronger voice.

No pivotal power is fundamentally opposed to the liberal world order. They take issue instead with the degree of influence they deserve in shaping that order and the U.S. dominance of it. All participate in and benefit from the liberal international institutions and regimes that the United States and Europe created after World War II. With the possible exception of Russia, the pivotal powers are more intent on trying to join or strengthen the liberal world order than on destroying it or creating their own structures.

As a part-architect, Europe is most satisfied with the current world order. Europeans are active in the leadership of every consequential global institution. As former French foreign minister Dominique de Villepin declared, "We are the guardians of an ideal . . . of a conscience that puts cooperation ahead of domination. And that must be the future for all the world." However, as Europe has become ever more vested in notions of multilateralism and interdependence, America's "go it alone" approach has put these two co-founders of the world order increasingly at odds. It is not just America's "no" votes that irk the Europeans. As Christoph Bertram commented, "No one is insisting that the U.S. sign the Kyoto protocol, but at least respect the desire of others to do so—don't crusade against it."

Europe has a vested interest in the multilateral system, where it knows it has voting heft. In international organizations, Europe can play both ends against the middle; that typically means twenty-five votes versus America's one. Europeans thus see multilateral institutions as a perfect platform for their "postmoderm" approach to power. The hope is that European "civilian power" will compensate for traditional military power and ensure European global influence over time.

Like Europe, Japan is a stalwart member of the international order. Japan is reliably supportive of the "rules-based" system and a very generous funder of it, being the second largest contributor to the U.N. That said, Toyko has not jumped at the chance to lead many new international initiatives.

India accepts the liberal world order and avers that it will help to build it. But Indians are chafing at their lack of voice in major institutions such as the U.N., the Security Council, the Asia-Pacific Economic Cooperation, the IMF, and others. As C. Raja Mohan has described it, many feel India has been "robbed of its rightful place at the high table in the international system," and that China's equities are better reflected. Delhi is determined to change that, and its frustration can lead to a narrow single-mindedness. For example, once India learned that the 2005 U.N. reform package was not going to include a permanent Security Council seat for India, its diplomats attempted to obstruct progress on key, substantive issues.

China's attitude toward the world order is a point of great debate in the U.S. Some conservatives argue that China is now or will inevitably emerge as a "revisionist" power, dissatisfied with the U.S. and Europe-created global order. But the facts do not support this view. On the contrary, American strategies of engaging and binding China have largely worked. Chinese attitudes toward the international system have changed dramatically over the last few decades. Now, assistant foreign minister He Yafei declares, "We are a maintainer and builder of the international system." Former deputy secretary of state in the George W. Bush administration Robert Zoellick agrees that China wants its rise to "complement, not replace" the current order.

From a starting point of near zero in the violent Maoist period of the 1960s, China's memberships in international governmental organizations have shot up to well past the world average. Once in these organizations, far from rejecting the norms, China has played largely within the rules. For example, in the WTO, China has shown no signs of wanting to weaken the regime. In fact, during the 2006 Doha WTO negotiations, the main concern of the U.S. delegation was that China, which would be a clear beneficiary of increased market access for goods, was not active enough! Beijing knows China's economic growth depends on global trade and global trade on a stable set of rules. The most important strategic decision the Chinese have made was to embrace globalization, and deepen their participation in the world economy, not detach themselves from it.

Stanford University professor Stephen Stedman, who was deeply engaged in the U.N. reform process in 2003–2005, calls China's behavior during the process "open-minded and supportive of strengthening the international order" but for its role in blocking Japan and India from securing permanent seats on the U.N. Security Council. Beijing also is now supporting the candidacy of Chinese nationals for positions of authority in international organizations. In November 2006, for example, Dr. Margaret Chan, a Hong Kong–based avian flu expert, won the campaign to become the head of the World Health Organization.

Why is Beijing integrating? In part because China has and will continue to benefit enormously from various economic dimensions of globalization, and in part because a stronger multilateral order could constrain America. China playing by the rules could also assuage other countries' fears of its growing power. Further, the experience of SARS showed China that nontraditional threats can be devastating, and can be addressed effectively only in concert with others. In short, China wants to join the international system because it works. The initial motivation is not as critical, though, as the fact that China is changing in the process. All this joining is "socializing" Chinese bureaucrats, according to Harvard's Alastair Iain Johnston, making China more sensitive to fitting in with the mainstream view. Today, China is reluctant to be exposed or isolated as the main obstacle to a generally accepted international action.

Evan Medeiros of the RAND Corporation observes this dynamic in China's attitude toward nonproliferation, which has changed markedly in the last two decades. China joined the Nuclear Suppliers Group (NSG) in 2004, capping a series of steps to bring its nuclear export control policies in line with international nonproliferation standards. At first, China assumed nonproliferation commitments in the early 1990s to improve its relations with America and specifically to gain access to U.S. trade, investments, and advanced industrial technologies. As China took those tactical steps, it built up constituencies of "intellectual entrepreneurs" inside the bureaucracy responsible for implementing nonproliferation policy. They began to make the case from the inside that the measures also contributed to China's national security. Though many factors were at work, this internal change was fostered, in part, by America's engagement strategy.

In Asia as well, China is now seen as a "status quo" power. That is remarkable given an earlier era in the 1950s and 1960s when China sought to destabilize regional governments by supporting armed insurgencies, had border conflicts with virtually every neighbor, and spread Maoism beyond its borders. China scholar David Shambaugh observes that China is now "the exporter of goodwill and consumer durables instead of weapons and revolution."

So while Chinese academics and policymakers still debate what China's ideal future world order is, there is little interest in a wholesale revision of the current international system, from which China benefits greatly. If anything, China is frustrated that it still occupies a second-class seat in many organizations and is treated with suspicion, especially by the U.S. The Chinese want to be taken more seriously and to be seen more positively.

Compared with the others, Russia is much more dissatisfied with the current world order. Russia's dance with the West and its liberal institutions has been ongoing for nearly twenty years, with less-than-stellar results for Moscow. Inclusion in international institutions was a centerpiece of the Clinton administration's recipe for Russia's post-communist transformation, whether promotion of free market economics through an IMF program, membership in the G8, or creation of the NATO-Russia Permanent Joint Council.

The outcomes were disappointing on both sides and fueled by wishful thinking. Russian elites pretended the country was promoting market and democratic reforms and the West pretended to believe it was happening. Underneath it all was the lack of consensus in the West and Russia about the nature and objectives of Russia's post-Soviet identity and integration.

Many of the 1990s reforms missed their mark, leaving Russians bitter and angry. Several components of the IMF-directed economic "shock therapy" that worked in Eastern Europe were only partially or poorly implemented in Russia. The difficulty of effecting drastic and massive reform helped lead to a prolonged period of inflation, which destabilized the economy, pushed millions of people (especially pensioners and others on fixed incomes) into poverty, and undermined the very notion of reform.

Time and again, in the immediate post-Soviet era, Russia was granted privileged treatment, but no prospect of real membership in either NATO or the EU. Even in the G8, Russia was relegated to a "junior member" role for many years, and NATO itself is still seen by the Russians as an explicit hedge by the U.S. Nothing the U.S. has done since has assuaged Russia's assumption that America sees it as a security threat.

But Russia is not prepared to walk away from every institution. Russia prizes its role on the U.N. Security Council, because it is the one forum in which Russia has equal footing with the U.S. and via its veto power can play the role of the spoiler. Perhaps with accession, the WTO will be another organization Russia is willing to embrace because the rules of the game are seen as less tilted toward the U.S. Such opportunities are crucial to satisfy Moscow's aspirations to restore Russia's great power status within the existing international framework and convince Russia that it has a real stake in the system.

In sum, every pivotal power supports the current world order to some degree, though every one, including the United States, will naturally seek to limit the degree to which specific rules impinge on its national interests and will strive to influence future rules, when given the chance.

10. The pivotal powers want more influence and respect on the world stage, but are reluctant to shoulder more responsibility or bear added costs for the sake of the world order.

Though they all support the world order, free-rider tendencies characterize pivotal power interactions, as theory would predict. Why should they take on the burden of repairing failed states, policing sea-lanes, or ending civil wars when the U.S. will likely do the work?

Japan is a case in point. Japan certainly wants to be treated as a great power and a leader in Asia, and has been willing to step up at crunch time. Tokyo dispatched troops to Iraq, held a major donor's conference for Afghanistan reconstruction, and is a generous distributor of foreign aid. What is less clear is whether Tokyo is prepared to incur the costs of becoming more influential in the global system. Japan traditionally avoids leadership roles in diffusing international crises—even those that affect it. Changing their approach would require stronger political ties in the region, which, in turn, would involve Japan confronting its history squarely. That move, and further opening its economy, are difficult steps many observers doubt it will take. So while there is great potential for the United States and Japan to join together and work in other spheres, such as the convergence of regulatory standards in intellectual property for example, a lack of political will on both sides has prevented that. In the end, rhetoric about Japan's greatness and entitlement may outstrip its practical willingness to attain that status, possibly creating a disjunction that nationalists could exploit.

Likewise, India has been willing to commit significant resources to certain multinational efforts like U.N. peacekeeping, but it has not been inclined to step forward to take the lead in solving international crises beyond the South Asia region. Along with not wanting to spend resources unnecessarily, China's fear of spooking its neighbors and the U.S. and its uncertainty about the value of being a global leader drive China's relatively low-key approach to global affairs. While China is guided by its notion of becoming a responsible great power, it has been selective in choosing the responsibilities it will accept. Russia is even less forthcoming. Moscow simply doesn't want responsibility for the world's problems.

At the other end of the spectrum is Europe, which sees a responsibility in sharing the burdens of tackling global challenges. However, even it has been reluctant to pay the price to scale up the "hard power" capacity that it would need to intervene in major global crises.

So while all of the pivotal powers surely want a seat at the table, it is unclear how much they are willing to pay for the privilege.

There are two final observations about the pivotal powers and the United States. Pivotal power policymakers often know America better than American officials know them. Because of our open society, many elites have visited or studied in the U.S. Because of America's cultural exports, some aspects of American society are known almost everywhere. And because of its global role, U.S. actions are reported on regularly in every pivotal power.

Also, the pivotal powers have long memories. Indians will raise a thirty-seven-year-old bitter recollection of the U.S. decision to dispatch an additional carrier to the Bay of Bengal during the 1971 war with Pakistan—a symbol of U.S. hostility to India. Japanese remember well the inflammatory rhetoric of the 1980s that Americans have long forgotten. Europeans talk about the standoff over control of the Suez Canal as though it happened yesterday.

What do the pivotal powers want? While we have not done justice to these large, complex powers whose internal constituencies seek different things, at a broad level, the list is surprisingly consistent. The pivotal powers want recognition, respect, and greater prestige. They want more influence and freedom to pursue their national interests. They want good relationships with the U.S., but not at the expense of their own welfare. They want to expand their options by broadening their relationships with one another and other countries. They are more than willing to work with the U.S. and with one another. The pivotal powers are not out to unseat the U.S. as the world's sole super-power but they don't want to be dictated to, either. To the extent they check U.S. ventures, it is usually out of fear, concern, and competing interests, not out of contempt or belligerence. American arrogance and disrespect strengthen the anti-American voices inside each country. The pivotal powers want a functioning global order because it serves their interests.

Finally, America's view of itself as well-meaning, generous, reluctant to use force, and vulnerable contrasts sharply with the view among the billions of citizens in pivotal power countries of America as self-centered, stingy, trigger-happy, and invincible. Actions that seem trivial to us (who remembers U.S. congressional opposition to China's 2000 Olympics bid?) matter a lot to them.

American actions are a key factor in determining the direction of internal debate that will shape pivotal power views. America drives these relationships.

Now push comes to shove, so to speak. We have argued so far in this book that we cannot know which, whether, or how fast the pivotal powers will continue to grow. Demographics, climate, political stability, and myriad other factors Americans do not control will conspire to shape their futures.

We have also shown that the pivotal powers affect what Americans care about in both positive and harmful ways, but that the benefits are more substantial, broad, or immediate and the harm is more nebulous, indirect, narrow, or distant. The pivotal powers help the U.S. battle the largest security threats it now faces in terrorism, disease, and proliferation of nuclear and other dangerous materials. The pivotal powers benefit from the world order and fight side by side with the U.S. against global killers that heed no authority.

None poses a direct security threat to America today, and their growth supports overall U.S. economic growth. The pivotal powers do not undermine U.S. liberal democracy at home and do not present a serious ideological challenge outside our borders either.

Finally, we know that the pivotal powers want stable and positive relations with the United States, and the United States is largely in the driver's seat in steering these relationships. For now, none seeks to unseat the U.S. as sole superpower. However, the pivotal powers are challenging U.S. leadership and prestige, as well as making it more difficult for the U.S. to get its way in all matters. America is seeing its operational freedom erode.

Our analysis suggests, first and foremost, that the U.S. has to tackle some tough problems at home to ensure its prosperity longer-term. That said, what should the U.S. strategy be toward the pivotal powers?

7. The Way Forward: Strategic Collaboration

The official digest of United Nations business contains this entry for October 25, 2005:

Vote on Outer Space Arms Race

The draft resolution on the prevention of an arms race in outer space . . . was approved by a recorded vote of 160 in favour to 1 against . . . as follows:

In favour: Afghanistan, Albania, Algeria, Andorra, Angola, Antigua and Barbuda, Argentina, Armenia, Australia, Austria, Azerbaijan, Bahrain, Bangladesh, Barbados, Belarus, Belgium, Belize, Benin, Bhutan, Bolivia, Bosnia and Herzegovina, Botswana, Brazil, Brunei Darussalam, Bulgaria, Burkina Faso, Burundi, Cambodia, Cameroon, Canada, Cape Verde, Chile, **China***, Colombia, Congo, Costa Rica, Côte d'Ivoire, Croatia, Cuba, Cyprus, Czech Republic, Democratic People's Republic of Korea, Denmark, Djibouti, Dominica, Dominican Republic, Ecuador, Egypt, El Salvador, Eritrea, Estonia, Ethiopia, Finland,* **France***, Georgia,* **Germany***, Greece, Grenada, Guatemala, Guinea, Guinea-Bissau, Guyana, Haiti, Honduras, Hungary,*

*Iceland, **India**, Indonesia, Iran, Iraq, Ireland, Italy, Jamaica, **Japan**, Jordan, Kazakhstan, Kenya, Kuwait, Kyrgyzstan, Lao People's Democratic Republic, Latvia, Lebanon, Lesotho, Liberia, Libya, Liechtenstein, Lithuania, Luxembourg, Madagascar, Malawi, Malaysia, Maldives, Mali, Malta, Mauritius, Mexico, Federated States of Micronesia, Monaco, Mongolia, Morocco, Mozambique, Myanmar, Nepal, Netherlands, New Zealand, Nicaragua, Niger, Nigeria, Norway, Oman, Pakistan, Panama, Paraguay, Peru, Philippines, Poland, Portugal, Qatar, Republic of Korea, Republic of Moldova, Romania, **Russian Federation**, Saint Lucia, Saint Vincent and the Grenadines, Samoa, San Marino, Saudi Arabia, Senegal, Serbia and Montenegro, Sierra Leone, Singapore, Slovakia, Slovenia, Solomon Islands, South Africa, Spain, Sri Lanka, Sudan, Suriname, Sweden, Switzerland, Syria, Thailand, The former Yugoslav Republic of Macedonia, Timor-Leste, Togo, Tonga, Tunisia, Turkey, Turkmenistan, Ukraine, United Arab Emirates, **United Kingdom**, Uruguay, Uzbekistan, Venezuela, Viet Nam, Yemen, Zambia, Zimbabwe.*

Against: United States.

We have grown accustomed to this scene: America on one side, the rest of the world on the other. Since the end of the Cold War, but most strikingly in the last seven years, the United States has been a bull in the china shop of international cooperation. When it suits, America tramples the established rules and gores initiatives before they ever come to a vote. For those that survive this trampling and goring, this "America against the world" pattern is typical.

In this case, America managed not only to cement the already widely held view that it is not genuinely committed to nonproliferation and disarmament (a view that makes getting cooperation on North Korea and Iran's nuclear programs difficult) but also to alienate all the world's strongest powers—China, Russia, and India, which sponsored the bill, and Japan and Europe, which voted for it.

Why this vote? At the time, the U.S. delegate explained that there was no need for an arms control agreement because there was no prospect of an arms race in outer space. That reasoning did not hold much water with the 160 opposing countries, especially for the forty with active space programs. If the whole world thought an arms control regime was necessary, even if it was premature, why wouldn't the U.S. go along?

The answer came almost exactly a year later when the Bush administration quietly released its National Space Policy, the first in ten years. Emphasizing the need for the U.S. to retain its "freedom of action," the policy rejected any arms control agreements that might impair America's right to do what it wanted in space.

This policy is one of dozens of examples of the Bush administration following a strategy rooted in America's primacy. Primacy relies on the coercive leverage that comes from being the strongest player in a system. In the words of neoconservative commentator Charles Krauthammer, a strategy of primacy argues "explicitly and unashamedly for . . . sustaining America's unrivaled dominance for the foreseeable future." In this case, the logic was that with its head start, the U.S. would become so superior in space that no other country would even bother to compete. America would "own" space and make it safe for other countries.

Other countries were not grateful. After the release of the National Space Policy, *The Times* of London headline read "America Wants It All—Life, the Universe and Everything." The foreign editor of Hong Kong's *South China Morning Post* wrote that "Someone has to be the first to make space as unsafe as Earth and there are few as qualified as the Bush Administration." The experts too have doubts about whether this strategy will work and, at the time, suggested that it could trigger the exact competition the U.S. was trying to prevent. Likely a coincidence, but a telling one, about a month after the U.S. policy was released, President Putin signed into law the India-Russia space cooperation pact. Then about three months later, on January

11, 2007, China shot down an aging weather satellite using a ballistic missile, something no country had done since the 1980s.

The False Promise of Primacy

You might have assumed that the U.S. would have thought twice about advocating primacy in space at a time when the carnage and chaos of Iraq were serving up daily painful examples of the pitfalls in a strategy built around unilateral military might. Yet it is hard for anyone, let alone our leaders, nurtured as they were on the Cold War, to accept that overwhelming power is no longer the sole linchpin of U.S. security.

After all, it was not supposed to be this complicated. For most of the last five hundred years, the amount of power, ultimately military power, that a country had was the key variable to its security. When nation-states were one another's only threat, an obsession with relative power made sense. Once the Soviet Union disappeared, neoconservatives argued that America had all it needed to keep itself safe—a singularly enormous and effective military.

Until then, and through the Clinton years, the bargain implicit in the world order had been that in return for the commitments of other nations to abide by the rules, the U.S. would make other countries more secure by embedding its overwhelming power in those same rules. It would serve as the protector and arbiter of the rules-based order. America heeded President Harry Truman's call "to recognize—no matter how great our strength—that we must deny ourselves the license to do always as we please." This arrangement gave U.S. power its legitimacy.

Neocons wanted to throw these shackles off as quickly as they could. With its unparalleled strength, the United States didn't need other countries, didn't need rules, and didn't need legitimacy. International institutions were a liability. "An entangling web of interdependence," Krauthammer wrote, would "tie down Gulliver with myriad strings that diminish his overweening power." In 2002, the Bush administration made retaining American primacy an explicit goal of American foreign policy. As President Bush explained in a speech at West Point in 2002, "America has, and intends to keep, military strengths beyond challenge . . . thereby making the destabilizing arms races of other eras pointless."

You have to make strategy for the world you have, not the world you wish you had, but American strategic paradigms have lagged. Primacy is not what it used to be. Today, America's gravest and most immediate threats do not come from great nations. All pivotal powers are caught together in the vortex of globalization. They need one another economically, and nuclear weapons make direct war among them nearly unthinkable. Border-crossing threats like terrorists, infectious disease, failed states, and regimes with WMD that reject the world order are their common enemies. Alone, nation-states cannot bring security to their own citizens any longer. For this reason, argues Brent Scowcroft, former national security advisor to Presidents Gerald Ford and George H. W. Bush, the world is at a turning point on the order of the Industrial Revolution.

In practice, the strategy of primacy failed to deliver. While the fact of being the world's only superpower has substantial benefits, a national security strategy based on using and retaining primacy has not made Americans more secure. America's mighty military has not been the answer to terrorism, disease, climate change, or proliferation. Iraq, Iran, and North Korea have become more dangerous in the last seven years, not less.

Worse than being ineffective with transnational threats and smaller powers, a strategy of maintaining primacy is outright counterproductive when it comes to the pivotal powers. If America makes primacy the main goal of its national security strategy, then why shouldn't the pivotal powers do the same? A goal of primacy signals that sheer strength is most critical to security. America cannot trumpet its desire to dominate the world militarily and then question why China is modernizing its armed forces.

The strategy built around primacy can lead to the dangerous dynamics of the "security dilemma," as we discuss later in this chapter. A
focus on primacy also shifts attention away from the underlying fun-
damentals of the American economy and society. The distribution of
power within the international system is always changing as some
states grow faster or slower compared to America. Preoccupation
with America's position may distract our politicians from doing what
they can at home to invest in America's future well-being.

Finally, a focus on primacy discourages cooperation, the cooperation America most needs. A goal of primacy undermines U.S. leadership, which is critical to making the world a better place. It sets up an
implicit confrontation that will encourage others to frustrate our
goals because it implies that America ultimately opposes other countries' growth.

Containment

Indeed, a complement to the primacy strategy is one of great power
"containment." Many who advocate primacy also advocate containment for any big, fast-rising power. Today, a vocal minority advocates
the containment of China (no other pivotal power at the moment).

John Mearsheimer at the University of Chicago writes that the
United States should "do what it can to slow the rise of China."
Mearsheimer argues that a rising power will, because of the nature of
the international system, inevitably target the dominant power in
order to protect itself. Decades from now, when China's armed forces
are formidable, and it has major political clout and worldwide interests, it will be too late for the U.S. to act. Washington neocons reach
similar conclusions for different reasons. They argue that because
China is an authoritarian state expanding its military, it will come to
threaten the U.S. and so should be slowed now, economically and
even militarily.

Containment is not a wise or workable strategy for China. First,
the U.S. does not have the wherewithal to contain China and every

other potential adversary at the same time. What if it chooses the wrong target? Over time, Russia or another power could become threatening. Containment could inadvertently waste scarce political and economic resources by putting American eggs in only one basket.

As we discussed earlier, there is no guarantee in China's rise. Some analysts predict, for instance, that China's economy will overtake America's to become the world's largest by 2050. Others warn that by then large swaths of Shanghai will be submerged under the rising tides of climate change.

To the extent that China does not now intend to confront the U.S. and has no expansionist inclinations, containment could push Beijing in that direction. Trying to stifle China's growth would guarantee its animosity and encourage it to stymie the U.S. agenda. Further, if the U.S. confronts China without justification in the eyes of the other powers, it will lead to American isolation. If, on the other hand, China were to act aggressively, neighbors would rush to America's side. China's proximity makes it far more threatening to Russia, Japan, South Korea, India, the Southeast Asian nations, and Australia than to us.

Further, China's internal political development will affect its foreign policy. As we discussed earlier, many conservative and liberal theorists believe that mature democracies will not go to war with one another. From this point of view, if it could get through a treacherous transition period, a richer China could be better for U.S. security in the long run, because many studies have shown a link between the growth of a large middle class and political liberalization.

Finally, what could the United States actually do to slow down China? As Francis Fukuyama and G. John Ikenberry write, "there is no feasible strategy for weakening China." Unilateral American economic sanctions would slow bilateral trade, and harm China's economy, but it would adjust. Also, between Chinese ownership of U.S. debt, U.S. industry operations in China, and cheap consumer imports, America is highly vulnerable to disruptions of the economic relationship. A protectionist tit-for-tat could spark a U.S. recession or worse. That is a large price to pay to thwart a very uncertain, distant threat. It is sensible, as we discuss later, for the U.S. to maintain close strategic relationships and troops in Asia, but provocative military actions will only speed China's military growth.

Even if America could somehow be certain that China would one day endanger key U.S. interests, and it found a way effectively to weaken China, it would still carry huge risks. If China's growth slowed even moderately, unemployment there could skyrocket, leading to instability and, from there, possible political chaos. As "Afghanistan x 1,000," China could become a staging ground for unimaginable mischief with rogue nuclear proliferators running amok and broken public health systems leaving virulent disease to thrive. "If there is any fundamental truth in the field of terrorism," says terrorism expert Brian Jenkins, "it's that the collapse of government is not good for controlling terrorism." World financial markets would undoubtedly quake if the largest and fastest-growing economies clashed. In general, pivotal power downturns can be as or more harmful to U.S. interests than their rapid growth.

No matter what the final outcome, a nation of some 1.5 billion people would become deeply resentful of the U.S. The ascent of China's most nationalist and fire-breathing leaders would be guaranteed. History's losing great powers do not stay down for long, and they do not forget their enemies.

This is not to say confrontational strategies will never be appropriate. As we discuss below, America has to be prepared in case a hostile big power emerges and watch for signs of trouble. William Perry, the former secretary of defense, along with Harvard professor and former Assistant Secretary of Defense Ashton Carter suggest a list of actions by China that could call for a shift of U.S. strategy. They include: Beijing putting defense spending first in the Chinese budget, an attempt to match or exceed the U.S. nuclear force in numbers, and the foreign basing of Chinese troops. No signs of these developments are present today. In the meantime, the U.S. should conserve its limited money and attention.

We are not suggesting, of course, that America's strength is a liability. On the contrary, America needs to invest anew in its ability to secure safety and prosperity for its citizens. We are instead suggesting that America give up an ineffective and provocative strategy that makes primacy itself the goal. The welfare of Americans depends more on a stable, liberal world order than on America being the strongest power by a fixed, enormous margin. America does not need unlimited freedom of action; it needs effective action. Today, for better or worse, effective action against our true adversaries is necessarily a collective endeavor. American world leadership is the key to our future safety and success—not American primacy.

Rising Power Strategies

Strategies should seek to shape the world, not just react to it. Also, in the words of one Japanese thinker, a strategy should "prevent the worst (saiaku) while trying to construct the best (saizen)." A pivotal power strategy should leverage the strengths of the pivotal powers to shape a future world that maximizes American security, prosperity, and values, but also prepare the U.S. to deter and defend against any future pivotal power aggression.

Of course, as we have discussed, there are many reasons to believe that America clashing with a pivotal power is unlikely. Never have big powers had so many reasons to feel they are joined together in a common enterprise. Moreover, war between a rising power and the dominant power has not been inevitable historically. Peaceful power transitions have occurred, including when the Dutch Republic gave way to Britain in the 1700s and later when Britain relinquished its role as the dominant power to the U.S. Perhaps, as we all wish, we have entered an era of major war obsolescence.

But who knows. In the past, the stronger and richer states became, the more their global responsibilities and commitments grew, the more able and willing they were to fight for their interests, the more they viewed the reigning power as a threat. Even if China's intentions toward America were completely benign now, and vice versa, as Robert Jervis has said, "Minds can be changed, new leaders can come to power, values can shift, new opportunities and dangers can arise." States exist in a world where no higher authority can protect one from another. Nationalism is a strong force in all pivotal power countries, small disputes can escalate, and it remains true that misperceptions can trigger conflict.

Strategic Collaboration

In general, dominant powers like the U.S. have reacted to a growing power in a variety of ways, ranging from the most hostile—preventive war—as when Sparta initiated the Peloponnesian Wars—to the most accepting—conciliation, as when the British ceded dominance to the United States at the turn of the twentieth century.

We advocate a pragmatic strategy in between these two extremes, called "strategic collaboration." While the U.S. needs a specific, nuanced bilateral strategy toward each pivotal power, we suggest here an overarching framework for those relationships. Strategic collaboration has four elements:

Compound American strengths;
Construct close relationships with pivotal powers;
Collaborate with the pivotal powers to solve global problems; and
Cover our bets.

Compounding American Strengths

First and foremost, America must put its own house in order. America's assets are so great that if our leaders make sensible choices, Americans can remain prosperous and safe no matter the trajectories of the pivotal powers.

American politicians, for reasons we will discuss in the next chapter, will tend to lay the blame for economic problems at the doorstep of another country, but there is much America needs to do to build its own capacity to prosper in the future. Rather than creating foreign demons, America must slay those at home. As we highlighted earlier, several familiar problems need sustained and creative attention, including better educating our children so the U.S. can continue to be an innovation-rich economy; ensuring our long-term fiscal strength; establishing a better health care system so businesses keep jobs here and workers can be more entrepreneurial; helping workers cope with job churn; living our values in reality as well as rhetorically; and reducing our oil dependency to bring down our trade deficit, address the climate crisis, and pressure pivotal powers to do the same.

America's military must remain strong, but, as we discussed in Chapter 2, it has to be redesigned to focus on today's threats, especially terrorists, and long-term, indeterminate pivotal power threats. This means investing in leap-frog technologies and shortening the Pentagon's procurement process so technologies are not obsolete by the time they are delivered. Washington also must shift some funds to nonmilitary national security spending as we discuss later in this chapter.

Americans cannot hope to provide opportunities for good lives for their children and grandchildren based on investments their grandparents made. America's primary focus needs to be on changing the country it has the power to change. America's choices at home are critical to its future prosperity.

The remaining elements of strategic collaboration focus on foreign policy. Because the pivotal powers largely want what Americans want, because America needs their help to counter real threats, because their trade keeps the U.S. economy humming, because America does not want them to go their own way, because none are ideological competitors or implacable aggressors, our strategy of strategic collaboration seeks to draw the pivotal powers nearer to the U.S. and to embed them deeply into the world order.

Constructing Close Relationships

The second element in strategic collaboration is constructing respectful, positive, and stable bilateral relationships with the pivotal powers. A productive, mature working relationship that one would have with an office colleague or teammate is the model; friendship is not necessary. Building such relationships will take six steps—reassure the pivotal powers, show respect, ramp up contact, remove chronic irritants, reward positive behavior, and rank key U.S. interests.

REASSURE THE PIVOTAL POWERS   First, America needs to reassure the pivotal powers that it welcomes their growth, and wants to keep relations constructive and stable. America should presume pivotal powers are "with us," because they usually are. Day-to-day disagreements, though fierce at times, cannot be permitted to call the essential character of the relationship into question.

This framing is consequential. How Americans and pivotal powers think of each other affects their interactions. For instance, while the underlying conditions had been gradually improving for years, America's relationship with India turned on a dime in 2000 because President Clinton and then President Bush concluded it made sense to begin treating India as a potential friend. Those decisions sparked a whole set of new, joint policy initiatives.

SHOW RESPECT   Next, the tone and trappings of pivotal power relationships have to signal respect. Diplomatic niceties cost America little, but go a long way in pivotal power homelands. As a general rule, pivotal power leaders should be accorded the highest-level welcome the U.S. has to offer—the state visit. (China's president was not given this in 2006.) In international forums, pivotal power diplomats cannot be left feeling that they were "treated like dirt" by the American delegation, as Europeans complained during discussions over the Biological Weapons Convention in 2001.

While we should not hide our differences, our officials need to choose their words carefully. Former Secretary of Defense Donald Rumseld's comments in 2003, lumping Germany in with Cuba and Libya as countries that refused to act in Iraq, still sting diplomats there. Officials should avoid delivering speeches that make a pivotal power wonder if you are trying to start a new Cold War, as Vice President Dick Cheney did in a May 2006 speech about Russia, delivered from a former Soviet republic, Lithuania. Pivotal powers crave respect. Instead of withholding it, America should meet that desire and leverage it.

RAMP UP CONTACT To successfully bring all pivotal powers firmly into America's orbit will mean listening, and talking—a lot. Developing common agendas with other pivotal powers and resolving differences will require constant diplomacy, often grueling, and frequently miserable. America will need to listen to pivotal powers much more and try even harder to understand their motivations and priorities. U.S. embassies and consulates in pivotal powers need to overcome their appearance of armed fortresses and reengage with society. Every other sort of exchange—educational, business, cultural—should also be ramped up. The greater number of Americans who know, first-hand, that regular human beings live in pivotal power countries, the better.

REMOVE CHRONIC IRRITANTS Changing American rhetoric is not enough. Whenever possible, the U.S. should work creatively with pivotal powers to remove the chronic irritants in the bilateral relationships. Usually this will be quite tricky—irritants are chronic for a reason. For example, when the Bush administration took steps to welcome India into the nuclear club, it compromised on an issue high on India's agenda, making a more productive bilateral relationship possible. Yet at the same time, the policy shift struck a serious blow to the global nonproliferation regime. Resolving key differences with pivotal powers will involve hard choices.

Two Cold War policy holdovers, NATO enlargement and Taiwan, neuralgic to Russia and China respectively, deserve regular scrutiny. Designed to deter and defend against Soviet aggression in Europe, NATO did not disappear with the end of the Cold War as Russia might have liked. Instead, the U.S. has pushed successfully for enlargement eastward, now with the possibility of including Georgia and Ukraine. For a rough sense of Moscow's unease, imagine Russia negotiating a military alliance with Mexico and Canada, including positioning military equipment in those neighbors.

Because NATO's original mission is obsolete, the organization could be formally refocused toward the new threats the U.S. and Europe face. A globalized NATO that includes members beyond Europe could remove a key irritant in the U.S.-Russian relationship and at the same time increase the capacity and efficiency of NATO when it is greatly needed.

Similarly, America's leaders should always be willing to think creatively and flexibly about how to deal with the perpetually difficult issue of Taiwan to decrease the likelihood of armed conflict and reassure China that America's goal is not to keep it divided.

Even if America does not end up being able to change its policy in these cases, Washington could get credit and diplomatic leverage in pivotal power capitals for being willing to bring these topics to the table.

REWARD POSITIVE BEHAVIOR Washington needs to think about incentives it can provide to pivotal powers to be the responsible, proactive stakeholders they say they want to be and that America wants them to be. At a minimum, it should acknowledge positive steps. Secretary of State Condoleezza Rice appropriately applauded China when it broke with tradition to sanction North Korea over its nuclear test, saying, "It is an extraordinary thing for China to be now where it is." Washington needs to practice that kind of positive recognition to balance its more frequent criticism.

RANK KEY U.S. INTERESTS Finally, to maintain productive, stable relationships, America should make very clear to pivotal powers on which issues the success of the bilateral relationship will be judged—which issues, that is, are truly vital to the U.S. at a given time. Over the past year, America has asked China, for example, to revalue its currency, pressure the regime in Sudan, grant more religious freedom to its citizens, curb intellectual property violations, reduce its carbon emissions, be more transparent about its military buildup, and help solve the North Korean and Iranian nuclear problems. These are all valid, important demands, but America is less likely to get movement on any of them, and may send confusing signals about what it takes to have a constructive relationship with the U.S., if all are given equal weight. Prioritizing the truly vital issues will require more discipline within the U.S. government, as now various departments—State, Treasury, Defense—carry their own messages to Beijing. Also, U.S. demands are likely to be more effective when framed as problems both countries want to solve.

U.S. relationships with Europe and Japan already follow the model of mature, stable relations we suggest, though emphasis of shared goals with Europe could be more routine, and America's relationship with Japan broader. Engagement with India is more serious now than in memory, but could be solidified and deepened. In contrast, as the above examples show, recent American messages to China and Russia have been a confusing array of demands, insults, and advice.

Strategic collaboration would call for a shift in American rhetoric toward China and Russia, with unambiguous statements and actions that demonstrate U.S. intent for the relationships to be constructive, dense, and stable. The disagreements and divergent viewpoints would remain, and hedging would continue, but they would be put in the context of forward-looking relationships where common interests were emphasized and advanced.

A strategic collaboration strategy would mean trying to reduce trade restrictions and proposing a clear path to "market status" for these countries, not imposing additional export controls (though restrictions on the most sensitive weapons technology should remain). Military-to-military contacts also should continue to expand. As Admiral William J. Fallon, former senior commander of the Pacific Command, argued, "It's in the interest of our country to engage with these people and not just . . . find things to quibble over."

Washington should always endeavor to keep small squabbles from escalating. America should not act at the first sign of menace, aware that superpowers are prone to exaggerate the gravity of another's transgression. An excellent example of this was when Defense Secretary Robert Gates took the air out of a caustic speech by President Putin in 2007 by commenting afterward: "As an old Cold Warrior, one of yesterday's speeches almost filled me with nostalgia for a less complex time. Almost," Gates said. "We all face many common problems and challenges that must be addressed in partnership with other countries, including Russia," he continued. "One Cold War was quite enough."

Let us be clear that building stable, constructive relationships with other pivotal powers does not mean perpetual capitulation. Within this positive framework, the U.S. must defend its own interests with vigor, not give up something for nothing, hold pivotal powers to their word, and expect bitter disagreements. At times, American differences with pivotal powers could be profound, and strategic. When (but only when) its vital or highly important interests are at stake— interest on which America would be willing to spend the blood of its soldiers—should it put the constructive nature of pivotal power relationships on the line.

FRIENDS WITH BENEFITS Constructive relationships with all pivotal powers will have considerable benefits. First, open, stable relationships will continually reassure the pivotal powers about U.S. goodwill, restraint, and judgment, reducing their concerns about U.S.

power. Recognizing that the emergence of a hostile competitor can result as much from U.S. actions as from those of pivotal powers, a close relationship will give them no added reasons for distrust. In the 1990s, for example, India went along with China's then theme of resisting U.S. hegemony partly as "insurance against the uncertainty in Indo-US relations," explains C. Raja Mohan. Conversely, close relationships will also give pivotal powers frequent opportunities to reassure America with words and actions that they mean no harm.

Regular interactions, including between American and pivotal power militaries, will reduce the chances of misunderstandings or miscalculations. As we write, for example, Chinese and American military commanders have no method for reaching each other in an emergency. When U.S. Pacific Commander Admiral Fallon tried in July 2006 to reach his Chinese counterpart with urgent concerns about a North Korean missile test, his call was returned with a public statement a full twenty-four hours later.

Closer relationships will provide valuable intelligence about the internal workings and strategic thinking of each pivotal power. America should keep the pivotal powers close to its side, where it can see them, monitoring for signs of changes in their posture toward the U.S. or its interests. This will also help Washington to develop a much more nuanced understanding of these powers and what makes them tick, knowledge it will need to navigate effectively in the decades to come. Further, a collaborative framework may help strengthen the forces of moderation within the domestic political environment of the pivotal powers. In some cases, a positive relationship with America may help make it politically harder for pivotal powers to oppose U.S. interests.

Strategic collaboration preserves political and financial capital for the threats America faces today and those that may appear tomorrow. It will also limit the unintended security consequences that big power hostilities inevitably generate.

Close relationships will also put the U.S. in a better position to influence pivotal power foreign policy. Each of the pivotal powers is pondering its own evolving role and profile on the international stage. The United States can play a hand in shaping their priorities as their interests expand, because, from its own experience, America is intimately familiar with the demands, dilemmas, and desires that come with being a great power. (For example, lending or donating funds to a corrupt government with no strings attached may seem like an attractive strategy until you experience your first coup.) America should seek to engage especially the reemerging powers China and Russia in conversations (not lectures) about the kind of world they *should* want, and the reasons international norms have developed as they have. The U.S. ought to work with Europe, Japan, India, and other major democracies like Brazil and Australia to establish liberal norms of rule of law, transparency, accountability, and individual rights as the norms for all countries. Tapping into peer pressure will help steer Chinese and Russian evolution. Over the long term, notes scholar John Ikenberry, "it is far more effective . . . to shape the interests and orientations of other states rather than directly shape their actions through coercion and inducements."

Daily, tactical cooperation on urgent issues like terrorism and avian flu would likely continue even through rocky relationships with pivotal powers. To leverage the shared interests of pivotal powers and use their new power to make the world safer and more prosperous in a significant way, however, will require deep, stable relationships. In order to realize the promise of this rare historical alignment among the pivotal powers, the U.S. must lead the way, by showing with its actions that it understands pivotal powers are on its side.

Collaborating with the Pivotal Powers

With a foundation of productive relationships with pivotal powers, America can lead them to use their strength, ideas, and friendships to solve serious global problems. This is the third component of strategic collaboration. The U.S. would embed pivotal powers further in the world order and collaborate with them to strengthen it. The U.S. should push a positive, proactive agenda with the pivotal powers that creates a better world for all.

WHAT'S SO GREAT ABOUT THE WORLD ORDER? International norms and institutions, which organize interactions among states, underlie much of the peace and prosperity Americans enjoy today. They have helped to solve a number of the world's pressing challenges. The only ways people have figured out how to coordinate collective action on a problem that affects many countries is through a set of common rules, a central institution that holds information and coordinates actions, a network of officials from different countries, or a combination of the three. On a practical level, the U.S. fashioned or greatly influenced all the international rules, whether about nonproliferation, development, trade, or anything else, to reflect its values, and often, its own particular interests.

Imagine the world without the World Health Organization to monitor outbreaks of Ebola, monkeypox, and avian flu and coordinate the response. Without the World Trade Organization (and its predecessor, the GATT) giving countries a forum to determine jointly free trade rules, worldwide GDP would be a fraction of what it is. If it had not been for the Nuclear Non-Proliferation Treaty and its enforcement arm, the International Atomic Energy Agency (IAEA), the world could have thirty nuclear powers today instead of nine. The world's economies could have witnessed many more destabilizing financial crises but for the work of the International Monetary Fund. If there were no International Energy Agency to coordinate the use of emergency oil reserves, the world economy would be even more a hostage to OPEC. Only webs of law enforcement officials from around the world can catch terrorists, drug dealers, and pirates.

Finally, without the U.N., who would have organized elections in war-torn Afghanistan and Iraq? Without U.N. peacekeepers,

Lebanon, Haiti, and Liberia would be even less stable. Multilateral organizations manage everything from air traffic rules to refugee flows.
Importantly, the current set of institutions and rules that comprises
the world order are liberal, reflecting America's beliefs in the rule of
law, transparency, accountability, and individual rights. Broadly, the
world order also makes U.S. power legitimate when Washington con-
forms to established procedures. As John Ikenberry observes: "The
most enduringly powerful states are those that work with and
through institutions."

The world order that America launched in 1945 has delivered
many benefits, but it is crumbling. All of its major institutions are
embattled, peppered with calls for reform. Many criticisms, including
from the United States, ring true. Bureaucratic sclerosis does plague
many of these bodies. They were designed for a world with fifty nations, not two hundred. Some institutions or conventions were
flawed from the start. Unsolved problems gnaw away at others. There
is a yawning gap between the scale of world issues today and the capacity of the institutions built to address them. The biggest problem
with the world order, however, is that it has lost its leader and steward.
America is eating its young.

A strategic collaboration strategy understands that the pivotal
powers are, in important respects, allies in the quest to maintain an
orderly world. As large, market-driven powers, they want what Americans want: better standards of living, peace, and predictability. Even
more than that, most of them, most of the time, want an order not
dramatically different in character from one that the U.S. created
in its own image. Because national interests differ, there will never
be complete alignment. Europe will lobby for stricter consumer
protection standards, for example. China will avoid transparency
when it can.

Yet the pivotal powers share a broad consensus that the nation-
state is the best vehicle for international politics, that open markets
create prosperity and most goods and services should flow freely

across borders, that many international institutions are worth supporting and reforming, that technology can bring positive change,
and that proliferation of nuclear weapons, terrorists, and disease
must be countered. A majority of the big powers—Europe, India, and
Japan—endorse liberal democracy as the best form of government.
Rhetorically, even Russia and China do. Stronger pivotal powers that
support the existing world order but try to realize their own agenda
are far preferable to weak ones that could not assist with current challenges even if they so chose. The benefits of peaceful, law-abiding big
powers outweigh the disadvantages of their increased influence.

Shoring up the system of institutions, norms, and rules preserves
U.S. power, makes life better for Americans today, and creates a world
in which Americans can thrive even as they increasingly share the
stage in the decades and centuries to come. How do we get it done?
There are three essential ingredients to being able to solve successfully
most world problems: pivotal power participation, a system of common rules, and American leadership.

THE C6 In order for the pivotal powers to collaborate on shoring up
the world order, they need to be able to discuss crises and challenges
together. Remarkably, today not a single international organization
offers them a forum. The U.N. Security Council excludes Japan and
India; the G8 excludes India and China; the OECD excludes India,
China, and Russia, as does NATO.

The world needs a pivotal power forum to include them all. It
would make the most sense for the pivotal powers—let's call them the
"C6," the Core Six—to become the permanent members of the U.N.
Security Council (which currently includes America, China, Russia,
France, and Britain—the P5) by adding Japan and India and reducing
the number of seats allocated to Europe. This body already has the
worldwide mandate to address security issues, but reform has proven
extremely contentious.

If reform of the Security Council does prove a bridge too far and to avoid creating a whole new international bureaucracy, the C6 could instead become an additional forum of the G8, the group of the world's largest economies. Over time, we would expect that the C6 would become the principal forum of the G8, addressing both economic and security challenges. In meetings focused narrowly on a particular topic, and with a minimum of scripted speeches and lofty rhetoric, the pivotal powers would discuss and coordinate actions to tackle the world's toughest problems. Over time, if the identity of the world's most powerful actors shifts, so too should the membership of the C6.

Each pivotal power wants either more influence or more recognition or both. By encouraging them to become members of the pivotal power club, or, as former Deputy Secretary of State Robert Zoellick emphasized in his discussions with China, "responsible stakeholders" in the international system, America harnesses pivotal power nationalism and pride, but channels it in a productive direction. Pivotal powers are already engaged in the world, and the next step is convincing them that with their power comes responsibility for the common good. They should become, with America, stewards of the global order. America's line to China and Russia has been "Show us you are responsible, and we may let you in." Instead America's message ought to be: "We see that you are trying to act responsibly most of the time, and we both want to strengthen the world order. Join us as a partner." With the C6, all pivotal powers would be formally made a part of the establishment and expected to contribute.

The C6 would work on a "pay to play" basis. In exchange for the prestige and influence of being included in the C6, every power would pledge to solve shared problems and shoulder responsibility for international initiatives. They would be held to account by their peers, and the rest of the world, for their willingness to participate constructively. Getting the reemerging powers India, China, and Russia to contribute financially, given their domestic priorities and needs, will be a key challenge for the U.S.

The C6 has some parallels to the Concert of Europe. In 1815, after the Napoleonic Wars, the great powers of Europe assembled in Vienna to develop mutual understanding that would keep the peace because, explains historian Richard Elrod, "only the great powers possessed the resources, the prestige, and the vision to contend with the transcendent concerns of peace or war, of stability or disorder." The Concert of Europe became the forum for solving collectively the serious issues of the day (namely, threats to its members), and was successful at preventing major power war in Europe for several decades. It was essentially the first time in history when nation-states consciously attempted to find an alternative to either the hegemony of one state or the anarchy of each state looking out only for its own survival. The Concert derived its energy from a consensus on the part of the great powers on the need for order. Then, as we hope now, vying pivotal powers were able to join together in their collective self-interest.

A pivotal power forum provides a number of advantages. Foremost, all the pivotal powers would be involved in tackling any major world problem—a necessary first step to a lasting solution. With a small group of the world's biggest powers, coordination on issues would be less likely to hamper progress, and it would be harder for powers to shift responsibility from one to another. The C6 would be the forum in which the United States could gradually push toward building a consensus on the rules of the road for pivotal powers, toward, as Richard Haass, president of the Council on Foreign Relations calls it, a "shared definition of legitimacy" that reflects liberal norms. The forum would allow the established powers America, the EU, and Japan to help define for their neighbors China, India, and Russia what being a responsible stakeholder means.

WHAT COULD THE PIVOTAL POWERS DO? What couldn't they do? There is no shortage of intractable problems facing humanity. The agenda ought to begin with items where pivotal powers share the most common ground. Nonproliferation is one area in need of immediate attention. Big powers share vulnerability to an attack by a weapon of mass destruction. If America closes ranks with the pivotal powers, hostile states like Iran could not duck through the gaps between them. As we laid out in Chapter 2, together the pivotal powers have major potential leverage, important contacts, and considerable expertise when it comes to Iran. None wants Iran to go nuclear.

"Iran has figured that the U.S. has alienated China and Russia," says Vali Nasr of the Council on Foreign Relations, and thus does not expect effective multilateral action to be forthcoming. The U.S. has squashed creative, though imperfect, ideas from Russia and Europe because they required direct talks with Tehran. If the U.S. could be more flexible, big power consensus could put Iran in a box with little chance for escape. A deal whereby the pivotal powers provide security assurances to Iran and grant its NPT rights to develop a limited capability to enrich uranium, in exchange for its acceptance of unannounced and intrusive inspections, is just one possible solution.

The Iran case illustrates why, on a broader level, the pivotal powers should drive the effort to refashion the Nuclear Non-Proliferation Treaty. The NPT is based on a bargain that in exchange for countries without nuclear weapons committing not to seek them (and letting inspectors in without notice to check), they are permitted to conduct peaceful, civilian nuclear research, and the nuclear powers are committed to gradually disarm. In a situation thick with irony, the U.S. has been alone in casting votes with Iran and North Korea to stall progress on strengthening the NPT.

If the U.S. position changes, and careful thought given to how to handle India's relationship to the rules, a reformed NPT could continue to be effective. As outlined by former secretaries of state George Shultz and Henry Kissinger, former Secretary of Defense William Perry, and former Senator Sam Nunn, steps would include finding a way to control and eventually remove the weaponizable uranium that is produced in civilian research reactors, yet guaranteeing that uranium for nuclear power reactors would be available at a reasonable price. To convince nonnuclear states to accept further controls, the U.S. would have to lead the nuclear pivotal powers to gradually reduce their nuclear forces. If the U.S. reengages, the pivotal powers could also push to achieve a robust Biological Weapons Convention with a binding verification regime.

Genocide in Sudan could not survive a pivotal power push to end it, and with a forum like the C6, the pivotal powers would have a harder time shifting blame for their inaction from one to the other. The pivotal powers could make a truly reconstructed and stable Afghanistan their joint aim. Finding more effective ways to battle HIV/AIDS is also in their mutual interest.

Energy is another area ripe with potential for pivotal power cooperation. The nuclear fusion project ITER is a promising model. As we discussed in the Introduction, every pivotal power is investing in the first ever truly international, large-scale, independent scientific research effort in the history of the world. America, China, Russia, India, Japan, and South Korea will each pay about 9 percent of the construction costs. The EU, as host, will contribute about 45 percent. For the next ten years all these countries will together test the possibility of this nonpolluting, renewable energy source. Along similar lines, China held an energy summit in December 2006, drawing together energy officials from all the pivotal powers save Russia. It makes infinite sense for every pivotal power to work together on the energy problem that plagues them all.

A pivotal power forum will not produce instant progress. Disputes over tactics and priorities will scuttle many efforts. But with over half the world's population between them, the combined commitment of the pivotal powers could make progress on any initiative. Where the pivotal powers go, other nations will follow. Their collective drive could become the fulcrum to move the rest of the world. If the pivotal powers can agree to a solution, it will be far easier to get other countries to go along.

With that in mind, other states should always be encouraged to work with the C6 based on their willingness to contribute. For example, South Korea is a member of the fusion project ITER and paying an equal share.

USE OF FORCE The United States should establish the expectation that the pivotal powers will discuss plans by any of the group to use force. If the U.S. sets the precedent, the pivotal powers will find it more difficult to use their militaries without previous consultation. Thus, while the U.S. should never give up its option to use force unilaterally, it should seek significant pivotal power support (though not necessarily an endorsement from each), as well as the blessing of a major global or regional security organization, for any large-scale military operation.

America has had to do this in the past (albeit grudgingly), to avoid derailing pivotal power relationships, to legitimize its actions, and for practical reasons. For example, in 1999, after leading a NATO-led air campaign in Kosovo designed to circumvent Russian opposition in the U.N., the U.S. recognized it needed Russian help to negotiate a cease-fire with Serbian president Slobodan Milosevic. Ultimately, at Moscow's insistence, the U.S. went back to the U.N. Security Council for a mandate authorizing the mission; Milosevic's surrender and Russian troop involvement quickly followed.

BEYOND THE C6 Not every issue will lend itself to the C6 agenda. Along with the C6, other new bodies or networks will be necessary to support an effective world order. For example, East Asia needs a regional security framework to help reduce tensions. Critically, existing global institutions also need to evolve to allow the pivotal powers the voices they deserve. Some express concern that international norms will be somehow "watered down" if international institutions include powers like China or Russia. The question is worth asking, and prophylactic measures may make sense, but the evidence supporting this concern is scarce. Rather, it seems that when they embed themselves in the world order, pivotal powers are shaped by its norms. We cited in the last chapter one example of how China moved from being an unabashed proliferator to a member in good standing of a multitude of international nonproliferation regimes. Warnings that China's entry would destroy the WTO have similarly not come to pass.

LEADING POWER LEADING Collaboration to build a better world also demands U.S. leadership. Pivotal powers will not come together to solve major international problems, in the C6 or any other forum, and no other nations will join in, unless the world's leading power leads. No pivotal power can step into the breach.

Nowadays, though, America is in the world's doghouse. To earn its leadership privileges back, America needs legitimacy, because without it, 300 million people cannot lead 6.5 billion citizens who are more informed about world events than ever. To retrieve legitimacy, America must act again, under the rules, and for the good of all.

A few bold gestures might help to convince the world that primacy is not America's goal and that it wants to work with other countries to reform the world order. While it would require careful consideration, America could, for example, announce that it will never be the first to use a nuclear weapon in a conflict. The reasons America has not made this commitment to "no first use" in the past—for example, to deter the Warsaw Pact from using its superior conventional forces to attack Western Europe—are gone. Alternatively, America could commit itself to serious steps on climate change. Even so, American leaders will have to expect skepticism from a bitter world for some time to come.

PASS THE BALL America also has to adopt a different conception of leadership. For a long time, America has been team captain and coach rolled into one—calling all the shots and making them too. America has to become a leader that is truly willing to share responsibility. No longer can America conceptualize, design, test, sell, organize, implement, and monitor every last international initiative. As we know from the last chapter, a steady source of resentment of America is the view that Washington pays little attention to the interests of other countries in making international policy decisions.

Pivotal powers must become, with the U.S., architects of the world order. Pivotal powers will not be America's lapdogs; they will not run and pay for initiatives or institutions they had no part in crafting. Further, they will often have important ideas, perspectives, expertise, and relationships to contribute to problem solving. Prestige and recognition are what pivotal powers crave, and the U.S. will want to share the limelight to entice them onto the field. While this will not come naturally to the U.S., it will lead to more optimal burden sharing. The model should be Bosnia, where America has paid about $1 billion of the $5 billion in reconstruction aid, not Iraq where the proportions are inverted. Being choosy with its own international commitments will also help America preserve its resources.

On the other hand, America's failed policy toward North Korea's nuclear program prior to 2007 is a cautionary example of what can happen when the U.S. delegates too much to pivotal powers. According to former U.S. envoy to North Korea Charles "Jack" Pritchard, because Iraq was consuming so much of the Bush administration's time, and because the administration was divided about how to approach North Korea, with many enamored of "regime change," it attempted to make China the surrogate for U.S. leadership through the Six Party Talks. Though unsuccessful, bringing the pivotal powers China, Japan, and Russia into the negotiations was surely the right approach, if for the wrong reason.

China worked hard to bring the parties together, but also took advantage of the forum for its own diplomatic gain. In the end, only with direct and sustained U.S. engagement could the parties forge an agreement to freeze North Korea's nuclear program. Pivotal power involvement cannot substitute for U.S. leadership. Every sticky problem that troubles America needs both. Washington must therefore be engaged enough for problems to get solved, yet not so involved that it discourages pivotal power responsibility or overspends its own finite resources.

A LEAGUE OF THEIR OWN What if the United States does not lead the group of pivotal powers to solve international crises? What if instead of drawing pivotal powers into the existing world order, it continues to hold some at bay? They may become "free radicals," or attempt to construct their own order. The meetings of the newly formed East Asia Summit in December 2005 and 2006, spurred on by China, included Japan, India, and every country in Asia but not the United States, the reigning Pacific power—a development unthinkable only a few years earlier. In the 1990s, in frustration over their underrepresentation at the International Monetary Fund, Asian countries threatened to form their own "Asian Monetary Fund." Similarly, despite heavy-handed efforts by the U.S. to undermine the International Criminal Court, European leadership brought the court to life. (Later this put the U.S. in the very awkward position of opposing efforts to refer the Sudanese leaders committing genocide in Darfur to the court.) China and Russia, along with the Central Asian republics, but not America, discuss security matters and conduct military exercises through the Shanghai Cooperation Organisation.

While these efforts do not have major strategic ramifications now, over time, alternate structures may reduce U.S. influence and give pivotal powers platforms to deny U.S. interests altogether. America should want big powers playing on its team, not forming a league of their own.

The only effective option to build a safe and prosperous world is deep, regular, consistent cooperation of nation-states, of a degree not yet ever seen. If the pivotal powers do not work together, threats will deepen. "Failure to rescue the present order," says Kishore Mahbubani, a highly respected policy voice from Singapore, "will result in a turbulent world." Because of their global nature, these challenges must be met collectively or they will be met weakly.

Covering Our Bets

The final prong of strategic collaboration recognizes that despite America's best efforts, the future could hold an aggressive pivotal power bent on thwarting vital U.S. goals. Therefore, America must continue to deter other power centers from disrupting the U.S.-led world order, to deny them the ability to harm major U.S. interests, and to ensure the U.S. is prepared to defend its interests if deterrence fails.

This calls for covering our bets, but the path of hedging is a treacherous one. We thus recommend "selective hedging"—steps designed to allow the U.S. to retain its diplomatic and military leverage, but not broadly targeted at any one power. The United States should hedge against certain *futures*, like China attacking Taiwan without provocation or India launching a preemptive strike against Pakistan, not against certain *powers* per se. Selective hedging includes three elements—better intelligence about pivotal powers, a hub-and-spokes model for U.S. relationships, as well as maintaining a highly capable, forward-deployed military.

INTELLIGENCE America knows relatively little about the pivotal powers. "We get along with China," Charlene Barshefsky, the former U.S. trade representative, says, "but typically we are ships passing in the night." America needs to allocate more resources to all the many forms of intelligence gathering and, more important, analysis, to get a deeper understanding of pivotal power strategic frameworks, priorities, and plans. A constant flow of information will enable Washington to negotiate more effectively and gauge changes in the pivotal powers' intentions toward the U.S. and the world order.

HUB-AND-SPOKES As the U.S. develops active, constructive relations with each pivotal power, and pulls them into the C6 to solve problems and build the world order anew, it should strive to maintain richer relationships with each pivotal power than those powers have with each other. Relationships with one power would not be directed specifically at balancing other powers, but that would be the ultimate effect. For example, strengthening relations with Japan and India hedges against aggressive Chinese steps. Closer ties with China hedges against misguided actions by Russia and Japan, and so on. A hub-and-spokes approach will reduce the odds of an anti-U.S. coalition forming and ensure allies in the case of pivotal power aggression.

A hub-and-spokes model will be extraordinarily hard to pull off. First, if pursued in a heavy-handed way, such efforts will smack of containment and cause more harm than good. When China sees the U.S. "cheerleading" Japan's remilitarization, it may respond by modernizing its military more quickly, resulting in a security dilemma, as we discuss below. Second, as America pulls closer to one power, others will become nervous. If Washington makes the positive gestures toward China that we suggest above, Japan and India will worry more about their relationships with the U.S.

Further, pursuing a hub-and-spokes model will require persuading the pivotal powers not to gang up against the U.S. even though unchecked power, whoever wields it, is a potential threat to others. Theorists argue, and centuries of European history show, that "balancing" against the dominant power is far more common than bandwagoning with it. (For this reason, many credit Otto von Bismarck for being a genius to make a hub-and-spokes approach work for a strong Germany while he was chancellor.) Today, nascent arrangements between Russia and China, China and India, and the EU and China, among others, are never openly, but always implicitly, aimed at the United States.

America's blessed geography makes a hub-and-spokes arrangement feasible because states actually balance against *threats*, not against pure power. Sitting atop one another, the pivotal powers are inherently more threatening to each other than the U.S. is to them. Despite a warming trend, most of these bilateral relationships are filled with mistrust. Pivotal powers have fought some eighteen wars with each other since 1800, not counting those between individual European countries. Moreover, balancing is difficult to coordinate.

Finally, while cultivating each pivotal power, America must take care not to exacerbate tensions in their relationships. Pivotal powers quietly appreciate America's role in keeping the peace among them, a role it must continue to play. A war between pivotal powers would be a phenomenal security disaster. Pivotal powers getting along is a necessary prerequisite for the C6 to be effective.

SMALL SPOKES Beyond the thick spokes connecting the U.S. to the pivotal powers are America's connections to small and mid-size nations, especially in big power neighborhoods. While pivotal powers will strive to have political clout in their own backyard, the United States will not want to let those trends radically reduce its own influence, especially with the U.S. worldwide network of treaty allies such as Australia, South Korea, the Philippines, and Thailand. The U.S. should avoid making smaller countries "choose" between a good relationship with the U.S. and one with their powerful neighbor, but should continue to provide security, trade, and other benefits.

BEING THERE Having a highly capable, technologically sophisticated military is the most effective hedge against pivotal power mischief. Constantly improving U.S. military capabilities is essential, and a forward-deployed presence in Asia and Europe remains wise.

Hedging too aggressively can trap America and pivotal powers in the risky quicksand of the security dilemma. It will always seem safer on the surface for the U.S. to acquire more capability, ever more targeted, to respond to future scenarios. Yet actions that America takes, merely to defend itself, can make the pivotal powers feel less secure. They will respond by improving their capacity to protect themselves. Those changes, in turn, could trigger a U.S. response, and so on, in a downward spiral of distrust that eventually makes the U.S. less secure.

Similarly, America may feel it needs to stand firm in even minor spats with the pivotal powers or risk inadvertently encouraging their aggression by appearing weak. Those American signals of toughness may well confirm a pivotal power's suspicions that America is unreasonable and aggressive. The result can be a self-perpetuating rivalry that is difficult to reverse.

An example of the security dilemma in action is ballistic missile defense. The United States argues that it must deploy this system to protect U.S. territory from hostile states with missiles, like North Korea. China and Russia complain that an effective missile defense system will upset the strategic balance and allow the U.S. to achieve "nuclear blackmail" because retaliating against an American first strike would be impossible. In reaction to America's missile defense plans, therefore, China is protecting its deterrent by building up its missile arsenal and developing a submarine-launched ballistic missile capacity. Hawks portray this buildup as an arms race when it is actually, at least in part, a reaction to a defensive U.S. system. (Washington tried to diffuse this issue with Russia by offering to share missile defense technology and operations of the radar sites but no understanding had been reached as of this writing.)

Further, some scenarios for which America may be tempted to over-hedge, such as a possible conflict over Taiwan, are not primarily determined by the military balance. Deterring China from attacking Taiwan is about the credibility of the American commitment. If Beijing does not believe that the U.S. will actually spill American blood to defend Taiwan, it does not matter how big an armada America has stationed nearby. Peace across the Taiwan Strait is therefore principally a political question, not a military one.

There is another fine line here. America needs a military of excellence, one well prepared and well equipped to handle a variety of plausible scenarios. At the same time, it should refrain from needlessly targeting or provoking the pivotal powers. In conversations with their counterparts, American officials should leave no doubt about their defensive intentions and objectives. How elements of hedging are perceived in pivotal power capitals is crucial. Most of all, then, hedging must be tightly paired with the positive messages of strategic collaboration described above, so America does not inadvertently create the future it means to guard against.

This last prong of the strategic collaboration strategy has focused on the possibility of conflict with pivotal powers, but that is not the only future to hedge against. The U.S. must be equally concerned about pivotal power failure, whose effects are much harder to predict.

Costs of Strategic Collaboration

Strategic collaboration has costs, as any strategy does. The outcome will be, in the words of Richard Haass, "a little less sovereignty" and a little less control in exchange for a more stable, coherent world. The United States will have to agree to be bound by the same solutions, policies, institutions, and rules it establishes along with the pivotal powers. When America makes its power safe for the world, the world will be safer for America.

We break the costs of our strategy into four categories: process costs, policy compromises, harm to pride, and budgetary shifts. The process-related costs are most familiar, as America's traditional response to foreign policy issues has been negotiation. As we mentioned earlier, strategic collaboration requires more intense and more deft U.S. diplomacy. America will need to negotiate with pivotal powers over the terms of large-scale operations or initiatives. More consultation may seem like a small price to pay, but we can attest to the exasperation of senior officials headed into their fourth round of talks with Russian diplomats—renowned for reveling in backroom wrangling.

In some cases, this additional diplomacy will mean the U.S. cannot act as quickly as it might like. Sometimes delay can generate significant, even life-or-death, consequences (as in the case of Darfur).

In those rare cases when process costs become harmful to U.S. policy preferences, because time is of the essence, the U.S. will have to weigh the heavy costs associated with acting alone against the costs triggered by the delay.

Strategic collaboration will also mean conceding on U.S. policy preferences, likely more so than in the past. At the very least, we can expect more instances, as in the WTO, where America is forced to live by its own principles, and occasionally must absorb blows to the interests of domestic constituencies (like steel manufacturers or Boeing). America will have a particularly tough hill to climb when its position is markedly different from the other pivotal powers, on issues like Cuba, Israel, and Iraq. Similarly, as mentioned earlier, it took a great deal of U.S. pressure at the IMF to secure a bailout for its neighbor Mexico in 1998. As pivotal powers gain strength, it could be even harder to convince them to take costly actions that benefit the United States disproportionately.

However, in many instances, the U.S. would not see its preferences fully implemented whether it joined a pivotal power solution or not. American business operations overseas are still affected by the Kyoto Protocol, despite the Bush administration's stance against it. Further, regulatory measures taken by California and the Northeast states mean many U.S. businesses are paying anyway. The question therefore is how much greater the costs would be if the U.S. joined the international consensus. Strategic collaboration often will mean taking the hit earlier, requiring a larger down payment, to shore up the world order.

The third kind of cost, to U.S. pride, should theoretically be easy to overcome, but in practice may prove most difficult. Just as the pivotal powers, America too craves recognition. Admitting mistakes, or backing down from a stated position, is painful for politicians, as events in Washington illustrate daily. A long history of America viewing itself as "exceptional"—different, even superior, to other countries—makes mea culpas particularly hard. America can take solace in knowing, though, as nineteenth-century British writer John Ruskin suggested, "In general, pride is at the bottom of all great mistakes."

A final cost is measured directly in dollars. For America to build the right relationships with pivotal powers and solve tough global problems, it will need to devote more of its budget to nonmilitary national security spending, both for diplomats and for C6 initiatives for the common, and American, good. While such spending has increased in dollar terms, it has shrunk as a percentage of the discretionary federal budget and remains meager, even though the world has become infinitely more complex and dangerous. As we see in Figure 7.1, America now spends a paltry 4 percent of its entire national security budget on nondefense, non-homeland-security items. That includes the entire State Department, all foreign embassies, the whole foreign aid budget, student exchanges, all of it. The United States spends more on sorghum subsidies (just over $500 million) than on all of the State Department's educational and cultural exchange programs combined ($486 million). The entire Defense Department budget for language and cultural training—$181 million—amounts to less than the cost of one F-35 fighter plane. Even a doubling of the nondefense national security budget would amount to a pittance compared to what is spent on defense. It is not just a question of increased funding; what is devoted to foreign assistance needs to be spent in a more coordinated way.

Are these costs worth it? We have no doubt. Not only will the strategic collaboration strategy help the U.S. fund and implement solutions to the world's problems, but it may free up resources for reinvestment at home because other powers will bear some of the costs. The era of full freedom of action is over, if it ever really existed, and by joining pivotal powers to the world order, that order, which ultimately benefits America, grows stronger.

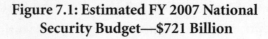

**Figure 7.1: Estimated FY 2007 National
Security Budget—$721 Billion**

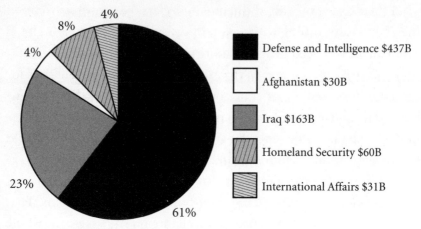

SOURCE: P.J. Crowley, *Time to Act*, Center for American Progress Report, 2006, 4, http://www.american progress.org/issues/2007/01/pdf/911.pdf.

Now Is the Time

Now is the time for America to bind pivotal powers to itself and to the world order. Why now? First, the pivotal powers are pushing to have more influence in international institutions, not opting out. For some, the period during which they can be successfully pulled into the liberal international order is finite. As Russia expert Coit Blacker laments, "We may be close to the point of no return with Russia."

Second, America remains by far the strongest power in the international system. With great tools of persuasion at its disposal, America has disproportionate impact on the solutions or institutions that will result. As America reengages with institutions it has belittled of late, it will be taking a key step toward preserving its own, still huge, leverage within them in the face of growing pivotal power clout. Because institutions and principles have inertia behind them, they could reflect U.S. priorities and values even beyond the time when overwhelming American dominance would sustain them. For example, if the U.S. led the effort to develop a harmonized set of international guidelines for life sciences research and securing dangerous pathogens now, it would be much more difficult for another power to replace them later because the more they were used, the more countries would grow accustomed to them and the more useful they would become. Conversely, if the U.S. disengages, as it largely has over climate change, it may have less and less influence over the emerging international order. At the same time, if America pushes too hard for international rules that will lock in special benefits to itself, others will resist. That is where having pivotal powers take the lead can be especially useful.

Strategic collaboration seeks a balance between maximizing the benefits America can draw from pivotal power relationships with careful hedging against an uncertain future. It focuses American attention on investing at home to give future Americans the best chance for secure and prosperous lives. It avoids wasting resources on threats that may not materialize. It deters and prepares for pivotal power aggression, while not encouraging it. It honors their need for recognition by giving them a voice in the future of the world, yet demands responsibility in return. It increases American knowledge about the other powers in case of a future conflict and minimizes chances of misperception. It reduces incentives for pivotal powers to thwart the U.S. agenda. It strengthens the liberal world order that benefits Americans.

No strategy toward big powers will guarantee success in such a complex and fluid international arena. But strategic collaboration stands the best chance of securing a peaceful future in a world that supports American interests.

We are in this world together with the pivotal powers. In many ways, they hold our fate in their hands, and we hold theirs. They cannot conquer us, and we cannot conquer them. America should build relationships that maximize cooperation and stability that benefit all.

We have a chance to strike a world-changing deal. Now, while no irreconcilable differences plague its relationships with pivotal powers, America can forge a new positive, proactive concert among them. It will not be cost free, but is designed to pay off in a windfall for American peace and prosperity in the decades to come, even in a future when America is not the sole superpower. There is only one right way to approach pivotal powers in the twenty-first century—draw them near.

8. Making It Happen

In the previous chapter, we outlined the strategy we think the United States should take toward the pivotal powers. Among other steps, strategic collaboration demands stable relationships with the pivotal powers and a commitment to working with them to solve the most pressing global problems. It will also require America to tackle domestic challenges rather than seeking convenient external scapegoats. Here we discuss some of the biggest political obstacles to our approach and thoughts on overcoming them.

The Wise and Willing

Let's begin with something that is not an obstacle—American public opinion. Strategic collaboration will not be a hard sell with the American people. When we started to frame this chapter, we presumed one of the biggest challenges would be American culture. Our political system and economy are based on paradigms of competition. Elections are "winner take all" and capitalism depends on companies trying to best each other. The sports we play and TV shows we watch are similarly competitive. We thought the true American—"Joe Six-Pack"—would wave his flag, chant "We're number one!," and reflexively bash rising foreign powers.

It turns out that Joe is a rare character. Steve Kull, a prominent pollster, tried to find him in the 1990s. At the time, Congress was debating America's support for the United Nations, and a few conservative Republicans, like Representative Helen Chenoweth of Idaho, were calling for the U.S. to withdraw altogether from the organization. So Kull and his team decided to visit her district to find the constituents Chenoweth's staff claimed were fully supportive of her stance.

In 1996, on a spring day in Boise, Kull gathered a focus group of twelve residents precisely chosen to reflect the demographics of the district. Expecting to find a hotbed of anti-U.N. sentiment, Kull asked the question: Who here thinks the U.S. should withdraw from the U.N.? One person raised his hand and another voiced tentative agreement. A few minutes later, a man suggested the U.N. should have its own standing army that America could help fund. Kull decided to ask the group if they agreed with the idea, which would greatly empower the U.N. To his shock, eight people raised their hands. Later polls confirmed what he learned in Boise. Even in districts electing radically unilateralist members of Congress, most Americans wanted instead to engage with the rest of the world in a constructive way.

More recent polling continues to bear this out. Americans seem unconvinced of the benefits of going it alone and are highly attuned to U.S. interdependence. Though a majority think that maintaining superior military power is a very important foreign policy goal, 87 percent of Americans in a 2006 poll rejected the view that because America is so strong "insecurity in other parts of the world" would not impact U.S. security significantly. A whopping 80 percent responded that goodwill toward the U.S. was "important" and rejected the view that the U.S. need not worry about what other countries think of it.

Decade after decade, polling reveals Americans as consistently dedicated multilateralists. In a 2006 poll sponsored by the Chicago Council on Global Affairs, 75 percent of Americans said that the

United States "should do its share to solve international problems together with other countries" rejecting both the view that America should take on these problems solo, and the position that the U.S. should withdraw from such efforts altogether. In fact, as we see in Figure 8.1, Americans surveyed in a 2005 BBC poll agreed by wide margins with citizens from the other pivotal powers that the "best framework for ensuring peace and stability" was either a system led by the United Nations or a system led by a "balance of regional powers." Only 10 percent of the Americans surveyed chose a "system led by a single or two world powers."

Figure 8.1: Ensuring Peace and Stability in the World
What is the best framework for ensuring peace and stability?

- A System Led by the United Nations
- A System Led by a Balance of Regional Powers
- A System Led by a Single or Two World Powers

Country	United Nations	Balance of Regional Powers	Single or Two World Powers
Germany	68	21	7
China	51	36	9
Great Britain	47	40	5
France	46	34	9
Brazil	36	45	15
India	33	37	28
Japan	33	29	2
United States	33	52	10
Russia	28	33	25
Total	42	36	12

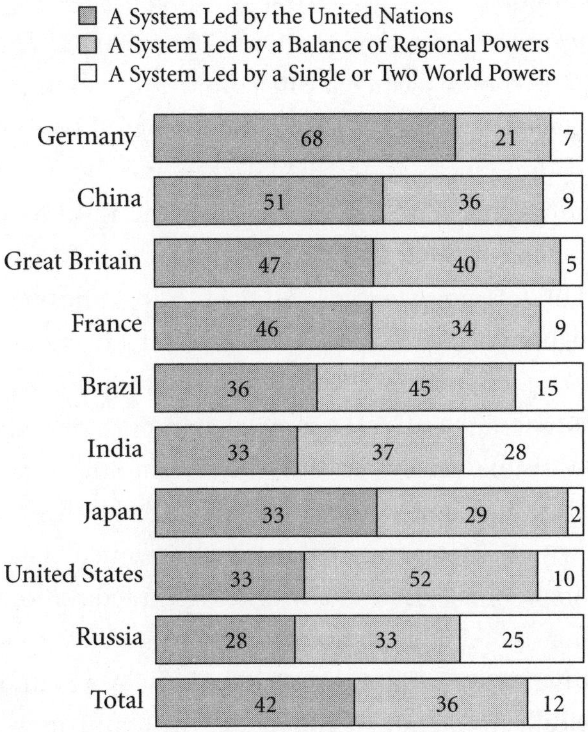

SOURCE: BBC, 12/2005

Findings by the Pew Research Center are in line with these results. Roughly three-quarters of Americans surveyed in 2004 said the U.S. should "play a shared leadership role," in the world while only 11 percent said the United States should be the sole leader.

America's ill-fated unilateralism in Iraq is surely driving these attitudes today, but earlier sentiments were similar. According to Pew polling in 1993, 81 percent of Americans said America should have a shared leadership role in the world. Similarly, from 1964 to 1995, a strong majority of Americans (between 72 and 86 percent) consistently agreed with the statement that the U.S. "should take into account the views of its major allies" in its foreign policy decisions. During the same period, a steady majority of Americans disagreed with the statement that the U.S. "should go its own way in international matters, not worrying too much about whether other nations agree with it or not."

Substantial majorities today—between 70 and 90 percent—think the United States should participate in a broad range of international agreements, including several—Kyoto, the Biological Weapons Convention, the Comprehensive Test Ban Treaty, and the International Criminal Court—that have been rejected by the Bush administration. Fully 40 percent think that strengthening the U.N. should be a "very important foreign policy goal" of the U.S., beating out promoting human rights abroad (28 percent) and helping bring democracy to other countries (17 percent). Seventy-nine percent think strengthening the U.N. should be at least a somewhat important goal.

More remarkable yet, Americans endorse multilateralism even when its costs are highlighted. Sixty percent of Americans surveyed in 2006 agreed with the following statement: "the United States should be more willing to make decisions within the United Nations even if this means that the United States will sometimes have to go along with a policy that is not its first choice." Similarly, by a margin of two to one, Americans would rather "cooperate with countries as often as we can, even if this means we have to compromise on occasion";

nearly 70 percent think the U.S. should comply with adverse decisions of the World Trade Organization. Majorities are also in favor of expanding the U.N. Security Council to include other powerful countries like India, Germany, and Japan, even though the expansion would dilute U.S. influence. Of course, agreeing with an abstract notion of cooperation is different from weighing the actual costs that have to be borne in a specific case, but Americans start off with a constructive mind-set.

Americans do not hold negative views of the pivotal powers either. Americans view Europe, Russia, Japan, and India in generally favorable terms. American attitudes toward China are fairly nuanced. A narrow majority of Americans held favorable impressions of China in 2006, despite anti-China rhetoric emanating from Washington. A large majority (65 percent) in another 2006 poll favored "friendly cooperation" and engagement with China—the country they identified as most likely to gain the most influence in the coming years—and in 2005, 70 percent thought trade with China was beneficial.

In that same 2006 poll, Americans surveyed showed "strikingly low levels of concern" over the prospect that China could catch up with the United States economically, and only a third saw this as mostly negative. Majorities or pluralities of Americans thought that it was important to work with China and India on a variety of issues, from reducing greenhouse gas emissions to reducing competition over energy sources. However, when presented with a list of countries in a 2007 poll, Americans overwhelmingly chose China as America's chief economic rival, and a slim majority viewed China's growing economy as a threat to the U.S., signaling a possible shift in attitude. The area of major concern was China's potential rise as a military power; 75 percent of Americans saw such a development as mainly negative.

When compared to other threats, a relatively small percentage of Americans view China's rise as a world power as a critical threat to vital U.S. interests (36 percent). Far more Americans are concerned with potential threats like terrorism (74 percent), unfriendly states getting nuclear weapons (69 percent), disruption in energy supply (59 percent), epidemics (49 percent), and global warming (46 percent), as we see in Figure 8.2: (Interestingly, the percentage of Americans very concerned with the rise of China is about the same as Chinese very concerned with the U.S. military presence in Asia—about a third.)

In sum, Americans seem to endorse the basic thrust of our suggested approach toward pivotal powers. By overwhelming majorities,

Figure 8.2: Critical Threats to U.S. Vital Interests
Percentage who see each of the following as a critical threat to
U.S. vital interests in the next ten years.

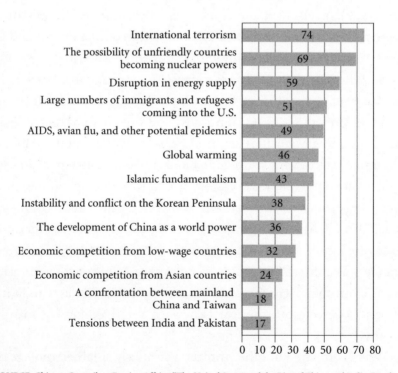

SOURCE: Chicago Council on Foreign Affairs, "The United States and the Rise of China and India: Results of a 2006 Multinational Survey of Public Opinion," October 2006, available at http://www.thechicagocouncil .org/Userfiles/file/GlobalViews06final.pdf (accessed October 25, 2006), p. 16.

Americans accept interdependence and value cooperation. They want the U.S. to be powerful, but don't presume other big countries to be the enemy. Out of loyalty or because they are told a compelling narrative, they will follow their leaders on a path that strays from these values, as they did with the war in Iraq. But not for very long, says Steve Kull. It is not the American public that stands in the way of America going in a new direction.

These statistics led us to wonder why there is such a disconnect between Americans' recognition of interdependence and support for multilateralism on the one hand and our unilateral policies and actions on the other. The answer lies in our political culture. We look here at the presidency, Congress, and the media.

The Buck Stops Here

Though many Bush administration foreign policy initiatives have been counterproductive, pivotal power relations have not been a disaster. Though some of our European allies and Moscow are estranged, relations with Japan and India have never been closer. With China, the administration has been somewhat schizophrenic and unfocused, but relations have remained stable. Nevertheless, the Bush administration has not leveraged the strength of the pivotal powers to build a more prosperous and safer world. Why hasn't it?

First, as we mentioned earlier, many who are or were on the president's team are mentally mired in the Cold War. They either genuinely believe or cynically argue that a large, growing China or resurgent Russia will inevitably become a threat. Though George W. Bush in the year 2000 preached humility in foreign policy, his team was enamored of unrestrained U.S. might. America has not led because our leaders did not think America needed followers. With that mind-set, working with the pivotal powers to strengthen the liberal world order was never on the agenda.

Then came the Iraq War, a disaster not only because it directly lessened U.S. security, but also because it has reduced America's capacity to attend to every other foreign policy priority. As we know from our work in the Clinton administration National Security Council, the amount of time that America's top national security leaders have is frustratingly finite. We saw that even the small-scale military operation in Kosovo sucked up the lion's share of America's foreign affairs energy for several months. Now with America's highest officials so preoccupied with Iraq, other initiatives cannot get airtime until they become crises.

The unbalanced power of the Pentagon and its civilian leadership in President Bush's first term has also contributed to a difficult climate for optimal pivotal power policy. Much of the attention of the growing Pentagon has been focused on terrorism, but conservative as well as progressive observers have suggested that some in the armed forces have "rediscovered" the China threat to justify Cold War–style weapons systems like destroyers, submarines, and fighter aircraft. There may be some truth in this, but, more important, defense officials are paid to worry about the next threat. They must take seriously that queasy sense that the U.S. will one day have less freedom of action and try to discern how U.S. interests could be compromised. Today, China seems like one of few possible significant state-based threats out there, and has a built-in flash point in Taiwan.

When the views of the Defense Department are balanced out by other parts of the government, there is no inherent problem with the Pentagon focusing on potential clashes. The departments of State and Treasury, as well as the CIA, have different perspectives on the pivotal powers and, in particular, less pessimistic views of China and its intentions. For example, in testimony before the Senate Armed Services Committee, Thomas Finger, chair of the National Intelligence Council, said recently the Chinese "appear to have decided that we are not an enemy." However, if the political leadership of the Defense Department is inclined to be confrontational, as it was in President Bush's first term, and is allowed to dominate interagency discussion, the outcome may be a policy that emphasizes potential disputes rather than the breadth of our deeply complicated, charged, and interdependent relationship with China.

Couples Counseling

While we fault the Bush administration for the giant foreign policy hole America has dug for itself, the obstacles to adjusting America's approach to pivotal powers go well beyond the current administration. Except on issues of war and peace that involve large numbers of U.S. troops, or on topics that motivate significant "single issue" domestic constituencies, foreign policy is too often the wallflower at the Washington policy dance. Off to the side, national security policymakers happily operate in a world unto themselves—often far removed from the rough-and-tumble of domestic politics—and as a result are not well schooled in how to implement and sustain policies that could be supported by an informed domestic electorate. The reverse is also true as those who work on domestic issues are content not to concern themselves with Byzantine issues like the U.N. protocol on pollutants.

Though both sides are satisfied with the traditional division of labor, the lines keep getting fuzzier. Nearly every foreign policy issue America faces is tied up in domestic policy and politics and vice versa. The U.S. trade deficit is tied to America's savings rate; American agents must track terrorists inside the U.S. and out; outbreaks of diseases need to be contained abroad but impact public health at home.

To change America's approach toward the pivotal powers, the two camps will need relationship counseling—especially within the White House. When we were at the National Security Council, literally only a fraction of our colleagues had even met, much less had a substantive discussion with, the "domestic side" of the White House—even though their offices were just one floor apart. It is time to rethink the structure and mandates of the National Security

Council, Homeland Security Council, National Economic Council, and Domestic Policy Council—the separate White House silos for coordinating policy matters. They need to be realigned, and staffs need incentives that will promote integration of foreign and domestic policy.

535 Cooks in the Kitchen

Even if we elect a wonderful president in 2008 who wants to forge a new pivotal power policy, he or she will have to sell it to a sometimes skeptical Congress. Many members of Congress don't consistently focus on issues involving the big powers. "The number of the 535 members who could *mispronounce* the name of China's currency is about fifty," says Charlie Cook, noted political analyst, half-jokingly.

The members who are focused on great power relations can shape the debate, but do not have strong incentives to make U.S. relationships with pivotal powers actually work. Because lawmakers do not have responsibility for the health of bilateral relations, it is politically safer and easier to be suspicious of emerging powers. "There's no political downside to castigating China," says James Sasser, a former Democratic senator and ambassador to China. "And some political negative if you defend China."

Historically, Congress has been far more allergic to international commitments than the American people. A comprehensive 2004 study shows that time and time again Congress's actions contradict popular support for multilateralism. Though there may be some genuine differences of opinion in different districts, members (like Helen Chenowith) routinely and incorrectly point to their constituents as the reason for rejecting such commitments. When strong majorities of the public, as well as American leaders inside the administration and out, wanted America to sign the Kyoto Protocol, join the International Criminal Court, and ratify the Comprehensive Test Ban Treaty, congressional action stymied those efforts.

Here we outline six reasons why Congress could challenge a more constructive approach toward the pivotal powers. First, generally in Congress (and especially in the House of Representatives), the extremes rule the middle. The passionate, be they moti-vated constituents, true believers, professional lobbies, or organized interest groups, are strong, disciplined, and often well funded. The middle is often agnostic. Thus, the outliers can pivot the debate in Congress. For example, when Jesse Helms became Chairman of the Senate Foreign Relations Committee in 1994, he was a driving force in pulling the entire debate about the U.N. far to the right of the public's position. As we will see later, Detroit similarly and successfully lobbied to enact some misguided legislation to address the "Japan threat." Redistricting, to the extent that it facilitates the election of ideologically extreme candidates, has contributed to this trend.

We see this playing out with China today. A coalition of defense contractors and hawks who fear China's military buildup has made common cause with those who deplore China's poor human rights record and blame Beijing for the erosion of America's manufacturing base. Together, they wield significant clout and can shift the political calculus, circumventing the majority who are less committed and the few brave moderates. "The stage is set for competitive China bashing," observes Sebastian Mallaby of the *Washington Post*. Indeed, Stephen Roach, Morgan Stanley's chief economist has counted twenty-seven pieces of anti-China legislation since the beginning of 2005.

The business lobby provides a countervailing force, but it is split many ways (between exporters and manufacturers, for example). Though all Americans benefit from low-priced Chinese goods and its cooperation on inspecting shipping containers for nuclear weapons, those advantages are diffuse. Meanwhile, job losses in a given locale, a persecuted dissident (especially one championed by a constituent), or the prospect of a violent clash at sea can get legislators fired up in a way that 99 cent socks cannot. On the other hand, the passage of

2006 legislation on a U.S.-India agreement on civilian nuclear cooperation, despite serious nonproliferation concerns, shows what can happen when a powerful constituency in favor of a pivotal relationship emerges. In this case, China hedgers concluded U.S.-India bilateral ties could be a counterweight to China's rise, U.S. business saw an opening for expanded trade and investment, and the increasingly politically powerful Indian-American community served as a natural advocate for further warming of relations.

Second, the way media dynamics work, as we discuss next, exacerbates the push toward congressional extremes. The White House grabs the bulk of attention on national security, which leaves members of Congress fighting for the scraps. The only way to get precious media coverage is to stake out an extreme position. Reasonable, middle-of-the-road speeches about China or India never see the light of day. A warning that China's navy is about to overtake America's, even if incorrect, can find its way to prime time. Further, expanded media coverage of congressional business (as on C-SPAN), though it contributes to transparency in public policy deliberations, also means members are aware they are "on stage" and are more inclined to stay true to their ideological base. Thus, the center of the debate slowly shifts, usually to the hawkish end spectrum; leaving those in the middle vulnerable to charges of appeasement.

Another factor contributing to polarization is the limits of time. The legislative workload has doubled since the 1950s while the incessant demands of fund-raising have continued to mount. With the nearly perpetual campaign cycle (especially for members of the House of Representatives), lawmakers have to be choosy—selecting only a few issues to understand thoroughly and committees on which to serve. On the others, they are apt to take direction from lobbyists bearing gifts, a member whose district is directly affected, or their party leaders. With textile tariffs, for example, the pain associated with lowering trade barriers is concentrated in a few districts, and members without a direct stake will stand on the sidelines, highly aware and sympathetic to the imperative of political survival of their colleagues. Further, there is significant political peril in voting against powerful national lobbies like labor organizations.

Fourth, scapegoating a foreign country for a largely domestic problem is one of the oldest tricks in the book. Members who want to convey the impression they are doing *something* about a given societal quandry can more easily point to what the other country has to do than address the underlying domestic problems. It is always more politically expedient to blame another government than point to one's own policy failures or admit the limited impact one member of Congress can have. Though the valuation of China's currency is a relatively minor factor in the U.S. trade deficit, criticizing Beijing is an easy political swipe. It involves only the scant time it takes to call a press conference. Actually changing American patterns of savings and consumption is exponentially more difficult, both politically and financially.

Fifth, the Pentagon is greatly influential on the Hill. Defense officials' concerns about the next big threat can spill over into the broader political debate. No member of Congress wants to be caught off guard on a potential threat and be criticized later for being asleep at the switch. The China hawks are represented on the powerful armed services committees, which are constantly briefed by the Pentagon, whose own intelligence operation readily turns up fodder for suspicion. The Defense Department also has a built-in grassroots presence, spread throughout 2,500 military installations around the country, which provide significant political capital in Congress. Further, the defense industry, the third side of the "iron triangle," showers the Hill with cash. In the 2004 election cycle, it contributed $13 million to candidates in both parties. By contrast, the State Department is notoriously ineffective at engaging the Hill, and has none of these advantages.

Last, the prevailing (and accurate) view in Congress is that foreign policy issues do not affect Americans' votes unless they rise to crisis proportions (e.g., Iraq), and members are therefore inclined to look more narrowly at the views of their specific electoral base on a given issue rather than the sentiment of the broader population within the district, state, or nation.

A 2004 survey of American leaders demonstrates that administration officials, congressional staffers, and societal leaders have not internalized Americans' support for multilateralism. For example, although 66 percent of the public surveyed said that the U.S. should address more issues through the U.N. system even if it means America will not get its way, only 22 percent of administration officials and, incredibly, 9 percent of congressional staffers (though both groups agreed with the statement) guessed correctly that a large majority of Americans would support that position. Similarly, where nearly 80 percent of the public supported the U.S. joining the International Criminal Court, only 17 percent of administration officials (a majority of whom agreed with that position) and 7 percent of congressional staffers (a majority who did not) guessed that a large majority of Americans would be in favor of the U.S. joining. Turns out we weren't the only ones who wrongly assumed the country is full of Joe- and Jane-Six-Packs.

Part of the explanation for this dichotomy is that politicians, correctly or incorrectly, assume that Americans' rhetorical support for multilateralism will fall by the wayside when real tradeoffs are at hand. As President Clinton once remarked, in the context of the U.N., the "real problem is not that people are opposed to the U.N. or opposed to us paying our fair share . . . [The] problem is that there's no penalty for not doing it, and there's always other competing claims on the dollar."

The Fourth Estate

Yet another hurdle to implementing strategic collaboration is today's media environment. For a variety of reasons, the fourth estate is more likely than ever to demonize big powers. Competition among media outlets continues to rise. So to break through the noise and attract big audiences, media companies have increasingly turned to sensational-ist, fear-based, personalized, and entertainment-oriented program-ming to achieve ratings. News coverage today typically includes a familiar mix of violence, heroism, scandal, a readily identifiable vil-lain, and conflict. The use of fear—"Can hand sanitizers kill your baby?"—as a hook to attract viewers' attention is commonplace. A 2000 Harvard study documented the rise of sensationalism in the media, in which news stories (across all outlets) with a moderate to high level of sensationalism rose from approximately 25 percent in the early 1980s to nearly 40 percent by 2000.

Why does this formula work? Human beings are naturally drawn to human drama—stories with high stakes, colorful characters, and plot lines clearly relevant to their lives. By using fear and vivid, nega-tive stories to attract attention, the media is tapping into the well-understood biases of viewers. "People tend to overvalue, over-retain, and over-attend to negative information in a well-demonstrated ef-fect called the 'negativity bias,' " explains Scott Gerwehr, director of the behavioral sciences program at Defense Group Inc. Evolutionary psychologists explain this bias by arguing that natural selection ad-vantages being sensitive to threats more than pleasures.

Like celebrity murder trials and prurient scandals, foreign policy crises can easily fit into the drama formula; Kim Jong Il's nuclear threats can be as compelling fodder as Paris Hilton's latest catfight. When world events do make it to the TV screen, the tyranny of the sound bite makes it nearly impossible to cover them in any depth. This helps explain why the media so often personalizes international crises, zeroing in on the personal travails of Saddam Hussein, Osama bin Laden, or Iran's president Mahmoud Ahmadinejad as a stand-in for complex geopolitical issues.

As anthropological research shows, societies must evaluate an endless stream of risks, and will typically react most strongly to dangers that offend moral principles (e.g., treatment of dissidents in China) or fuel criticism of groups that are disliked (e.g., communists). Public discussion of scares and counterscares then feeds a larger culture of fear.

That is why there is space to cover brutal repression of a particular journalist or activist, a growing military, or the stories of those who were laid off when their plant closed. As Joseph Quinlan, a Wall Street analyst, recently complained, "China is emerging as the most profitable market for U.S. goods, but I can't get the mainstream media interested in that story!"

Three more recent trends reinforce the potential demonizing power of the media: the rise of "opinionews," "newsertainment," and the agenda-setting power of the blogosphere.

OPINION AGE Those who may seek to demonize the pivotal powers will have a willing handmaiden in the form of "opinionews." Mixing editorial opinion with objective reporting was a journalism no-no when we grew up, but it's pervasive now. Fox News was in the vanguard of this trend, but to pull itself out of a ratings slump, CNN copied many of Fox's tactics.

Lou Dobbs is the paragon of this new brand of journalism. Dobbs has taken his virulently anti-immigration, anti-trade agenda and blunt, populist opinions right to the top of cable news. His ratings in 2006 in the sought-after twenty-five-to-forty-year-old demographic were up 40 percent over 2005. As *New York* magazine writer Kurt Andersen commented, "anti-Establishment anger is now a major part of the CNN brand."

A stinging Dobbs's lead-in on a story about a China intellectual property infringement case gives the flavor: "Tonight China and its unfair trade practices are stealing American innovation . . ." China has a dismal record on protecting intellectual property rights, but the picture is a complex and shifting one as we discussed in Chapter 4. However, in the world of opinionews, there is no time to debate the intellectual property rights issue fully; heated language and catchy sound bites rule.

In the world of print punditry too, we are more inclined to see articles like Robert Kaplan's cover story in the *Atlantic Monthly*, "How We Would Fight China," than "How One Day China and the U.S. Might Clash over Taiwan, but How Neither of Them Wants To and Since Both Have Nuclear Weapons and Are Very Interdependent, a Violent Clash Is Unlikely and Self-Defeating." As blogger Thomas Barnett sees it, "Without journalists like Kaplan, Americans might fear the world less, and if Americans feared the world less, who would read Bob Kaplan?"

NEWSERTAINMENT Another recent trend is the rise of "newsertainment"—shows whose main purpose is entertainment, but which use news events as fodder for their programming. For many viewers (including, we sheepishly admit, occasionally ourselves) these shows are their sole source of news. Jon Stewart's *The Daily Show*, *The Colbert Report*, late night talk shows like David Letterman and Bill Maher, and even *Entertainment Tonight* have created a whole new genre of programming that more viewers watch than all of the cable news networks combined. The result is more awareness and attentiveness to foreign policy issues than in the past, across a segment of the population that is typically uninterested in foreign policy.

In theory, connecting with a larger share of the American viewing public is a good thing, but the desire to find the entertaining story line may not be consistent with providing Americans a clear understanding of the issues at stake. While Stephen Colbert's term for China— "frenemy"—is poetic in its own way, China coverage on these shows tends to reinforce old stereotypes. Further, some studies of newsertainment viewers suggest that overall they tend to be less politically sophisticated, more skeptical of an activist U.S. foreign policy, and more easily motivated to "rally round the flag." Taken together, these attributes suggest that the growing number of such viewers may be more easily manipulated in times of crisis with a pivotal power, real or perceived.

CHOCK-O-BLOGS While millions of Americans tune into entertainment news, they also are turning to blogs for foreign policy information. The Bush administration's Internet director described the blogosphere as "instrumental, important and underestimated in its influence." Readership of blogs has skyrocketed; in the spring of 2007, the top political blog, Daily Kos and its companion site, Daily Kos Diaries, were together attracting more than one million visitors per day.

While blogs are not supplanting traditional media outlets, they do increasingly have the power to set the media's agenda. As the number of foreign correspondents based overseas continues to decline, the Internet allows anyone with a connection to fill that vacuum. According to John Hamilton, dean of Mass Communications at Louisiana State University, the result is that "traditional foreign correspondents no longer exercise hegemony over foreign news." More and more, traditional journalists are also turning to the blogosphere to determine "what matters" in the world. Under the right circumstances, blogs can shape the news agenda, but they are a double-edged sword. By increasing the diversity of voices involved in debating foreign affairs, blogs can help drive attention to neglected issues like Darfur, driving more traditional press coverage and public attention to the crisis. At the same time, blogs are prone to extremism and sensationalism, and stories posted to the Internet have fewer safeguards against inaccuracy or deliberate efforts to misinform.

TICK-TOCK The era of sound bite "insta-news" has real-world consequences because it greatly increases the time pressures for national security policymakers. In a period marked by complex risks and dangers, U.S. officials are under constant scrutiny from an ever-watchful media. A full, coherent story can be very hard to tell in the middle of an unfolding crisis. As we saw at the White House, policymakers have to devote time and energy taken from the crisis itself to continuously frame policy developments for reporters. Responding to the demands of a clamoring media also invariably impacts policymakers' ability to manage and reconcile delicate pivotal power diplomacy in such circumstances.

Perfect Storm

Worse, in a time of crisis, it is easy to see how the press and politicians can whip up American fears and bias. For the reasons we just discussed, lawmakers' incentives will be to allow the blame game to rage. The executive branch may not be inclined, or able, to fend off the attacks. The press will see the prospect of a ratings bounce. No one in this scenario would benefit from explaining the nuanced, dowdy reality. America's experience with Japan in the 1980s and 1990s demonstrates how these forces have come together in the past, resulting in harm to American's interests.

Side by side for decades, the U.S. knew it could count on Japan in the battle against communism in Asia. And yet, when Japan's economy seemed poised to eclipse America's in the 1980s, America lashed out. Struggling with a deep recession, and nearly 11 percent unemployment, America was bearing the brunt of a competitive wave unlike any it had felt before.

The auto industry became the poster child of the ailing economy. Between 1976 and 1981, imports of Japanese compact cars had increased by nearly 50 percent, representing over a quarter of all car sales in the U.S. With over 200,000 auto manufacturing jobs lost, the Reagan administration came under heavy pressure to act.

No one wanted to hear, or tell, the ugly truth—that the U.S. auto industry lacked any sizeable export market; that American auto manufacturers had chosen not to optimize their products for foreign customers; and most damaging, that they continued to produce cars that were increasingly unpopular at home. Instead, the government turned to protectionism. The result was the 1981–1984 voluntary export restraint (VER) agreement, whereby Japan agreed to limit the number of cars it exported to the U.S. to give Detroit some "breathing room."

Despite massive auto manufacturing job losses, Americans were not predisposed to blame Japan for their economic woes. In polling from the early 1980s, they were just as likely to point to high interest rates (70 percent) or high labor costs (61 percent) as the causes of U.S. economic malaise as foreign competition (64 percent). That is, until multiple forces saw advantage in fanning the flames of Japanophobia. Marketers saw an opportunity to convert American nationalism into sales of domestic products. Politicians found a fall guy and a way to rally the votes of American workers and unions. As an *Economist* editorial at the time aptly described, another accelerant was the establishment media, "lending credibility to quarter-baked economic thought . . . and turning misunderstandings and exaggerations into supposed facts." The spin cycle took hold. By 1989, nearly 70 percent of Americans saw Japan's economic power as a greater peril to the country's future than the Soviet military threat.

Then, suddenly, just two months after President George H. W. Bush's January 1992 collapse at the feet of Japanese Prime Minister Kiichi Miyazawa seemed to symbolize America's imminent economic retreat, the Tokyo stock market plunged to a five-year low. The meteoric rise of Japan Inc. had stalled, its real estate and banking sectors collapsed. Fears of Japanese hegemony quickly faded.

America was left with a legacy of poorly conceived policies enacted in political haste. In the case of autos, the voluntary export restraints certainly did help return the Big Three to profitability, but the regime led to higher car prices and had minimal impact on employment. In a sense, the VERs created a U.S. government–sanctioned cartel, in which the auto industry claimed temporary victory and the

American consumer lost out, paying upward of $1,000 or more per vehicle extra (when average vehicle prices were in the $10,000 range). In limiting the number of imports, Japanese auto manufacturers were able to charge higher prices for their vehicles. Reinvestment of their excess profits arguably helped accelerate their move up the food chain to sedans and later luxury vehicles.

In retrospect, it is surprising that the U.S. felt so threatened by a friendly country with half its population and a minimal military establishment. The fact that Japan had been a longtime ally did not insulate it from a political firestorm.

Instant Replay?

Today's target is China, and to a lesser extent, Russia. As noted earlier, the American public has been aware and largely comfortable with China's rise, though that might be changing; Russia doesn't register much on the popular radar. But in Washington, the mood ranges from apprehensive to antagonistic.

Congressional staffers are far more wary of China than their constituents (15 percent have a favorable impression versus 59 percent of the public, according to a 2005 poll). When we hear anything from Congress on China these days, it is likely to be about its military buildup or undervalued currency. Like Japan in the 1980s, observers will quietly note that China is somehow particularly alien. One senior Senate staffer caricatured a common reaction of panicky legislators: "Military build up. . . . These guys don't look like us. . . . Taiwan. . . . Oh, God!" Combined with the legacy of the Cold War and American distrust of non-democracies, the emotional case for anti-China sentiment is obvious.

The extent of the anti-China movement may not be apparent to readers outside the foreign policy arena, but various factions—right-wing commentators, ideological Cold Warriors, certain civilians in the Pentagon, and some labor and environment interests—have begun to lay the groundwork for a more confrontational stance. Table 8.1, which compares publications from today and during the 1980s, shows a clear resonance.

Likewise, Russia has become a popular target for congressional ire. With its newfound energy wealth, Russia's foreign policy activism in places like Iran is unsettling the foreign policy establishment; human rights and democracy concerns are worries, too. Similar to

Table 8.1: China vs. Japan Threat in Publications

CHINA	JAPAN
"China as No.1" Clyde Prestowitz *American Prospect* 16, no. 3 (March 2005)	*Japan as No. 1 (Lessons for America)* Ezra Vogel Harvard University Press (1979)
America's Coming War with China Ted Galen Carpenter Palgrave Macmillan (2006)	*The Coming War with Japan* George Friedman and Meredith Lebard St. Martin's Press (1991)
"How China Threatens America" Greg Mastel *The International Economy* 19, no. 2 (Spring 2005)	"The Danger from Japan" Theodore H. White *New York Times Magazine* (July 28, 1985)
Hegemon: China's Plan to Dominate Asia and the World Steven W. Mosher Encounter Books (July 2000)	"Japan, an Imminent Hegemon?" Koji Taira *Annals of the American Academy of Political and Social Science* (January 1991)
"The Chinese Invasion" *Los Angeles Times* editorial (July 3, 2005)	"Japan Invades Hollywood" *Newsweek* cover story (October 9, 1989)
In China's Shadow: The Crisis of American Entrepreneurship Reed Hundt Yale University Press (2006)	*In the Shadow of the Rising Sun: The Political Roots of American Economic Decline* William S. Dietrich Pennsylvania State University Press (1991)

China, there is a quiet coalescing between left and right about the Russia "problem."

The Tipping Point

As we saw in the case of Japan, the seeds of anti–pivotal power sentiment can grow quickly into a thicket of popular panic and hostility that ends in poor policies. What would push America over the edge again? A higher unemployment rate—unless we develop a credible social safety net. Despite Americans' broad acceptance of globalization, they also are well aware of its downside. In a December 2006 Pew poll, though many Americans acknowledge that trade is beneficial, "nearly half (48 percent) believe that free trade agreements lead to job losses in the U.S." (Only 12 percent say that trade agreements have led to more jobs.)

Americans want their government to protect them from such upheaval. A 2004 Chicago Council on Global Affairs poll showed 78 percent of the public believes protecting the jobs of U.S. workers should be a "very important" foreign policy goal. Only 41 percent of American leaders agree, and this disconnect has persisted between U.S. policymakers and the public since polling on this question began in 1974. This gap may also help explain why policymakers are not urgently seeking solutions to address the downside of globalization.

The angst from job loss is contagious. Back in 1995, when a neighbor lost his job because his company moved its Wisconsin operations to post-NAFTA Mexico, his story rattled the entire neighborhood. If his relatively comfortable middle-class existence could be upended because of cheaper labor elsewhere, it could happen to anyone. Even relatives with a vaguely internationalist outlook immediately became anti-trade. Today, the relatively new phenomenon of offshoring of service sector jobs adds to trade-related anxiety.

With a shrinking safety net to protect workers, a recession that brings higher unemployment may result in a replay of the 1980s, this time with China or perhaps India. In some ways, the conditions are even more ripe. Despite a relatively strong economic expansion, millions of middle-class workers are at increasing financial risk, forced to pay for health care and retirement out of stagnant or falling incomes. As former Treasury Secretary Larry Summers warns, "If the anxious middle's concerns about fairness are this serious when the unemployment rate is 4.4%, there will be far greater concerns whenever the economy next turns down." Increasing income volatility and longer periods of unemployment have become the norm, driving broad worker insecurity.

However, workers' expectations may also come to change. Generation Y workers, now under thirty and numbering close to seventy million, don't expect "lifetime" employment or even to stay in the same career for too long. Americans under thirty are also more likely to think free trade is good (68 percent), and half are inclined to say it has helped them financially. (By contrast those aged fifty to sixty-four are divided about the benefits—only 36 percent say trade is good—and more than half think trade has hurt them personally.) Further, as new economy business writer Dan Pink has commented, a fundamental shift in the American workplace is under way. Today one in four American workers—over thirty million Americans—earns a living through some form of independent employment (either self-employment, temp work, or jobs in microbusinesses with fewer than twenty employees), more than all U.S. manufacturing workers or Americans employed by government at all levels (including police and teachers). Changing expectations could impact the intensity of the debate at home.

Awareness and Action

What will it take to overcome these various hurdles and bring U.S. policy in line with the commonsense pragmatism of most Americans? We break out several of the most practical and achievable near-term, tactical solutions.

As the line between domestic and foreign policy issues continues to blur, and other powers get stronger while the world's problems get worse, it will become harder to ignore the principles of strategic collaboration that are already favored by most Americans. Until then, even a president who wants to set America on the right course has to overcome the objections of those forces that push America to the extremes.

A president can only promise abroad what he or she can deliver at home politically. The next president has two options for bringing all the naysayers along. First is the domestic equivalent of the Colin Powell doctrine of overwhelming force. When it is crunch time on a critical pillar of strategic collaboration, the administration should throw everything it has at the issue—as President Clinton did when it came to the vote on Permanent Normal Trade Relations (PNTR) for China that allowed it to join the WTO. In retrospect, it is hard to believe that this vote in Congress was ever in doubt given what was at stake, but the White House had to wage an epic battle that took great ingenuity and attention to secure a majority of Republican votes in the last year of Clinton's presidency. Fact sheets, press releases, and presidential statements blanketed Washington for several weeks in the spring of 2000; you could not throw a rock on Capitol Hill without hitting an administration official testifying or meeting with constituent groups about the importance of PNTR.

On very important issues, in addition to working with Congress, the president should also take his or her case directly to the American people, explaining why any short-term or narrow harm an agreement or treaty might pose cannot be allowed to stand in the way of the best interests of their children. Americans support multilateralism, and if authoritative voices can successfully "connect the dots" on why it matters, they can help lure congressional members in the agnostic middle to take sides. While it is not always feasible to use this tactic, it might be appropriate for bold measures like establishing the C6 or addressing climate change.

The other approach is to "think small," starting with narrow arrangements that can build gradually into binding commitments. For example, the Clinton administration wrestled with the International Criminal Court and, though it signed the treaty, declined to submit it to Congress for ratification because even with many safeguards, the military opposed it because of possible cases against American service personnel, and it was thus politically untenable. In hindsight, despite some strong voices advocating for the ICC in Congress, it might have been better to build on an existing, successful tribunal, turning it into a permanent court, which would have given legislators and the military time to observe its rules and recognize its benefits. Either tactic, be it blizzard or baby steps, requires a serious and sustained engagement by the executive branch with Congress and key constituent groups on issues on a constant basis and not just when there is a crisis. There has to be a rich, ongoing dialogue, as difficult as that can be to achieve.

Further, the president cannot shy away from defending the institutions and rules that make the world orderly. In the recent past, few politicians have risen to praise the U.N. or other bodies. As we have discussed, these organizations often carry our water, and, if they are to survive politically, America's leaders cannot be reticent about sharing the credit. Also, the executive branch must move aggressively to address the major source of American angst associated with the pivotal powers—employment-related disruption popularly associated with trade. Washington needs to ameliorate the perils of what economist Jared Bernstein has termed the "YOYO"—"you're on your own"—economy that prevails today. Ideas we discussed in Chapters 4 and 5 like wage insurance and portable health care, along with better opportunities for retraining, will help mitigate the impact of an economic downturn, create incentives for workers to take risks, and potentially reduce the likelihood of unwarranted political backlash against foreign countries. Nearly 90 percent of Americans say they would favor more free trade if they were confident the U.S. was making major efforts to retrain and educate workers. The Chairman of the House Financial Services Committee, Barney Frank, has proposed a "grand bargain" with corporate America—trading added protection for workers for Democrats' support of trade deals—suggesting a political path forward.

On the media front, policymakers must "get in the game" and leverage the opportunities created by the newly fragmented market. The ability of the president to set the agenda has waned, and the standard method of daily briefings to a small White House press corps reaches too limited an audience. The executive press operation needs to monitor and cultivate a whole new set of opinion shapers, both domestic and foreign. It needs to be creative about getting its message out through blogs, video games, social networking sites, short movies, and even music. A quick check of YouTube in the fall of 2007 pulled up a list of just over 276,000 videos on Iraq that had been posted and another three thousand on Darfur.

Not a Spectator Sport

Our recommendations so far have been for the executive branch, but that assumes a president who wants to set a new course. A forward-looking president will go a long way toward putting the U.S. on a better footing to achieve strategic collaboration and facilitate ties with the pivotal powers.

Thus when Americans are evaluating candidates in 2008 and beyond, they should be looking for a leader who can think in the long term and tell the difficult, subtle truth in the face of unappealing facts and fear mongers. He should want to lead the world, not just Americans; she has to be sincere enough to convince other countries' leaders that we are serious about turning over a new leaf. He must understand the importance of innovation, health care, education, and fiscal discipline to America's future prosperity and foreign policy and inspire Americans to take the bitter medicine now to enjoy more prosperous lives later. She has to be politically deft enough to forge a bipartisan consensus on pivotal power policy. Finally, he must never have had, or have by now thoroughly abandoned, a Cold War mind-set.

Beyond voting for a great leader, here are five steps that individual citizens could take to improve the environment for pivotal power policy. First is maintaining a healthy dose of skepticism about what they are told about pivotal powers. While many Americans may not generally be prone to media spin, it is hard not to listen when the drumbeat gets loud. When pundits opine on the certainty of the China threat, viewers ought to think twice and seek out the full picture. Second, citizens can help turn the tide against a sensationalist fear-based media by supporting those media outlets whose coverage is informative, even if that means paying for it when it is not required.

Third, more Americans should travel to the pivotal powers. Nothing is a substitute for seeing them firsthand, and the more Americans that understand these increasingly powerful nations, and understand that regular people live in them, the better off we all will be. (The reverse is also important; America must remain open to visitors from pivotal powers.)

Fourth, is demanding more accountability from elected officials. As we have shown, politicians will use voters' names in vain to pursue policies that contravene the wishes of the majority. Voters must begin to hold politicians' feet to the fire on foreign policy issues. We applaud the work of groups organizing more debate on national security beyond the New York–Washington corridor. There is room for additional efforts to undertake and share district or state polling on foreign policy issues with members of Congress to make it easier for those without a direct interest to do the right thing.

Finally, individual Americans must play a more active role in shaping the debate. This means contributing to blogs, getting involved with NGOs working on the issues, joining online petitions, posting videos, writing op-eds, and the like.

• • •

These steps are only a place to start. In the past, we have seen that a crisis—whether 9/11, the Vietnam War, or the Great Depression—has given Americans the jolt to overcome obstacles in their political system and turn the country in a whole new direction. Perhaps the Iraq War, and the perception of increased competition with the pivotal powers, will have the positive effect of lighting a fire under American policymakers. However, in the absence of such a motivating force, Americans must become that force themselves.

Conclusion

In 1997, Tiger Woods won the Masters, his first major golf tournament, by a record margin of twelve strokes. Even nongolfers like ourselves marveled at the feat. In less than one year of professional playing, Woods rose to number one in the official global golf rankings, the fastest-ever ascent. Then, at the height of his fame, Woods shocked the sports world by deciding to take time off from the tour to completely rework his swing—the very core of his winning game. In 1999, he came back and had a three-year run of the "most dominant golf ever played," breaking or tieing dozens of long-standing golfing records.

That did not stop him from reinventing himself yet again in 2004 to take advantage of new technology in both clubs and balls. "Tiger Woods wins four consecutive major championships," one journalist wrote incredulously, "and decides to change his swing because he wants to get better? The risk in making a change that pronounced can't be overstated." But Woods understands he's in heated competition with himself. "It's a never-ending struggle," he says. "No matter how good you play you can always play better." As Woods's coach Hank Haney once commented, "The thing that impresses me most about [Woods] is that he isn't interested in getting back to where he was in 2000 or whenever. He wants to be better than that."

America needs to follow in Tiger's footsteps. It too must find the courage to reinvent itself at the height of its power to continue its long run of prosperity and security. We must do the hard work of solving our problems at home. At the same time, America must also leverage the strength of pivotal powers to shore up the liberal world order, harnessing their talent and resources and driving their participation and responsibility. In this rare moment when our aspirations align with theirs, we can together construct a world we want our children and grandchildren to live in.

As we have seen, the growth of big powers brings America many opportunities. Pivotal powers are not direct military foes, but crucial partners in thwarting the lethal threats we all face. India is a key ally against terrorism; China is a partner in curtailing North Korea's nuclear program; Russia's influence is critical with Tehran; Europe is a champion of the liberal, rules-based world order; and Japan can show us all the way to reduce greenhouse gases. Though their increasing influence reduces America's full freedom of action, and flashpoints like Taiwan remain very dangerous, no pivotal power is the kind of ideologically driven enemy we faced during the Cold War.

While pivotal powers seek more influence and respect within the international system, they are not trying to usurp America's role as a superpower. Moreover, as President Clinton once said, ". . . America has found that it is the weakness of great nations, not their strength, that threatens [our] vision for tomorrow." Also, we do not really know which pivotal powers, if any, will continue to rise over time.

For those powers that are growing, their economic expansion bolsters our own in most ways. To the extent that shifting economic winds trigger pain and economic dislocation, the remedies are America's alone to administer. So when we find ourselves worrying about competition from China or India, it should spur us to better educate our children and help our workers compete effectively.

A new era of pivotal powers will mean difficult trade-offs and choices for America. We cannot simultaneously grow our economy and try to thwart the economic rise of others. We cannot cooperate effectively on developing alternative energy supplies while prohibiting others from buying our energy companies. We cannot retain sole control over international rules and also genuinely welcome the pivotal powers into the club.

We also cannot afford to see the world as it was or become preoccupied with defending the status quo. Nor can we succumb to what a famous Indian yogi called *tamas*, the "dark and heavy demon of inertia." To continue to thrive and prosper in this new era of pivotal powers, we have to relinquish the sense of entitlement that will lead us down a dead-end path of protectionism and hostility.

We've been in tougher spots before. The United States has withstood thirty-two recessions since 1857 (when they began tracking such statistics); ten major armed conflicts, six of which saw the deaths of more than ten thousand military personnel; four presidential assassinations and thirteen other attempts; multiple terrorist incidents on U.S. soil; and several mass social protests—from the debate over slavery to the women's and civil rights movements—that threatened the cohesion of the country. America faced each, transformed itself, and went on to excel. America has all that it needs: economic vitality, creative people, diverse populations, a risk-taking culture, flexible and cutting-edge companies, abundant natural resources, military strength, and the best system of government around.

The avenue to a truly safer and more prosperous world runs through the pivotal powers. With them, we can build a world where Americans will thrive, today and tomorrow.

Notes

INTRODUCTION

9 *None could have built ITER:* South Korea is also a partner. For more on ITER, "U.S. ITER Fact Sheet," Oak Ridge National Laboratory, U.S. ITER Project Office (2006); "U.S. Signs International Fusion Energy Agreement," U.S. Department of Energy Office of Public Affairs, November 21, 2006; Dr. Raymond L. Orbach, under secretary for science, U.S. Department of Energy (remarks at the signing of the ITER agreement), November 21, 2006; "A White-Hot Elephant," *Economist*, November 25, 2006; Daniel Clery, "ITER's $12 Billion Gamble," *Science* 314 (October 13, 2006): 238.

10 *The pure zero-sum days:* In this book, we take a catholic approach to international relations theory, pulling insights from the two major and one more recent school. We accept the primary tenets of realism that states are the central (but not only) actors in the international system; that the number of powerful states in that system influences considerably how they behave; and that, in the end, states can rely only on themselves for protection. States conduct their affairs "in the brooding shadow of violence," operating in a "self-help" system without a world government to enforce agreements, mediate disputes, or protect one state from another's aggression. Kenneth N. Waltz, *Theory of International Politics* (Boston: McGraw-Hill, 1979), 101. Further, realists posit, and we agree, that no state can ever really know another state's future intentions. Ibid., 102; John Mearsheimer, "The False Promise of Inter-

237

national Institutions," *International Security* 19, no. 3 (Winter 1994/ 1995): 10. We do not, however, accept the hard-line realist ("offensive realist") argument that state power is necessarily zero-sum and that relative power, military power, is all-determining. For an elaboration of this argument, John J. Mearsheimer, *The Tragedy of Great Power Politics* (New York: Norton, 2001). The more mainstream realists ("defensive realists") believe, as we do, that states actually seek security rather than power per se. Stephen M. Walt, *The Origin of Alliances* (Ithaca: Cornell University Press, 1987). In international politics, vulnerability is often the mother of violence. States can and will cooperate, and nonmilitary forms of power (diplomatic, ideological, cultural) matter greatly to a state's ability to achieve security.

We find persuasive the argument from liberalism—the second major school of international relations—that factors beyond relative power, such as domestic politics, economic relationships, and the presence of international institutions, shape how states act toward one another. For arguments on domestic politics, among others, Bruce Bueno de Mesquita and David Lalman, *War and Reason: Domestic and International Imperatives* (New Haven: Yale University Press, 1992); Richard Rosecrance and Arthur A. Stein, eds., *The Domestic Bases of Grand Strategy* (Ithaca: Cornell University Press, 1993); Jack Snyder, *Myths of Empire: Domestic Politics and International Ambition* (Ithaca: Cornell University Press, 1991); Andrew Moravcsik, "Taking Preferences Seriously: A Liberal Theory of International Politics," *International Organization* 51 (Autumn 1997): 513–53; Helen Milner, "Rationalizing Politics: The Emerging Synthesis of International, American, and Comparative Politics," *International Organization* 52 (Autumn 1998): 759–86. On economic relationships, Erik Gartzke, "The Capitalist Peace," *American Journal of Political Science* 51, no. 1 (January 2007): 166–91; John Oneal and Bruce Russett, "Assessing the Liberal Peace with Alternative Specifications: Trade Still Reduces Conflict," *Journal of Peace Research* 36, no. 4 (1999); Robert O. Keohane and Joseph S. Nye, *Power and Interdependence* (New York: HarperCollins, 1989). For the effect of international institutions, G. John Ikenberry, *After Victory: Institutions, Strategic Restraint, and the Rebuilding of Orders After Major Wars* (Princeton: Princeton University Press, 2001); Robert O. Keohane, "International Institutions: Can Interdependence Work?," *Foreign Policy* 110 (Spring

1998): 82–94; Robert O. Keohane and Lisa L. Martin, "The Promise of Institutionalist Theory," *International Security* 20, no. 1 (Summer 1995). For more on the theoretical debate between liberalism and realism generally, David A. Baldwin, ed., *Neorealism and Neoliberalism: The Contemporary Debate* (New York: Columbia University Press, 1993).

We are not the first to draw insights from both realism and liberalism—most policymakers are liberal realists or realist liberals. Recently, there have been new attempts to house ideas from both schools under one roof. Anatol Lieven and John Hulsman, *Ethical Realism: A Vision for America's Role in the World* (New York: Pantheon, 2006); Francis Fukuyama, *America at the Crossroads: Democracy, Power, and the Neoconservative Legacy* (New Haven: Yale University Press, 2006); Robert Wright, "An American Foreign Policy That Both Realists and Idealists Should Fall in Love With," *New York Times*, July 16, 2006.

Finally, we find the central insight of constructivism, the newest school of international relations theory, persuasive, which argues that how states act toward one another is driven by perceptions and shared mental states. Alexander Wendt, *Social Theory of International Politics* (Cambridge: Cambridge University Press, 1999).

10 *Through a combination of key traits:* The list of traits relevant to national power is adapted from Ashley Tellis et al., *Measuring National Power in the Postindustrial Age* (Santa Monica: RAND, 2000). Also George Perkovich, "Is India a Major Power?" *Washington Quarterly* (Winter 2003/2004). There is no clear consensus in the political science community on how to measure national power. Robert J. Art and David A. Baldwin, "Debate: Force, Fungibility, and Influence," *Security Studies* 8, no. 4 (Summer 1999): 173–83.

10 *The European Union has its own central government:* T. R. Reid, *The United States of Europe: The New Superpower and the End of American Supremacy* (New York: Penguin, 2004), 2.

10 *Further, a sense of European identity:* Ibid., 199–200.

11 *Japan has the world's second largest national economy:* "Status of Contributions to the Regular Budget, International Tribunals, Peacekeeping Operations and Capital Master Plan," United Nations (2006), http://www.globalpolicy.org/finance/tables/reg-budget/large06.htm (accessed January 3, 2007).

12 *On the contrary, these powers often further American security:* We use

"prosperity" as a stand-in for the "pursuit of happiness," for analysis purposes, understanding that they are not substitutes; when it comes to other big powers, the debate in the United States revolves around how they affect American economic success, not the more elusive components of happiness. Also, we appreciate that American interests in security, prosperity, and ideology are interrelated and cannot be fully parsed, as we have attempted to do here. Oil, for example, is primarily an economic issue, because, heart attacks at the pump notwithstanding, its price and availability do not threaten physical harm to Americans. That said, pivotal power relationships with oil-rich nations have security implications for the United States.

12 *Even so, five hundred years of history:* "Power transition" literature investigates this issue. Some theorists suggest a historical pattern in which a rising power will attack a dominant power when it has amassed adequate resources to take it on. For example, A. F. K. Organski and Jacek Kugler, *The War Ledger* (Chicago: University of Chicago Press, 1980). Other theorists suggest that it actually tends to be the dominant power that lashes out when it begins to fear a deep and irreversible decline. Dale C. Copeland, *The Origins of Major War* (Ithaca: Cornell University Press, 2000). Other useful sources include Robert Gilpin, *War and Change* (Cambridge: Cambridge University Press, 1981); Woosang Kim and James D. Morrow, "When Do Power Shifts Lead to War?," *American Journal of Political Science* 36, no. 4 (November 1992): 896–922; Douglas Lemke, "The Continuation of History: Power Transition Theory and the End of the Cold War," *Journal of Peace Research* 34, no. 1 (February 1997): 23–36.

13 *It could be different:* Among others, Richard Haass makes this point. Richard Haass, *The Opportunity: America's Moment to Alter History's Course* (New York: Public Affairs Press, 2005), 5–8.

13 *Alone these weapons pose:* John Lewis Gaddis, *The Long Peace: Inquiries into the History of the Cold War* (Oxford: Oxford University Press, 1987), 230. Robert Gilpin is also somewhat optimistic that nuclear weapons can contribute to peace among major powers. Gilpin, *War and Change*, 218. Of course, nuclear powers have fought in the past, and nuclear weapons do not prevent proxy conflicts such as those that characterized the Cold War. For an elaboration of the view that nuclear weapons do not necessarily change dynamics between states, Organski and Kugler, *The War Ledger*, 199–200.

13 *Commodities markets make conquering for land:* Multinationals import the assets, natural resources, and brains they need for much lower than the cost of war and conquest. Stephen Brooks, "The Globalization of Production and the Changing Benefits of Conquest," *Journal of Conflict Resolution* 43, no. 5 (October 1999). For more on how the modern global economy reduces the costs of conflict between states, Robert Jervis, "The Future of World Politics: Will It Resemble the Past?," *International Security* 16 (Winter 1991/1992): 49–50. Richard Rosecrance, "Power and International Relations: The Rise of China and Its Effects," *International Studies Perspectives* 7 (2006): 33; Josef Joffe, "Defying History and Theory," in *America Unrivaled: The Future of the Balance of Power,* ed. G. John Ikenberry (Ithaca: Cornell University Press, 2002), 169.

13 *A future great power that seeks to become safer:* Put another way, shared threats from outside the system of nation-states raise the costs of state-on-state violence.

13 *This security interdependence:* Francis Fukuyama, *America at the Crossroads: Democracy, Power, and the Neoconservative Legacy* (New Haven and London: Yale University Press, 2006), 67.

13 *Economic interdependence has grown deeper too:* For theoretical inquiries into the links between economic interdependence and conflict, Edward D. Mansfield and Brian M. Pollins, eds., *Economic Interdependence and International Conflict* (Ann Arbor: University of Michigan Press, 2003).

13 *Britain and Germany also traded heavily:* Robert J. Art, *A Grand Strategy for America* (Ithaca: Cornell University Press, 2003), 20–26; Richard Rosecrance, "A New Concert of Powers," *Foreign Affairs* (Spring 1992): 68.

13 *Not only is the level of worldwide trade:* Jervis, "The Future of World Politics," 49.

14 *Those relationships are much harder to replace:* Rosecrance, "Power and International Relations," 35.

14 *No pivotal power demands allegiance:* Some commentators also find it significant that international norms have shifted and now the international community has come to "oppose utterly" wars fought to seize permanently another country and its population. Anna Simons, "The Death of Conquest," *National Interest* (Spring 2003): 41.

14 *Interdependence is no guarantee:* Jervis, "The Future of World Politics," 51.

14 *Preparation for conflict:* This dynamic is known as the "security dilemma," and we discuss it further in Chapter 7.

15   *In the late 1800s:* S. C. M. Paine, *The Sino-Japanese War of 1894–1895: Perceptions, Power, and Primacy* (Cambridge: Cambridge University Press, 2003). Provides a detailed analysis of historical relations between China and Japan, and the impact on Russo-Japanese relations.

15   *Just a few decades later, fears of Bolshevik Russia:* Michael Howard, *The Continental Commitment* (London: Temple Smith, 1972); Brian Bond, *British Military Policy Between the Two World Wars* (Oxford: Clarendon Press, 1980). Offers a review of Britain's priorities during the interwar period.

15   *In nine short years:* Pam Woodall, "The New Titans," *Economist*, September 16, 2006, 4.

15   *It attracted over $70 billion:* Preliminary U.N. estimate as of January 2007. "UNCTAD Investment Brief, Number 1, 2007: Foreign Direct Investment Surged Again in 2006," United Nations Conference on Trade and Development (January 2007), http://www.unctad.org/en/docs/iteiiamisc20072_en.pdf (accessed April 11, 2007).

15   *and has been building a California's worth:* California's total interstate system is 2,457 miles. China added around 13,000 miles to its expressway system from 2001 to 2005. "China's Fast Expanding Road to Development," Agence France-Presse, April 6, 2006.

15   *Because America can tend to focus:* "The New Face of Globalization," *Economist*, November 19, 2005, 27.

15   *"The post-Cold War peace":* Bill Gertz, "Chinese Dragon Awakes," *Washington Times*, June 26, 2005.

16   *China's income gap:* Andrew Batson and Shai Oster, "As China Booms, the Poorest Lose Ground; Survey Showing Income Decline Among Bottom 10% Suggests New Wealth Isn't Filtering Down," *Wall Street Journal*, November 22, 2006.

16   *over 800 million of its citizens:* That is nearly 80 percent of India's population. "2006 World Development Indicators," World Bank (April 2006), http://devdata.worldbank.org/wdi2006/contents/Section2.htm (accessed March 11, 2007).

16   *Social unrest is on the rise:* Thomas Lum, "Social Unrest in China," *CRS Report for Congress*, May 8, 2006, 2.

16   *fresh water is in very short supply:* Georgina Lee, "Top Official Warns of Looming Water Crisis," *South China Morning Post*, November 7, 2006.

16   *the People's Republic is home to twenty:* Mark Magnier, "U.N. Report

Raises Pressure on China to Cut Pollution," *Los Angeles Times*, April 8, 2007.

16 *With its schools and demographic composition:* Manjeet Kripalani and Pete Engardio, "The Rise of India," *BusinessWeek Online*, December 8, 2003, http://www.businessweek.com/magazine/content/03_49/b38610 01_mz001.htm (accessed March 23, 2005).

16 *But Bollywood and Bangalore aside:* Somini Sengupta, "In Teeming India, Water Crisis Means Dry Pipes and Foul Sledge," *New York Times*, September 29, 2006.

16 *and nearly half the children:* Somini Sengupta, "Even Amid Its Wealth, India Finds, Half Its Small Children Are Malnourished," *New York Times*, February 10, 2007. For the original data, "UNICEF India Statistics" (Nutrition, 1996–2005), http://www.unicef.org/infobycountry/ india_india_statistics.html#23 (accessed April 12, 2007); UNICEF Sudan Statistics (Nutrition, 1996–2005), http://www.unicef.org/infoby country/sudan_statistics.html#23 (accessed April 12, 2007).

16 *"the United States is not":* Haass, *The Opportunity*, 21.

16 *Moreover, straight-line forecasts are limited:* Peter Katzenstein as quoted in G. John Ikenberry, *After Victory,* 7. Also, Charles F. Doran, "Why Forecasts Fail: The Limits and Potential of Forecasting in International Relations and Economics," *International Studies Review* (Summer 1999): 15. The choices of individual policymakers, with their own particular values and beliefs, also affect outcomes. Jervis, "The Future of World Politics," 41. Especially when interconnections are dense, as they are in international relations, the impact of any change is unpredictable. Robert Jervis, *System Effects* (Princeton: Princeton University Press, 1997). For more on chaos and complexity theory as related to strategy, Harry R. Yarger, *Strategic Theory for the 21st Century: The Little Book on Big Strategy*, Strategic Studies Institute, U.S. Army War College (February 2006).

16 *"[H]istory usually makes":* Robert Jervis, "The Future of World Politics: Will It Resemble the Past?," *International Security* 16 (Winter 1991/ 1992): 39.

18 *A remarkably consistent cast:* Paul Kennedy, *The Rise and Fall of the Great Powers: Economic Change and Military Conflict from 1500–2000* (New York: Random House, 1987), 149; Waltz, *Theory of International Politics*, 162.

19 *These institutions reflect and reinforce:* G. John Ikenberry and Anne-Marie Slaughter, "Forging a World of Liberty Under Law: U.S. National Security in the 21st Century," Princeton Project on National Security Papers (September 27, 2006), 23, http://www.wws.princeton.edu/ppns/report/FinalReport.pdf (accessed February 2007).

19 *Instead of leading, America has been busy alienating:* Former Deputy Secretary of State Richard Armitage in the Bush administration once characterized this foreign policy approach as "Look, fucker, you do what we want!" "A Falling Star," *Economist*, January 20, 2007, 44.

19 *Even though America is more dominant:* Many have made this observation. G. John Ikenberry, *After Victory*; Stephen M. Walt, *Taming American Power* (New York: Norton, 2005), 31–32.

1. SAFETY IN NUMBERS

23 *Carrying AK-47s and hand grenades:* Rajesh Mahapatra, "Police Commander at Parliament Recounts Terrorist Attack," Associated Press, December 15, 2001; Palash Kumar, "India Seeks to Avenge 'Terrorist' Attack on Democracy," Agence France-Presse, December 14, 2001.

23 *Six of the men eventually pleaded guilty:* Jerry Markon, " 'Va. Jihad' Case Hailed as Key in War on Terror," *Washington Post*, June 8, 2006.

23 *LeT has joined the global jihadist bandwagon:* "Lashkar-e Tayyiba (LeT)," Jane's World Insurgency and Terrorism, *Janes.com*, September 1, 2004 (accessed September 27, 2005).

24 *Osama bin Laden has reportedly asked LeT:* Gethin Chamberlain, "Investigators Reveal London Bomber's Links to Al-Qaeda," *Scotsman*, July 16, 2005; Kevin Sullivan, "Al-Qaeda Suspect Held in Britain; Zambia Deports Man Tied to Terrorist Camp in Oregon," *Washington Post*, August 8, 2005.

24 *"Among the many objects":* Alexander Hamilton, James Madison, John Jay, *The Federalist Papers,* http://www.foundingfathers.info/federalist papers/fed03.htm (accessed March 11, 2007). For more on Jay, Frank Monaghan, *John Jay* (New York: Bobbs-Merrill, 1935).

24 *Traditionally, when most national security experts discuss:* E.g., Kenneth N. Waltz, *Theory of International Politics* (New York: Random House, 1979). As our overall objective is to understand how pivotal powers affect what Americans care about, we look beyond the entrenched defini-

tion of security as freedom from threats of organized interstate violence to the territorial integrity of the U.S. For more on why it is appropriate to use this broader definition of security today, David P. Fidler, "Transnational Threats to National Security: Daniel Deudney's Case Against Linking Environmental Degradation and National Security," working paper for the Princeton Project on National Security, http://www.wws.princeton.edu/ppns/papers/Fidler.pdf (accessed April 11, 2007); Sarah Tarry, "Deepening and Widening: An Analysis of Security Definitions in the 1990s," *Journal of Military and Strategic Studies* 2, no. 1 (Fall 1999). For another critique of the state-centric focus of security studies, Richard K. Betts, "The Soft Underbelly of American Primacy: Tactical Advantages of Terror," *Political Science Quarterly* 117, no. 1 (Spring 2002): 19–38. For discussion of the framework of "human security" that focuses on the individual, rather than the state, as the primary consumer of security, W. E. Blatz, *Human Security: Some Reflections* (Toronto: University of Toronto Press, 1966).

25 *Each of these dire threats:* Note that this taxonomy is not attempting to be scientific or exhaustive. These categories make the discussion easier to organize and provide a framework to discuss rough priorities.

26 *The potential for "catastrophic damage":* Francis Fukuyama, *America at the Crossroads: Democracy, Power and the Neoconservative Legacy* (New Haven: Yale University Press, 2006), 67.

27 *Terrorists pose the most dire threat:* As a panel of high-ranking former government officials and experts put it, "The foremost challenge to U.S. national security today comes from violent extremists who, often in the name of Islam, seek to use catastrophic terror to achieve their goals." "Combating Catastrophic Terror: A Security Strategy for the Nation," Center for American Progress (October 2005), 1, http://www.american progressaction.org/site/pp.asp?c=klLWJcP7H&b=1138607 (accessed November 1, 2005). Some suggest a terrorist attack that targeted the main institutions of U.S. government, like the White House and Capitol, could even pose an *existential* threat to the U.S. government. Cyber attacks by terrorists are another concern, though perhaps not as life-threatening.

27 *The "gold standard in terror":* Daniel Benjamin, "What's New About the London Terror Plot," *slate.com*, August 10, 2006, http://www.slate.com/id/2147498/ (accessed April 6, 2007).

27 *In the last ten years:* We focus on the threat from extremist Islamic groups, though there are plenty of other terrorist organizations that also pose dangers for the U.S. or its allies, such as the FARC in Colombia and American extremist groups. Naturally, it's only a tiny minority of the Muslim faithful who condone the use of violence to further political ends.

27 *Now a diffuse jihadist network:* Bruce Hoffman, "Combating Al Qaeda and the Militant Islamic Threat" (testimony before the House Armed Services Subcommittee on Terrorism, February 16, 2006).

27 *a global problem in need:* "Combating Catastrophic Terror," 15.

27 *At the same time, the nuts-and-bolts:* Michael A. Sheehan, "Diplomacy," in *Attacking Terrorism: Elements of a Grand Strategy* (Washington, D.C.: Georgetown University Press, 2004), 99.

27 *Many are "self-starters," operating:* For a thorough discussion of these trends, Daniel Benjamin and Steven Simon, *The Next Attack* (New York: Henry Holt, 2005).

28 *As powerful as the U.S. is:* Sheehan, "Diplomacy," 100.

28 *"the U.S. simply could not replicate":* Brian Jenkins (senior advisor and counterterrorism expert at RAND), in discussion with Nina Hachigian, October 2005.

28 *U.S. human intelligence:* Douglas Jehl, "CIA Is Reviewing Its Policy for Recruitment," *New York Times,* June 8, 2005; Gary Thomas, "US Seeks to Revitalize Human Intelligence," *Voice of America,* May 5, 2005, http://www.globalsecurity.org/intell/library/news/2005/intell-050505-33 7d8164.htm (accessed November 20, 2005); U.S. House of Representatives, Permanent Select Committee on Intelligence, "H.R. 2475, 109th Congress, 2nd Session—Intelligence Authorization Act for Fiscal Year 2007."

28 *That leaves the U.S. "highly dependent":* Jenkins discussion.

28 *"VERY VERY VERY":* Former CIA counterterrorism expert, in e-mail exchange with Nina Hachigian, November 2005, emphasis in the original.

28 *The 2006 National Intelligence Estimate:* "Trends in Global Terrorism: Implications for the United States," National Intelligence Council, Declassified Key Judgments of the National Intelligence Estimate (April 2006), http://www.dni.gov/press_releases/Declassified_NIE_Key_Judg ments.pdf (accessed November 11, 2006). Others agree. "Intelligence

cooperation is the most important weapon in the struggle to contain the 'new' terrorism." Richard J. Aldrich, "Transatlantic Intelligence and Security Cooperation," *International Affairs* 80, no. 4 (2004): 752. Says Michael Sheehan, former deputy counterterror commissar for the New York City Police Department, "The most important counterterrorism activity since the fall of the Taliban has been the close cooperation of the CIA with foreign intelligence services." Michael Sheehan, "Walking the Terror Beat," *New York Times,* September 10, 2006.

28 *In 1995, the Buddhist cult:* Entry for Aum Shinrikyo in Wikipedia, http://en.wikipedia.org/wiki/Aum_Shinrikyo (accessed May 16, 2007).

29 *With the third largest Muslim population:* Indonesia has the largest Muslim population, followed by Pakistan (157 million) and India (144 million). *CIA World Factbook 2006* (Washington, D.C.: Central Intelligence Agency, 2006), http://www.odci.gov/cia/publications/factbook/geos/pk.html#People (accessed February 16, 2006).

29 *India has diligently monitored and countered:* Jay Solomon, "Despite U.S. Effort, Pakistan Remains Key Terror Hub," *Wall Street Journal,* July 22, 2005.

29 *The terrorist group LeT:* "The Kashmir Connection," *Jane's Terrorism & Security Monitor,* September 16, 2006.

29 *After 9/11, India:* Mohan Malik, "High Hopes: India's Responses to U.S. Security Policies," Asia Pacific Center for Security Studies, Special Assessment (March 2003), 3, http://www.apcss.org/core/BIOS/malik/malik.htm#PUBLICATIONS (accessed April 23, 2007).

29 *In June 2005, India and the U.S.:* "India and America's Common Cause: Informed Sources," *National Post* (Canada), July 20, 2005.

29 *India's pledge of "unlimited support":* C. Christine Fair, *The Counterterror Coalitions: Cooperation with Pakistan and India* (Santa Monica: RAND, 2004), 76–77. No doubt Delhi was also motivated by the disadvantages of the U.S. action in Pakistan.

29 *European countries have been high-profile partners:* Benjamin, "What's New."

30 *Some facets of counterterrorism will benefit:* Nora Bensahel, in discussion with Nina Hachigian, September 2005. These law enforcement and judicial measures are part of the EU's so-called Third Pillar. Nora Bensahel, *The Counterterror Coalitions: Cooperation with Europe, NATO, and the European Union* (Santa Monica: RAND, 2003).

31   *China is not on the front lines:* The Uighurs live in the vast northwestern province of Xingjian. A number of separatist Uighur groups have fought for several decades to establish an independent nation that would be known as East Turkistan and, over the last fifteen years, have killed some two hundred Chinese civilians. David M. Lampton and Richard Daniel Ewing, *The U.S.-China Relationship Facing International Security Crisis* (Washington, D.C.: Nixon Center, 2003), 11. The "War on Terror" has made it easier for China to characterize legitimate Uighur political organizing as terrorist activity.

31   *Nevertheless, Beijing stepped up:* Ibid.

31   *Beijing agreed to freeze:* Jia Qingguo, "Learning to Live with the Hegemon: Evolution of China's Policy Toward the US Since the End of the Cold War," *Journal of Contemporary China* 14, no. 44 (August 2005): 403.

31   *China has acceded to eleven of twelve:* U.N. Secretary-General, Extract from the Report of the Secretary-General on Measures to Eliminate International Terrorism (Doc. A/57/183)," December 10, 2002, http://www.un.org/law/terrorism/terrorism_table_update_12-2002.pdf (accessed November 20, 2005).

31   *Most important, China has signed up:* Lampton and Ewing, *The U.S.-China Relationship,* 8.

31   *"The container is the potential Trojan":* Michael Richardson, "Containing Trojan Horses," *Straits Times* (Singapore), December 8, 2004. Some terrorism experts conclude that Islamic terrorists are unlikely to use this method of delivery, as a valuable weapon would spend too much time outside of their direct control. Jenkins discussion.

31   *Because American ports are vulnerable:* For suggestions on how to improve port security, Stephen Flynn, "U.S. Port Security and the Global War on Terror," *American Interest* 1, no. 1 (Autumn 2005).

31   *Each year over 3.2 million containers:* Richardson, "Containing Trojan Horses"; Russell Barling, "Hong Kong Worries That Stricter Reporting Rules Will Reduce Efficiency," *South China Morning Post,* January 16, 2003.

31   *U.S. customs officials:* "China's Port of Shenzen Joins U.S. Container Security Initiative," globalsecurity.org, June 24, 2005, http://www.globalsecurity.org/security/library/news/2005/06/sec-050624-usia03.htm (accessed September 2, 2007).

31   *During the early stages of the campaign:* Ekaterina Stepanova, "War and Peace Building," *Washington Quarterly* 27, no. 4 (Autumn 2004): 127–36.

Moscow played "a key role" in providing supplies for Afghanistan's Northern Alliance and helped secure bases for U.S. troops in Central Asia.

31 *"unprecedented forms of intelligence sharing":* Alexander Vershbow, "Russia, NATO, and International Organizations" (remarks at the Institute of Scientific Information on Social Sciences, Russian Academy of Sciences, Moscow, May 26, 2003), http://www.usembassy.it/file2003_05/alia/A3052903.htm (accessed October 2, 2005).

31 *To find a foreign jihadist:* Russia's conduct in the intractable battle against the Muslim population in Chechnya, now always couched in the language of the "War on Terror," has led to ongoing human rights abuses. "Russian Federation Must End Torture, Ill-Treatment, 'Disappearances' and Arbitrary Detention in Chechnya," Amnesty International Public Statement, March 14, 2007, http://web.amnesty.org/library/Index/ENGEUR460092007?open&of=ENG-RUS (accessed April 14, 2007).

31 *Bruce Hoffman of Georgetown University:* Bruce Hoffman, "Combating Al Qaeda and the Militant Islamic Threat" (testimony before the House Armed Services Subcommittee on Terrorism, Unconventional Threats and Capabilities, February 16, 2006).

32 *the United States could learn:* Martin I. Wayne, "Inside China's War on Terrorism," Institute for National Strategic Studies, China Security Perspective Series, February 21, 2007, 2.

32 *pivotal powers may also be able:* Angel Rabasa et al., *Beyond Al Qaeda: The Global Jihadist Movement* (Santa Monica: RAND 2006), xxiii.

32 *"treating foreign intelligence services":* Jenkins discussion.

32 *Inadequate sensitivity to local political conditions:* For example, during Operation Rhyme discussed above, British authorities wished that U.S. officials had not been so specific when warning about the attack, as it compromised their surveillance of terror cells in Britain. Eric Lichtblau, "U.S. Warns of High Risk of Qaeda Attack," *New York Times*, August 2, 2004; Amy Waldman and Eric Lipton, "Rounding Up Qaeda Suspects: New Cooperation, New Tensions, New Questions," *New York Times*, August 17, 2004; Justin Davenport, "The Biggest Terror Plot Since 9/11," *Evening Standard*, August 17, 2004.

32 *Governments sometimes take big political hits:* Melissa Eddy, "German lawmakers set up committee to investigate secret agency's role in Iraq war," Associated Press, April 7, 2006.

32 *After all, says Jenkins:* Jenkins discussion.

33 *as an atomic blast in a dense urban area:* One study estimates that a nuclear blast centered in midtown Manhattan would kill, conservatively, on the order of 250,000 people and injure an additional 750,000 others. Michael V. Hynes, John E. Peters, David Orletsky, and David Shlapak, "Homeland Defense: Scenarios Used in the Analysis" (Santa Monica: RAND/AB-671-AF, 2002).

33 *Osama bin Laden has declared:* Osama bin Laden, interviewed by *PBS Frontline,* December 23, 1998, http://www.pbs.org/wgbh/pages/front line/shows/binladen/who/edicts.html (accessed May 13, 2005).

33 *the intelligence community is "extremely concerned":* Matthew Bunn and Anthony Wier, "Securing the Bomb: The New Global Imperatives," Nuclear Threat Initiative (May 2005), 9. In 2001, the CIA reported that al Qaeda "probably had access to nuclear expertise and facilities and that there was a real possibility of the group developing a crude nuclear weapon." Ibid, 10. For further evidence of terrorist interest in nuclear weapons, Graham Allison, *Nuclear Terrorism: The Ultimate Preventable Catastrophe* (New York: Times Books, Henry Holt, 2004), 19–42.

33 *"the need for international cooperation":* Michael Hynes (nonproliferation expert formerly with the RAND Corporation, now at Raytheon), in discussion with Nina Hachigian, October 2005.

33 *"Despite serious setbacks":* Joe Cirincione (vice president for national security, Center for American Progress), in e-mail exchange with Nina Hachigian, August 2006.

34 *Though the U.S. has already spent:* Brian Finlay and Andrew Grotto, *The Race to Secure Russia's Loose Nukes: Progress Since 9-11* (Washington, D.C.: Henry L. Stimson Center and the Center for American Progress, September 2005), 9.

34 *Senior Russian officials confirmed:* Bunn and Wier, "Securing the Bomb."

34 *The fissile material of choice:* In contrast, plutonium metallurgy is a tricky business, and getting plutonium to explode is also technologically complex. James Goodby et al., *Cooperative Threat Reduction for a New Era* (Washington, D.C.: National Defense University, September 2004), 2.

34 *According to a report from the National Defense University:* Finlay and Grotto, *The Race to Secure Russia's Loose Nukes,* 1.

34 *remains inadequately secured:* Goodby et al., *Cooperative Threat Reduction,* 2.

34 *Some 128 civilian nuclear research reactors:* Bunn and Wier, "Securing the Bomb," 15.

34 *The IAEA reports ten incidents:* "Incidents Involving HEU and Pu Confirmed to the ITDB, 1993–2005," International Atomic Energy Agency, http://www.iaea.org/NewsCenter/Features/RadSources/PDF/table1-2005.pdf (accessed March 11, 2007).

34 *In July 2001, for example, Paris police:* "Uranium Seized in France Could Have Made Low Grade Bomb," Nuclear Threat Initiative (July 2001), http://www.nti.org/db/nistraff/2001/20010550.htm (accessed November 11, 2005).

35 *Keeping nuclear materials out:* According to a study by the Lawrence Livermore National Laboratory, some 20 percent of Russian physicists, biologists, and chemists would consider working in countries such as North Korea and Iran. Finlay and Grotto, *The Race to Secure Russia's Loose Nukes,* 43.

35 *Nuclear programs under development:* The chances of detecting a clandestine nuclear program are very much larger—by a factor of five or so—in the early phases when a group is acquiring the materials and building the device than when it's complete and headed toward its target. Hynes discussion.

35 *"wouldn't need a Manhattan Project":* Ibid.

35 *Since the mid-1990s, China has greatly improved:* For more on the evolution of China's export control mechanisms, Evan S. Medeiros, *Chasing the Dragon: Assessing China's System of Export Controls for WMD-Related Goods and Technologies* (Santa Monica: RAND, 2005).

36 *Administration officials have frequently praised:* For example, John R. Bolton, *"Stopping the Spread of Weapons of Mass Destruction in the Asia-Pacific Region: The Role of the Proliferation Security Initiative"* (speech by John R. Bolton, U.S. Department of State, October 27, 2004).

36 *In August 2006, Tokyo police:* "Japan Arrests 5 in Iran Nuclear Case," United Press International, August 26, 2006.

36 *While much work remains to be done:* Finlay and Grotto, *The Race to Secure Russia's Loose Nukes,* 6.

36 *For the first time in a decade:* Nikolai Sokov, "CNS Analysis of the Russian Government's White Paper on WMD Nonproliferation," Center for Nonproliferation Studies (July 25, 2006), http://cns.miis.edu/pubs/week/060726.htm (accessed February 21, 2007).

36   *Russia is also the cofounder:* Abby Dell, "Anti-Nuclear Terrorism Strate-
     gies Discussed," *Arms Control Today,* July/August 2007; "Showing Initia-
     tive; Loose Nukes," *Economist,* June 16, 2007.

36   *The Europeans are also engaged:* Finlay and Grotto, *The Race to Secure
     Russia's Loose Nukes,* 47.

36   *India too has been increasingly willing:* C. Raja Mohan, *Crossing the Rubi-
     con* (New York: Palgrave Macmillan, 2003), 18.

36   *While it undermines the strength of the NPT:* R. Nicholas Burns, "India
     and Pakistan: On the Heels of President Bush's Visit" (remarks at Her-
     itage Lecture No. 927, March 13, 2006), www.heritage.org/Research/
     AsiaandthePacific/h1927.cfm (accessed August 25, 2006); Henry Sokol-
     ski, "Fissile Isn't Facile," *Wall Street Journal,* February 21, 2006.

37   *"U.S. policy itself":* Cirincione e-mail.

37   *In recent years, America has failed to ratify:* George Perkovich, "Bush's
     Nuclear Revolution: A Regime Change in Non-Proliferation," *Foreign
     Affairs* (March/April 2003).

37   *far from emphasizing disarmament:* James Clay Moltz, "Practical Steps
     for Improving U.S. Nonproliferation Leadership, Issue Brief," Center for
     Nonproliferation Studies (June 2005).

37   *The net effect was to slow the momentum:* Jenni Rissanen, "BWC Update
     a Turning Point to Nowhere? BWC in Trouble as US Turns Its Back on
     Verification Protocol," *Disarmament Diplomacy* 59 (July/August 2001),
     http://www.acronym.org.uk/dd/dd59/59bwc.htm (accessed December
     10, 2006).

37   *infectious diseases are the number one killer:* Michael Osterholm, "Prepar-
     ing for the Next Pandemic," *Foreign Affairs* (July/August 2005): 25;
     George Armelagos, "The Viral Superhighway," *Sciences* 38, no. 1 (1998).

37   *AIDS has already killed:* "Report on the Global AIDS Epidemic: Global
     Facts and Figures," UNAIDS (2006), http://data.unaids.org/pub/Glob
     alReport/2006/200605-FS_globalfactsfigures_en.pdf (accessed January
     3, 2007).

37   *A 2000 U.S. National Intelligence Estimate on the threat:* "The Global
     Infectious Disease Threat and Its Implications for the United States,"
     National Intelligence Council, National Intelligence Estimate (January
     2000), http://www.dni.gov/nic/special_globalinfectious.html (accessed
     March 11, 2007).

38   *During the last major "Spanish flu" influenza pandemic:* Laurie Garrett,
     "The Next Pandemic?," *Foreign Affairs* (July/August 2005) 5.

39 *In eighteen months:* Ibid., 5.

38 *The global death toll:* Ibid., 6.

38 *Recently linked to birds:* Ibid., 5–6.

39 *In 2007, for the first time in history:* "Urbanization: A Majority in Cities," United Nations Population Fund (UNFPA), December 15, 2005, http://www.unfpa.org/pds/urbanization.htm (accessed August 12, 2006).

39 *Now some 800 million people:* Stacey Knobler, Adel Mahmoud, Stanley Lemon, Leslie Pray, eds., *The Impact of Globalization on Infectious Disease Emergence and Control: Exploring the Consequences and Opportunities, Workshop Summary—Forum on Microbial Threats* (Washington, D.C.: National Academies Press, 2006) 23, http://www.nap.edu/catalog/11588.html (accessed May 22, 2007). Also, Jennifer Brower and Peter Chalk, *The Global Threat of New and Reemerging Infectious Diseases* (Santa Monica: RAND, 2003), 14.

39 *Disease-carrying mosquitoes:* Stacey Knobler, Adel Mahmoud, Stanley Lemon, Leslie Pray, eds., *The Impact of Globalization on Infectious Disease Emergence and Control: Exploring the Consequences and Opportunities, Workshop Summary—Forum on Microbial Threats* (Washington, D.C.: National Academies Press, 2006), http://www.nap.edu/catalog/11588.html (accessed August 25, 2006).

40 *The six-month SARS epidemic virtually shut down:* Osterholm, "Preparing for the Next Pandemic," 28.

40 *These travelers, in turn, seeded outbreaks:* Elizabeth M. Prescott, "SARS: A Warning," *Survival* 45, no. 3 (Autumn): 207–26.

40 *Once SARS emerged in rural China:* Osterholm, "Preparing for the Next Pandemic," 28.

40 *Another flu pandemic "cannot be avoided":* Ibid., 37.

40 *Dr. Nancy Cox, the chief influenza scientist:* "Responding to the Avian Influenza Pandemic Threat," Communicable Disease Surveillance and Response Global Influenza Programme, World Health Organization (2005), http://www.who.int/csr/resources/publications/influenza/WHO_CDS_CSR_GIP_05_8-EN.pdf (accessed October 1, 2005); "CDC Director Gerberding Cites Avian Flu as 'Very Ominous' Threat," American Association for the Advancement of Science (February 21, 2005), http://www.aaas.org/news/releases/2005/0221flu.shtml (accessed October 8, 2005).

40 *"This is the worst flu virus":* Andrew Jack, "Feeling the Strain," *Financial Times*, September 2, 2006.

40 *A worst-case scenario predicts sixteen million:* Garrett, "The Next Pandemic?," 4.

40 *The World Bank estimates an $800 billion:* Stephanie Nebehay, "Experts Warn of Human, Financial Bird Flu Toll," Reuters, November 7, 2005.

41 *"In short order":* Osterholm, "Preparing for the Next Pandemic," 31.

41 *Developed countries are only as secure:* Prescott, "SARS," 213.

41 *Commercial development along their traditional migration routes:* Garrett, "The Next Pandemic?," 10.

41 *In the case of A(H5N1):* "Transmission of Influenza A Viruses Between Animals and People," Centers for Disease Control and Prevention (October 17, 2005), http://www.cdc.gov/flu/avian/gen-info/transmission .htm (accessed August 25, 2006). Recent reports also indicate that human-to-human transmission may be less rare than previously thought. Donald G. McNeil, Jr., "Human Flu Transfers May Exceed Reports," *New York Times,* June 4, 2006.

41 *With the largest rural population in the world:* "World Urbanization Prospects, Data Tables and Highlights, 2003," U.N. Department of Economic and Social Affairs, http://www.un.org/esa/population/publica tions/wup2003/2003WUPHighlights.pdf#search=rural%20population %20percentages%20world (accessed November 15, 2005).

42 *China tried to cover up:* Still, in 2006, the Chinese Ministry of Agriculture handed over avian flu samples to the World Health Organization after years of delay only after a Chinese doctor was elected head of the WHO. Mary Ann Benitez, Kristine Kwok, and Cary Huang, "Beijing Ends Impasse over Bird Flu Samples; Virus Sent to US a Day After Chan Is Elected WHO Chief," *South China Morning Post,* November 11, 2006.

42 *American and Chinese officials had repeated meetings:* "China-US Bird Flu Seminar in Beijing Discusses Cooperation Mechanism," Xinhua News, November 2, 2005.

42 *China co-hosted a major avian flu:* The World Bank, International Pledging Conference on Avian and Human Influenza, Beijing, January 17–18, 2006, http://web.worldbank.org/WBSITE/EXTERNAL/PROJECTS/0,, contentMDK:207765526~pagePK:41367~piPK:51533~theSitePK:409 41,00.html (accessed March 11, 2007).

42 *The facility would become Asia's:* Andrew Yeh, "China to Boost Funds to Fight Lethal Diseases," *Financial Times,* April 10, 2006.

42 *Only effective government can prevent a pandemic:* Matt Pottinger, "Why

SARS Didn't Return," *Far Eastern Economic Review* 167, no. 14 (April 8, 2004).

42   *In 2005, China slaughtered millions:* Keith Bradsher, "Poultry Power: China, with Huge Flocks, Is at Big Flu Risk," *New York Times*, October 18, 2005.

43   *One of the teams that traced bats:* Lawrence K. Altman, "Two Teams Identify Chinese Bat as SARS Virus Hiding Place," *New York Times*, September 30, 2005.

43   *In general, the more states that go nuclear:* For more on the argument that a larger number of nuclear states makes the world less safe, and the counterarguments, Scott D. Sagan and Kenneth N. Waltz, *The Spread of Nuclear Weapons: A Debate Renewed* (New York: Norton, 2003).

44   *"the wicked nature":* "N. Korea's Statement in Full," *BBC News*, February 10, 2005, http://news.bbc.co.uk/2/hi/asia-pacific/4252515.stm (accessed February 21, 2007).

45   *"adversely impact":* John Holdren (remarks at the Global Challenges for U.S. Energy Policy: Economic, Environmental, and Security Risks, Brookings Institution, March 2004), http://www.brookings.edu/comm/op=ed/20040305environment.htm (accessed August 5, 2006). Eleven of the last twelve years (1995–2006) rank among the twelve warmest years since scientists began measuring global surface temperature in 1850. "Climate Change 2007: The Physical Science Basis: Summary for Policy Makers," Intergovernmental Panel on Climate Change (February 5, 2007), 5, http://www.ipcc.ch/SPM2feb07.pdf (accessed February 12, 2007). For more on global warming and its causes, Tim Flannery, *The Weather Makers* (New York: Atlantic Monthly Press, 2005).

45   *"could create risks":* Sir Nicholas Stern, "Stern Review on the Economics of Climate Change" (February 2007), http://www.hm-treasury.gov.uk/independent_reviews/stern_review_economics_climate_change/stern review_index.cfm (accessed March 3, 2007).

45   *American lives are directly at risk:* Thomas Karl and Kevin Trenberth, "Modern Global Climate Change," *Science* 302, no. 5651 (December 5, 2003): 1719–23; David Doniger, "It'd Be Cooler if We'd Lead," Center for American Progress (December 9, 2003), http://www.americanprogress.org/site/pp.asp?c=biJRJ8OVF&b=13866 (accessed August 28, 2006).

45   *The melting of Greenland's ice sheet:* Stefan Lovgren, "Warming to Cause Catastrophic Rise in Sea Level?," *National Geographic News*, April 26,

2004, http://news.nationalgeographic.com/news/2004/04/0420_0404
20_earthday.html (accessed August 28, 2006).

45 *That melting is happening much more quickly:* John Collins Rudolf, "The
Warming of Greenland," *New York Times*, January 16, 2007.

45 *American security could also be threatened: National Security and the
Threat of Climate Change* (Washington, D.C.: CNA Corporation, 2007),
http://securityandclimate.cna.org/report/National%20Security%20
and%20the%20Threat%20of%20Climate%20Change.pdf (accessed
April 16, 2007).

45 *Unlike the rest of the world's rich countries:* "A Lost Opportunity for Environmental Leadership: U.S. Must Lead the Charge on Climate Change,"
Center for American Progress (March 27, 2007), http://www.american
progress.org/issues/2007/03/climate_change.html (accessed May 16,
2007).

45 *As long as the U.S. resists:* Bryan Walsh, "The Impact of Asia's Giants,"
Time, March 26, 2006.

46 *NASA scientist James Hansen:* "Warming Expert: Only Decade Left to
Act in Time," *MSNBC News Services*, September 14, 2006, http://msnbc
.msn.com/id/14834318/ (accessed September 21, 2006).

47 *"an immense amount of experience":* Joseph Romm (former principal
deputy assistant secretary for energy efficiency and renewable energy,
U.S. Department of Energy; senior fellow, Center for American Progress,
and author of *Hell and High Water: Global Warming—The Solution and
the Politics*), in discussion with Nina Hachigian, August 2006.

47 *"blessed among the nations":* Jules Jusserand as quoted in Stephen M.
Walt, *Taming American Power* (New York: Norton 2005), 39.

47 *As Figure 1.3 suggests:* As the diagram shows, America's aircraft carriers
are substantially larger than almost all the other nation's aircraft carriers. The Navy likes to call the big Nimitz class carriers "4.5 acres of sovereign and mobile American territory." There are eleven active carriers
now. The John F. Kennedy was decommissioned, leaving the U.S. with
one conventionally powered aircraft carrier, the Kitty Hawk, and ten
nuclear-powered carriers: the Enterprise and nine Nimitz-class vessels.
A 10th Nimitz-class carrier, the George H.W. Bush, has been launched,
but not yet commissioned. It will be commissioned in November 2008,
but at that point the Kitty Hawk will have been decommissioned, so
America will continue to have eleven carriers (and will go down to ten in
around 2013, when the Enterprise is decommissioned, until the first of a

new carrier class, the Gerald R. Ford, is commissioned in 2015). Roger Cliff (senior political scientist at the RAND Corporation) in discussion with Nina Hachigian, June 2007.

48 *Even if pivotal powers coalesced:* Josef Joffe, "Defying History and Theory," in *America Unrivaled: The Future of the Balance of Power,* ed. G. John Ikenberry (Ithaca: Cornell University Press, 2002), 163.

48 *The U.S. spends more on its military each year:* "US Military Spending vs. the World," Center for Arms Control and Non-Proliferation (February 5, 2007), http://www.armscontrolcenter.org/archives/002279.php (accessed March 3, 2007). Russia's total expenditures in 2004 were 93 billion. *CIA World Factbook 2005* (Washington, D.C.: Central Intelligence Agency, 2005).

48 *Washington's nonwar military budget:* "Russian government adopts preliminary 2008–2010 budget parameters," *Russian News and Information Agency RIA Novosti,* March 22, 2007, http://en.rian.ru/russia/20070322/62421395.html<http://www.cbr.ru/eng/analytics/Rus0706e.pdf> (accessed March 20, 2007); "Fiscal 2008 Department of Defense Budget Press Release," U.S. Department of Defense (February 5, 2007), http://www.dod.gov/comptroller/defbudget/fy2008/2008_Budget_Roll out_Release.pdf (accessed March 28, 2007).

China's official defense budget for 2007 is about $45 billion, but most U.S. analysts believe the actual number is quite a bit higher. Jim Yardley and David Lague, "Beijing Accelerates Its Military Spending," *New York Times,* March 5, 2007. The real figure is probably in the range of $100 billion, about 20 percent of America's. "Annual Report to Congress: Military Power of the People's Republic of China," U.S. Department of Defense (2007). http://www.defenselink.mil/pubs/pdf/070523-China-military-powerfinal.pdf (accessed June 5, 2007). For more on China's defense spending, James C. Mulvenon et al., *Chinese Responses to U.S. Military Transformation and Implications for the Department of Defense* (Santa Monica: RAND, 2006), 19.

48 *"China has the greatest potential":* "Quadrennial Defense Review Report," U.S. Department of Defense (February 6, 2006), 29, http://www.defenselink.mil/qdr/report/Report20060203.pdf (accessed March 12, 2007).

48 *More than half of Americans surveyed:* "The New Face of Globalization," *Economist,* November 19, 2005.

48 *In terms of its nuclear arsenal:* "Annual Report to Congress: Military

Power of the People's Republic of China," U.S. Department of Defense (2007), 18–20.

49   *In comparison, though, the U.S. has:* Amy F. Wolf, "U.S. Strategic Nuclear Forces: Background, Developments, and Issues," Congressional Research Service (October 17, 2006), http://www.fas.org/sgp/crs/nuke/RL33640.pdf (accessed April 12, 2007).

50   *Its mothballed aircraft carrier:* The PLA has been refurbishing one of the other two carriers—the Varyag—for as-yet-unclear purposes. The latest DoD report on Chinese military power has a good summary of China's aircraft carrier situation. "Annual Report to Congress: Military Power of the People's Republic of China," U.S. Department of Defense (2007), 24. If China decided to build a carrier, it would have its first in 2020, and would be inviting an expensive naval arms race with the U.S. that it knows it could not win. Robert S. Ross, "Assessing the China Threat," *National Interest* (Fall 2005): 86.

50   *Though with the help of Russia:* James Hackett, ed., *The Military Balance 2007* (Abingdon, U.K.: Routledge Journals for the International Institute for Strategic Studies, 2007), 348.

50   *The United States has fifty-five:* "Submarine Forces, United States," Jane's Underwater Warfare Systems, Jane's Information Group (March 1, 2005), http://juws.janes.com/public/juws/index.shtml (accessed January 3, 2007).

50   *China has only about four hundred:* The exact makeup of China's fighter aircraft inventory is debated, but, by one count, includes 116 Su-27 air-to-air fighters, seventy-three Su-30s, and about sixty-two J-10s. Hackett, ed., *The Military Balance 2007*, 350.

50   *"The idea that China":* Military analyst at the RAND Corporation, in discussion with Nina Hachigian, October 2005.

50   *China appears to be spending increasing percentages:* For more on the motivations behind China's modernization, Joseph W. Prueher, Harold Brown, and Adam Segal, *Chinese Military Power* (New York: Council on Foreign Relations, 2004); Michael D. Swaine, "China's Regional Military Power," in David Shambaugh, ed., *Power Shift: China and Asia's New Dynamics* (Berkeley: University of California Press, 2005); David Shambaugh and Richard Yang, eds., *China's Military in Transition* (Oxford: Oxford University Press, 1997); Andrew and Nathan and Robert S. Ross, *The Great Wall and the Empty Fortress: China's Search for Security* (New York: Norton, 1997).

51 *Using sensible assumptions about economic growth:* Based on estimates using market exchange rates. Keith Crane et al., *Modernizing China's Military: Opportunities and Constraints* (Santa Monica: RAND, 2005), 229; "Annual Report to Congress: Military Power of the People's Republic of China," U.S. Department of Defense (2005), 21.

51 *Russian newspapers have reported malnutrition:* Eugene B. Rumer and Celeste A. Wallander, "Russia: Power in Weakness," *Washington Quarterly 27*, no. 1 (Winter 2003): 60.

51 *To say that big countries cannot:* This phenomenon is discussed in the 2005 National Defense Strategy. "National Defense Strategy of the United States of America," U.S. Department of Defense (March 2005), http://www.dami.army.pentagon.mil/offices/dami-zxg/National%20Defense%20Strategy%20Mar05-U.pdf (accessed August 29, 2006).

2. INDIRECT THREATS: THE QUEASY FEELING

54 *"the sheer volume of diplomacy":* David Shambaugh, "China's New Engagement with the Region," *Wall Street Journal*, February 10, 2004. For more on China's diplomacy in Asia, David Shambaugh, ed., *Power Shift: China and Asia's New Dynamics* (Berkeley: University of California Press, 2005); Robert G. Sutter, *China's Rise in Asia: Promises and Perils* (London: Roman & Littlefield, 2005); David Shambaugh, "China Engages Asia," *International Security* 29, no. 3 (Winter 2004/2005).

54 *"expanding multilateral organizations":* Evan Medeiros, in discussion with Nina Hachigian, February 2007.

55 *"China is running circles around us":* J. Stapleton Roy (remarks at the launch of the John L. Thornton China Center at the Brookings Institution), September 20, 2005.

55 *"China, once a revolutionary threat":* "Power at Stake," *Australian*, October 25, 2003.

55 *Asian neighbors see China's economic growth:* "China's Neighbors Worry About Its Growing Military Strength," Six Nation Pew Global Attitudes Survey, Pew Global Attitudes Project (September 21, 2006).

55 *First, China's growing influence in Asia:* Sutter, *China's Rise in Asia*, 17.

55 *In some cases, as Andrew Hoehn:* Andrew Hoehn, in discussion with Nina Hachigian, October 2006.

55 *Over time, China's military modernization:* Despite the fact that Australia is a staunch American ally, for example, its foreign minister made

it clear publicly in 2004 that the United States could not assume Australia would automatically help the U.S. defend Taiwan against Chinese aggression. Mohan Malik, "The China Factor in Australia-US Relations," *China Brief* 5, no. 8 (April 12, 2005), http://www.jamestown .org/publications_details.php?volume_id=408&issue_id=329&article_ id=2369588 (accessed August 15, 2006).

55 *"whether China chooses peace or coercion"*: Colin Powell as quoted by Richard N. Haass (remarks to the National Committee on U.S.-China Relations, December 5, 2002), http://www.state.gov/s/p/rem/15687 .htm (accessed January 4, 2006).

56 *"China's rise in Asia"*: Robert Sutter, *China's Rise: Implications for U.S. Leadership in Asia* (Washington, D.C.: East-West Center Washington, 2006), 64, http://www.eastwestcenter.org/stored/pdfs/PS021.pdf (accessed March 28, 2007).

56 *China's diplomacy and trade overtures:* Ibid., 63.

56 *"the top security position"*: Robert Sutter, "Why Rising China Can't Dominate Asia" (testimony before the U.S.-China Economic and Security Review Commission Hearing "China's Role in the World: Is China a Responsible Stakeholder?," August 3, 2006).

56 *The only places where Chinese and Indian companies:* For a fuller discussion of China's energy policy, David Zweig and Bi Jianhai, "China's Global Hunt for Energy," *Foreign Affairs* (September/October 2005); Erica Downs, "The Chinese Energy Security Debate," *China Quarterly* 177 (March 2004).

57 *"We have been producing"*: Zweig and Bi, "China's Global Hunt for Energy," 33.

57 *An August 2006 deal has China helping:* Jonathan Watts, "Chavez Says China Deal 'Great Wall' Against U.S.," *Guardian*, August 25, 2006, http://www.guardian.co.uk/venezuela/story/0,,1858631,00.html?gursr c=rss&feed=1 (accessed January 3, 2007).

57 *Chinese investment in Africa:* Harry Broadman, *Africa's Silk Road: China and India's New Frontier* (Washington, D.C.: World Bank, 2007), 91–104.

57 *two-way trade increased to nearly $55 billion:* Yaroslav Trofimov, "In Africa, China's Expansion Begins to Stir Resentment," *Wall Street Journal*, February 2, 2007.

57 *Beijing predicts that Chinese foreign direct investment:* Neil Ford, "Power

Struggle: Boosting Competition for Africa's Energy," *Jane's Intelligence Review* (January 1, 2007).

57 *"vital to the stability":* Princeton N. Lyman, "China's Rising Role in Africa" (presentation to the U.S.-China Commission, July 21, 2005), http://www.cfr.org/publication/8436/ (accessed January 3, 2007).

57 *Its president cautioned Beijing:* Françoise Crouigneau and Richard Haiult, "World Bank Hits at China Over Lending," *Financial Times*, October 23, 2006.

58 *In sum, China complicates existing U.S. relationships:* Dr. Ernest J. Wilson III, "China's Role in the World: Is China a Responsible Stakeholder in Africa?" (testimony before the U.S.-China Economic and Security Review Commission Hearing, August 3–4, 2006).

58 *"a more competitive":* Jeffrey Gentleman, "The World: Across Africa, A Sense That U.S. Power Isn't So Super," *New York Times*, December 24, 2006.

58 *Having Russian backing makes some countries:* Eugene B. Rumer and Celeste A. Wallander, "Russia: Power in Weakness," *Washington Quarterly* 27, no. 1 (Winter 2003): 59.

58 *"spending billions of dollars":* "President Urges Nation to Counter Enemies' Cultural Invasion," Iranian Republic News Agency (Tehran), January 10, 2007, http://www.irna.com/en/news/view/line-24/0701109098144106.htm (accessed February 21, 2007).

58 *If Tehran some years from now:* William Broad and David Sanger, "With Eye on Iran, Rivals Also Want Nuclear Power," *New York Times*, April 15, 2007.

58 *Because American companies are prohibited:* "China Is Now Iran's Biggest Energy Buyer, Europe Steps Up Oil Activity," *Asharq Al Awsat*, January 20, 2005; "Iran: Country Analysis Brief," Energy Information Administration (August 2006), http://www.eia.doe.gov/emeu/cabs/Iran/Background.html (accessed February 21, 2007).

59 *Russia has been selling billions of dollars of weapons:* Ali A. Jalali, "The Strategic Partnership of Russia and Iran," *Parameters* 31, no. 4 (Winter 2001/2002): 98–112.

59 *In 2005, European governments provided $18 billion:* Steven R. Weisman, "Europe Resists U.S. on Curbing Ties with Iran," *New York Times*, January 30, 2007.

59 *In 2006, Washington sanctioned six Chinese:* Wade Boese, "U.S. Sanctions

Nine Companies for Iran Trade," *Arms Control Today* (January/February 2006), http://www.armscontrol.org/act/2006_01-02/JANFEB-sanctions.asp?print (accessed January 30, 2007); Shirley A. Kan, "China and Proliferation of Weapons of Mass Destruction and Missiles: Policy Issues," Congressional Research Service (January 6, 2006).

59 *Russia and China have weighed in:* For more on China's Iran policy, Dingli Shen, "Iran's Nuclear Ambitions Test China's Wisdom," *Washington Quarterly* 29, no. 2 (Spring 2006): 55.

60 *China and Russia may want to foster a strategic partnership:* Subodh Atal, "The New Great Game," *National Interest* 81 (Fall 2005): 103.

60 *Despite its growing relationship with the United States:* Ibid., 104.

60 *"Europe might also see China":* "Report of the Working Group on Grand Strategic Choices," Princeton Project on National Security (2005), 20.

60 *Both claim the right:* For more on resource competition in the East China Sea, "Energy Policy Act 2005, Section 1837: National Security Review of International Energy Requirements," U.S. Department of Energy (February 2006), 29.

61 *China has also deployed one thousand peacekeepers:* "A Quintet, Anyone?," *Economist*, January 13, 2007, 37.

61 *India played a vital:* Xenia Dormandy, "Is India, or Will It Be, a Responsible Stakeholder?," *Washington Quarterly* 30, no. 3 (Summer 2007): 120.

61 *Similarly, now that India's economy has taken off:* C. Raja Mohan, "India and the Balance of Power," *Foreign Affairs* (July/August 2006): 20.

62 *"U.S. treatment of allies":* Eric Heginbotham and Christopher Twomey, "America's Bismarckian Asia Policy," *Current History* 104, no. 683 (September 2005): 244.

62 *The U.S. should reinsert itself in the economic growth:* Charlene Barshefsky (former U.S. trade representative), in discussion with the authors, June 2006.

62 *America must be able to defend itself from attacks:* "America's National Interests," Commission on America's National Interests (July 2000), 52, http://www.nixoncenter.org/publications/monographs/nationalinterests.htm (accessed March 23, 2006).

63 *Much of the increase in spending:* David C. Gompert and James Dobbins, "Outside View: A Far Too Costly Pentagon," United Press International,

February 27, 2006; Max Boot, "The Wrong Weapons for the Long War," *Los Angeles Times*, February 8, 2006, http://www.cfr.org/publica tion/9803/wrong_weapons_for_the_long_war.html (accessed August 29, 2006). For budget numbers, Defense Department fact sheet, Office of Management and Budget, http://www.whitehouse.gov/omb/budget/ fy2007/defense.html (accessed January 3, 2007).

64 *The department's base proposed budget:* Defense Department fact sheet.

64 *An important way to prepare:* Thomas S. Szayna et al., *The Emergence of Peer Competitors: A Framework for Analysis* (Santa Monica: RAND, 2001), 2, fn 3; Lawrence Korb, "The Best Weapons Money Can Buy," *Los Angeles Times*, August 13, 2005, http://www.americanprogress.org/ site/apps/nl/content3.asp?c=biJRJ8OVF&b=681083&ct=1327177 (accessed August 29, 2006).

64 *The Pentagon has not made anywhere:* Kori Schake, "Jurassic Pork," *New York Times*, February 9, 2006. Also "Measuring the Moment: Innovation, National Security and Economic Competitiveness," Task Force on the Future of American Innovation (November 2006), 5, http://future ofinnovation.org/PDF/BII-FINAL-HighRes-11-14-06_nocover.pdf (accessed July 11, 2007).

64 *"It's always been bad":* Leslie Wayne, "Spending More for Less Is Frequent in Weapons Projects Since 9/11," *New York Times*, July 11, 2006.

64 *The Government Accountability Office determined in 2006:* The poster child for waste is the Comanche helicopter, into which the Pentagon poured nearly $7 billion before scrapping it in 2004. Liz Sidoti, "Congress, Pentagon Rein in Weapons Costs," Associated Press, October 1, 2005.

64 *Contractors involved in the F-22:* Wayne, "Spending More for Less."

65 *Other necessary national security:* For specific recommendations for U.S. counterterror policy, Daniel Benjamin and Steven Simon, *The Next Attack* (New York: Holt, 2005), Part III.

65 *Nor . . . will it be easy politically to make the necessary shift:* For more on the politics of national security budgets, Gordon Adams, "The Politics of National Security Budgets," Policy Analysis Brief, Stanley Foundation (February 2007), http://www.stanleyfoundation.org/publications/ pab/pab07natsecbudget.pdf (accessed April 9, 2007).

3. THE BATTLE OF IDEAS?

66 *Here we focus on the principles:* Alexis de Tocqueville, *Democracy in America* (New York: New American Library, 2001). Written after his travels across the U.S. in 1830–1831.

66 *In the wake of 9/11, the federal government:* "H.R. 3162—USA Patriot Act of 2001: Section 215. Access to Records and Other Items Under the Foreign Intelligence Surveillance Act," United States Congress (2001). Of particular concern are provisions that allow the FBI to gather data from an individual's library and personal records (including medical) without prior court approval, and restrict those served with such an order from disclosing it. Several of these provisions are being challenged in court. For more on civil liberties in the post-9/11 world, Richard C. Leone and Greg Anrig, eds. *Liberty Under Attack: Reclaiming Our Freedoms in an Age of Terror* (New York: Public Affairs, 2007).

67 *"content merely to stand":* Robert J. Art, *A Grand Strategy for America* (Ithaca: Cornell University Press, 2003), 70.

67 *And even the Russians:* Dmitri Trenin (deputy director, Carnegie Moscow Center), in discussion with Mona Sutphen, October 24, 2006.

67 *Most European governments spend:* "Public Social Expenditure as a % of GDP," Organization for Economic Cooperation and Development (Social Expenditure Database, 2006).

68 *The export of liberal democracy:* Josef Joffe, *Uberpower: The Imperial Temptation of America* (New York: Norton, 2006), 46.

68 *U.S. policies to this end have fallen:* Ibid., 114.

68 *In America's earliest days:* Thomas Jefferson, "Inaugural Address" (March 4, 1801). President Jefferson captured the sentiment of the period with his oft-quoted approach to U.S. foreign affairs, "peace, commerce, and honest friendship with all nations, entangling alliances with none."

68 *although the expansionist impulse:* Robert Kagan, *Dangerous Nation: America's Place in the World from Its Earliest Days to the Dawn of the Twentieth Century* (New York: Knopf, 2006).

68 *By the eve of World War I:* President Woodrow Wilson, "Address to Joint Session of Congress, Sixty-Fifth Congress, 1st Session, Senate Document No. 5" (April 1917).

68 *Since the end of World War II:* "Presidential Inaugural Addresses," Amer-

ican Presidency Project, University of California at Santa Barbara, http://www.presidency.ucsb.edu/index.php (accessed February 21, 2007).

68 *Over the years, the United States has moved:* Henry R. Nau, *Identity and Power in American Foreign Policy* (Ithaca: Cornell University Press, 2002), 11 and Chapter 3; Monten, "The Roots of the Bush Doctrine," 114–17.

68 *"If Americans know one thing for certain":* Michael Hirsh, *At War with Ourselves* (Oxford: Oxford University Press, 2003), 159.

69 *Later, Jimmy Carter focused on promoting:* "Country Report on Human Rights Practices 2005, Overview and Acknowledgement," U.S. Department of State, http://www.state.gov/g/drl/rls/hrrpt/2005/61551.htm (accessed May 7, 2007).

69 *Ronald Reagan founded the National Endowment for Democracy:* "About Us," National Endowment for Democracy Web site, http://www.ned .org/about/about.html (accessed January 3, 2007).

69 *At the end of the Cold War, Bill Clinton:* James Dobbins, "Haiti: A Case Study in Post–Cold War Peacekeeping" (remarks at the Institute for the Study of Diplomacy Conference on Diplomacy and the Use of Force, September 21, 2005).

69 *"the survival of liberty":* George W. Bush, "Inaugural Address" (January 20, 2005).

69 *Advocates of the "democratic peace" theory:* For arguments supporting the "democratic peace theory," Randall Schweller, "Domestic Structure and Preventive War: Are Democracies More Pacific?," *World Politics* 44, no. 2 (January 1992): 235–70; David Lake, "Powerful Pacifists: Democratic States and War," *American Political Science Review* 87, no. 1 (March 1992): 2–37; John Owen, "How Liberalism Produces Democratic Peace," *International Security* 19, no. 2 (Fall 1994): 87–126; Michael Ward and Kristian Gleditsch, "Democratizing for Peace," *American Political Science Review* 92, no. 1 (March 1998): 51–61. For a debate between detractors and proponents, *Debating the Democratic Peace*, Michael E. Brown, Sean M. Lynn-Jones, and Steven E. Miller, eds. (Cambridge: MIT Press, 1996); Bruce Russett, Christopher Layne, David E. Spiro, and Michael W. Doyle, "The Democratic Peace," *International Security* 19, no. 4 (Spring 1985): 164–84.

69 *Others believe that liberalism is an antidote:* "Declassified Key Judgments of the National Intelligence Estimate 'Trends in Global Terrorism: Im-

plications for the United States,' " Office of the Director of National Intelligence (April 2006), www.dni.gov/press_releases/Declassified_NIE_Key_Judgments.pdf (accessed July 11, 2007).

69 *Yet others focus on more philosophical motivations:* Monten, "The Roots of the Bush Doctrine," 120–23.

69 *"unlike most other nations":* Charles Kupchan (professor of international affairs, Georgetown University, and senior fellow and director of European studies, Council on Foreign Relations), in discussion with Mona Sutphen, September 14, 2006.

69 *On the one hand, bringing democracy to other countries:* "The United States and the Rise of China and India: Results of a 2006 Multination Survey of Public Opinion," Chicago Council on Global Affairs (October 2006), 17, 18, 30, http://www.thechicagocouncil.org/UserFiles/File/Glo balViews06Final.pdf (accessed March 23, 2007).

69 *On the other, Americans clearly:* Ibid.

70 *For the most part, Americans:* Art, *A Grand Strategy for America*, 69–71.

70 *We can only hope:* For their part, a decisive majority of Americans reject using force to install democratic governments. "The United States and the Rise of China and India," 30.

70 *The EU is a staunch promoter of shared values:* "The EU's Human Rights and Democratisation Policy," European Commission (February 2006), http://ec.europa.eu/comm/external_relations/human_rights/intro/ind ex.htm (accessed March 23, 2006).

70 *"the most enduring example":* C. Raja Mohan, *Crossing the Rubicon* (New York: Palgrave Macmillan, 2003), 58.

71 *Delhi may take a lower-key approach:* Ashley Tellis (senior associate, Carnegie Endowment for International Peace), in discussion with Nina Hachigian, October 2006.

71 *and India is warming:* C. Raja Mohan, "Balancing Interests and Values: India's Struggle with Democracy Promotion," *Washington Quarterly* 30, no. 3 (Summer 2007): 99–115.

71 *Recently, Delhi:* Ibid., 110.

71 *Another positive trend is the work of Japanese NGOs:* Emily Perkin, "NGOs as Political Actors: A Japanese Approach?," Overseas Development Institute, November 30, 2006, http://www.reliefweb.int/rw/rwb. nsf/db900SID/KHII-6WA9EM?OpenDocument (accessed January 3, 2007).

71 *"The Chinese communist party today":* David Shambaugh, "Return to

the Middle Kingdom?," in Shambaugh, ed., *Power Shift: China and Asia's New Dynamics* (Berkeley: University of California Press, 2005), 25.

71 *"Beijing does not seek to spread":* Bates Gill (Freeman Chair in China Studies, Center for Strategic and International Studies), in discussion with Nina Hachigian, June 2006.

71 *The same is true for Russia:* Ariel Cohen, "Putin's Legacy and United Russia's New Ideology," Backgrounder No. 1940, Heritage Foundation (June 2006), http://www.heritage.org/Research/RussiaandEurasia/bg 1940.cfm (accessed February 21, 2007).

72 *First is the idea that as China's alternative economic development model:* Joshua Cooper Ramo, "The Beijing Consensus," Foreign Policy Centre (May 2004), 11–12. The approach articulated by China is said to emphasize an innovation-led economy; a development plan that ensures the equitable distribution of the benefits of growth; and finally, a modicum of political and economic independence.

72 *Some argue that under the banner:* Georgie Anne Geyer, "Eyes on the China Model," *Washington Times*, April 22, 2006.

73 *Its Confucius Institutes teach Mandarin:* Raymond Li, "Putonghua Becomes a Top Export Commodity," *South China Morning Post*, November 14, 2006.

73 *Democracy theorists have long argued:* Cynthia McClintock, review of *The Democratic Century*, by Seymour Martin Lipset and Jason Lakin, *Journal of Democracy* 6, no. 2 (April 2005): 163; Charles Boix and Susan Stokes, "Endogenous Democratization," *World Politics* 55 (July 2003): 517–49; Adam Przeworski, Michael E. Alvarez, Jose Antonio Cheibub, and Fernando Limongi, *Democracy and Development: Political Institutions and Well-Being in the World, 1950–1990* (Cambridge: Cambridge University Press, 2000).

73 *Chinese views on sovereignty are born:* For more on traditional Chinese views of sovereignty, Gerald Chan, *Chinese Perspectives on International Relations: A Framework for Analysis* (New York: St. Martin's, 1999), 75–80.

73 *However, it is not alone in its devotion:* Stephen D. Krasner, *Sovereignty: Organized Hypocrisy* (Princeton: Princeton University Press, 1999). Krasner calls sovereignty a fiction, but it has been a popular one.

73 *The United Nations was founded on this notion:* Michael Clough, "Darfur: Whose Responsibility to Protect?," Human Rights Watch World Report (January 2005), 6.

73 *China did not vote against American intervention:* Gordon Fairclough and Neil King, Jr., "Behind China's Stance on North Korea," *Wall Street Journal*, November 6, 2006.

74 *Further, with its 1,861 troops:* "Monthly Summary of Contributors of Military and Civilian Police Personnel," U.N. Department of Peacekeeping Operations (February 2007), http://www.un.org/Depts/dpko/dpko/contributors (accessed April 4, 2007).

74 *China blocked U.N. Security Council efforts:* Evelyn Leopold, "Russia, China Block Sudan Sanctions," Reuters, April 17, 2006.

74 *abstained (along with Russia and Qatar):* "Security Council Expands Mandate of UN Mission in Sudan to Include Darfur," Resolution 1706, Security Council 5519th Meeting, U.N. Department of Public Information, August 31, 2006.

74 *President Hu Jintao took the unprecedented step:* Guy Dinmore and Mark Turner, "China's Role Over Darfur Defended," *Financial Times*, April 13, 2007.

74 *In February 2005, India's Oil and Natural Gas Corporation:* "Sudan Woos Indian Oil Firms with 'Special Treatment' Promise," *Alexander's Gas and Oil, News and Trends: Africa* 10, no. 12 (June 7, 2005), http://www.gasandoil.com/goc/news/nta52537.htm (accessed January 20, 2006).

74 *In January 2005, French oil concern Total:* "Sudan Country Analysis Brief," U.S. Department of Energy, Energy Information Administration (March 2006), http://www.eia.doe.gov/emeu/cabs/Sudan/Background.html (accessed April 2007).

74 *Instead, the People's Republic has probably concluded:* Susan Rice, Anthony Lake, and Donald Payne, "We Saved Europeans, Why Not Africans?," *Washington Post*, October 2, 2006.

75 *The military junta there has kept:* "2006 Country Reports on Human Rights Practices, Burma," U.S. Department of State (released March 6, 2007), http://www.state.gov/g/drl/rls/hrrpt/2006 (accessed July 11, 2007).

75 *China has embraced this neighbor to the southeast:* Larry Jagan, "Jiang Boosts China-Burma Link," *BBC News Online*, December 16, 2001, http://news.bbc.co.uk/1/hi/world/asia-pacific/1714119.stm (accessed April 2, 2007).

75 *China's concern about northern Burma:* M. Taylor Fravel, "Regime Insecurity and International Cooperation: Explaining China's Compromises in Territorial Disputes," *International Security* 30, no. 2 (2005): 63.

75 *Cross-border trade and investment has flourished:* Allen Clark, "Burma in 2002: A Year of Transition," *Asian Survey* 43, no. 1 (January/February 2003): 131.

75 *the Chinese currency is now the principal:* Michael Vatikiotis and Bertil Lintner, "New Asian Dollar: The Growing Reach of China's Renminbi," *Far Eastern Economic Review*, May 29, 2003.

75 *In 2006, during the first visit of an Indian president to Rangoon:* Jill Mc-Givering, "India Signs Burma Gas Agreement," *BBC News Online*, March 9, 2006, http://news.bbc.co.uk/1/hi/world/south_asia/4791078 .stm (accessed April 2, 2007).

75 *French energy giant Total:* "Total in 2005—Annual Report: Exploration and Production," Total (2005), 29, http://www.total.com/en/finance/re sults_presentations/rp_2005 (accessed February 28, 2007).

75 *In January 2007, the Russians and Chinese vetoed:* Amy Kazmin and Mark Turner, "U.S. Seeks to Step-up Pressure on Burma," *Financial Times Online*, June 2, 2006.

76 *In its quest for access to Zimbabwe's gold:* Princeton N. Lyman, "China's Rising Role in Africa" (Presentation to the U.S.-China Commission, July 21, 2005), http://www.cfr.org/publication/8436/#_edn7 (accessed January 3, 2007); Abraham McLaughlin, "A Rising China Counters US Clout in Africa," *Christian Science Monitor*, March 30, 2005; Joshua Eisenman, "Zimbabwe: China's African Ally," *China Brief* 5, no. 15 (July 5, 2005): 9–11.

76 *"if we deal with the United States":* Carrie Grace, "China's Rise Leaves West Wondering," *BBC News Online*, August 16, 2006, http://news.bbc .co.uk/2/hi/asia-pacific/4797903.stm (accessed April 2, 2007).

76 *Some argue China should prepare itself for a backlash:* Victor Mallet, "The Ugly Face of China's Presence in Africa," *Financial Times*, September 14, 2006; Elizabeth C. Economy and Karen Monaghan, "The Perils of Beijing's Africa Strategy," *International Herald Tribune*, November 2, 2006.

76 *During President Hu's February 2007 trip to Africa:* Michelle Faul, "China Acknowledges Downside in Africa," Associated Press, February 8, 2007.

77 *Further, though Chinese investments in Africa are up substantially:* Harry Broadman, *Africa's Silk Road: China and India's New Frontier* (Washington, D.C.: World Bank, 2007), 91–104; "World Investment Report 2006—Box II.I Asian FDI in Africa," U.N. Conference on Trade and Development (2006), 43.

77 *"I have spent my whole career":* Jeffrey Bader (director of the John L. Thornton China Center and senior fellow in Foreign Policy Studies, the Brookings Institution), in discussion with Nina Hachigian, October 2006. For an example of exhortations and pressure not working, see Jia Qingguo's account of early attempts by the Clinton administration to get tough with China on human rights. Jia Qingguo, "Learning to Live with the Hegemon: Evolution of China's Policy Toward the US Since the End of the Cold War," *Journal of Contemporary China* 14, no. 44 (August 2005): 398–99.

78 *"Our hopes":* Susan L. Shirk, *China: Fragile Superpower* (Oxford: Oxford University Press, 2007), 261.

78 *Public upbraidings on human rights:* For a review of the debate between those who say the U.S. should serve as a model for others and those that favor more activism, Robert W. Tucker, "Exemplar or Crusader? Reflections on America's Role," *National Interest* 5 (Fall 1986): 64–75; Gideon Rose, "Democracy Promotion and American Foreign Policy: A Review Essay," *International Security* 25, no. 3 (Winter 2000/2001): 186–203.

78 *"in China's modern history":* Wang Jisi, "From Paper Tiger to Real Leviathan: China's Images of the United States Since 1949," in Carola McGiffert, ed., *Chinese Images of the United States* (Washington, D.C.: CSIS, 2005), 10.

78 *In a 2006 poll:* "Russians Support Putin's Re-Nationalization of Oil, Control of Media, but See Democratic Future," World Opinion and Levada Center Poll, Program on International Policy Attitudes (July 10, 2006).

78 *"A liberal democracy":* Ibid.

78 *Similarly, polling shows that 78 percent of Chinese:* "The United States and the Rise of China and India," 34.

78 *"They have not had to struggle just to survive":* Li Xiaoping, "Chinese Media Professionals' Views of America," in McGiffert, ed., *Chinese Images of the United States,* 84.

79 *"Al-Qaeda seeks America's":* Daniel Byman, "Al Qaeda as Adversary: Do We Understand Our Enemy?," *World Politics* 56, no. 1 (2003): 147.

79 *"humiliat[ing] and slaughter[ing]":* Ibid.

79 *Their ultimate objective of reasserting:* John Parachini, "Symposium: Diagnosing Al Qaeda," interview by *Frontpage Magazine/RAND,* August 18, 2003, http://www.frontpagemag.com/Articles/ReadArticle.asp?ID=9416 (accessed September 11, 2006).

79   *"a Caliphate would not have":* "Mapping the Global Future: Report of the National Intelligence Council's 2020 Project," National Intelligence Council (December 2004), 91, http://www.dni.gov/nic/NIC_2020_proj ect.html.

79   *To the extent that the campaign against terrorists:* For more on the importance of addressing terrorist ideology, Angel Rabasa et al., *Beyond Al Qaeda: The Global Jihadist Movement* (Santa Monica: RAND, 2006).

80   *"As a people, we have oscillated":* Henry A. Kissinger, *American Foreign Policy* (New York: Norton, 1977), 200.

80   *For that reason and many:* For overview of recent issues in U.S. democracy promotion, see Thomas Carothers, *Critical Mission: Essays on Democracy Promotion* (Washington, D.C.: Carnegie Endowment for International Peace, 2004).

80   *For one thing, the amount America spent per capita:* James Dobbins et al., *America's Role in Nation-Building: From Germany to Iraq* (Santa Monica: RAND, 2003), 160.

80   *Today, fewer than 20 percent:* Thomas Carothers, "The End of the Transition Paradigm," *Journal of Democracy* 13 (January 2002): 9.

80   *Most are stuck in a semi-authoritarian:* Thomas Carothers as cited in Francis Fukuyama, *America at the Crossroads: Democracy, Power and the Neoconservative Legacy* (New Haven: Yale University Press, 2006), 58.

80   *"undercuts the higher ends they seek":* Francis Fukuyama, "The Imperative of State Building," *Journal of Democracy* 15, no. 2 (April 2004): 19.

81   *"In the world we have":* Michael McFaul (director of the Center for Democracy, Development and the Rule of Law at the Freeman Spogli Institute for International Studies at Stanford University), in remarks at workshop hosted by Stanford University's Center for International Security and Cooperation and the Stanley Foundation, November 8–10, 2006.

81   *"[d]emocracy promotion has come to be seen overseas":* Thomas Carothers, "The Backlash Against Democracy Promotion," *Foreign Affairs* (March/April 2006): 64.

81   *This same backlash dynamic:* Richard Lapper, "Venezuela and the Rise of Chavez: A Background Discussion Paper," Council on Foreign Relations (November 22, 2005), http://www.cfr.org/publication/9269/venezuela_ and_the_rise_of_chavez.html (accessed March 23, 2006).

81   *"this catastrophic path":* Kenneth Roth, "Filling the Leadership Void: Where Is the European Union?," Human Rights Watch World Report 2007 (New York: Human Rights Watch, 2006), 7–8.

82   *"any government under stress":* Jeffrey Bader discussion.

82   *Hypocrisy, real or even apparent:* Stephen M. Walt, *Taming American Power* (New York: Norton, 2005), 100.

82   *undermines our legitimacy:* Ibid., 167.

82   *In addition, concludes analyst:* Wang Jisi, "China's Search for Stability with America," *Foreign Affairs* (September/October 2005): 42.

82   *Venezuela's record on political rights:* "Freedom in the World 2007—Table of Independent Countries: Comparative Measures of Freedom," Freedom House (January 17, 2007), http://www.freedomhouse.org/template.cfm?page=15 (accessed February 21, 2006).

82   *For example, in 2001:* Joel Campagna, "Between Two Worlds: Qatar's Al Jazeera Satellite Channel Faces Conflicting Expectations," CPJ Press Freedom Reports (October 2001).

82   *proclamations about the need for independent media:* Linda Heard, "Al Jazeera, 'For Sale' Is a Bad Sign for All," *Al Jazeera*, February 2, 2005, http://www.aljazeerah.info/Opinion%20editorials/2005%20Opionion%20Editorials/February/2%20o/A1%20Jazeera%20for%20sale%20is%20a%20sad%20sign%20for%20all%20By%20Linda%20S%20Heard.htm (accessed February 21, 2006).

82   *"the most enduring factor":* Qazi Hussain Ahmad, head of Pakistan's Jamaat-e-Islami movement, as quoted in Walt, *Taming American Power*, 174.

82   *"pursuing democracy as a matter of principle":* Carothers, "Backlash Against Democracy Promotion," 67.

83   *Despite America's recent shaky record:* Michael McFaul, "Democracy Promotion as World Value," *Washington Quarterly* 28, no. 1 (Winter 2004/2005): 148.

83   *Seventy percent of Americans:* "Americans on Promoting Democracy," Chicago Council on Foreign Affairs, Program on International Policy Attitudes (September 29, 2005), 10.

83   *America also has to realize:* G. John Ikenberry and Anne-Marie Slaughter, *Forging a World of Liberty Under Law: U.S. National Security in the 21st Century*, Princeton Project on National Security Papers (September 27, 2006), http://www.wws.princeton.edu/ppns/report/FinalReport.pdf (accessed February 21, 2007).

83   *Only slow, small, and steadfast steps:* Thomas Carothers and Sheri Berman, "How Democracies Emerge," *Journal of Democracy* 1, no. 1

(January 2007): 18, http://www.journalofdemocracy.org/articles/gratis/Carothers-18-1.pdf (accessed May 16, 2007).

84　*That there is a "trust gap":* Richard L. Armitage and Joseph S. Nye, *The U.S.–Japan Relationship: Getting Asia Right Through 2020* (Center for Strategic and International Studies, 2007), 4.

4. U.S. PROSPERITY AND THE PIVOTAL POWERS

85　*"When I have my union":* "American Airlines 'Insources' Maintenance Work," National Public Radio (NPR), *All Things Considered*, December 7, 2006, http://www.npr.org/templates/story/story.php?storyId=6594273 (accessed February 21, 2007).

86　*The mechanics' contract comes up again:* Ibid. Also, Trebor Banstetter, "Sky's the Limit," *Dallas Star-Telegram*, February 2, 2007.

86　*There is a tension between the two things:* As Stanford economist Paul Romer has observed, "Everyone wants economic growth, but nobody wants change." Quoted in Thomas L. Friedman, *The World Is Flat* (New York: Farrar, Straus & Giroux, 2005), 339.

86　*"There is no choice but to embrace change":* McKinsey and Company Leadership Breakfast, "Panel Debates Offshoring," http://www.mckinsey.com/ideas/Offshoring/roundtable/pdf/offshoring_breakfast_panel.pdf (accessed May 14, 2006).

87　*To economists, the notion of nations "competing":* Paul Krugman, *Pop Internationalism* (Cambridge: MIT Press, 1996), 9.

87　*As South Korea's GDP per capita grew:* Global Financial Data, *"Real GDP Per Capita, 1953–2005,"* GFD Database, www.globalfinancialdata.com (accessed February 19, 2006).

87　*One study predicts that U.S. GDP:* Erik Britton and Christopher T. Mark, Sr., *The China Effect: Assessing the Impact on the US Economy of Trade and Investment with China*, China Business Forum (January 2006), 17, http://www.chinabusinessforum.org/pdf/the-china-effect.pdf (accessed June 7, 2007).

88　*Another suggests that the American economy:* Scott C. Bradford, Paul L. E. Grieco, and Gary Clyde Hufbauer, "The Payoff to America from Global Integration," in *The United States and the World Economy*, ed., C. Fred Bergsten (Washington, D.C.: Institute for International Economics, 2005), 68. For more on gains due to U.S. economic integration into the world economy, Grant D. Aldonis, Robert Z. Lawerence, and Matthew J. Slaughter, "Succeeding in the Global Economy," The Financial Services Forum, June 26, 2007, 18–28.

88 *A world where great power economies:* Tom Petruno, "Emerging Nations Powering Global Economic Boom," *Los Angeles Times*, May 14, 2006.

88 *"The emerging economies":* "Coming of Age," *Economist*, January 21, 2006.

89 *During 2000–2005, U.S. exports:* Calculations based upon data from U.S. Census Bureau, "Annual Trade Highlights: 2005 Highlights, Foreign Trade Statistics," http://www.census.gov/foreign-trade/statistics/highlights/annual.html (accessed February 18, 2006); "U.S. Total Exports to Individual Countries, 1998–2004," U.S. Department of Commerce, International Trade Administration (March 2005), http://www.ita.doc.gov/td/industry/otea/usfth/aggregate/H04T06.html (accessed February 18, 2006).

89 *In 2005, India was the fastest-growing:* "US Exports to India Have Doubled Since 2003," Progressive Policy Institute, September 21, 2005, http://www.ppionline.org/ppi_ci.cfm?knlgAreaID=108&subsecID=900003&contentID=253537 (accessed February 22, 2007).

89 *Many American companies:* Michael Bazeley, "Net Giants Bet Big on China's Potential," *San Jose Mercury News*, August 14, 2005; Keith Naughton, "The Great Wal-Mart of China," *Newsweek*, October 30, 2006, http://www.msnbc.msn.com/id/15364026/ (accessed March 28, 2007); Clay Chandler, "Inside the New China: Part Communist, Part Capitalist—and Full Speed Ahead," *Fortune*, October 4, 2004, http://money.cnn.com/magazines/fortune/fortune_archive/2004/10/04/8186805/index.htm (accessed March 28, 2007).

89 *"makes almost as much money":* Chandler, "Inside the New China."

89 *Starbucks CEO Howard Schultz:* Howard Schultz, in discussion with Nina Hachigian, March 2006.

89 *If General Motors avoids bankruptcy:* William H. Overholt, "Globalization's Unequal Discontents," *washingtonpost.com*, December 21, 2006; "GM Tops 100,000 in China Sales," *CNNMoney.com*, February 2, 2007, http://money.cnn.com/2007/02/02/news/companies/gm.reut/index.htm (accessed February 21, 2007).

89 *While its U.S. sales dropped:* "GM, Ford Show Strong Growth," *People's Daily Online*, January 9, 2007, http://english.peopledaily.com.cn/200701/09/eng20070109_339419.html (accessed February 21, 2007).

89 *American agriculture is also:* Peter Coy, "Asian Competition: Is the Cup Half Empty—Or Half Full?," *BusinessWeek*, August 22, 2005.

90 *Toward the end of 2006, Westinghouse:* "Westinghouse Scores China Nuclear Deal," *Financial Times*, December 17, 2006.

90 *More exports mean more wealth:* For an attempt to quantify this, Erica L. Groshen, Bart Hobjin, and Margaret M. McConnell, "US Jobs Gained and Lost Through Trade: A Net Measure," *Current Issues*, Federal Reserve Bank of New York (August 2005), www.newyorkfed.org/re search/current_issues (accessed February 21, 2006).

90 *The gains from these new markets:* Pam Woodall, "The New Titans," *Economist*, September 16, 2006.

90 *Chinese demand:* Ian Bremmer, "Are the U.S. and China on a Collision Course?," *Fortune*, January 24, 2005, 52.

90 *Cheap manufacturing abroad:* "From T-shirts to T-bonds," *Economist*, July 28, 2005. Also "Unnaturally Low," *Economist*, October 2, 2004.

90 *Michael Cox of the Dallas Federal Reserve Bank:* W. Michael Cox and Richard Alm, *Myths of Rich and Poor: Why We're Better Off Than We Think* (New York: Basic Books, 1999), 14–15.

90 *In total, a Morgan Stanley Study:* Friedman, *The World Is Flat*, 120.

90 *That amounts to $521 in disposable income:* Another study estimates the annual gains to the U.S. economy as $70 billion. C. Fred Bergstein, Bates Gill, Nicholas R. Lardy, and Derek Mitchell, *China: The Balance Sheet: What the World Needs to Know Now About the Emerging Superpower* (New York: Public Affairs Press, 2006), 116.

90 *European firms held $1.4 trillion:* European Union, "Europe and America: An Economic Union," *eufocus Newsletter* (2005), 8.

91 *"international competition helps upgrade productivity":* Michael E. Porter, *The Competitive Advantage of Nations* (New York: Free Press, 1990), 8.

91 *innovate faster and improve their products:* Jeffrey Garten, "A New Threat to America, Inc.," *BusinessWeek*, July 25, 2005, 114.

91 *One study suggests that U.S. manufacturing productivity:* Britton and Mark, *The China Effect*, 20.

91 *"Competition with China":* Richard W. Fisher, "China's Economic Growth" (remarks before the Annual Symposium on Critical Global Markets, June 14, 2005).

91 *"Sure Chinese companies":* Deloitte CEO Bill Parrett, "At the Crossroads of Globalization: Choices and Challenges for America and China"

(speech at Indiana University, March 16, 2005), www.deloitte.com (accessed December 5, 2005).

91 *China may be the most open:* China's ratio of imports to GDP has soared since 1978 and is now roughly twice that of the U.S. and three times that of Japan. Only small economies like South Korea have similarly high ratios. Also, China's import tariffs have dropped from more than 50 percent in 1982 to 10 percent in 2005 and compared to developing countries are relatively low (and much lower than India's). For a useful analysis of this point, Bergsten et al., *China: The Balance Sheet*, 83–87.

92 *"so onerous they violate":* Neil C. Hughes, "A Trade War with China?," *Foreign Affairs* (July/August 2005): 99.

92 *Every day, American officials cooperate:* For more on the future importance of international networks of government officials, Anne-Marie Slaughter, *A New World Order* (Princeton: Princeton University Press, 2004).

92 *Moreover, over the longer term:* For a recent example, Adam Posen and Daniel K. Tarullo, "Report of the Working Group on Economics and National Security," Princeton Project on National Security (2005), 5, http://www.wws.princeton.edu/ppns/conferences/reports/fall/ENS.pdf (accessed April 9, 2007).

92 *It turns out that when it comes to happiness:* Isabel V. Sawhill (remarks at Center for American Progress panel, "Moving on Up? Economic Mobility in America," April 2006) http://streaming.americanprogress.org/events/2006/2006_04_26_moving_on_up/5.sawhill.320.240.mp4.html (accessed November 3, 2006); "Are We Happy Yet?," Pew Research Center, Social Trends Report (February 13, 2006), http://pewresearch.org/social/pack.php?PackID=1 (accessed November 3, 2006); Robert H. Frank, "Does Absolute Income Matter?" (paper prepared for "The Paradoxes of Happiness in Economics" conference, Milan, March 21, 2003), http://www.law.berke ley.edu/centers/bclbe/Courses/216.4lepsych .papers/Frank.Rober.Happiness%20Surveyed.03.htm (accessed November 3, 2006).

93 *If or when China's economy grows:* Woodall, "The New Titans," 12.

93 *"It's all our fault":* Coy, "Asian Competition."

93 *Technological innovation necessarily:* China is not immune to this phenomenon. It lost fifteen million manufacturing jobs in the seven years between 1995 and 2002, compared to the U.S.'s two million, because of

efficiency gains. Friedman, *The World Is Flat*, 118; also John Berry, "Some Lost Jobs May Never Come Back," *Washington Post*, November 29, 2003.

93 *The U.S. has gone:* Carolyn Dimitri, Anne Effland, and Neilson Conklin, "The 20th Century Transformation of U.S. Agriculture and Farm Policy," U.S. Department of Agriculture Economic Research Service, *Electronic Information Bulletin*, No. 3 (June 2005), http://www.ers.usda; "Portrait of the USA", U.S. State Department, March 2003, http://usinfo.state.gov/usa/infousa/facts/factover/ch5.htm (both accessed May 13, 2007).

94 *Meanwhile, farming output:* Ian D. Wyatt and Daniel E. Hecker, "Occupational Changes During the 20th Century," U.S. Bureau of Labor Statistics, Monthly Labor Review (March 2006), http://www.bls.gov/opub/mlr/2006/03/art3full.pdf (accessed May 13, 2007).

94 *"has closely followed":* Lael Brainard and Robert E. Litan, "Services Offshoring, American Jobs and the Global Economy," *Perspectives on Work*, Winter 2005, 9.

94 *In the last ten years:* Richard W. Fisher, "China's Economic Growth" (remarks before the Annual Symposium on Critical Global Markets, June 14, 2005).

94 *"Someone will always":* Mark Warner speech at a gathering in Los Angeles, February 2006.

94 *Offshoring, whereby firms:* Offshoring is transferring internal tasks overseas, even within the same company. Outsourcing, in contrast, involves transferring an internal business function to another company, domestic or foreign.

94 *"the normal adjustment process":* McKinsey & Company, Leadership Breakfast, "Panel Debates Offshoring," http://www.mckinsey.com/ideas/Offshoring/roundtable/pdf/offshoring_breakfast_panel.pdf (accessed May 14, 2006).

94 *Though it is of little comfort:* Catherine Mann, "Globalization of IT Services and White Collar Jobs: The Next Wave of Productivity Growth," *Institute for International Economics Policy Briefs*, No. PB03-11 (December 2003).

94 *McKinsey's Diana Farrell estimates:* Martin N. Baily and Diana Farrell, April 2004, 2–5; Clyde Prestowitz, *Three Billion New Capitalists* (New York: Basic Books, 2005), 204–205 offers a critique of this study.

95 *The low prices fed demand:* Friedman, *The World Is Flat*, 235.

95 *U.S. firms that employ highly skilled:* Brainard and Litan, "Services Off-shoring, American Jobs and the Global Economy."

95 *The hawkish U.S.-China Economic:* "U.S.-China Trade, 1989–2003: Impact on Jobs and Industries, Nationally and State-by-State," U.S.-China Economic and Security Review Commission (January 2005), http://www.uscc.gov/pressreleases/2005/05_01_11pr.htm (accessed May 14, 2006).

95 *Forrester Research predicts:* John C. McCarthy, "Near-Term Growth of Offshoring Accelerating," Forrester Research, May 14, 2004, as cited in Linda Levine, "Offshoring (a.k.a. Offshore Outsourcing) and Job Insecurity Among US Workers," *CRS Report for Congress*, May 2, 2005, 8–9.

95 *In the one month:* "Job Openings and Labor Turnover: February 2007," U.S. Department of Labor, Bureau of Labor Statistics, http://www.bls.gov/news.release/pdf/jolts.pdf (accessed April 10, 2007).

95 *Some 25,000 jobs:* Aldonas, Lawrence, and Slaughter, "Succeeding in the Global Economy," 29, 44.

95 *Losses to offshoring:* Brainard and Litan, "Services Offshoring, American Jobs and the Global Economy," 9.

95 *Moreover, there is a limit to the number:* McKinsey Global Institute estimates that only 11 percent of service jobs, which account for 80 percent of U.S. employment, in the neighborhood of twelve million jobs, could ever—even theoretically—be outsourced. Diana Farrell and Jason Rosenfeld, "US Offshoring: Rethinking the Response," McKinsey Global Institute (December 2005), 5. Princeton University economist Alan S. Binder, on the other hand, estimates the number could be as high as forty million in the next decade. Importantly, he stands firmly opposed to protectionism. David Wessel and Bob Davis, "Job Prospects: Pain from Free Trade Spurs Second Thoughts; Mr. Blinder's Shift Spotlights Warnings of Deeper Downside," *Wall Street Journal*, March 28, 2007.

95 *Many jobs just have to be done face-to-face:* For more on the distinction between "personal" services that cannot be offshored and "impersonal" services that can, Alan Blinder, "Offshoring: the Next Industrial Revolution?," *Foreign Affairs* (March/April 2006): 113.

95 *Regulatory barriers and skilled labor shortages:* Diana Farrell and Jason

Rosenfeld, "US Offshoring: Rethinking the Response," 4, http://www
.mckinsey.com/mgi/publications/rethinking.asp (accessed May 14, 2006).

96 *Foreign corporations employ:* Senator Mitch McConnell (R-KY), floor
statement on S1637, the Jumpstart Our Business Strength Act, March 4,
2004.

96 *14 percent higher wages than American firms:* James K. Jackson, "Outsourcing and Insourcing Jobs in the US Economy," *CRS Report for Congress*, May 4, 2005, 17.

96 *Japan's Toyota accounts:* "Toyota Reaches 15 Million Mark in North
American Production," press release (February 2006), http://www.toy
ota.com/about/news/manufacturing/2006/02/01-1-FifteenMillion.html
(accessed February 8, 2007); Steve Schifferes, "Toyota: An All American
Car Company?," *BBC News*, January 12 2007, http://news.bbc.co.uk/
1/hi/business/6247479.stm (accessed February 8, 2007).

96 *When their jobs go overseas:* Lori G. Kletzer, "Job Loss from Imports:
Measuring the Costs," *Institute for International Economics* (September
2001), 40, http://www.iie.com/publications/chapters_preview/110/3iie
2962.pdf (accessed April 2, 2007).

96 *Part of the reason:* Prestowitz, *Three Billion New Capitalists*, 205; also
Woodall, "The New Titans," 14.

96 *Boeing employs Russian aeronautical engineers:* Friedman, *The World Is
Flat*, 14, 195–96.

96 *"Globalization can explain":* Paul Krugman, "The Disappearing Middle," *New York Times*, October 20, 2002. In 2006, the average income
for the bottom 20 percent of households was $10,655 compared to
$159,583 for those in the top 20 percent—the highest percentage dis-
parity, 1,500 percent, on record.

96 *A 2007 Center for American Progress report explains:* Center for American
Progress Task Force on Poverty, "From Poverty to Prosperity: A National
Strategy to Cut Poverty in Half," April 2007, 2. http://www.american
progress.org/projects/poverty/index.html (accessed May 13, 2007).

96 *The vast majority:* Aldonas, Lawrence, and Slaughter, "Succeeding in the
Global Economy," 37.

96 *Even with heavy tariffs and quotas:* "Agriculture Reform Key to Global
Trade Talks, U.S. Official Says," U.S. Department of State, Bureau of
International Information Programs, January 16, 2004, http://usinfo
.state.gov/xarchives/display.html?p=washfile-english&y=2004&m=Jan

uary&x=20040116140138zemogb1.713198e-02<http://usinfo.state.gov/ xarchives/display.html?p=washfileenglish&y=2004&m=Jan uary&x=20040116140138zemogb1.713198e-02> (accessed March 29, 2007).

97 *Also, studies have shown that the poorest Americans:* I. M. Destler, *American Trade Politics*, 4th ed. (Washington, D.C.: International Institute for Economics, 2005), 311.

97 *Protectionist policies are politically popular:* Quote of Robert Rubin in Edward Luce, "Out on a Limb: Why Blue Collar Americans See Their Future as Precarious," *Financial Times*, May 3, 2006; quote of Senator Clinton in Edward Luce and Krishna Guha, "Seeking Shelter: Why Democrats Are in Retreat from Their Free Trade Record," *Financial Times*, November 3, 2006.

97 *Currently, the U.S. spends far less:* Farrell and Rosenfeld, "US Offshoring," 12.

97 *Federal spending devoted:* Destler, *American Trade Politics*, 326.

97 *One idea, wage insurance:* Lori G. Kletzer and Howard Rosen, "Reforming Unemployment Insurance for the Twenty-first Century Work Force," Hamilton Project Discussion Paper, September 2006, http://www1.hamiltonproject.org/views/papers/200609kletzer=rosen .pdf (accessed June 3, 2007).

97 *The current unemployment insurance:* Ibid.

97 *Another idea gaining currency:* Gene Sperling, "A Progressive Framework for Social Security Reform," Center for American Progress Report, January 10, 2005, http://www.americanprogress.org/kf/social%20security %20-%20sperling%20web%20final.pdf (accessed May 13, 2007).

97 *Economist Alan Binder of Princeton University suggests:* Wessel and Davis, "Job Prospects."

97 *A recent report:* Aldonas, Lawrence, and Slaughter, "Succeeding in the Global Economy," 49.

97 *Firms could make up for 70 percent:* Farrell and Rosenfeld, "US Offshoring," 12.

98 *Developing a more educated pool:* Brainard and Litan, "Services Offshoring," 11–12.

98 *Intel opened a large new chip facility:* Thomas L. Friedman (remarks at McKinsey and Company Leadership Breakfast, "Panel Debates Offshoring").

98 *"Virtually every entrepreneur":* Friedman, *The World Is Flat*, 287.

98　*America has slipped:* "The Development of Broadband Access in OECD Countries," Organization for Economic Cooperation and Development (2001), http://www.oecd.org/dataoecd/48/33/2475737.pdf (accessed May 13, 2007); also "OECD Broadband Statistics to June 2006," http://www.oecd.org/document/9/0,2340,en_2649_34223_37529673_1_1_1_1,00.html (accessed May 13, 2007).

98　*That is two-thirds of the entire federal budget today:* Felix Rohatyn and Warren Rudman, "It's Time to Rebuild America," *Washington Post,* December 13, 2005; "Guiding Principles for Strengthening America's Infrastructure," Center for Strategic and International Studies, Commission on Public Infrastructure (March 27, 2006).

98　*In the 1980s:* Gene Koretz, "The Buying of America: Should We Be Worried?," *BusinessWeek,* May 9, 1988.

98　*In reality, Japanese investors:* In 1990 Japan held only 21 percent of foreign direct investment in the U.S. (Britain held 27 percent), and between 1978 and 1987 Japanese investors acquired only ninety-four companies, far fewer than European countries. Mack Ott, "Foreign Investments in the United States," *The Concise Encyclopedia of Economics,* Library of Economics and Liberty, http://www.econlib.org/library/Enc/Foreign InvestmentintheUnitedStates.html (accessed May 13, 2006).

99　*Europe's direct investments:* Thomas Anderson, "Foreign Direct Investment in the United States," *Survey of Current Business,* June 2005, 31.

99　*Some of the biggest names:* T. R. Reid, "Buying American? Maybe Not," *Washington Post,* May 18, 2002.

99　*The fact that this trend:* For more on the Committee on Foreign Investment in the United States (CFIUS) process, Douglas Holtz-Eakin, "You Can't Be CFIUS," *Wall Street Journal,* July 13, 2006, http://www .cfr.org/publication/11105/you_cant_be_cfius.html (accessed February 21, 2007).

99　*American mayors understand this:* Ron Scherer, "An Outsourcing Reversal: Chinese Firms in the US," *Christian Science Monitor,* January 28, 2005.

99　*When it became clear that this:* Remarks of Henry Levine (former U.S. consul general in Shanghai and deputy assistant secretary of commerce for Asia), at workshop hosted by Stanford University's Center for International Security and Cooperation and the Stanley Foundation, November 8–10, 2006.

99　*IBM also ended up owning:* John Spooner and Michael Kanellos, "IBM

Sells PC Group to Lenovo," *CNET News.com*, December 8, 2004, http://news.com.com/IBM+sells+PC+group+to+Lenovo/2100-1042_3-5482284.html (accessed February 21, 2007).

99 *Americans are sure to hear:* For more on Chinese motivations in buying foreign firms, Friedrich Wu, "The Globalization of Corporate China," *NBR Analysis*, December 2005. For more on the trend of Indian companies buying foreign entities, Joe Leahy, "Unleashed: Why Indian Companies Are Setting Their Sights on Western Rivals," *Financial Times*, February 7, 2007.

100 *London is now seen:* "Interim Report of the Committee on Capital Markets Regulation," Committee on Capital Markets Regulation, November 30, 2006, http://www.capmktsreg.org/pdfs/11.30Committee_Interim_ReportREV2.pdf (accessed February 21, 2007); "Down on the Street," Special Report, *Economist*, November 25, 2006.

100 *We focus in this section:* For more on the issue of resource security in general, Michael Klare, "The New Geography of Conflict," *Foreign Affairs* (May/June 2001): 49. For more on rare earth elements, David Lague, "China Corners the Market in a High-tech Necessity," *International Herald Tribune*, January 22, 2006.

101 *Oil is critical:* "The Oiloholics," *Economist*, August 27, 2005.

101 *"pale in comparison":* David R. Francis, "China's Risky Scramble for Oil," *Christian Science Monitor*, January 20, 2005, http://www.csmonitor.com/2005/0120/p16s01-cogn.htm (accessed July 11, 2006).

101 *Japan comes in third:* "Top World Oil Consumers—2005," U.S. Energy Information Administration, http://www.eia.doe.gov/emeu/cabs/top worldtables3_4.html (accessed March 26, 2007).

101 *Misperceptions and "mythology":* Mikkal Herberg (energy expert at the National Bureau of Asian Research), in discussion with Nina Hachigian, January 2006.

101 *While it may seem logical:* Modern contracts for oil contain provisions that recalculate the price regularly.

102 *Though China's oil investments:* "Energy Policy Act 2005, Section 1837: National Security Review of International Energy Requirements," U.S. Department of Energy (February 2006), 28.

102 *these deals ultimately bring:* Daniel Yergin, "Ensuring Energy Security," *Foreign Affairs* (March/April 2006): 77. On the other hand, on the margins, these deals may also be driving up costs in the oil business by offering more for exploration rights, for example.

102 *"Congress does not understand":* Herberg discussion.

102 *Despite Congress's assertion:* We explore in Chapter 8 why Congress adopts such policies. But for the successful bidder, Chevron, lobbying may have been cheaper than outbidding CNOOC.

102 *If Unocal's oil went to China:* James Surowiecki, "All the Oil in China," *New Yorker*, July 11, 2005.

102 *Even though coal provides:* "Energy Policy Act Report," U.S. Department of Energy, 4–5.

102 *and is likely to double its usage:* James Kendell, "World Oil Consumption by Region, Reference Case, 1990–2025," Energy Information Administration (March 2005), www.eia.doe.gov/oiaf/pdf/worldenergydemand .pdf (accessed February 27, 2006). Also, "International Energy Outlook 2005," Energy Information Administration (July 2005), http://www.eia .doe.gov/oiaf/ieo/excel/ieoreftab_4.xls (accessed February 27, 2006).

103 *India too could be importing:* Calculated using data from: "Table A4: World Oil Consumption by Region, Reference Case, 1990–2030," International Energy Outlook 2006, U.S. Department of Energy, Energy Information Administration; "Table E4: World Oil Production by Region and Country, Reference Case, 1990–2030," International Energy Outlook 2006; "Table A5: World Natural Gas Consumption by Region, Reference Case, 1990–2030," International Energy Outlook 2006; "Table 9: Natural Gas," International Energy Outlook 2006 (Chapter 4), http:// www.eia.doe.gov/oiaf/ieo/nat_gas.html (accessed April 11, 2007).

103 *In addition to industrial growth:* Flynt Leverett and Jeffrey Bader, "Managing China-U.S. Energy Competition in the Middle East," *Washington Quarterly* (Winter 2005/2006): 189.

103 *If China followed a similar pattern:* Lester Brown, *Plan B 2.0: Rescuing a Planet Under Stress and a Civilization in Trouble* (New York: Norton, 2006). To provide the roads, highways, and parking lots to accommodate such a vast fleet, China would have to pave an area equal to the land it now plants in rice. It would need 99 million barrels of oil a day. The world currently produces 84 million barrels per day and may never produce much more. "China Forcing World to Rethink its Economic Future," Earth Policy Institute, January 5, 2006, http://www.earthpolicy .org/Books/PB2/index.htm (accessed March 23, 2006).

103 *The consensus among geologists:* Richard Heinberg, *The Party's Over: Oil, War and the Fate of Industrial Societies* (Canada: New Society Publishers, 2005), 95, 113.

104 *Yet oil expert Daniel Yergin:* Daniel Yergin, "It's Not the End of the Oil Age," *Washington Post*, July 31, 2005.

104 *Moreover, there is lots:* Heinberg, *The Party's Over*, 185–86.

104 *Also, as the price of oil rises.* James Bartis et al., *Oil Shale Development in the United States: Policies and Prospects* (Santa Monica: RAND, 2005), http://www.rand.org/pubs/monographs/2005/RAND_MG414.pdf (accessed August 28, 2006). But Heinberg, *The Party's Over*, 127, for obstacles to using shale and tar sands.

104 *Today's increased demand has eliminated:* The status of the dollar is another concern commentators raise when it comes to oil prices. Oil is sold exclusively in dollars. Some suggest that China's influence may cause oil producers to move to a basket of currencies instead, thus diminishing the role of the dollar. Leaving aside the fact that China owns hundreds of billions of dollars in Treasuries and so has little financial motivation to see the dollar slide, OPEC has for decades toyed with the idea of moving away from the dollar. Whenever the dollar depreciates, the debate is revived. China could be a factor in this scheme, but not the cause. We discuss the dollar below.

104 *In China it was less:* Calculated using data from: "International Energy Annual 2004," Table 1.2, World Petroleum Data, U.S. Department of Energy, Energy Information Administration, http://www.eia.doe.gov/emeu/international/oilconsumption.html (accessed May 16, 2006); International Energy Annual 2004 Appendix, Table B.1, http://www.eia.doe.gov/iea/popgdp.html; "Top World Oil Consumers, 2005," http://www.eia.doe.gov/emeu/cabs/topworldtables3_4.html (accessed May 16, 2006); "Key Development Data and Statistics for the U.S. and China," World Bank, http://web.worldbank.org/WBSITE/EXTERNAL/DATASTATISTICS/0,contentMDK:20535285~menuPK:1192694~pagePK:64133150~piPK:64133175~theSitePK:239419.00.html (accessed May 16, 2006).

105 *Eighty percent:* David Zweig and Bi Jianhai, "China's Global Hunt for Energy," *Foreign Affairs* (September/October 2005): 25.

105 *"China's energy strategy":* Xuecheng Liu, "China's Energy Security and Its Grand Strategy," Policy Analysis Brief, Stanley Foundation (September 2006), 12.

105 *A Chinese naval capacity:* Bill Gertz, "China Builds Up Strategic Sea Lanes," *Washington Times*, January 18, 2005, http://www.washtimes.com/national/20050117-115550-1929r.htm (accessed February 19,

2006); Henry Chu, "China's Footprint in Pakistan," *Los Angeles Times*, April 1, 2007.

105 *In general, the United States should encourage:* Mikkal E. Herberg, "Asia's Energy Insecurity: Cooperation or Conflict," in *Strategic Asia 2004–2005,* National Bureau of Asian Research (2004), 368.

105 *China and India must become partners:* The membership for the IEA is the same as for the OECD—industrialized democracies. Membership for China is inappropriate at this juncture, but partnership is absolutely essential. Kenneth Lieberthal and Mikkal Herberg, "China's Search for Energy Security: Implications for U.S. Policy," *NBR Analysis* 17, no. 1 (April 2006): 33.

105 *Together, as energy expert:* Zweig and Bi, "China's Global Hunt." However, American oil companies have had a history of convincing the U.S. government to request price increases from OPEC when the price was perceived to be too low. Sheikh Ahmed Zaki Yamani, oil minister of Saudi Arabia and RAND expert, James Bartis, in interview with *ABC News Radio*, February 17, 2003.

105 *In January 2006, India and China:* Richard McGregor, "China and India Forge Alliance on Oil Supplies," *Financial Times*, January 12, 2006.

106 *What is needed and missing:* Emma Chanlett-Avery, "Rising Energy Competition and Energy Security in Northeast Asia: Issues for U.S. Policy," *CRS Report for Congress*, February 9, 2005, 16.

106 *Not only should the U.S. allow:* Leverett and Bader, "Managing China," 198.

106 *U.S. companies are already:* "Energy Policy Act Report," U.S. Department of Energy, 11.

106 *If the U.S. were to attempt a blockade:* If oil tankers were diverted to other ports, prices would eventually return to normal or even diminish as more supply hit the market, but the damage from the spike would already be done. Some question whether the U.S. Navy actually could block oil tankers, as the ocean lanes are wide and alternative routes around Indonesia exist. Bernard Cole, "China's Developing Martime Power and Energy Security at Sea" (presentation at conference, "China's Search for Energy Security and Strategic Implications for the U.S.," National Bureau of Asian Research, September 27–28, 2005).

106 *China and India:* Energy Information Administration, International Energy Annual 2004, Table E.1g, Energy Intensity, http://www.eia.doe.gov/iea/wecbtv.html (accessed June 11, 2007).

107 *Afterward, a tube sucks:* Martin Fackler, "The Land of Rising Conservation," *New York Times*, January 6, 2007.

107 *In 2006, China and India:* "U.S. and India Sign Historic Agreement on FutureGen Project," U.S. Department of Energy press release, April 3, 2006, http://www.energy.gov/news/3420.htm (accessed February 21, 2007); "U.S. and China Announce Cooperation on FutureGen and Sign Energy Efficiency Protocol at U.S.-China Strategic Economic Dialogue," U.S. Department of Energy press release, December 16, 2006, http://www.energy.gov/news/4535.htm (accessed February 21, 2007).

107 *The Environmental Protection Agency:* Terence Chea, "China's Growing Air Pollution Reaches U.S.," Associated Press, July 28, 2006, http://abcnews.go.com/Technology/wireStory?id=2250133 (accessed September 21, 2006).

107 *Dozens of creative ideas are on the table:* "Energy Security in the 21st Century: A New National Strategy," National Security Task Force on Energy (July 2006), http://www.americanprogress.org/atf/cf/%7bE24FE4-9A2B-43C7-A521-5D6FF2E06E03%7d/ENERGY_SECURITY_REPORT.PDF (accessed August 20, 2006).

107 *"conservation has worked":* Yergin, "Ensuring Energy Security," 81.

107 *Trade deficits are another sticky issue:* For a more detailed, but readable, discussion of these dynamics, Prestowitz, *Three Billion New Capitalists* 164–94.

107 *Reasonable people can differ:* Albert Keidel, "China's Currency: Not the Problem," Policy Brief No. 39, Carnegie Endowment (June 2005); Gary Clyde Hufbauer and Yee Wong, "China Bashing 2004," Institute for International Economics Policy Brief, No. PB04-05 (September 2004).

108 *In any case, the trade deficit:* Keidel, "China's Currency," 5. Keidel also points out that speculative currency flows exacerbate the yuan-dollar balance. Those flows, in turn, are encouraged by U.S. policymakers' demands that China revalue.

108 *small relative to the trade deficit:* "Petrodollar Power," *Economist*, December 9, 2006.

108 *Moreover, almost 60 percent:* Neil C. Hughes, "A Trade War with China?," *Foreign Affairs* (July/August 2005): 94.

108 *Also, component parts:* Bergsten et al., *China Balance Sheet*, 89.

108 *The share of America's:* Calculated using figures from U.S. International

Trade Commission Dataweb Version 2.8.4. http://dataweb.usitc.gov/ (accessed July 11, 2007).

108 *In the category:* "China and US Trade: Lost in Translation," *Economist,* May 17, 2007.

109 *That inflow, in turn, increases demand:* This can happen even when the federal budget is nearly balanced, as it was in the late 1990s under President Clinton, because of a net inflow of foreign investment. Today the imbalance has much to do with America's need to borrow money to consume.

109 *In order for the trade deficit to be smaller:* For more on the relationship between the trade and budget deficits, Craig Elwell, "The U.S. Trade Deficit: Causes, Consequences, and Cures," *CRS Report for Congress,* September 15, 2005; Marc LaBonte and Gail Makinen, "The Budget Deficit and the Trade Deficit: What Is Their Relationship?," *CRS Report for Congress,* March 24, 2005; "Causes and Consequences of the Trade Deficit: An Overview," Congressional Budget Office, March 2000, http://www.cbo.gov/showdoc.cfm?index=1897&sequence=0 (accessed February 3, 2007).

109 *In 2005, American households:* Paul Krugman, "Debt and Denial," *New York Times,* February 13, 2006.

109 *America has careened from a $236 billion:* "Revenues, Outlays, Surpluses, Deficits, and Debt Held by the Public, 1962 to 2006," Office of Management and Budget, Congressional Budget Office, http://www.cbo.gov/budget/historical.pdf (accessed February 19, 2007); also "Basic Questions and Answers About the Deficit," Center on Budget and Policy Priorities, October 30, 2006, http://www.cbpp.org/10-30-06bud.htm (accessed February 19, 2007).

109 *Interest payments alone on the nearly $9 trillion:* "The Debt Tax," Hope Street Group (November 2003), http://www.hopestreetgroup.org/publications/DebtTaxFinal.pdf (accessed February 26, 2006). Figures updated according to "Debt to the Penny and Who Holds It," U.S. Department of Treasury, Treasury Direct, http://www.treasurydirect.gov/NP/BPDLogin?application=np (accessed April 16, 2007); "Interest Expense on the Debt Outstanding," U.S. Department of Treasury, Treasury Direct, http://www.treasurydirect.gov/govt/reports/ir/ir_expense.htm (accessed March 23, 2006); "Budget of the United States Government FY2006," Office of Management and Budget, http://www.whitehouse

.gov/omb/budget/fy2006/tables.html (accessed March 23, 2006); "Households and Families," 2005 American Community Survey, Table S1101, U.S. Census Bureau http://factfinder.census.gov/servlet/ST Table?_bm=y&-geo_id=01000US&-qr_name=ACS_2005_EST_G00_ S1101&-ds_name=ACS_2005_EST_G00_&-_lang=en&-_caller=geo select&-state=st&-format= (accessed March 23, 2006).

109 *"superpower living on credit":* Paul Krugman, "China Unpegs Itself," *New York Times,* July 22, 2005.

109 *To finance its budget deficit:* "Sizing up the Deficit," *Washington Times,* April 26, 2005, http://washingtontimes.com/op-ed/20050415-084659-3981r.htm (accessed February 19, 2006).

110 *China and Japan account:* Calculated using data from: "Total Liabilities to Foreigners by Type and Country: China, Mainland (41408)," U.S. Department of the Treasury, http://www.ustreas.gov/tic/lb_41408.txt (accessed April 11, 2007); "Total Liabilities to Foreigners by Type and Country Japan (42609)," U.S. Department of the Treasury, http://www.ustreas.gov/tic/lb_42609.txt (accessed April 11, 2007); "Major Foreign Holders of Treasury Securities," U.S. Department of the Treasury, http://www.ustreas.gov/tic/mfh.txt (accessed April 11, 2007).

110 *Like a massive company store:* "A Fair Exchange?," *Economist,* October 2, 2004; also Niall Ferguson, "Our Currency, Your Problem," *New York Times Magazine,* March 13, 2005, 22.

110 *"Borrowing to consume"* Jacob Weisberg, "The Perils of Bush's Binge Borrowing," *Financial Times,* February 9, 2006.

110 *While the ratio:* Former Treasury Secretary Robert Rubin warns that "a day of serious reckoning" is near. Joseph Stiglitz, the Nobel Prize–winning economist, is "very worried." The former chairman of the Federal Reserve Board, Paul Volcker, predicts we face a 75 percent chance of a major financial crisis by 2009. These quotes and a fuller analysis of the twin deficits in Peter G. Peterson, *Running on Empty* (New York: Farrar, Straus & Giroux, 2004), xiii. Also Mark Glassman, "Fall into the Trade Gap," *SmartMoney.com,* February 11, 2006; Jonathan Jacoby, "Attention to Deficit Disorder: US Trade Deficit Demands Long Term Focus," Center for American Progress, February 13, 2007, http://www.american progress.org/issues/2007/02/trade.html (accessed February 21, 2007).

110 *Federal Reserve chairman Ben Bernanke:* Krishna Guha, Eoin Callan, and Tony Tassell, "Bernake Warns US of 'Fiscal Crisis' Fear," *Financial Times,* January 19, 2007.

110   *The tax cuts of 2001:* "Basic Questions and Answers About the Deficit," Center on Budget and Policy Priorities, October 30, 2006, http://www.cbpp.org/10-30-06bud.htm (accessed February 3, 2007).

110   *The Fed might not be able:* Weisberg, "The Perils of Bush's Binge Borrowing."

110   *"I think the greatest threat":* Nicholas D. Kristof, "A Glide Path to Ruin," *New York Times,* June 26, 2005.

111   *U.S. credibility is low:* Posen and Tarullo, "Report of the Working Group on Economics and National Security," 9.

111   *"Competition from Japan":* John Yochelson (former president of the Council on Competitiveness), in discussion with Nina Hachigian, December 2005.

112   *China knows it eventually needs:* Keith Bradsher, "Consumer Demand at Home Keeps China's Factories Humming, and Hiring," *New York Times,* October 21, 2005, Robert J. Samuelson, "China's Trade Time Bomb," *Washington Post,* May 9, 2007.

113   *A recent law banning lead and mercury:* Marla Cone, "Europe's Rules Forcing US Firms to Clean Up," *Los Angeles Times,* May 16, 2005.

113   *Other examples include regulations:* Stuart Eizenstat and Ruben Kraiem, "In Green Company," *Foreign Policy* (September/October 2005): 92; Brandon Mitchener, "Rules, Regulations of Global Economy Are Increasingly Being Set in Brussels," *Wall Street Journal,* April 23, 2002.

113   *Japan, India, and the EU:* "Snapshot of WTO Cases Involving the US," Office of the U.S. Trade Representative, October, 18, 2006, http://www.ustr.gov/assets/Trade_Agreements/Monitoring_Enforcement/Dispute_Settlement/WTO/asset_upload_file962_5696.pdf (accessed February 24, 2007); "Japan-US Relations: Issues for Congress," Congressional Research Service, March 21, 2005, http://fpc.state.gov/documents/organization/46431.pdf#search=japanu.s.%20tension (accessed February 25, 2006).

113   *In the Doha Round, India and Brazil:* William Hawkins, "WTO Talks Move in China's Direction," *China Brief* 6, no. 1 (January 3, 2006), http://jamestown.org/publications_details.php?volume_id=415&issue_id=3571&article_id=2370617 (accessed May 13, 2006).

113   *China has brought actions:* George J. Gilboy, "The Myth Behind China's Miracle," *Foreign Affairs* (July/August 2004): 37.

113   *What is encouraging is that:* China is also promoting Linux, an

open-source operating system to avoid licensing Microsoft's software. Michelle Kessler, "US Firms: Doing Business in China Tough, but Critical," *USA Today*, August 17, 2004. For more on China's standards, Ann Weeks and Dennis Chen, "Navigating China's Standards Regime," *China Business Review Special Report* (May/June 2003), http://china businessreview.com/public/0305/weeks.html (accessed February 11, 2006).

114 *In the case of cell phones:* Steven W. Popper and Caroline S. Wagner, *New Foundations for Growth: The U.S. Innovation System Today and Tomorrow* (Santa Monica: RAND, 2002), 46.

114 *Losses from illegal copyright:* "2007 Special 301 Report," International Intellectual Property Alliance, February 12, 2007, http://www.iipa.com/pdf/IIPA2007Special301TableofEstimatedTradeLossesandPiracyLevels for20052006draft012907.pdf (accessed April 12, 2007).

114 *The natural evolution of China:* "Thinking for Themselves," *Economist*, October 22, 2005.

114 *After the U.S., China:* "Third Annual BSA and IDC Global Software Piracy Study," Business Software Alliance, May 2006, 8–9.

114 *Bill Gates predicts:* Reuters, "Gates: Beating Asian Piracy to Take a Decade," January 27, 2006, http://news.yahoo.com/s/zd/170141 (accessed February 16, 2006).

114 *America cannot have:* Charlene Barshefsky (former U.S. trade representative), in discussion with the authors, June 2006.

115 *Paradoxically, the growing:* Deanne Julius, "US Economic Power: Waxing or Waning?," *Harvard International Review* (Winter 2005–2006): 18.

115 *Despite the increase in trade:* Paul Krugman, *Pop Internationalism* (Cambridge: MIT Press, 1996), 9.

115 *Trade with China:* Christian Weller (Senior Fellow, Center for American Progress) in discussion with Nina Hachigian, May 2007.

115 *It's America's fear:* Krugman, *Pop Internationalism*, 67–68.

5. REPAIRING THE INNOVATION ENGINE

116 *Even slight improvements:* For example, Britain began with a higher per capita income than the U.S. in 1870, but it grew slower—just one-half of one percentage point slower over the next 125 years. That tiny gap meant that Americans enjoy higher incomes today, such is the relentless nature of compound growth. Paul Romer, "Innovation: The New Pump

of Growth," *Blueprint* (December 1, 1998). Here is another example of compounding: An investment banker asks to be paid by putting one penny on the first square of a chessboard, two on the second, four on the third, etc. If both black and white squares are used, the penny will grow to $92 million. Try it yourself. Paul M. Romer, "Economic Growth," in *The Concise Encyclopedia of Economics*, http://www.econlib.org/LIBRARY/Enc/EconomicGrowth.html (accessed February 6, 2006).

116 *The linchpin to U.S. economic growth:* Michael E. Porter, *The Competitive Advantage of Nations* (New York: Free Press, 1990), 6.

117 *"[T]he key to productivity growth":* Diana Farrell, "Panel Debates Offshoring" discussion at McKinsey & Company Leadership Breakfast, http://www.mckinsey.com/ideas/Offshoring/roundtable/pdf/offshoring_breakfast_panel.pdf (accessed May 14, 2006); Steven W. Popper and Caroline S. Wagner, *New Foundations for Growth: The U.S. Innovation System Today and Tomorrow* (Santa Monica: RAND, 2002), 1. As Popper and Wagner put it, "The startling transformation of the U.S. economy over the past twenty years has made it clear that innovations based upon scientific and technological advances have become a major contributor to our national well-being."

117 *and many have argued:* Council on Competitiveness, *Innovative America: Thriving in a World of Challenge and Change* (2004), Executive Summary.

117 *Technological improvements:* Committee on Prospering in the Global Economy of the 21st Century, *Rising Above the Gathering Storm: Energizing and Employing America for a Brighter Economic Future* (Washington, D.C.: National Academies Press, 2007), 205, http://books.nap.edu/openbook.php?record_id=11463&page=R1 (accessed July 11, 2007).

117 *As Stanford economist Paul Romer:* Romer, "Economic Growth."

117 *Second, unlike in commodities markets:* Michael E. Porter, "Location, Competition and Economic Development: Local Clusters in a Global Economy," *Economic Development Quarterly* 14, no. 1 (February 2000): 15–34.

118 *For example, first movers:* Porter, *Competitive Advantage*, 47, 64.

118 *The U.S. and Great Britain:* Peter J. Hughill, "The Route to the Techno-Industrial World Economy and the Transfer of German Organic Chemistry to America Before, During and Immediately After World War I," *Comparative Technology Transfer and Society* 3, no. 2 (August 2005).

118   *For starters, the superiority:* Mary Jo Nye, *From Chemical Philosophy to Theoretical Chemistry: Dynamics of Matter and Dynamics of Disciplines, 1800–1950* (Berkeley: University of California Press, 1993), 168.

119   *The language of chemistry:* L. F. Haber, *The Chemical Industry During the Nineteenth Century* (Oxford: Oxford University Press, 1958), 129.

119   *The academic environment:* C. E. McClelland, *State, Society, and University in Germany, 1700–1914* (New York: Cambridge University Press, 1980), 173.

119   *These links in turn:* Ashish Arora, Ralph Landau, and Nathan Rosenberg, eds., *Chemicals and Long-Term Economic Growth* (New York: Wiley, 1998), 518.

119   *Germany's technology lead:* Ibid., 65.

119   *With less than 5 percent:* Richard B. Freeman, "Does Globalization of the Scientific/Engineering Workforce Threaten U.S. Economic Leadership?," *National Bureau of Economic Research,* Working Paper No. 11457 (2005), 1, http://www.nber.org/papers/w11457 (accessed July 12, 2006).

119   *China's $93 billion:* China's R&D calculated using purchasing power parity data; 1983 figure in 2000 dollars. "Science, Technology and Industry Outlook 2006, Statistical Annex, Table 1, Key Figures on Research and Development," Organization for Economic Cooperation and Development (December 2006); "National Patterns of R&D Resources—Historical Database for National Patterns," National Science Foundation (2004 data update), http://www.nsf.gov/statistics/nsf06327/pdf/tabd.pdf (accessed May 13, 2006).

119   *China placed 49th:* "The Global Competitiveness Report 2005–2006," World Economic Forum, http://www.weforum.org/site/homepublic .nsf/Content/Global+Competitiveness+Programme%5CGlobal+Com petitiveness+Report (accessed May 7, 2006).

119   *In 2005, India and China:* This comparison found in Richard Florida, "The World Is Spiky," *Atlantic Monthly,* October 2005. Figures updated using data from "Patents by Country, State, and Year—Utility Patents," U.S. Patent and Trademark Office (December 2005), http://www.usp to.gov/web/offices/ac/ido/oeip/taf/cst_utl.htm (accessed August 20, 2006); "Calendar Year 2005: Preliminary List of Top Patenting U.S. Universities," U.S. Patent and Trademark Office, http://www.uspto.gov/ web/offices/ac/ido/oeip/taf/top05univ.htm (accessed August 20, 2006).

119   *and most of the world's best research institutions:* Committee on Prospering in the Global Economy, *Rising Above the Gathering Storm,* 70.

119   *There is more foreign-funded R&D:* Ibid., 194, 210.

119   *and scientific articles by Americans:* Ibid., 70.

120   *The U.S. also leads:* Adam Segal, "Is America Losing Its Edge? Innovation in a Globalized World," *Foreign Affairs* (November/December 2004): 3.

120   *Beyond the numbers:* Popper and Wagner, *New Foundations for Growth.*

120   *"There is no God-given right":* Alcoa executive, in discussion with Nina Hachigian, February 2006.

120   *In 2006, Google established:* Tom Koehler, "Boeing Active in Technology Research Around the World," *Boeing Frontiers* 3, no. 8 (December 2004/January 2005).

120   *Boeing's Moscow Design Center:* Thomas L. Friedman, "Will Russia Bet on Its People or Its Oil Wells?," *New York Times*, February 16, 2007.

120   *"We came to India":* Pete Engardio, "A New World Economy," *Business-Week Online*, August 22, 2005, http://www.businessweek.com/magazine/content/05_34/b3948401.htm (accessed May 13, 2006).

120   *While it has a long road to travel:* Edward Cody, "In China, Dreams of Bright Ideas," *Washington Post*, June 17, 2006. For a discussion of the many hurdles on China's innovation path, Geoff Dyer, "How China Is Rising Through the Innovation Ranks," *Financial Times*, January 4, 2007.

121   *National spending in China on all R&D:* "Measuring the Moment: Innovation, National Security and Economic Competitiveness," Task Force on the Future of American Innovation (November 2006), 14, http://futureofinnovation.org/PDF/BII-FINAL-HighRes-11-14-06_nocover.pdf (accessed January 3, 2007); Committee on Prospering in the Global Economy, *Rising Above the Gathering Storm*, 72; also Kathy Chen and Jason Dean, "Low Costs, Plentiful Talent Make China a Global Magnet for R&D," *Wall Street Journal*, March 13, 2006.

121   *Its R&D spending is now second:* Dyer, "How China Is Rising."

121   *In 1997, China had fewer than fifty:* Freeman, "Globalization of the Scientific/Engineering Workforce," 9.

121   *Bill Gates asserts:* Thomas L. Friedman, *The World Is Flat* (New York: Farrar, Straus & Giroux, 2005), 266.

121   *Procter & Gamble runs:* Chen and Dean, "Low Costs."

121   *"China is not an innovative economy":* Dyer, "How China Is Rising."

121   *Plagiarism plagues research:* Ibid.

122   *Steven Popper, an innovation expert:* Steven Popper (innovation economist at the RAND Corporation), in discussion with Nina Hachigian, February 2006.

122 *If labs evaluated one thousand:* Romer, "Economic Growth."

122 *In general, the more innovation there is:* Ibid.

122 *American companies have been conducting:* "R&D Investments by Multi-national Companies," Science and Engineering Indicators 2004, National Science Foundation (May 2004), http://www.nsf.gov/statistics/seind04/c4/c4s5.htm#c4s512 (accessed May 16, 2006); "Monitoring Industrial Research: The 2005 EU Industrial R&D Scoreboard," European Commission (2005), http://eurosfaire.prdFr/7pc/doc/1139409651_scoreboard2005_key_findings_vol1.pdf (accessed June 20, 2006). Of the world's top 942 companies in 2004, EU companies accounted for 31.1 percent of R&D investment spending against 38 percent by U.S. companies.

122 *Moreover, in many areas of science:* Popper and Wagner, *New Foundations for Growth*, 72.

122 *In subatomic physics:* Dennis Overbye, "China Pursues Major Role in Particle Physics," *New York Times*, December 5, 2006.

123 *American and EU scientists:* European Union, "Working Together for New Discoveries," *eufocus newsletter* (July 2005), 6.

123 *This is exactly what has happened:* Karen A. Rasler and William R. Thompson, *The Great Powers and Global Struggle—1490–1990* (Lexington: University Press of Kentucky, 1994), Overview and Chapter 5.

123 *All great powers have been keen innovators:* At their apex, nearly all the world's great powers were renowned for cutting-edge innovation. Between the seventh and eleventh centuries, the Islamic "golden age" produced many advances in science and technology like the "Canons of Medicine" used by European doctors for over six hundred years. In the fifteenth and sixteenth centuries, the Ottoman Empire successfully leveraged early advances in artillery technology to build an empire stretching from Europe to the Middle East and North Africa. Dutch shipbuilding prowess, and their innovative design of efficient cargo carriers, helped propel the tiny nation to become a leading power from the 1620s to 1660s. On the Islamic "Canons of Medicine," James McClellan and Harold Dorn, *Science and Technology in World History: An Introduction* (Baltimore: Johns Hopkins University Press, 1999), 103–15; on Muslim science and technological achievements, PBS Global Connections, "The Middle East: Science and Technology, Historic Innovation, Modern Solutions," http://www.pbs.org/wgbh/

globalconnections/mideast/themes/science/index.html (accessed July 11, 2006); on Ottoman innovation, William Cleveland, *A History of the Modern Middle East* (Boulder Westview, 2000); for a description of Dutch naval technology and supremacy, George Raudzens, *Empires: Europe and Globalization, 1492–1788* (Gloucestershire, U.K.: Sutton, 1999), Chapter 5.

123   *Beyond tea and gunpowder:* "China and Europe 1500–2000 and Beyond: China's Contribution to the West," Asia for Educators, Columbia University (2004).

123   *Iron production was fully under way:* Robert Hartwell, "Markets, Technology and the Structure of Enterprise in the Development of the 11th Century Iron and Steel Industry," *Journal of Economic History* 26, no. 1 (March 1966): 34.

124   *The largest vessels:* McClellan and Dorn, *Science and Technology in World History,* 126–27.

124   *By comparison, Christopher Columbus's ships:* F. W. Mote, *Imperial China: 900–1800* (Cambridge: Harvard University Press, 1999), 614.

124   *It was an ill-fated decision:* McClellan and Dorn, *Science and Technology in World History,* 126–27.

124   *In the specific case of shipbuilding:* John K. Fairbank and Edwin O. Reischauer, *China: Tradition and Transformation* (Boston: Houghton Mifflin, 1989), 199–200.

124   *Others focus on cultural factors:* Nathan Sivin, "Science and Medicine in Chinese History" (1990), http://ccat.sas.upenn.edu/~nsivin/writ.html (accessed February 21, 2006).

125   *Britain had gone from being the laggard:* Paul Kennedy, *The Rise and Fall of the Great Powers: Economic Change and Military Conflict from 1500–2000* (New York: Random House, 1989), 149.

125   *At the height of its power:* Niall Ferguson, *Empire: The Rise and Demise of the British World Order and Lessons for Global Power* (New York: Basic Books, 2004), ix.

125   *It was easier and cheaper:* Ibid., 385.

125   *Like the U.S. today, the dominant orthodoxy:* Aaron Friedberg, *The Weary Titan: Britain and the Experience of Relative Decline, 1895–1905* (Princeton: Princeton University Press, 1988), 92–95.

125   *The government consciously pursued:* Kennedy, *The Rise and Fall of the Great Powers,* 153.

125 *By the turn of the twentieth century, savvy:* Friedberg, *The Weary Titan,* 292–93.

125 *So limited was the belief:* Ibid., 38–41.

125 *After 1903, Englishmen tended:* Ibid., 296.

126 *Many argued the nation could not afford:* Joseph Nye, *Bound to Lead: The Changing Nature of American Power* (New York: Basic Books, 1990), 61, 63.

126 *Compulsory primary education:* David Landes, *The Unbound Prometheus: Technological Change and Industrial Development in Western Europe from 1750 to the Present* (Cambridge: Cambridge University Press, 1969), 340–43.

126 *The first public grant:* Peter Mathias, *The First Industrial Nation: The Economic History of Britain 1700–1914* (London: Methuen & Co. 1983), 389.

126 *And even as some observers understood:* Friedberg, *The Weary Titan,* 298.

126 *As a share of GDP:* "Measuring the Moment: Innovation, National Security and Economic Competitiveness," Task Force on the Future of American Innovation, November 2006, 9, http://futureofinnovation.org/ PDF/BII-FINAL-HighRes-11-14-06_nocover.pdf (accessed May 13, 2007); also Committee on Prospering in the Global Economy, *Rising Above the Gathering Storm,* 137–39.

127 *"increasingly risk-adverse":* Committee on Prospering in the Global Economy, *Rising Above the Gathering Storm,* 32–33.

127 *Likewise, private funding for R&D:* Task Force on American Innovation, "Measuring the Moment," 9.

127 *Only 5 percent of funding is devoted:* Ibid., 12.

127 *A smaller share of American undergraduates:* Committee on Prospering in the Global Economy, *Rising Above the Gathering Storm,* 31; also Freeman, "Globalization of the Scientific/Engineering Workforce." The number of students in China studying engineering is regularly overstated, however. Pete Engardio, "Engineering: Is the U.S. Really Failing?," *BusinessWeek,* December 27, 2005.

127 *Tuition is up, but scholarship funds are shrinking:* Committee on Prospering in the Global Economy, *Rising Above the Gathering Storm,* 31.

127 *Yet the number of jobs requiring:* National Science Board, *Science and Engineering Indicators 2006* (Arlington: National Science Foundation, 2006), http://www.nsf.gov/statistics/seind06/ (accessed July 12, 2007).

127 *"If you took all 'foreigners' out of Silicon Valley,"*: Byron Auguste (director at McKinsey & Company), in discussion with Nina Hachigian, November 2005.

127 *"flocking back from top"*: Chen and Dean, "Low Costs."

127 *In 2006, two prominent cancer researchers*: Wayne Arnold, "Science Haven in Singapore," *New York Times*, August 17, 2006.

127 *A recent book*, Flight Capital: David Heenan, *Flight Capital: The Alarming Exodus of America's Best and Brightest* (Mountain View: Davies-Black, 2005).

127 *A troubling OECD study:* "Learning for Tomorrow's World," Organization for Economic Cooperation and Development (2003), http://www .pisa.oecd.org (accessed July 12, 2006).

128 *A recent blue-ribbon commission:* Committee on Prospering in the Global Economy, *Rising Above the Gathering Storm*, 25.

128 *and that "the scientific and technical":* Ibid., 3.

128 *The Hart-Rudman Commission:* Executive Summary, Report of the U.S. Commission on National Security/21st Century (January 31, 2001), http://www.apfn.org/apfn/security.htm (accessed February 23, 2006).

128 *"how you can raise your bar"*: Friedman, *The World Is Flat*, 190.

128 *The best thinkers in the country:* Examples of such studies include: Popper and Wagner, *New Foundations for Growth* (2002); Committee on Prospering in the Global Economy, *Rising Above the Gathering Storm*; Kent H. Hughes, "Facing the Global Competitiveness Challenge," *Issues in Science and Technology Online* (Summer 2005), http://www.issues .org/21.4/hughes.html (accessed August 30, 2006).

128 *A periodic report card:* Every four years, the military conducts a comprehensive review of strategies, assets, and threats, known as Quadrennial Defense Review (QDR), which helps direct funding and training priorities for the future.

128 *Most critical, though, are investments:* A key strategic resource necessary for America's prosperity has become intellectual capital—educated people and their ideas. James J. Duderstadt and Farris W. Womack, *Beyond the Crossroads: The Future of the Public University in America* (Baltimore: Johns Hopkins University Press, 2003), 215, 219.

129 *Intel chairman Craig Barrett:* Craig Barrett, "Why America Needs to Open Its Doors Wide to Foreign Talent," *Financial Times*, January 31, 2006.

129   *It has been twenty-five years:* Among them Michael Porter's influential 1990 book, *The Competitive Advantage of Nations* (New York: Simon & Schuster, 1990); Senator John Glenn's 2000 report, *Before It's Too Late: A Report to the Nation from the National Commission on Mathematics and Science Teaching for the 21st Century*; National Academies, "Committee on Prospering in the Global Economy of the 21st Century" (2005); Task Force on the Future of American Innovation, *Measuring the Moment: Innovation, National Security and Economic Competitiveness* (2006); Committee on Pre-College Education in Mathematics, Science, and Technology, *Educating Americans for the 21st Century: A Report to the American People and the National Science Board* (2003); U.S. Congress Office of Technology Assessment, *Educating Scientists and Engineers: Grade School to Grad School* (1988).

129   *The Teaching Commission:* The Teaching Commission, *Teaching at Risk: Progress and Potholes* (Spring 2006), http://www.theteachingcommission .org/press/pdfs/ProgressandPotholes.pdf (accessed September 4, 2006).

129   *Another blue-ribbon panel:* "Renewing Our Schools, Securing Our Future," Center for American Progress (August 2005), http://www.ameri canprogress.org/projects/education/report.html (accessed April 11, 2007).

129   *Other experts suggest new charter schools:* Edward Gresser, Paul Weinstein, Jr., and Will Marshall, "Raising Our Game: A National Competition Strategy," Progressive Policy Institute, (June 2006), http://www .ppionline.org/documents/Raising_Game_062906.pdf (accessed September 4, 2006); Committee on Prospering in the Global Economy, *Rising Above the Gathering Storm*, 165–66.

130   *"Civilizations die from suicide":* Patrick J. Buchanan, *States of Emergency: The Third World Invasion and Conquest of America* (New York: St. Martin's Press, 2006), 1.

130   *"The only thing":* Jon Stewart, *The Daily Show with Jon Stewart*, September 18, 2006.

6. THE POWERS' PERSPECTIVES

132   *In China's case, such bifurcated attitudes:* Carola McGiffert, ed., *Chinese Images of the United States* (Washington, D.C.: CSIS, 2005), xv.

132   *Chinese analysts will remind:* World Bank, *World Bank Development Indicators 2006—Table 1.1, Size of Economy* (Washington, D.C.: International Bank for Reconstruction and Development, 2006), http://dev

data.worldbank.org/wdi2006/contents/index2.htm (accessed March 23, 2007).

132 *At the same time, the sense that China is destined:* Zhang Yunling and Tang Shiping, "China's Regional Strategy," in David Shambaugh, ed., *Power Shift: China and Asia's New Dynamics* (Berkeley: University of California Press, 2005), 49.

132 *The Chinese public is confident:* "The United States and the Rise of China and India: Results of a 2006 Multination Survey of Public Opinion," Chicago Council on Global Affairs (2006), 33.

132 *In India, the mood:* Journalist Dileep Padgaonkar, as quoted in C. Raja Mohan, *Crossing the Rubicon* (New York: Palgrave Macmillan, 2003), 267.

132 *While Indians readily admit:* UNDP, *Human Development Report—2006* (New York: U.N. Development Programme, 2006), http://hdr.undp.org/hdr2006/statistics (accessed February 21, 2007).

132 *"India's greatness":* C. Raja Mohan (professor at the S. Rajaratnam School of International Studies of Nanyang Technological University in Singapore), in discussion with Nina Hachigian, October 2006.

132 *This sense of entitlement:* Mohan, *Crossing the Rubicon*, 58.

132 *In recent polling, Indians declared themselves:* "The United States and the Rise of China and India," 40.

133 *"Bigger, tougher, stronger":* Thom Shanker and Jim Rutenberg, "Bush Begins Advanced Course on the Ways of Putin," *New York Times*, July 14, 2006.

133 *The Bush team was inclined:* Masha Lipman, "The Russian Revival," *Daily Times*, August 10, 2006, http://www.carnegie.ru/en/pubs/media/74565.htm (accessed November 28, 2006).

133 *Putin's comment reflected:* Stephen E. Hanson, "Strategic Partner or Evil Empire?," *Strategic Asia* (2004/2005): 169.

133 *Russians see themselves as the third:* "Americans and Russians Agree US Is No. 1 but Disagree on the Up and Comers," Program on International Policy Attitudes (July 10, 2006), http://www.worldpublicopinion.org/pipa/articles/views_on_countriesregions_bt/225.php?nid=&id=&pnt=225&lb=btvoc (accessed February 10, 2007).

133 *The debate inside Russia:* Hanson, "Strategic Partner or Evil Empire?," 169.

133 *For Putin, strengthening the power:* For a thorough analysis of Putin's conception of "*gosudarstvennost*," ibid., 169–73.

133 *However, for all of Putin's recent swagger:* Thomas E. Graham, Jr., *Russia's*

Decline and Uncertain Recovery (Washington, D.C.: Carnegie Endowment for International Peace, 2002), Chapter 5.

133 *This lack of confidence lingers:* Lilia Shevtsova, "Imitation Russia," *The American Interest* (November/December 2006), http://www.carnegie.ru/en/pubs/media/74848.htm (accessed April 23, 2007).

134 *Europeans seek to be:* Christoph Bertram (German foreign policy scholar and former director of the German Institute for International and Security Affairs in Berlin), in discussion with Mona Sutphen, November 2006.

134 *"Europeans today":* Robert Kagan, *Of Paradise and Power: America and Europe in the New World Order* (New York: Knopf, 2003), 55.

134 *Europeans have more appetite:* Bertram discussion.

134 *"huge economy":* Gerald L. Curtis (Burgess Professor of Political Science and former director of the East Asian Institute at Columbia University), in discussion with Nina Hachigian, November 2006.

134 *A recent poll also shows:* "World Powers in the 21st Century: The Results of a Representative Survey in Brazil, China, France, Germany, India, Japan, Russia, the United Kingdom, and the United States," Bertelsmann-Stiftung, June 2, 2006, 13.

134 *For Japan, a permanent seat:* Curtis discussion.

134 *"The U.S. has been secure":* Dr. Jia Qingguo, in discussion with Nina Hachigian, June 2006.

135 *"unassailably powerful":* Salman Haidar (former Indian foreign secretary), in discussion with Nina Hachigian, July 2006.

135 *"part of the future of the world":* Ibid.

135 *But while India seeks a prominent role:* Mohan, *Crossing the Rubicon*, 236.

135 *India wants to move from being a reactive power:* Dr. S. Narayan (former economic advisor to prime minister and finance and economic affairs secretary in the Indian government), in discussion with Nina Hachigian, November 2006; Mohan, *Crossing the Rubicon,* 263.

136 *"Russia today is not":* Dmitri Trenin, "The End of the Affair: Russia Leaves the West," *Foreign Affairs* (July/August 2006).

136 *As longtime Russia expert Susan Eisenhower:* Susan Eisenhower (president of the Eisenhower Group and chairman emeritus of the Eisenhower Institute), in discussion with Mona Sutphen, November 2006.

136 *From these two experiences:* Dmitri Trenin (deputy director, Carnegie Moscow Center), in discussion with Mona Sutphen, October 2006.

136 *As U.S. strategic interests in the Caucasus:* Ilan Berman, "The New Battleground: Central Asia and the Caucasus," *Washington Quarterly* (Winter 2004/2005): 59.

136 *the U.S. should expect more of this confrontational behavior:* Shevtsova, "Imitation Russia."

136 *"Russia is still trapped":* Mark Medish (vice president for studies, Carnegie Endowment for International Peace), in discussion with Mona Sutphen, November 2006.

137 *"Its main goal":* Stephen Sestanovich (professor of international affairs, Columbia University School of International and Public Affairs), in discussion with Mona Sutphen, October 2006.

137 *Europe relies primarily on its "soft power":* Franco Algieri, "A Weakened EU's Prospects for Global Leadership," *Washington Quarterly* (Winter 2006/2007): 109.

137 *In much of the world, European foreign assistance:* T. R. Reid, *The United States of Europe: The New Superpower and the End of American Supremacy* (New York: Penguin, 2004), 189–90.

137 *Its desire to have a stable:* Jia Qingguo, "Learning to Live with the Hegemon: Evolution of China's Policy Toward the US Since the End of the Cold War," *Journal of Contemporary China* 14, no. 44 (August 2005): 406. Bates Gill suggests a broader framework for China's foreign policy goals. Bates Gill, "China's Evolving Regional Security Strategy," in Shambaugh, ed., *Power Shift*, 248. For more on the sources of Chinese international relations thinking, Alastair Iain Johnston and Robert S. Ross, eds., *New Directions in the Study of China's Foreign Policy* (Stanford: Stanford University Press, 2006); Gerald Chan, *Chinese Perspectives on International Relations: A Framework for Analysis* (New York: St. Martin's, 1999); Avery Goldstein, *Rising to the Challenge: China's Grand Strategy and International Security* (Stanford: Stanford University Press, 2005); Ashley Tellis and Michael Swaine, *Interpreting China's Grand Strategy: Past, Present, and Future* (Santa Monica: RAND, 2000).

137 *With as many as three hundred separate mass protests:* Jin Canrong (associate dean, School of International Studies, Renmin University), in discussion with Nina Hachigian, June 2006.

138 *Building superior military power in Asia:* "The United States and the Rise of China and India," 35, 42.

138 *When ranking threats to China's vital interests:* Ibid., 35.

138 *In every pivotal power:* These terms taken from Wang Jisi, "From Paper Tiger to Real Leviathan: China's Images of the United States Since 1949," in McGiffert, ed., *Chinese Images of the United States,* 10.

138 *In India, Japan, and Russia:* "America's Image Slips, but Allies Share US Concerns Over Iran, Hamas," Pew Global Attitudes Survey (June 13, 2006), 10, http://pewglobal.org/reports/display.php?PageID=825 (accessed April 22, 2007).

138 *According to another poll:* Zhao Mei, "Chinese Views of America," in McGiffert, ed., *Chinese Images of the United States,* 73. Unlike in the past, the Chinese government is not deliberately trying to encourage negative opinions of the United States. Wang, "From Paper Tiger to Real Leviathan."

138 *By comparison, far fewer citizens of the Muslim world:* "America's Image Slips," 10.

139 *Dropping from 78 percent in 2000:* Ibid., 1.

139 *Russians and Chinese have:* Ibid.

139 *In every pivotal power but Japan:* Ibid., 3.

139 *Foreign governments find it more difficult:* Stephen M. Walt, *Taming American Power* (New York: Norton, 2005), 176.

139 *Moreover, if anti-Americanism persists:* Richard N. Haass, *The Opportunity: America's Moment to Alter History's Course* (New York: Public Affairs Press, 2005), 203.

139 *"The doubt in the American system":* Bertram discussion.

139 *Europeans think the United States "continues to shoot itself":* Charles Grant (director, Centre for European Reform), in discussion with Mona Sutphen, November 2006.

139 *leading many to conclude the U.S.:* Richard Morningstar (former U.S. ambassador to the European Union), in discussion with Mona Sutphen, October 2006.

139 *Within Europe, solid majorities:* "US Image up Slightly; but Still Negative," Pew Global Attitudes Survey (June 23, 2005), 23.

139 *Michael Maclay, a former senior advisor:* Maclay discussion.

140 *"the bigger worry":* Ibid.

140 *Even still, over 70 percent of the Russian public:* "US Image up Slightly," 23.

140 *Elites concede that Russia benefits:* Medish discussion.

140 *"Moscow is extremely bitter":* Roald Sagdeev (director emeritus of Russia's Space Research Institute and former Duma member), in discussion with Mona Sutphen, October 2006.

140   *In the case of China:* Evan Medeiros, "Strategic Hedging and the Future of Asia-Pacific Stability," *Washington Quarterly* (Winter 2005/2006): 148. For more on historic anti-Americanism in China, Wang, "From Paper Tiger to Real Leviathan."

140   *"insatiable, domineering country":* Wang, "From Paper Tiger to Real Leviathan," 16.

140   *The Iraq War is proof:* Medeiros, "Strategic Hedging," 148.

140   *"Many Chinese still view":* Wang Jisi, "China's Search for Stability with America," *Foreign Affairs* (September/October 2005): 39.

140   *Even though many Chinese analysts:* Alastair Iain Johnston, "Is China a Status Quo Power?," *International Security* 27, no. 4 (Spring 2003): 32.

140   *A 2006 poll found that a strong majority in China:* "The United States and the Rise of India and China," 53.

141   *Further, they admit that seeing another nation:* Ibid., 54.

141   *The consensus in China:* Jeffrey Bader (director of the John L. Thornton China Center and senior fellow in Foreign Policy Studies, the Brookings Institution), in discussion with Nina Hachigian, October 2006.

141   *And while Beijing is worried:* Jia discussion.

141   *America's might has benefited:* Mohan Malik, "High Hopes: India's responses to US Security Policies," Asia Pacific Center for Security Studies, Special Assesment (March 2003), http://www.apcss.org/core/BIOS/malik/malik.htm#PUBLICATIONS (accessed April 23, 2007).

141   *"cannot even afford":* Curtis discussion.

141   *In each, majorities believe America wants:* "The United States and the Rise of China and India," 52; also, "US Image up Slightly," 23.

141   *Officials and analysts from every pivotal power:* Gong Li, "The Official Perspective: What Chinese Government Officials Think of America," in McGiffert, ed., *Chinese Images of the United States*, 30.

141   *According to a hierarchical:* Wang, "From Paper Tiger to Real Leviathan," 20.

142   *Instead, the United States shows "contempt":* Feng Changhong, "How to View U.S. Strategic Thinking," in McGiffert, ed., *Chinese Images of the United States*, 33, 39.

142   *The expression Chinese:* The Chinese transliteration is "Zhi Xu Zhouguan Fanghuo Buxu Baixing Diandeng."

142   *Chinese often ask:* Wang, "From Paper Tiger to Real Leviathan," 17, 21. As Wang puts it, because the U.S. justifies its actions only in terms of

American interests, it "puts those Chinese who want to defend US foreign policy in an embarrassing position because they are hardly able to present a United States that works to serve the interests of other nations."

142 *Europeans' plea is for the U.S.:* Bertram discussion.

142 *From the Russian point of view:* Trenin discussion.

142 *"[Russians] see the United States":* Coit Blacker (director of Freeman Spogli Institute for International Studies at Stanford University), in discussion with Mona Sutphen, November 2006.

142 *Despite its misgivings:* Bergsten, *China: The Balance Sheet*, 122.

142 *A stable relationship with America:* Jia, "Learning to Live with the Hegemon," 406.

143 *Indians were "congenitally anti-American":* Ashley Tellis (senior associate, Carnegie Endowment for International Peace), in discussion with Nina Hachigian, October 2006.

143 *Following a 1971 meeting:* "Nixon's Dislike of 'Witch' Indira," *BBC News online*, June 29, 2005, http://news.bbc.co.uk/2/hi/south_asia/463 3263.stm (accessed February 2007).

143 *A close relationship is also an "entrée card":* Frank Wisner (vice chairman, AIG, and former U.S. ambassador to India), in discussion with Nina Hachigian, July 2006.

143 *Because "no page in history turns neatly":* Wisner discussion; Haidar discussion.

144 *"There is no support here":* Mohan discussion.

144 *In particular, India is wary:* We discuss the containment strategy and its flaws in the next chapter.

144 *"the United States will fight China":* Stephen P. Cohen, "India: America's New Ally?," Brookings Institution (July 18, 2005), http://www.brook ings.edu/views/op-ed/cohens/20050718.htm (accessed April 23, 2007).

144 *Though segments of the policy community:* Mohan, *Crossing the Rubicon*, 266.

144 *Shared interests in modernizing the Muslim world:* Mohan discussion.

144 *In the case of Russia:* Hanson, "Strategic Partner or Evil Empire?," 166.

144 *As Dmitri Trenin has observed:* Trenin discussion.

144 *"U.S. took advantage":* Sagdeev discussion.

144 *In reality, neither side was willing:* Angela Stent, "America and Russia: Paradoxes of Partnership" in Alexander Moytl, Blair Ruble, and Lilia

Shevtsova, eds., *Russia's Engagement with the West: Transformation and Integration in the 21st Century* (Armonk: M. E. Sharp, 2005), 260.

144 *Now, Russia is ultimately pragmatic:* Trenin, "Russia Leaves the West."

144 *only lead to dissatisfaction:* Shevtsova, "Imitation Russia."

145 *The extent and degree of European comfort:* Philip H. Gordon (senior fellow in Foreign Policy Studies at the Brookings Institution), in discussion with Mona Sutphen, October 2006; Philip H. Gordon and Jeremy Shapiro, *Allies at War: America, Europe and the Crisis over Iraq* (New York: McGraw-Hill, 2004), 26.

145 *Generally, though, there is an assumption:* Bertram discussion.

146 *In India, to use Stephen Cohen's taxonomy:* Stephen P. Cohen, "India: America's New Ally?," Brookings Institution, July 18, 2005, http://www.brookings.edu/views/op-ed/cohens/20050718.htm (accessed October 10, 2006).

146 *Those on the fence want the United States to demonstrate:* Narayan discussion.

146 *In the last camp are the emotional hard-liners:* China has a few neoconservatives who inform the policy debate as well. Mark Leonard, "China's Long and Winding Road," *Financial Times,* July 9, 2005.

147 *"are not a secret":* Ashton B. Carter and William J. Perry, "China's Rise in American Military Strategy," Preventive Defense Project, Aspen Strategy Group (October 16, 2006), 1 (emphasis in the original), http://bcsia .ksg.harvard.edu/BCSIA_content/documents/DearColleagueandCarter PerryASGChina_October2006.pdf (accessed April 6, 2007).

147 *Across the spectrum, Chinese policy elites:* Zhao Mei, "Chinese Views of America," 70; "China Eyes Stronger Military Against Threats," Reuters, July 26, 2006.

147 *To this day, worldly, America-friendly Chinese:* Yong Deng, "Hegemon on the Offensive: Chinese Perceptions on US Global Strategy," *Political Science Quarterly* 116, no. 3 (2001): 352.

147 *America's clear, constant, and public disapproval:* Bergsten, *China: The Balance Sheet,* 124–25.

147 *The loss of Taiwan in 1895:* Thomas Christensen, "Posing Problems Without Catching Up," *International Security* 25, no. 4 (Spring 2001): 15.

147 *A very popular view in China:* Wang, "From Paper Tiger to Real Leviathan," 17; for polling on this issue, Zhao Mei, "Chinese Views of America," 71.

147 *"woke up a thousand ghosts":* Kishore Mahbubani (former Singapore diplomat and dean of the Lee Kuan Yew School of Public Policy at the National University of Singapore), in discussion with Nina Hachigian, June 2005.

148 *Even those who claim that more independence from the United States:* Justin Vaisse (French historian and affiliated scholar in foreign policy at the Brookings Institution), in discussion with Mona Sutphen, October 2006.

148 *As leading French:* Ibid.

148 *However, Iraq taught Europe:* Jean-Yves Haine, "Idealism and Power: The New EU Security Strategy," *Current History* (March 2004): 109.

148 *"across the political landscape":* Sagdeev discussion.

148 *There is a perception:* Trenin discussion.

149 *U.S. policies, like the outdated Jackson-Vanik Amendment:* Sagdeev discussion.

149 *Post-9/11, both sides thought counterterror cooperation:* Hanson, "Strategic Partner or Evil Empire?," 176.

149 *Though it is no longer fashionable to be pro-U.S.:* Shevstova, "Imitation Russia."

149 *The "neo-autonomists" would keep:* For an informative discussion of this debate, Richard J. Samuels, "Japan's Goldilocks Strategy," *Washington Quarterly* (Autumn 2006): 111.

149 *Pacifists would:* Ibid.

149 *"Everything Americans":* Susan L. Shirk, *China: Fragile Superpower* (Oxford: Oxford University Press, 2007) 261; Jia discussion.

149 *In an instant, U.S. actions can put those arguing:* Jia discussion. Jia warns in an earlier article, "Should the US revert back to a policy that treats China as an enemy or potential enemy . . . this may force China to treat the US as such." Jia, "Learning to Live with the Hegemon," 407.

149 *Russians similarly see the agenda:* Stent, "America and Russia," 272.

149 *"the main impetus":* Michael McFaul, "Russia and the West: A Dangerous Drift," *Current History* (October 2005): 104, 684.

150 *"The answer to that":* Ratan Tata (CEO of Tata Group, one of India's largest conglomerates) in discussion with Nina Hachigian, December 2005.

150 *For example, while India and Russia:* Mohan, *Crossing the Rubicon,* 129–33.

151 *"Strategic partners":* "India keen to expand n-ties with Russia," News RIN.ru, January 24, 2007, http://www.news.rin.ru/eng/news///9837/3// (accessed June 20, 2007).

151 *Moscow is Delhi's largest defense partner:* Somini Sengupta, "Putin in India: Visit Is Sign of Durability of Old Ties," *New York Times,* January 25, 2007; "India, Russia Discussing Developing 5th Generation Fighter," *Rediff India Abroad,* December 22, 2005, http://www.rediff.com/news/2005/dec/22jet.htm (accessed November 13, 2006).

151 *Space agreement made Russian law:* Russian president Vladimir Putin signed the Indo-Russian space cooperation agreement into law in November 2006. "Russia's Putin Clears Space Pact with India," *BBC News Worldwide,* November 6, 2006.

151 *Bilateral trade:* Trade statistics, Japanese Ministry of Finance, http://www.customs.go.jp/toukei/suil/csv/d42ca006.csv (accessed July 30, 2007).

151 *Japan is largest investor in Russian oil and gas:* James Brooke, "Quietly, Japan and Russia Mend Ties," *New York Times,* January 11, 2005.

151 *Free trade agreement:* Negotiations on the agreement began in November 2006, with a deal expected in 2007. "Russia-EU Free Trade Agreement to Be Discussed in 2007," *mosnews.com,* July 3, 2006, http://mosnews.com/money/2006/07/03/russiaeutrade.shtml (accessed October 29, 2006).

151 *Major military exercise held:* Named "Peace Mission 2005," the exercise included nearly ten thousand troops. Ariel Cohen and John J. Tkacik, Jr., "Sino-Russian Military Maneuvers: A Threat to U.S. Interests in Eurasia," Backgrounder No. 1883, Heritage Foundation, September 20, 2005; Mark Magnier and Kim Murphy, "An Exercise Fit for Sending U.S. a Message," *Los Angeles Times,* August 17, 2005; "Hu, Putin Reaffirm 'Strategic Alliance' at Summit Talks," Agence France-Presse, February 7, 2005.

151 *"Eight-fold" initiative issued:* "Eight-fold Initiative for Strengthening Japan-India Global Partnership," Ministry of Foreign Affairs of Japan, http://www.mofa.go.jp/region/asia-paci/india/partner0504.html#eight (accessed May 13, 2007); Amit Baruah, "India and Japan Plan to Work as 'Partners Against Proliferaton,' " *Hindu,* April 30, 2005, http://www.hindu.com/2005/04/30/stories/2005043006030100.htm (accessed November 3, 2006); "Japan to Pursue Trade Deals with India, China:

Paper," Reuters, January 2, 2006, http://www.boston.com/news/world/asia/articles/2006/01/03/japan_to_pursue_trade_deals_with_india_china_paper/?rss_id=Boston.com+%2F+News (accessed November 3, 2006).

151 *India is the largest:* "Outline of Japan's ODA to India," Ministry of Foreign Affairs of Japan, http://www.mofa.go.jp/region/asia-paci/india/pmv0504/oda_i.pdf.

151 *In 2006 the U.K. proposed India and EU:* "India, E.U. Should Sign Free Trade Deal: U.K.," *Hindu,* January 17, 2006, http://www.hindu.com/2006/01/17/stories/2006011703131700.htm (accessed November 3, 2006). The suggestion was made by the visiting U.K. trade minister, Ian Pearson, to Indian commerce and industry minister Kamal Nath, who said India would be "open" to the idea.

151 *Memorandum of understanding on training and employment:* India and the European Commission on, November 27, 2006, signed a memorandum of understanding to strengthen dialogue and exchange on employment and social affairs. "EU, India Sign MoU on Training and Employment," *IndiaDaily,* November 27, 2006, http://www.indiadaily.com/breaking_news/82874.asp (accessed November 29, 2006).

151 *Major summit in November 2006:* "China, India Expand Economic Ties," Associated Press, November 22, 2006. Also, silk road border trade resumed after forty-four years. Anil K. Joseph, "Sino-India Trade Set to Cross Record $20 Billion," *Rediff India,* April 17, 2006, http://us.rediff.com/money/2006/apr/17china.htm?q=bp&file=.htm (accessed November 3, 2006); "India-China Trade Link to Reopen," *BBC News,* June 19, 2006, http://news.bbc.co.uk/1/hi/world/south_asia/5093712.stm (accessed November 3, 2006).

151 *Border deal signed:* "China and India sign Border Deal," *BBC News,* April 11, 2005, http://news.bbc.co.uk/1/i/world/south_asia/4431299.stm (accessed November 13, 2006).

151 *Agreed in June:* "India and China to conduct first joint army exercises," Agence France-Presse, June 7, 2007.

151 *EU ranks 2nd in Japan's imports:* Numbers take into account Japanese production in China, and are from 2004 and 2005; "Bilateral Trade Relations: Japan," The EU and the World: External Trade, European Commission, http://ec.europa.eu/trade/issues/bilateral/countries/japan/index_en.htm (accessed November 3, 2006).

151 *2006 summit in Beijing ends 5-year:* Wenran Jiang, "China's Renewed Summit Diplomacy with Japan," *China Brief* 21, no. 6 (October 25, 2006), Jamestown Foundation, http://jamestown.org/images/pdf/cb_006_021.pdf (accessed October 29, 2006).

151 *In 2006 began considering:* "China, Japan Consider Free Trade Talks," Associated Press, November 2, 2006, http://biz.yahoo.com/ap/061102/china_japan_free_trade.html?.v=1 (accessed November 3, 2006). China is already Japan's largest trading partner, while Japan is China's second largest trading partner. Paul Blustein, "China Passes U.S. in Trade with Japan," *Washington Post*, January 27, 2005, http://www.washingtonpost.com/wp-dyn/articles/A40192-2005Jan26.html (accessed November 3, 2006).

151 *China is EU's 2nd largest trading partner:* "Bilateral Trade Relations: China," European Commission, http://ec.europa.eu/trade/issues/bilateral/countries/china/ index_en.htm (accessed November 3, 2006).

151 *Similarly, Russia and China flirt:* Susan Shirk (director of the University of California Institute on Global Conflict and Cooperation and former deputy assistant secretary of state for East Asia), in discussion with Nina Hachigian, October 2006.

152 *Such concern about China is shared:* James Kanter, "Poll Reflects Growing Fear of China's Military," *Boston Globe*, September 22, 2006.

152 *Further, for all their recent friendliness:* Mohan, *Crossing the Rubicon*, 210.

152 *The Indians think they should have a lot:* "The United States and the Rise of China and India," 33, 40.

152 *According to recent Pew polling:* "US Image up Slightly," 29–30.

153 *In a different poll:* "23 Nation Poll: Who Will Lead the World?," Program on International Policy Attitudes, April 6, 2005, http://www.worldpublicopinion.org/pipa/articles/views_on_countriesregions_bt/114.php?nid=&id=&pnt=114&1b=btvoc (accessed February 21, 2007).

153 *Tokyo is most supportive:* Samuels, "Japan's Goldilocks Strategy," 120.

153 *Many Chinese believe the decline of U.S. primacy:* Wang, "From Paper Tiger to Real Leviathan," 40.

153 *Because of America's staying power:* For more on China's policies toward the U.S., C. Fred Bergsten, Bates Gill, Nicholas R. Lardy, and Derek Mitchell, *China: The Balance Sheet: What the World Needs to Know Now About the Emerging Superpower* (New York: Public Affairs Press, 2006);

David Lampton, *Same Bed, Different Dreams: Managing U.S.-China Relations, 1989–2000* (Berkeley: University of California Press, 2002); Denny Roy, "China's Reaction to American Predominance," *Survival* 45, no. 3 (Autumn 2003): 57–78.

153 *Beijing is framing its path:* Zheng Bijian, "China's 'Peaceful Rise' to Great-Power Status," *Foreign Affairs* (September/October 2005): 18–24; Yong Deng and Thomas G. Moore, "China Views Globalization: Toward a New Great-Power Politics?," *Washington Quarterly* (Summer 2004): 123; Robert G. Sutter, *China's Rise in Asia: Promises and Perils* (London: Roman & Littlefield, 2005), 266.

153 *Chinese thinkers claim that China:* Zheng, "China's 'Peaceful Rise.' "

153 *"not so good for the unipolar power":* Montek Ahluwalia (India's deputy minister of planning), in discussion with Nina Hachigian, October 2006.

153 *At the same time, India would deeply regret:* Wisner discussion.

153 *"Russia is realistic":* Trenin discussion.

153 *Russians are not instinctively opposed to U.S. power:* Eisenhower discussion.

154 *"the hegemon is":* Vaisse discussion.

154 *Europeans presume that Europe will inevitably become:* John Van Oudenaren, "Unipolar Versus Unilateral," *Policy Review* 124 (April/May 2004).

154 *though some analysts have noted that Europe's preference:* Ibid.

155 *"We are the guardians":* Reid, *The United States of Europe*, 193.

155 *"No one is insisting":* Bertram discussion.

155 *In international organizations, Europe can:* Reid, *The United States of Europe*, 189.

155 *The hope is that European "civilian power":* Andrew Moravcsik, "How Europe Can Win Without an Army," *Financial Times*, April 3, 2003.

155 *India accepts the liberal world order:* Xenia Dormandy, "Is India, or Will It Be, a Responsible Stakeholder?" *Washington Quarterly* 30, no. 3. (Summer 2007): 117–130.

155 *"robbed of its rightful place":* Mohan, *Crossing the Rubicon*, 80.

155 *For example, once India learned:* Remarks of Stephen Stedman (professor of political science, Stanford University), in workshop hosted by Stanford University's Center for International Security and Cooperation and the Stanley Foundation, November 8–10, 2006.

156 *Some conservatives argue that China:* For a version of this argument, see

Robert Kagan, "The Illusion of 'Managing' China," *Washington Post*, (May 15, 2005).

156   *Chinese attitudes toward the international system:* For a thorough analysis on the question of China's attitudes toward the international order, Johnston, "Is China a Status Quo Power?," 5; Medeiros, "Strategic Hedging," 148.

156   *"We are a maintainer":* Joseph Khan, "China, Shy Giant, Shows Signs of Shedding Its False Modesty," *New York Times*, December 9, 2006.

156   *"complement, not replace":* Robert Zoellick, "A Global Mission for China and America," *Financial Times*, January 23, 2007, 13.

156   *From a starting point of near zero:* Johnston, "Is China a Status Quo Power?," 13.

156   *In fact, during the 2006 Doha WTO negotiations:* Remarks of Henry Levine (former deputy assistant secretary of commerce for Asia and former U.S. consul general in Shanghai), at workshop hosted by Stanford University's Center for International Security and Cooperation and the Stanley Foundation, November 8–10, 2006.

156   *The most important strategic decision the Chinese:* Zheng, "China's 'Peaceful Rise,' " 20.

156   *"open-minded":* Stedman remarks.

157   *In part because China has and will continue to benefit:* Deng and Moore, "China Views Globalization"; Walt, "Taming American Power," 144–152.

157   *the experience of SARS:* Deng and Moore, "China Views Globalization," 127–28.

157   *All this joining is "socializing" Chinese bureaucrats:* Alastair Iain Johnston, "The Social Effects of International Institutions of Domestic and Foreign Policy Actors," in Daniel Drezner, ed., *The Interaction of Domestic and International Institutions* (Ann Arbor: University of Michigan Press, 2001).

157   *Today, China is reluctant:* Bergsten, "China: The Balance Sheet," 141.

157   *China joined the Nuclear Suppliers Group:* Evan S. Medeiros, *Reluctant Restraint: The Evolution of China's Nonproliferation Policies and Practices* (Stanford: Stanford University Press, 2007).

157   *They began to make the case from the inside:* Ibid.

158   *"the exporter of goodwill":* David Shambaugh, "Return to the Middle Kingdom?," in Shambaugh, ed., *Power Shift*, 24.

158   *The Chinese want to be taken more seriously:* Jia discussion.

158 *Inclusion in international institutions was a centerpiece:* Stent, "America and Russia," 265.

158 *Russian elites pretended:* Manfred Hueterer and Heidi Reisinger as cited in Ibid.

158 *Several components of the IMF-directed:* Mark Kramer, "The Changing Economic Complexion of Eastern Europe and Russia: Results and Lessons of the 1990s," *SAIS Review* 2, no. 19 (1999): 26–29.

158 *The difficulty of effecting:* Ibid.

159 *Time and again:* Trenin discussion.

159 *Even in the G8, Russia was relegated:* As evidence, Russians point to the 1991 U.S. National Security Strategy (the comprehensive report to Congress outlining the broad strategic vision of the President and the U.S.), which acknowledged the diminished threat from a disintegrating Soviet Union but still argued that "the size and orientation of Soviet military forces must . . . remain critical concerns to the United States and . . . the European system still require[s] a counterweight to Soviet military strength. It is our responsibility as a government to hedge against the uncertainties of the future."

160 *So while there is great potential:* Matthew Goodman and Michael Green, "Why Saying 'Sayonara' Is the Hardest Thing to Do," *Financial Times*, June 27, 2006.

160 *While China is guided by its notion:* Zhang and Tang, "China's Regional Strategy," 49–50.

160 *Moscow simply doesn't want:* Trenin discussion.

161 *Indians will raise a thirty-five-year-old:* Mohan, *Crossing the Rubicon*, 236.

162 *Finally, America's view of itself:* Derek Mitchell, "U.S. Self Image," in McGiffert, ed., *Chinese Images of the United States*, 134.

7. THE WAY FORWARD: STRATEGIC COLLABORATION

165 *Against: United States:* Israel abstained and several other nations were absent. "Prevention of Outer Space Arms Race, Mediterranean Security Among Issues, As Disarmament Committee Approves Seven More Texts" 60th General Assembly, 1st Committee, 19th Meeting (PM), October 25, 2005, http://www.un.org/News/Press/docs/2005/gadis3310.doc.htm (accessed April 23, 2007).

166 *The answer came almost exactly:* The policy was released on a Friday at

5:00 P.M. before the Columbus Day weekend. Marc Kaufman, "Bush Sets Defense as Space Priority," *Washington Post*, October 18, 2006.

166   *Emphasizing the need:* "U.S. National Space Policy," Office of Science and Technology Policy, August 31, 2006, http://www.ostp.gov/html/US%20 National%20Space%20Policy.pdf (accessed April 23, 2007).

166   *"explicitly and unashamedly":* Charles Krauthammer, "The Unipolar Moment Revisited—United States World Dominance," *National Interest*, 70 (Winter 2002): 17.

166   *"America Wants It All":* Bronwen Maddox, "America Wants It All—Life, the Universe and Everything," *The Times* (London), October 19, 2006.

166   *"Someone has to be the first":* Peter Kammerer, "Master of the Universe?," *South China Morning Post*, October 20, 2006; Viktor Volodin and Nikolai Poroskov, "Bush's Space Appetites; Washington's Zone of Interests Now Encompasses the Whole Universe," *Defense and Security* (Russia), October 20, 2006.

166   *The experts too have doubts:* Harvard's Will Marshall writes: "[W]eaponizing space is no solution. Doing that would be like watching brave Achilles unsheathing his knife and turning it on himself." William Marshall, "Weapons in Outer Space," *Boston Globe*, July 5, 2006.

166   *Likely a coincidence:* According to the Russian space agency, the agreement was designed in part to end the monopoly of the "Pentagon-controlled" GPS system. "Putin Signs Pact with India into Law," www.domain-b.com, November 7, 2006, http://www.domain-b.com/ economy/infrastructure/space/20061107_space.html (accessed January 20, 2007).

167   *Yet it is hard for anyone:* For a discussion of the benefits of American primacy, Stephen M. Walt, *Taming American Power* (New York: Norton, 2005), 40; Samuel P. Huntington, "Why International Primacy Matters," *International Security* 17, no. 4 (Spring 1993): 68–83. Also Robert J. Art, *A Grand Strategy for America* (Ithaca: Cornell University Press, 2003), 90–92.

167   *It would serve as the protector:* Kishore Mahbubani, "The Impending Demise of the Postwar System," *Survival* 47, no. 4 (Winter 2005/ 2006): 9.

167   *"to recognize":* Harry S. Truman, address in San Francisco at the closing session of the United Nations Conference, June 26, 1945, http://

www.presidency.ucsb.edu/ws/index.php?pid=12188 (accessed July 12, 2006).

167 *This arrangement gave:* G. John Ikenberry, *After Victory: Institutions, Strategic Restraint, and the Rebuilding of Orders After Major Wars* (Princeton: Princeton University Press, 2001).

167 *Neocons wanted to throw:* The Clinton years were wasted, in their view, pandering to the international community and deploying American troops on humanitarian missions. Charles Krauthammer argued in 2002 that American security interests "will require the aggressive and confident application of unipolar power rather than falling back, as we did in the 1990s, on paralyzing multilateralism." Krauthammer, "The Unipolar Moment Revisited," 17.

167 *"An entangling web":* Ibid., 12.

168 *In 2002, the Bush administration made:* The relevant language is "Our forces will be strong enough to dissuade potential adversaries from pursuing a military build-up in hopes of surpassing, or equaling, the power of the United States." *The National Security Strategy of the United States of America* (2002), http://www.whitehouse.gov/nsc/nss.pdf (accessed April 21, 2007). For a description of Secretary of Defense Donald Rumsfeld's ideas of primacy, Michael Hirsh, *At War with Ourselves: Why America Is Squandering Its Chance to Build a Better World* (New York: Oxford University Press, 2003), 42.

168 *"America has":* "President Bush Delivers Graduation Speech at West Point," Office of the White House Press Secretary, June 1, 2002, http://www.whitehouse.gov/news/releases/2002/06/20020601-3.html (accessed October 9, 2006).

168 *For this reason, argues Brent Scowcroft:* Scowcroft argues that the Industrial Revolution generated the need for protections within nations, like antitrust laws, workers' rights, and food safety inspections, to rein in the excesses of capitalism. Now, nation-states can no longer provide protections that their citizens expect. Therefore, international cooperation between nations must be strengthened. Brent Scowcroft in discussion with Mona Sutphen and Nina Hachigian, July 2006.

168 *In practice, the strategy of primacy:* Our conclusions about primacy were shaped in discussions with James B. Steinberg, dean of the LBJ School of Public Policy at the University of Texas at Austin and former deputy national security advisor. Also, G. John Ikenberry and Charles A. Kupchan, "Liberal Realism: The Foundations of a Democratic Foreign Policy,"

National Interest, Fall 2004; G. John Ikenberry and Anne-Marie Slaughter, "Forging a World of Liberty Under Law: U.S. National Security in the 21st Century," Princeton Project on National Security (September 27, 2006), 13, http://www.wws.princeton.edu/ppns/report/Final Report.pdf (accessed February 21, 2007); Robert Jervis, "International Primacy: Is the Game Worth the Candle?," *International Security* 17, no. 4 (Spring 1993): 52–67.

168   *America cannot trumpet:* Moreover, it is now clear that America cannot be so militarily superior as to discourage other countries from investing in their own military power.

169   *The distribution of power:* Thomas S. Szayna et al., *The Emergence of Peer Competitors: A Framework for Analysis* (Santa Monica: RAND, 2001), 49.

169   *It sets up an implicit confrontation:* Despite America's overwhelming power, other nations have found all kinds of ways of thwarting American aims. Walt, *Taming American Power.*

169   *Indeed, a complement to the primacy strategy:* For a summary of different forms of containment in today's context, Francis Fukuyama and G. John Ikenberry, "Report of the Working Group on Grand Strategic Choices," Princeton Project on National Security (2005), 21, http://www.wws .princeton.edu/ppns/conferences/reports/fall/GSC.pdf (accessed May 8, 2006).

169   *"do what it can":* This is the classic "offensive realist" position. John J. Mearsheimer, *The Tragedy of Great Power Politics* (New York: Norton, 2001), 402.

170   *Trying to stifle China's growth:* Richard N. Haass, *The Opportunity: America's Moment to Alter History's Course* (New York: Public Affairs Press, 2005), 21; Szayna et al., *The Emergence of Peer Competitors*, 51.

170   *If, on the other hand:* William C. Wohlforth, "The Stability of a Unipolar World," *International Security* 24, no. 1 (Summer 1999): 31.

170   *From this point of view, if:* The literature on this thesis is large and full of controversy. For the argument that wealth helps consolidate (but does not cause a transition to) democracy, Adam Przeworski, Michael E. Alvarez, José Antonio Cheibub, and Fernando Limongi, *Democracy and Development: Political Institutions and Well-Being in the World, 1950–1990* (Cambridge: Cambridge University Press, 2000). For the argument that wealth actually encourages transitions from authoritarian to democratic government, Charles Boix and Susan C. Stokes, "Endogenous Democratization," *World Politics* 55, no. 4 (July 2003): 514–49.

170 *"there is no feasible strategy":* Fukuyama and Ikenberry, "Report of the Working Group on Grand Strategic Choices," 25.

171 *to weaken China:* As China scholar Kenneth Lieberthal has argued: "[Al]though a strong, dynamic China will challenge American patience, skill and interests, a failed China would produce even less welcome problems." Kenneth Lieberthal, "A New China Strategy," *Foreign Affairs* (November/December 1995): 36–37.

171 *"If there is any fundamental truth":* Brian Jenkins (senior advisor and counterterrorism expert at RAND), in discussion with Nina Hachigian, October 2005.

171 *World financial markets:* There is also a moral question regarding the humanitarian disaster that would result.

171 *No matter what the final outcome:* As a RAND study puts it: "If the hegemon reacts with more force and conflict than are warranted, then it may strengthen that proto-peer's determination to become a peer and a competitor." Szayna et al., *The Emergence of Peer Competitors*, 51.

171 *History's losing great powers:* Even losers in major power wars, like a phoenix, tend to rise from their ashes and catch up quickly with winners. Abramo Fimo Kenneth Organski and Jacek Kugler, *The War Ledger* (Chicago: University of Chicago Press, 1980), 145.

171 *They include:* Ashton B. Carter and William J. Perry, "China on the March," *National Interest* (March/April 2007): 20.

172 *"prevent the worst":* From testimony by Tanaka Akihiko, professor at the University of Tokyo, to the Diet, quoted in Richard J. Samuels, "Japan's Goldilocks Strategy," *Washington Quarterly* (Autumn 2006): 121. Harry R. Yarger, *Strategic Theory for the 21st Century: The Little Book on Big Strategy*, Strategic Studies Institute, U.S. Army War College, February 2006, http://www.strategicstudiesinstitute.army.mil (accessed August 20, 2006).

172 *Never have big powers:* Raymond Aron, "The Dawn of Universal History," excerpted in *National Interest* (Spring 2003): 49. We discuss the reasons for this—the shared threats of terrorism, small, hostile states, disease, and others—in the Introduction.

172 *Perhaps, as we all wish:* For one argument along these lines, John Mueller, *Retreat from Doomsday: The Obsolescence of Major War* (New York: Basic Books, 1988).

172 *In the past, the stronger and richer:* Robert Gilpin, *War and Change in World Politics* (Cambridge: Cambridge University Press, 1981), 22–25.

173 *"Minds can be changed":* Robert Jervis, "Cooperation Under the Security Dilemma," *World Politics* 30, no. 2 (January 1978): 168.

173 *States exist in a world:* Kenneth Waltz, one of America's most influential foreign policy thinkers, explains: "Because some states may at any time use force, all states must be prepared to do so—or live at the mercy of their militarily more vigorous neighbors." Kenneth N. Waltz, *Theory of International Politics* (New York: Random House, 1979), 102.

173 *Nationalism is a strong force:* Robert Jervis, "War and Misperception," *Journal of Interdisciplinary History* 18, no. 4 (Spring 1988): 675.

173 *In general, dominant powers:* This terminology is from Randall L. Schweller, "Managing the Rise of Great Powers: History and Theory," in Alastair Iain Johnston and Robert S. Ross, eds., *Engaging China: The Management of an Emerging Power* (London: Routledge, 1999), 1–31. Scholars have categorized strategies dominant powers use to address rising powers in various ways. For another taxonomy, Szayna et al., *The Emergence of Peer Competitors*. We discuss "power transition" theory, which investigates the likelihood of war when a rising power gains strength, in a note on page 40 for note 12.

173 *We advocate a pragmatic strategy:* Strategic collaboration is consistent with most mainstream proposals for U.S. grand strategy. For example, it could be part of a "selective engagement" strategy that seeks to keep the U.S. involved in consequential world problems, or an "offshore balancing" posture, which suggests the U.S. withdraw from struggles that do not affect its vital or very important interests. For more on possible grand strategies, Robert J. Art, *A Grand Strategy for America* (Ithaca: Cornell University Press, 2003).

173 *Compound American strengths:* A strategy similar to "strategic collaboration" is a "co-option," which a RAND report describes this way: "The co-opt strategy is a hedging strategy designed to lower the potential for the proto-peer to compete with the hegemon. The strategy has a fair amount of conflict-imposition elements and the hegemon does not shy away from disputes with the proto-peer, though cooperative aspects form the majority of the hegemon's policies." Szayna et al., *The Emergence of Peer Competitors*, 57. This strategy is also similar to "binding," described in Schweller, "Managing the Rise of Great Powers," 13.

175 *America should presume:* Richard Haass suggests viewing big powers "less as rivals and more as partners." Richard N. Haass, *The Opportunity: America's Moment to Alter History's Course* (New York: Public Affairs Press, 2005), 17.

175 *How Americans and pivotal powers:* Constructivist theory emphasizes this. Alexander Wendt, *Social Theory of International Politics* (Cambridge: Cambridge University Press, 1999).

175 *For instance, while the underlying conditions:* For more on the speech by President Clinton that "transformed the atmosphere of Indo-U.S. relations," C. Raja Mohan, *Crossing the Rubicon* (New York: Palgrave Macmillan, 2003), 93–94.

175 *In international forums:* Walt, *Taming American Power*, 284, fn 100. For a discussion of the damage hostile rhetoric can inflict, independent of its content, Alastair Iain Johnston, "Is China a Status Quo Power?," *International Security* 27, no. 4 (Spring 2003), 54.

176 *Former Secretary of Defense:* For his original comment, "Protests Await Rumsfeld's Arrival in Germany," *Deutsche Welle*, February 7, 2003, www.dw-world.de/popups/popup_printcontent/0,773989,00.html (accessed December 4, 2006).

176 *Officials should avoid*: Neil Buckley, "Cheney Remarks Spark Talk of 'New Cold War,' " *Financial Times*, May 6, 2006; also, Stephen Boykewich, "Cheney Says Liberty at Risk in Russia," *Moscow Times*, May 5, 2006.

176 *Every other sort of exchange:* For specific recommendations on how to boost U.S.-China interactions, Bates Gill and Melissa Murphy, "Meeting the Challenges and Opportunities of China's Rise: Expanding and Improving Interaction Between American and Chinese Policy Communities," CSIS, October 2006, http://www.csis.org/component/option .com_csis_pubs/task.view/id.3529/type.1/ (accessed February 21, 2007).

177 *A globalized NATO:* For a fuller discussion of a "global" NATO concept, James Goldgeier and Ivo Daalder, "Global NATO," *Foreign Affairs* (September/October 2006): 105.

177 *"It is an extraordinary thing":* Gordon Fairclough and Neil King, Jr., "Behind China's Stance on North Korea," *Wall Street Journal*, November 6, 2006.

179 *"It's in the interest":* Audrey McAvoy, "Navy Leader Cites Progress with China," *Honolulu Star-Bulletin*, June 13, 2006. Military-to-military relationships ought to be pursued according to "value-based reciprocity" whereby each side obtains equal benefits. Perry and Carter, *China on the*

March, 22. An appropriate military relationship with China can reduce tensions, making it possible to prevent future crises. Appropriate transparency on the American end may also persuade the Chinese to be more open about their strategic intentions and operating procedures, and also may deter the Chinese by revealing to them the technological prowess and pro-fessionalism of the U.S. military. A military relationship allows for cooperation with China in order to respond effectively to threats from third parties, for example terrorist groups. Further, a military relationship creates opportunities for U.S. military officers to gain insight into the strategic thinking of the Chinese military and may also yield intelligence-gathering opportunities. For more on military to military relations with China, Kevin Pollpeter, *U.S.-China Security Management: Assessing the Military-to-Military Relationship* (Santa Monica: RAND, 2004), http://rand.org/pubs/monographs/2004/RAND_MG143 .pdf (accessed May 10, 2006); Kurt Campbell and Richard Weitz, "The Limits of U.S.-China Military Cooperation: Lessons from 1995–1999," *Washington Quarterly* (Winter 2005/2006): 177.

179 *America should not act:* Jervis, "Cooperation Under the Security Dilemma," 172; Szayna et al., *The Emergence of Peer Competitors*, 56, 59.

179 *"As an old Cold Warrior":* Robert Gates, U.S. Secretary of Defense, "Transcript: Prepared Remarks at 43rd Munich Security Conference," *Washington Post*, February 12, 2007, http://www.washingtonpost.com/ wp-dyn/content/article/2007/02/12/AR2007021200572.html (accessed April 25, 2007).

179 *First, open, busy relationships:* Walt, *Taming American Power*, 226.

180 *Recognizing that the emergence:* Szayna et al., *The Emergence of Peer Competitors*, xv.

180 *"insurance against the uncertainty":* Mohan, *Crossing the Rubicon*, 145.

180 *unintended security consequences:* America's funding of mujahadeen to fight the Soviets in Afghanistan and subsequent rise of al Qaeda is one such example among many.

181 *The U.S. ought to work:* G. John Ikenberry and Anne-Marie Slaughter, "Forging a World of Liberty Under Law: U.S. National Security in the 21st Century," Princeton Project on National Security, September 27, 2006, 25, http://www.wws.princeton.edu/ppns/report/FinalReport.pdf (accessed February 10, 2007). This report suggests a "Concert of Democracies" to strengthen security cooperation among liberal democracies. While we think it is useful to work with democracies on a variety

of issues, including developing these norms as we have said, China and Russia have to be on the inside of solutions to major world problems or the solutions are unlikely to be effective.

181   *"it is far more effective":* Ikenberry, *After Victory,* 53.

182   *The U.S. would embed:* This recommendation is similar to an aspect of Richard Haass's doctrine of "integration." Haass, *The Opportunity.*

182   *The only ways people:* For more on networks in the international order, Anne-Marie Slaughter, *A New World Order* (Princeton: Princeton University Press, 2004).

182   *On a practical level:* For example, Stephen Walt makes the point that the WTO's dispute resolution mechanism depends, in part, on the ability of aggrieved parties to retaliate, something the U.S. is better able to do than any other nation. Walt, *Taming American Power,* 50. The world order keeps the costs of enforcing these beneficial norms lower. G. John Ikenberry, "Democracy, Institutions, and American Restraint," in G. John Ikenberry, ed., *America Unrivaled: The Future of the Balance of Power* (Ithaca: Cornell University Press, 2002), 222.

182   *If it had not been for the Nuclear Non-Proliferation Treaty:* Joe Cirincione (vice president for National Security, Center for American Progress), in e-mail exchange with Nina Hachigian, August 2006; Ambassador Thomas Graham, Jr., "The Significance of the NPT" (testimony before the Bipartisan Task Force on Nonproliferation, U.S. House of Representatives, June 18, 2003).

183   *Importantly, the current set:* For more on the benefits of a liberal world order, Fukuyama and Ikenberry, "Report of the Working Group on Grand Strategic Choices," 10; Ikenberry and Slaughter, "Forging a World of Liberty Under Law," 23.

183   *Broadly, the world order:* For more on different kinds of world order—balance of power, hegemonic, or constitutional—Ikenberry, *After Victory.*

183   *"The most enduringly powerful":* Ibid., 20.

183   *There is a yawning gap:* Mark Malloch Brown, deputy secretary-general of the United Nations (remarks at the "Power and Superpower in the 21st Century" conference hosted by the Century Foundation and Center for American Progress, June 6, 2006), http://www.security peace.org/pdf/brown_remarks.pdf (accessed February 21, 2007).

183   *Even more than that:* Or they are at least not willing to risk or sacrifice much to change the status quo. For more on this distinction, Robert

Jervis, *Perception and Misperception in International Politics* (Princeton: Princeton University Press, 1976), 48–54.

184 *The benefits of peaceful:* Fukuyama and Ikenberry, "Report of the Working Group on Grand Strategic Choices," 22.

184 *The world needs a pivotal power forum:* This group could expand if new pivotal powers emerge, but its ability to be effective is tied to its small size.

184 *It would make the most sense:* It also makes sense to eliminate the power of the veto in the U.N. Security Council and replace it with a supermajority or three-fourths vote of the membership, at least for some kinds of resolutions. Ikenberry and Slaughter, "Forging a World of Liberty Under Law," 23.

184 *If reform of the Security Council:* William Antholis (director of Strategic Planning, Brookings Institution), suggested this in remarks at a workshop hosted by Stanford University's Center for International Security and Cooperation and the Stanley Foundation, November 8–10, 2006. Reforming current G8 membership would likely be too difficult politically.

185 *In meetings focused narrowly:* The head of state meetings would have to be at least twice a year because the agendas of yearly G8 meetings are too easily derailed by outside events. Meetings of cabinet-level officials would occur in between. Continuity among the diplomats who represent the pivotal powers at the meetings would be useful to build trust and understanding. Stephen Garrett, "Nixonian Foreign Policy: A New Balance of Power—or a Revived Concert?," *Polity* 8, no. 3 (Spring 1976): 406.

185 *By encouraging them to become members:* Michael Green (professor, Georgetown University; former senior director for Asia, National Security Council), in discussion with Nina Hachigian, November 2006. Also Robert B. Zoellick, "Whither China: From Membership to Responsibility?" (remarks at the National Committee on U.S.-China Relations, September 21, 2005).

186 *"only the great powers":* Richard B. Elrod, "The Concert of Europe: A Fresh Look at an International System," *World Politics* 28, no. 2 (January 1976): 164.

186 *The Concert of Europe became:* Some say the system ended in 1848, others 1871. Garrett, "Nixonian Foreign Policy," 394.

186 *It was essentially the first time:* Ibid., 395.

186 *The Concert derived:* Ibid., 416.

186 *Then, as we hope now:* For more on the Concert of Europe as a possible model for today, Haass, *The Opportunity*, 15; also Charles A. Kupchan, "Hollow Hegemony or Stable Multipolarity?," in Ikenberry, ed., *America Unrivaled*, 79.

186 *"shared definition of legitimacy":* Haass, *The Opportunity*, 23.

187 *"Iran has figured,":* Vali Nasr (Iran expert at the Council on Foreign Relations), in discussion with Nina Hachigian, April 2007.

187 *A deal whereby the pivotal powers:* Scott D. Sagan, "How to Keep the Bomb from Iran," *Foreign Affairs* (September/October 2006): 45, 58–59. Also Ray Takeyh, "Time for Détente with Iran," *Foreign Affairs* (March/April 2007).

188 *To convince nonnuclear states:* See George P. Shultz, William J. Perry, Henry A. Kissinger, and Sam Nunn, "A World Free of Nuclear Weapons," *Wall Street Journal*, January 4, 2007; Jean du Preez, "Half Full or Half Empty? Realizing the Promise of the Nuclear Nonproliferation Treaty," *Arms Control Today*, December 2006, http://www.armscontrol.org/act/2006_12/DuPreez.asp (accessed January 15, 2006).

188 *If the U.S. reengages:* For more on the Biological Weapons Convention, "The 2006 Biological Weapons Convention Review Conference: Articles and Interviews on Tackling the Threats Posed by Biological Weapons," Arms Control Association, November 2006, http://www.armscontrol.org/pdf/BWCreaderWebVersion.pdf (accessed April 11, 2007); "The Biological Weapons Threat and Nonproliferation Options: A Survey of Senior U.S. Decision Makers and Policy Shapers," Center for Strategic and International Studies, November 2006, http://www.csis.org/media/csis/pubs/061129_biosurvey.pdf (accessed April 11, 2007).

188 *Along similar lines, China:* Shai Oster, "China Aims to Engage Top Energy Users in Forum," *Wall Street Journal*, December 15, 2006.

189 *Ultimately, at Moscow's insistence:* Alexander Nitkin, "Partners in Peacekeeping," *NATO Review*, Winter 2004. Even in Iraq, the U.S. realized the need for a UN Security Council resolution, because the World Bank and other lenders would not fund reconstruction projects without one. Paul Blustein, "U.S. Plans for Iraqi Economy Hit Friction," *Washington Post*, April 11, 2003.

189 *For example, East Asia needs:* Many have commented on the need for a NATO- or OSCE-like organization in East Asia to address China-Japan and Japan–South Korea tensions as well as the North Korea problem.

Fukuyama and Ikenberry, "Report of the Working Group on Grand Strategic Choices," 23. As long as the pivotal powers have their own forum, "multi-multilateralism" is the right result. Francis Fukuyama, *America at the Crossroads: Democracy, Power, and the Neoconservative Legacy* (New Haven: Yale University Press, 2006), 168.

189 *Critically, existing global institutions:* The pivotal powers want a greater voice in the shape and direction of the International Monetary Fund, for example. The U.S. should and does welcome the fact that other countries want to buy into a global institution it created. Yet while the U.S. agrees that China, India, Russia, and other growing economies should be allocated proportionately more voting rights, measured in "shares," it wants the additional shares to come largely out of Europe's hide. Doing so allows the U.S. to preserve its veto power but dooms the rebalancing efforts. Ironically, this is veto power the U.S. cannot use because decisions are nearly always made informally and by consensus, according to a former IMF executive director. Trading in a nearly meaningless veto right for a stable and financially balanced institution that benefits the U.S. seems sensible.

189 *Some express concern:* C. Fred Bergstein, Bates Gill, Nicholas R. Lardy, and Derek Mitchell, *China: The Balance Sheet: What the World Needs to Know Now About the Emerging Superpower* (New York: Public Affairs Press, 2006), 141.

190 *Pivotal powers will not:* As Kenneth Waltz says, "If the leading power does not lead, others cannot follow." Kenneth N. Waltz, *Theory of International Politics* (Boston: McGraw-Hill, 1979), 210.

190 *To earn its leadership:* Kishore Mahbubani, "The Impending Demise of the Postwar System," *Survival* 47, no. 4 (Winter 2005/2006): 8.

190 *To retrieve legitimacy:* Listen to the Germans on this. Josef Joffe, editor of *Die Ziet*, recommends that America "do good for others in order to do well for yourself." Josef Joffe, "Defying History and Theory," in Ikenberry, ed., *America Unrivaled*, 180. Former German foreign minister Joschka Fisher argued in a 2006 speech at Stanford University that record levels of anti-Americanism in every pivotal power are not shouts of "We hate you!" but cries of desperation akin to "Wake up, Dad!"

190 *The reasons America has not:* Keir A. Leiber and Daryl G. Press, "The Rise of U.S. Nuclear Primacy," *Foreign Affairs* (March/April 2006): 52.

190 *Even so, American leaders:* Mark Malloch Brown, the deputy secretary-general of the United Nations, warned in a 2006 speech: "[T]here is cur-

rently a perception among many otherwise quite moderate countries that anything the U.S. supports must have a secret agenda aimed at either subordinating multilateral processes to Washington's ends or weakening the institutions, and therefore, put crudely, should be opposed without any real discussion of whether they make sense or not." Mark Malloch Brown, "Power and Superpower in the 21st Century."

190 *No longer can America:* Stephen M. Walt, "Keeping the World Off-Balance," in Ikenberry, ed., *America Unrivaled,* 145. For more on leaders sharing responsibility, Max DePree, *Leadership Is an Art* (New York: Dell, 1989), 9.

191 *a steady source of resentment:* "16-Nation Survey," Pew Global Attitudes Project—June 23, 2005, 23. As Francis Fukuyama points out, "Being willing to work within a multilateral framework does not mean accepting support only on your terms; that is just another form of unilateralism." Fukuyama, *America at the Crossroads,* 173.

191 *The model should be Bosnia:* Through mid-2006, America had spent $20 billion in Iraq (just on reconstruction) and all other countries combined spent less than $4 billion. Curt Tarnoff, "Iraq: Recent Developments in Reconstruction Assistance," Congressional Research Service Report for Congress, June 15, 2006, http://www.fas.org/sgp/crs/mid east/RL31833.pdf (accessed October 17, 2006); Onur Ozlo, "Iraqi Economic Reconstruction and Development," CSIS, April 21, 2006, http://www.csis.org/media/csis/pubs/060421_onuriraqireconstruct.pdf (accessed October 17, 2006).

191 *According to former U.S. envoy:* Charles J. Pritchard (president of Korea Economic Institute, former special envoy to the Democratic People's Republic of North Korea), in discussion with Nina Hachigian, December 2006.

192 *In the 1990s, in frustration:* Emad Mekay, "Washington Moves to Preempt 'Asian IMF,' " *Asia Times,* June 11, 2005.

192 *Later this put:* Elena Beylis, "Why the International Criminal Court Needs Darfur More than Darfur Needs the ICC," *Jurist,* June 3, 2005, http://jurist.law.pitt.edu/forumy/2005/06/why-international-criminal-court-needs.php.

192 *"Failure to rescue":* Mahbubani, "The Impending Demise of the Postwar System," 8.

193 *We thus recommend "selective hedging":* "Selective hedging" is similar in thrust to Bill Perry and Ash Carter's "prudent hedging," which they rec-

ommend as an element of China policy. Carter & Perry, "China on the March," 16.

193 *The United States should hedge:* Eric Heginbotham (political scientist at the RAND Corporation), in discussion with Nina Hachigian, October 2006. For a discussion of hedging in U.S.-China relations, Evan S. Medeiros, "Strategic Hedging and the Future of Asia-Pacific Stability," *Washington Quarterly* 29, no. 1 (Winter 2005/2006): 145–67.

193 *"We get along with China":* Charlene Barshefsky, in discussion with Nina Hachigian and Mona Sutphen, April 2006.

194 *When China sees the U.S. "cheerleading":* Richard J. Samuels, "Japan's Goldilocks Strategy," *Washington Quarterly* 29, no. 6 (Fall 2006): 111–127.

194 *Theorists argue, and centuries:* For more on balancing and bandwagoning, Stephen M. Walt, *The Origins of Alliances* (Ithaca: Cornell University Press, 1987). Coordinating alliances against the dominant power is very difficult, however. Wohlforth, "The Stability of a Unipolar World," 29.

194 *For this reason, many credit:* For more on Bismarckian strategies for the U.S., Eric Heginbotham and Christopher P. Twomey, "America's Bismarckian Asia Policy," *Current History* (September 2005): 243. See also Josef Joffe, "Defying History and Theory," in Ikenberry, ed., *America Unrivaled*, 159.

194 *Sitting atop one another:* Walt, *The Origins of Alliances*; William C. Wohlforth, "U.S. Strategy in a Unipolar World," in Ikenberry, ed., *America Unrivaled*, 107–8.

195 *Pivotal powers have fought:* Kristian Gleditsch, "A Revised List of Wars Between and Within Independent States, 1816–2002," *International Interactions* 30 (2004): 231–62, http://weber.ucsd.edu/~kgledits/papers/gleditsch2004ii_corrected.pdf (accessed May 8, 2006).

195 *Moreover, balancing:* Wohlforth, "U.S. Strategy in a Unipolar World," 100.

195 *A war between pivotal powers:* For a full discussion of why pivotal power war would be harmful to U.S. interests, Art, *A Grand Strategy*, 56–58.

195 *Constantly improving U.S. military capabilities:* Military assets in Japan, for example, caution China against aggressive actions toward Taiwan and reduce Japan's need for increased defense spending and its own nuclear weapons, actions that would reduce China's security and push it

toward greater military investments. For an argument in favor of robust U.S. military presence in Asia, Ashley J. Tellis and Michael Wills, eds., *Strategic Asia 2005–06: Military Modernization in an Era of Uncertainty* (Seattle: National Bureau of Asian Research, 2005). A buildup and hardening of military assets on Guam is likewise sensible for a variety of Asian contingencies. A European presence assures our allies that the U.S. will consult them when it decides to use those assets. Some argue that U.S. troops in Europe continue also to "shorten the shadow of German power." Joffe, "Defying History and Theory," 165.

195 *Hedging too aggressively:* For more on the "security dilemma," Jervis, "Cooperation Under the Security Dilemma," 167–214; Charles Glaser, "The Security Dilemma Revisited," *World Politics* 50, no. 1 (October 1997): 171–201.

195 *They will respond by improving:* For more on this dynamic, Jervis, "Cooperation Under the Security Dilemma," 182; Jervis, *Perception and Misperception*, 58–114.

195 *Those changes, in turn:* Jervis, *Perception and Misperception*, 58–114.

196 *The result can be:* Szayna et al., *The Emergence of Peer Competitors*, xvi, 69.

196 *Hawks portray this buildup:* Some argue that the intent of the missile defense system is not, in fact, defensive, but that it is meant as a component in America's drive for nuclear primacy. In any event, it is not in America's interests for Chinese leaders—faced with the prospect of an imminent American attack, real or fictional—to feel pressured with their nuclear weapons to "use it or lose it." The U.S. could size and shape missile defense to make it clear that China and Russia are not targets, it could pledge not to undertake a nuclear first strike, or it could abandon an overpriced and, to date, unproven system. For more on these issues, Keir A. Leiber and Daryl G. Press, "The Rise of U.S. Nuclear Primacy," *Foreign Affairs* (March/April 2006): 52.

197 *Most of all, then, hedging:* Without reassurances of America's good intentions to accompany hedging, pivotal powers will tend to view strategy toward them as more sinister and less driven by uncertainty than America claims. Johnston, "Is China a Status Quo Power?," 53.

197 *"a little less sovereignty":* Richard Haass, *The Opportunity*, 33.

197 *The United States will have to agree:* Ikenberry, *After Victory*, 57. For more on other nations' attempts to "bind" the U.S. Walt, *Taming American Power*, 144–52.

199 *While such spending:* A comprehensive report on these issues is Larry Nowels, "Foreign Policy Budget Trends: A Thirty-Year Review," *CRS Report for Congress*, June 20, 2006. Also, "International Affairs Budget Update 2/5/07," U.S. Global Leadership Council, http://www.usglobal leadership.org/index.php?option=com_content&task=view&id=67&It emid=43 (accessed April 15, 2007).

199 *The United States spends more on:* For 2005. "Sorghum Subsidies by Year, US Total," Environmental Working Group, Farm Subsidies Database, December 16, 2006, http://www.ewg.org/farm/progdetail.php?fips= 00000&progcode=sorghum (accessed February 21, 2007).

199 *than on all of the State Department's:* Fiscal Year 2008 Budget Request, Summary and Highlights, International Affairs Function No. 150, 3, www.usaid.gov/policy/budget/cbj2008/fy2008cbj_highlights.pdf (accessed May 2, 2007).

199 *The entire Defense Department budget for language:* Max Boot, "The Wrong Weapons for the Long War," *Los Angeles Times*, February 8, 2006, http://www.cfr.org/publication/9803/wrong_weapons_for_the_long_ war.html (accessed August 29, 2006).

199 *It is not just a question:* Currently, U.S. aid is doled out by dozens of U.S. agencies without clear objectives or priorities. For an analysis of this problem and useful suggestions for addressing it, see Lael Brainard, ed. *Security By Other Means: Foreign Assistance, Global Poverty and American Leadership* (Washington, D.C.: Brookings Institution Press and CSIS, 2007).

200 *"We may be close":* Coit D. Blacker (director of the Freeman Spogli Institute for International Studies at Stanford University), in discussion with Nina Hachigian, July 2006.

200 *Because institutions and principles have inertia:* Ikenberry, *After Victory*, 5, 16, 47, 54.

200 *For example, if the U.S. led:* This is a summary of the phenomenon known as "increasing returns." Ibid., 232.

201 *Conversely, if the U.S. disengages:* Walt, *Taming American Power*, 147.

8. MAKING IT HAPPEN

204 *At the time, Congress was debating:* There always has been, and probably always will be, a political constituency suspicious of any international commitments. Walter Russell Mead, *Special Providence: American For-*

eign Policy and How It Changed the World (New York: Routledge, 2002), 225. On the other hand, America has been aggressively internationalist since its earliest days: Robert Kagan, *Dangerous Nation: America's Place in the World from Its Earliest Days to the Dawn of the Twentieth Century* (New York: Knopf, 2006).

204 *Even in districts electing radically unilateralist:* Steven Kull and I. M. Destler, *Misreading the Public: The Myth of a New Isolationism* (Washington, D.C.: Brookings Institution, 1999), 202–3, http://brookings.nap .edu/books/0815717652/html/203.html#pagetop (accessed December 12, 2006); Steven Kull (remarks at the Stanley Foundation conference, "Leveraging American Strength in an Uncertain World," December 7, 2006).

204 *Though a majority think that maintaining superior:* "The United States and the Rise of China and India: Results of a 2006 Multination Survey of Public Opinion," Chicago Council on Global Affairs (2006), http:// www.thechicagocouncil.org/UserFiles/File/GlobalViews06Final.pdf (accessed October 25, 2006).

204 *87 percent of Americans in a 2006 poll:* "Americans Assess US International Strategy," Program on International Policy Attitudes, December 7, 2006, 7, www.worldpublicopinion.org/pipa/pdf/dec06/USIntlStrat egy_Dec06_rpt.pdf (accessed June 4, 2007).

204 *A whopping 80 percent responded:* Ibid., 9.

204 *75 percent of Americans:* "The United States and the Rise of China and India," 14.

205 *Americans surveyed in a 2005:* "Poll of 9 Major Nations Finds All, Including U.S., Reject World System Dominated by Single Power in Favor of Multipolarity," Program on International Policy Attitudes, June 12, 2006, http://www.worldpublicopinion.org/pipa/articles/views_on_ countriesregions_bt/208.php?nid=&id=&pnt=208&lb=brglm (accessed June 4, 2007). The full survey is available at http://www.bertelsmann -stiftung.de/bst/en/media/xcms_bst_dms_19189_19190_2.pdf (accessed June 4, 2007).

206 *Findings by the Pew Research Center:* Another 9 percent thought the U.S. should not play a leadership role in the world. "Foreign Policy Attitudes Now Driven by 9/11 and Iraq," Pew Research Center for the People and the Press, and the Council on Foreign Relations, August 18, 2004, 11, http://people-press.org/reports/pdf/222.pdf (accessed June 4, 2007).

206   *According to Pew:* "America's Place in the World: An Investigation of the Attitudes of American Opinion Leaders and Public about International Affairs," The Pew Research Center for the People and the Press, November 2, 1993, 7, http://people-press.org/reports/pdf/19931102.pdf (accessed June 12, 2007).

206   *"should take into":* "Public Opinion of the U.N.: Strong Support, Strong Criticism," The Pew Research Center for the People and the Press, June 25, 1995, 9, http://people-press.org/reports/pdf/19950625.pdf (accessed June 12, 2007).

206   *"should go its own way":* Ibid., 9–10.

206   *Substantial majorities:* "The United States and the Rise of China and India," 19.

206   *Fully 40 percent think that strengthening:* "The United States and the Rise of China and India," 17. Also, "Public More Internationalist than in 1990s: Terrorism Worries Spike, War Support Steady," Pew Research Center for the People and the Press, December 12, 2002, http://people-press .org/reports/print.php3?ReportID=166 (accessed November 3, 2006).

206   *Sixty percent of Americans surveyed in 2006:* Ibid., 18; "American Attitudes Toward National Security, Foreign Policy, and the War on Terror," the Security and Peace Initiative and the Marttila Communications Group (2005), 18, http://www.securitypeace.org/index.asp?typeid=8& pgid=82 (accessed December 12, 2006).

206   *Similarly, by a margin of two to one:* "American Attitudes Toward National Security, Foreign Policy, and the War on Terror," 11.

207   *nearly 70 percent think the U.S. should comply:* "Hall of Mirrors: Perceptions and Misperceptions in the Congressional Foreign Policy Process," Chicago Council on Foreign Affairs, October 1, 2004, 11, http://65 .109.167.118/pipa/pdf/oct04/HallofMirrors_Oct04_rpt.pdf (accessed November 3, 2006).

207   *Majorities are also in favor of expanding:* "The United States and the Rise of China and India," 20–21.

207   *Americans do not hold negative views:* "American Attitudes Toward China," Zogby International poll sponsored by the Committee of 100, February 2005, 31, http://www.committee100.org/publications/survey/ C100_PhaseI_031805.pdf (accessed December 12, 2006).

207   *A narrow majority of Americans held favorable impressions:* "America's Image Slips, but Allies Share U.S. Concerns over Iran, Hamas," Pew

Global Attitudes Survey, June 13, 2006, 8, http://pewglobal.org/reports/pdf/252.pdf (accessed October 25, 2006).

207 *A large majority (65 percent) in another poll favored:* "The United States and the Rise of China and India," 15, 37.

207 *in 2005, 70 percent thought trade with China:* "American Attitudes Toward China."

207 *In that same 2006 poll:* "The United States and the Rise of China and India," 37.

207 *Majorities or pluralities of Americans:* "The United States and the Rise of China and India," 58.

207 *However, when presented:* "UPI/Zogby Poll: 75% Say China Top Economic Rival," press release, *Zogby International*, May 23, 2007.

207 *The area of major concern:* Ibid.

207 *Far more Americans are concerned with potential threats:* Ibid., 16, 35.

210 *Much of the attention of the growing Pentagon:* Bryan Bender, "Tensions Stir Ahead of Bush's China Visit," *Boston Globe*, November 14, 2005.

210 *"appear to have decided":* Dr. Thomas Finger, director, National Intelligence Council, "Annual Threat Assessment" (testimony before the Senate Armed Services Committee, February 27, 2007), http://www.dni.gov/testimonies/20070227_transcript.pdf (accessed July 11, 2007).

210 *However, if the political leadership:* For example, former Defense Secretary Donald Rumsfeld delivered at least one speech that was perceived in the region as more confrontational than the general tenor of the Sino-American relationship at the time. "China: Rumsfeld's 'Blistering Attack' Marks 'Significant' Shift," U.S. Department of State International Information Programs Foreign Media Reaction, June 13, 2005, http://www.globalsecurity.org/wmd/library/news/china/2005/wwwh60513.htm (accessed April 30, 2007).

212 *"The number of the 535 members":* Charlie Cook (editor and publisher of the Cook Political Report), in discussion with Nina Hachigian, December 2006.

212 *"There's no political downside":* Holly Yeager, "China Finds Few Friends in Congress," *Financial Times*, August 4, 2005.

212 *When strong majorities of the public:* "Hall of Mirrors," 3–6.

213 *Thus, the outliers can pivot:* Mancur Olson, *The Logic of Collective Action: Public Goods and the Theory of Groups* (Cambridge: Harvard University Press, 1971).

213 *Redistricting, to the extent that it:* Nancy E. Roman, "Both Sides of the Aisle: A Call for Bipartisan Foreign Policy," Council Special Report No. 9, Council on Foreign Relations (September 2005), 37, http://www.cfr.org/content/publications/attachments/Bipartisan_CSR.pdf (accessed April 30, 2007).

213 *"The stage is set":* Sebastian Mallaby, "Trade and the China Card," *Washington Post*, March 6, 2006.

213 *Indeed, Stephen Roach:* "Rich Man, Poor Man," *Economist*, January 20, 2007, 15.

213 *Though all Americans benefit:* This is the classic political problem with free trade—diffuse benefits but concentrated costs. I. M. Destler. *American Trade Politics*, 4th ed. (Washington: Institute for International Economics, 2005), 4.

214 *Further, expanded media coverage:* Michael Schiffer (program officer at the Stanley Foundation and former aide to Senator Dianne Feinstein, D-CA), in discussion with the authors, February 2007.

214 *The legislative workload has doubled:* This is when measured using metrics like the number of committee meetings or floor votes. Roman, "Both Sides of the Aisle," 43.

214 *On the others, they are apt:* The lack of engagement between the parties on tough issues adds to this dynamic. Ibid., 32–33.

215 *The Defense Department:* Gordon Adams, "The Politics of National Security Budgets," *Policy Analysis Brief, The Stanley Foundation*, February 2007, 5–7. Other political advantages the Defense Department has over State include a unified budget authority, an ability to demonstrate tangible results of its work, and a system that rewards its professionals for learning about how the American domestic political system works.

215 *In the 2004 election cycle:* William D. Hartung and Michelle Ciarrocca, "The Ties That Bind: Arms Industry Influence in the Bush Administration and Beyond," World Policy Institute, Special Report (October 2004), 1, http://www.worldpolicy.org/projects/arms/reports/TiesThatBind.html (accessed December 21, 2006).

215 *Last, the prevailing (and accurate) view in Congress:* Schiffer discussion.

216 *Similarly, where nearly 80 percent of the public:* "Hall of Mirrors," 12.

216 *the "real problem is":* Michael Hirsh, *At War With Ourselves* (Oxford: Oxford University Press, 2003), 91.

217 *Competition among media outlets:* One facet of this competition is in-

tense efforts to generate media "stampedes" that bring audience share, ratings, and ultimately revenue. David Bollier, "Can Serious Journalism Survive in the New Media Marketplace?," in *The Cato Report on Journalism and Society*, 1999, 26.

217 *The use of fear:* Matthew Baum, *Soft News Goes to War: Public Opinion and American Foreign Policy in the New Media Age* (Princeton: Princeton University Press, 2003), 7–8.

217 *A 2000 Harvard study documented:* Thomas E. Patterson, "Doing Well and Doing Good: How Soft News and Critical Journalism Are Shrinking the News Audience and Weakening Democracy, and What News Outlets Can Do About It," Joan Shorenstein Center on the Press, Politics and Public Policy, Harvard University (2000), 2–4.

217 *Human beings are naturally drawn:* Scott Gerwehr (director, behavioral sciences program at Defense Group Inc.), in discussion with Nina Hachigian, January 2006.

217 *"People tend to overvalue":* Among other studies, Tiffany A. Ito, Jeff T. Larsen, N. Kyle Smith, and John T. Cacioppo, "Negative Information Weighs More Heavily on the Brain: The Negativity Bias in Evaluative Categorizations," *Journal of Personality and Social Psychology* 75, no. 4 (1998): 887–900.

217 *As anthropological research shows:* Discussion of Mary Douglas's research, in Barry Glassner, *The Culture of Fear: Why Americans Are Afraid of the Wrong Things* (New York: Basic Books, 1999), xxvi.

218 *Public discussion of scares:* Ibid., xxviii.

218 *"China is emerging":* Joseph Quinlan (managing director and chief market strategist at Banc of America Capital Management), in discussion with Nina Hachigian, May 2007.

218 *Dobbs has taken his virulently:* Kurt Andersen, "The Lou Dobbs Factor," *New York Magazine*, December 4, 2006.

218 *"anti-Establishment anger":* Ibid.

218 *"Tonight China":* "Terror Arrests; Homeland Security; No Boundaries; Sanders and Paul Discussion," *Lou Dobbs Tonight*, transcript, June 9, 2005, http://transcripts.cnn.com/TRANSCRIPTS/0506/09/ldt.01.html (accessed April 30, 2007).

219 *In the world of print punditry:* Robert Kaplan, "How We Would Fight China," *Atlantic Monthly*, June 2005. For a refutation of this piece, Thomas P. M. Barnett, "Kaplan's Strategic Lap Dance for the US Navy

and Pacific Command," *Newsletter from Thomas P. M. Barnett*, May 16, 2005, http://www.thomaspmbarnett.com/weblog/archives2/001802 .html (accessed February 3, 2007).

219 *"Without journalists like Kaplan"*: Barnett, "Kaplan's Strategic Lap Dance."

219 *Another recent trend:* Baum, *Soft News Goes to War*, 2.

219 *The result is more awareness:* Ibid., 5–6.

219 *In theory, connecting with a larger share:* Ibid., 284.

219 *but the desire to find the entertaining story line:* Patterson, "Doing Well and Doing Good."

219 *Further, some studies of:* Baum, *Soft News Goes to War*, 223.

220 *"instrumental, important":* Daniel W. Drezner and Harry Farrell, "Web of Influence," *Foreign Policy* (November/December 2004), http://www .foreignpolicy.com/story/cms.php?story_id=2707&popup_delayed=1 (accessed April 30, 2007).

220 *the top political blog:* "The TTLB Blogosphere Ecosystem, Ranking by Traffic," http://truthlaidbear.com/TrafficRanking.php?start=1 (accessed April 30, 2007).

220 *While blogs are not supplanting:* "Online Papers Modestly Boost Newspaper Readership; Maturing Internet News Audience Broader than Deep," Biennial News Consumption Survey, Pew Research Center for People and the Press (July 30, 2006), 1; Amanda Lenhart, "Blogging: A Portrait of the Internet's New Storytellers," Pew Internet and American Life Project (July 19, 2006), 5.

220 *As the number of foreign correspondents:* John Maxwell Hamilton and Eric Jenner, "The New Foreign Correspondence," *Foreign Affairs* (September/October 2003).

220 *"traditional foreign correspondents":* Ibid.

220 *More and more, traditional journalists:* Drezner, "Web of Influence."

220 *Under the right circumstances:* Ibid.

220 *By increasing the diversity of voices:* Warren Strobel, "The Media: Influencing Foreign Policy in the Information Age," The Making of U.S. Foreign Policy, *U.S. Foreign Policy Agenda: An Electronic Journal of the U.S. Department of State* 5, no. 1 (March 2000): 38–39.

220 *At the same time, blogs are prone:* Hamilton, "The New Foreign Correspondence."

220 *The era of sound bite:* Strobel, "The Media: Influencing Foreign Policy," 37–38.

221 *Side by side for decades:* Yukio Okamoto, "Japan and the United States: The Essential Alliance," *Washington Quarterly* 25, no. 2 (2002): 60–61.

221 *Struggling with a deep:* Adam Clymer, "Joblessness Causing Stress and Gloom About Nation, *New York Times,* February 2, 1983.

221 *Between 1976 and 1981, imports:* Robert W. Crandall, "The Effects of U.S. Trade Protection for Autos and Steel," *Brookings Papers on Economic Activity* 1987, no. 1 (1987): 276.

221 *No one wanted to hear:* Gilbert Winham, "We Are Driven: The Auto Crisis," *Foreign Policy* (Summer 1981): 157.

222 *In polling from the early 1980s, they were just as likely to point to:* Clymer, "Joblessness Causing Stress."

222 *Marketers saw an opportunity:* Adam Snyder, "Japan Fights Back," *AdWeek,* December 3, 1990.

222 *"lending credibility":* "America's Japanophia," *Economist,* November 18, 1989.

222 *By 1989, nearly 70 percent of Americans:* Mark Vamos, "What Americans Think of Japan Inc.," *BusinessWeek,* August 7, 1989.

222 *In the case of autos:* Crandall, "The Effects of U.S. Trade Protection for Autos and Steel," 280.

222 *but the regime led to higher car prices:* Ibid., 287.

222 *In a sense, the VERs created:* Ibid., 277; "Average Price of a New Car, 1970–2003," National Income and Product Accounts—Underlying Detail Estimates for Motor Vehicle Output, U.S. Department of Commerce, Bureau of Economic Analysis, 2004.

223 *In limiting the number of imports:* John C. Ries, "Windfall Profits and Vertical Relationships: Who Gained in the Japanese Auto Industry from VERs?," *Journal of Industrial Economics* 41, no. 3 (September 1993): 274.

223 *reinvestment of their excess profits:* Lael Brainard (vice president and director, Global Economy and Development, the Brookings Institution), in discussion with Mona Sutphen, February 2007.

223 *Congressional staffers are far more wary:* "American Attitudes Toward China, Phase II," Zogby International Poll sponsored by the Committee of 100, April 2005, http://www.committee100.org/publications/survey/phase2/English_pressrelease.pdf (accessed December 27, 2006).

223 *"Military build up":* Senior Senate staffer, in discussion with Nina Hachigian, September 2005.

223 *Combined with the legacy of the Cold War:* For more on the political

dynamics of U.S. China policy, Aaron L. Friedberg, "The Future of US-China Relations: Is Conflict Inevitable?" *International Security* 30 no. 2, (Fall 2005): 7–45.

225 *Despite Americans' broad acceptance of globalization:* Mark Penn and Tom Freedman, "The Emerging Politics of Globalization," polling undertaken for the Democratic Leadership Council (January 2007), 8, http://www.ndol.org/ndol_ci.cfm?kaid=108&subid=206&contentid=254134 (accessed April 30, 2007).

225 *In a December 2006 Pew poll:* "Free Trade Agreements Get a Mixed Review," Pew Research Center (December 19, 2006), 1.

225 *A 2004 Chicago Council on Global Affairs poll:* "Global Views 2004: American Public Opinion and Foreign Policy," Chicago Council on Global Affairs (2004), 42.

225 *Only 41 percent of American leaders agree:* Ibid.

225 *Today, the relatively new phenomenon:* Alan S. Blinder, "Offshoring: The Next Industrial Revolution?," *Foreign Affairs* (March/April 2006).

226 *Despite a relatively strong economic expansion:* Mortimer Zuckerman, "America's High Anxiety," *U.S. News & World Report*, December 17, 2006.

226 *"If the anxious middle's concerns":* Ibid.

226 *Increasing income volatility:* Jason Bordoff, Michael Deich, and Peter Orszag, "A Growth Enhancing Approach to Economic Security," Hamilton Project, Brookings Institution, September 2006, 4, http://www.brookings.edu/views/papers/200609economicsecurity.htm (accessed April 30, 2007).

226 *Generation Y workers:* Stephanie Armour, "Generation Y: They've Arrived at Work with a New Attitude," *USA Today*, November 8, 2005.

226 *Americans under thirty:* "Foreign Policy Attitudes Now Driven by 9/11 and Iraq," Pew Research Center for People and the Press, August 18, 2004, 34.

226 *By contrast those aged fifty to sixty-four:* Ibid.

226 *Today one in four American workers:* Daniel H. Pink, *Free Agent Nation: The Future of Working for Yourself* (New York: Warner, 2001), 44–45.

227 *Until then, even a president who wants:* For a more in-depth discussion of the trap of idealist rhetoric and its limitations in a more complex world, Anatol Lieven and John Hulsman, *Ethical Realism: A Vision for America's Role in the World* (New York: Pantheon, 2006).

228 *these organizations often carry our water:* Mark Malloch Brown, "Power and Superpower: Global Leadership in the 21st Century" (remarks at a conference co-sponsored by the Center for American Progress and the Century Foundation, June 6, 2006), http://www.securitypeace.org/pdf/brown_remarks.pdf (accessed April 30, 2007).

228 *"YOYO":* Jared Bernstein, "All Together Now: Common Sense for a Fair Economy," Economic Policy Institute (Washington: Berrett-Koehler, 2004).

228 *Nearly 90 percent of Americans say:* "Americans on Globalization—A Study of US Public Attitudes," Program on International Policy Attitudes (PIPA), March 28, 2000, 24; Penn and Freedman, "The Emerging Politics of Globalization," 1.

228 *The chairman of the House Financial Services Committee:* Michael Kranish and Ross Kerber, "Rep. Frank Offers Business a Grand Bargain," *Boston Globe*, November 19, 2006.

229 *The ability of the president:* Jeffrey Peake, "Presidential Agenda Setting in Foreign Policy," *Political Research Quarterly* 54, no. 1 (March 2001): 69.

CONCLUSION

233 *In 1999, he came back:* Alan Shipnuck, "Back to the Future," *Sports Illustrated*, January 31, 2005.

233 *That did not stop him:* Scott Ostler, "Tiger Finds the Sweetest Swing of All—So Far," *San Francisco Chronicle*, July 16, 2005.

233 *"Tiger Woods wins four consecutive":* Randall Mell, "New Swing Illustrates Tiger's Will," *Buffalo News*, August 3, 2005.

233 *But Woods understands:* Douglas Lowe, "Search for Perfection Threatens to Leave Pack Fighting for Scraps," *The Herald* (Glasgow), July 19, 2005.

233 *"It's a never-ending struggle":* Ibid.

233 *"The thing that impresses me":* Ostler, "Tiger Finds the Sweetest Swing of All."

234 *"America has found":* As quoted in Strobe Talbott, *Engaging India* (Washington, D.C.: Brookings Institution, 2004), 200.

235 *"dark and heavy demon of inertia":* C. Raja Mohan, *Crossing the Rubicon* (New York: Palgrave Macmillan, 2003), 267.

235 *To continue to thrive:* Todd Thomson, "Asia's Dance of the Twin Elephants," *Financial Times*, March 1, 2006.

235   *The United States has withstood thirty-two recessions:* National Bureau of Economic Research, "Business Cycle Expansions and Contractions," National Bureau of Economic Research, http://www.nber.org/cycles .html (accessed January 2007).

235   *ten major armed conflicts:* "Principal Wars in Which the United States Participated: US Military Personnel Serving and Casualties," U.S. Department of Defense, http://www.globalsecurity.org/military/ops/casu alties.htm (accessed April 30, 2007).

235   *over two dozen terrorist incidents:* Joseph McCann, *Terrorism on American Soil: A Concise History of Plots and Perpetrators from the Famous to the Forgotten* (Boulder: Sentient, September 2006).

Index

Page numbers in *italics* refer to figures and tables.

Belgium, 111
Benjamin, Daniel, 27
Bensahel, Nora, 30
Berlin Wall, 1
Bernanke, Ben, 110
Bernstein, Jared, 228
Bertram, Christoph, 139, 155
Binder, Alan, 97
bin Laden, Osama, 24, 33, 217
biological weapons, 19
Biological Weapons Convention, 19,
    37, 175, 188, 206
Bismarck, Otto von, 194
Blacker, Coit D., 142, 200
Blackwell, Ron, 86
blogs, 220, 230
Boeing, 96, 120, 198
    Moscow Design Center of, 120
Bonner, Robert, 31
Bosnia, 191
Brainard, Lael, 94
Brazil, 11, 58, 91, 113, 181
Brin, Sergey, 127
Brookings Institution, 77, 94
"bunker buster" bombs, 37
Burchette, Dennis, 85
Burger King, 87, 99
Burma, 75
Bush, George H. W., 168, 222
Bush, George W., 16, 55, 69, 81, 175,
    209, 210–11
    Putin's 2002 summit with, 31, 133
    second Inaugural Address of, 69
    on U.S. primary, 167–68
Bush (G. W.) administration, 156, 176,
    191, 198, 206, 220, 226
    "Anything but Clinton" policy of, 2
    foreign policy failures of, 209–11
    National Space Policy of, 166
    primary strategy of, 167–69

BusinessWeek, 93
butterfly effect, 16
Byman, Daniel, 79

C6 forum, 184–86, 188, 189–90, 193,
    199, 227
California, University of, 119
Canada, 99, 122, 177
capitalism, 66, 93, 203
    as economic model, 67–68
Carnegie Endowment, 81, 134, 136
Carothers, Thomas, 81, 82–83
Carter, Ashton, 171
Carter, Jimmy, 69
cell phone market, 113–14
Center for American Progress, 2, 33, 61,
    96, 129
Center for Asia Pacific Policy at RAND,
    2
Centers for Disease Control, 40
Central Intelligence Agency (CIA), 12,
    28, 210
CERN collider, 122–23
Chain of Pearls, 105
Chan, Margaret, 157
Chávez, Hugo, 57, 81
Chechnya, 28, 31
chemical industry, 118–19
Chemical Weapons Convention, 35
Cheney, Dick, 176
Chenoweth, Helen, 204, 212
Chicago Council on Global Affairs
    survey, 204–5, 225
China, Imperial, 123–24
China, People's Republic of:
    Africa policy of, 56–57, 72, 74,
        76–77, 137
    anti-Americanism in, 135
    Belgrade embassy bombing and, 135
    Burma and, 75

hantavirus, 37
Hart-Rudman Commission on
    National Security for the 21st
    Century, 128
Harvard University, 127, 217
health care, 16, 17, 98, 129, 174, 228,
    229
Heginbotham, Eric, 62
Helms, Jesse, 213
Herberg, Mikkal, 101, 102
He Yafei, 156
Hezbollah, 58
highly enriched uranium (HEU),
    34–35
Highs, Thomas, 124–25
Hilton, Paris, 217
Hirsh, Michael, 68
HIV, 42, 188
Hoehn, Andrew, 55
Hoffman, Bruce, 31–32
Holdren, John, 44–45
Holiday Inn, 99
Homeland Security Council, 212
Homeland Security Department, U.S.,
    30
Hong Kong, 31, 40, 100
House of Representatives, U.S., 213,
    214
    Financial Services Committee of,
    229
"How We Would Fight China"
    (Kaplan), 219
Hubbert, M. King, 103
Hu Jintao, 55, 74, 76, 81, 150
human intelligence (HUMINT), 28
human rights, 66–67, 68, 69, 72, 77–78,
    81–82, 206, 224
Human Rights Watch, 81
Hurd, Douglas, 139
Hussein, Saddam, 217

hydrogen fuel cells, 106–7
Hynes, Michael, 33, 35

IBM, 98, 99
Iceland, 128
Ikenberry, G. John, 60, 170, 181, 183
immigration, 2
India:
    China as threat to, 170
    democracy and, 75, 83, 132, 184
    demographic composition of, 16
    in East Asia summit, 192
    economic rise of, 2, 86, 87, 91, 113,
        131, 226
    global aspirations of, 58, 134,
        135–36, 138, 160
    greenhouse gas emissions in, 45–46
    innovation and, 119, 120, 121
    intellectual property rights in, 114
    Iran and, 59
    in ITER partnership, 9, 188
    Japan's Eight-fold initiative with, 150
    Kashmir conflict and, 23, 29, 61
    liberal world order and, 152, 153–56,
        181, 184
    military capacity of, 47
    Nepal crisis and, 61, 70–71
    nonproliferation and, 36, 165
    offshoring and outsourcing to, 3, 93,
        95
    oil issue and, 57, 74, 101–7
    Parliament building attack and, 23
    pivotal powers' relationship with, 60,
        150–51, *151*, 185, 186, 194
    population of, 9
    Russia's space pact with, 166
    self-perception of, 132, 133
    terrorism threat and, 23–24, 28–29,
        32, 234
    U.S. as viewed by, 138–39, 161, 181

U.N. and, 182–83
use of force and, 189
U.S. leadership and, 190–92, 206
U.S. strengths and, 173–74
Sudan, 16, 74, 178, 188, 192
Suez Crisis (1956), 145, 161
Summers, Larry, 226
Sutter, Robert, 56
Sweden, 122, 127
Syria, 35

Taiwan, 51, 54, 55, 60, 61, 62, 73, 83,
    137, 143, 147–48, 177, 193, 196,
    210, 234
Taliban, 31
tamas, 235
tariffs, 96–97
Tata, Ratan, 150
Teaching Commission, 129
technology, 2, 13, 26, 64, 66, 100, 117,
    184
  income stratification and, 96
  innovation and, 117, 118–19
  job displacement and, 93–94
Tellis, Ashley, 143
terrorism, terrorists, 1, 13, 52, 53, 79,
    128, 138, 140, 162, 168, 171, 181,
    183, 210, 211, 234, 235
  China and threat of, 28, 31, 32,
    34–36
  European Union and, 28, 29–30
  India and, 29
  interdependence of intelligence
    services and, 29–33
  Japan and, 28–29
  NIE on, 28
  nuclear proliferation and, 34–35
  Russia and, 28
  threat of, *17,* 23–28, *26,* 207–8
  U.S. values and ideals and, 66–67

textile industry, 96–97
  British, 124–25
Thailand, 55, 195
Times (London), 166
tokamak nuclear reactor, 9
Toshiba Corporation, 90
Total (oil company), 74
Toynbee, Arnold, 130
Toyota, 96
Transportation Workers Union, 85
Treasury Bonds, U.S., 110
Treasury Department, U.S., 178, 210
Trenin, Dmitri, 67, 136, 144, 153–54
Truman, Harry S., 167
tsunami disaster of 2005, 56
Turkey, 138

Ukraine, 34, 83, 136, 148, 177
unemployment, 225–26
unemployment insurance, 97
United Kingdom, *see* Great Britain
United Nations, 11, 18, 32, 44, 59, 61,
    81, 83, 143, 160, 213, 216, 228
  conservative opposition to, 204
  General Assembly of, 73
  Security Council of, 54, 57, 74, 75,
    134, 155–56, 159, 184–85, 189, 207
  space race resolution of, 164–67
  strategic collaboration and, 182–83
United States:
  anti-U.N. sentiment of, 204
  arms control and, 164–67
  Belgrade embassy bombing and, 135
  budget surpluses and deficits of,
    109–10, 115
  capital markets of, 120
  China and global ideology of, 67,
    72–75
  China and global relations of, 1, 54,
    56–58

About the Authors

NINA HACHIGIAN is a Senior Vice President at the Center for American Progress and a Visiting Scholar of the Center for International Security and Cooperation at Stanford University. Earlier, she spent five years at RAND as the Director of the Center for Asia-Pacific Policy and a Senior Political Scientist. From 1998 to 1999, she was on the staff of the National Security Council. A coauthor of several monographs and book chapters about geopolitics and technology in Asia, her writings have appeared in *Foreign Affairs*, *The Washington Quarterly*, *The New York Times*, and the *Los Angeles Times*, among others.

MONA SUTPHEN is a Managing Director at Stonebridge International LLC, a Washington-based international business strategy firm. A former diplomat, she served at the U.S. Embassy in Bangkok and in Sarajevo, where she worked on the implementation of the Dayton Peace Agreement. Later, she served as Special Assistant to U.S. National Security Advisor Samuel R. Berger and as an advisor to U.N. Ambassador Bill Richardson.